Engendering the State

Why have states been slower to incorporate women's human rights norms domestically than other human rights norms?

Why has the diffusion of these norms varied so greatly between states?

Why are some states more responsive and exert more effort than others to comply with these norms?

Engendering the State seeks to explain these key issues and argues that the gender-biased identity of many states represents the most significant barrier to diffusion. It also explores how particular norms have diffused into certain states at specific points in time, as a consequence of international and domestic pressure.

The author:

* addresses the limitations of existing explanations of international norms
* develops case studies of Germany, Spain, Japan and India, which provide a new perspective on comparative analysis of Europe and Asia
* develops alternative arguments to explain cross-national variation in the influence of international norms of sexual discrimination
* addresses the theoretical and practical implications of the argument.

This book is essential reading for all those with an interest in women's human rights, gender studies and international studies.

Lynn Savery is a Postdoctoral Fellow in the Department of International Relations, Research School of Pacific and Asian Studies at the Australian National University.

Routledge studies in critical realism
Edited by Margaret Archer, Roy Bhaskar, Andrew Collier, Kathryn Dean, Nick Hostettler, Jonathan Joseph, Tony Lawson, Alan Norrie and Sean Vertigan.

Critical realism is one of the most influential new developments in the philosophy of science and in the social sciences, providing a powerful alternative to positivism and post-modernism. This series will explore the critical realist position in philosophy and across the social sciences.

Also published by Routledge:
Critical realism: interventions
Edited by Margaret Archer, Roy Bhaskar, Andrew Collier, Kathryn Dean,
Nick Hostettler, Jonathan Joseph, Tony Lawson, Alan Norrie and Sean
Vertigan.

Critical Realism
Essential readings
*Edited by Margaret Archer,
Roy Bhaskar, Andrew Collier,
Tony Lawson and Alan Norrie*

**The Possibility of Naturalism, 3rd
edition**
A philosophical critique of the
contemporary human sciences
Roy Bhaskar

Being and Worth
Andrew Collier

**Quantum Theory and the Flight
from Realism**
Philosophical responses to
quantum mechanics
Christopher Norris

From East to West
Odyssey of a soul
Roy Bhaskar

Realism and Racism
Concepts of race in sociological
research
Bob Carter
Rational Choice Theory
Resisting colonisation
*Edited by Margaret Archer and
Jonathan Q. Tritter*

Explaining Society
Critical realism in the social
sciences
*Berth Danermark, Mats Ekström,
Jan Ch. Karlsson and Liselotte Jakobsen*

Critical Realism and Marxism
Edited by Andrew Brown,
Steve Fleetwood and
John Michael Roberts

Critical Realism in Economics
Edited by Steve Fleetwood

Realist Perspectives on
Management and Organisations
Edited by Stephen Ackroyd and
Steve Fleetwood

After International Relations
Critical realism and the
(re)construction of world politics
Heikki Patomaki

Capitalism and Citizenship
The impossible partnership
Kathryn Dean

Philosophy of Language and the
Challenge to Scientific Realism
Christopher Norris

Transcendence
Critical realism and God
Margaret S. Archer, Andrew Collier and
Douglas V. Porpora

Critical Realist Applications in
Organisation and Management
Studies
Edited by Steve Fleetwood and
Stephen Ackroyd

Making Realism Work
Realist social theory and empirical
research
Edited by Bob Carter and Caroline New

Rethinking Marxism
From Kant and Hegel to Marx and
Engels
Jolyon Agar

Engendering the State

The international diffusion of women's human rights

Lynn Savery

Routledge
Taylor & Francis Group

LONDON AND NEW YORK

First published 2007
by Routledge
2 Park Square, Milton Park, Abingdon, Oxon OX14 4RN

Simultaneously published in the USA and Canada
by Routledge
270 Madison Ave, New York, NY 10016

Routledge is an imprint of the Taylor & Francis Group, an informa business

© 2007 Lynn Savery

Typeset in Baskerville by Wearset Ltd, Boldon, Tyne and Wear
Printed and bound in Great Britain by TJI Digital, Padstow, Cornwall

British Library Cataloguing in Publication Data
A catalogue record for this book is available from the British Library

Library of Congress Cataloging in Publication Data
A catalog record for this book has been requested

ISBN10: 0-415-42877-7

ISBN13: 978-0-415-42877-4

2006037799

In loving memory of my dear friend Sharron Lee 1964–2001 and Jasper the spoodle 1998–2004

Contents

Preface

This book was prompted by my interest in, or rather bemusement at, the furore surrounding the term 'gender' at the United Nations Conference on Women in Beijing in 1995. As the battle over definitional clarification of the term raged, I wondered whether such events mattered very much. In particular, I wondered whether international women's human rights had any bearing on state behaviour and, in turn, women's lives. Surprisingly little attention has been paid to this question. What I do in this study is explore the relationship between international norms of sexual non-discrimination and state behaviour. I argue that, despite the significant barrier of the gender-biased corporate identity of states, particular norms diffuse into particular states at particular points in time as a result of international and domestic pressure, or a combination of both.

This book would never have seen the light of day without the support of a great many friends and colleagues. I owe a tremendous debt of gratitude to Chris Reus-Smit for his intellectual guidance, challenging questions and constant encouragement. Chris has shepherded me through numerous intellectual travails, and his unstinting attention to this book, in its many drafts, has been invaluable. I am also indebted to Heather Rae for her thoughtful comments and sound advice at various stages of this book. My thanks go to Paul Keal, Greg Noble and Greg Fry for their insightful comments and encouragement, and to Joel Quirk, Shogo Suzuki, Sarah Graham, Nicky George and Thuy Do for their intellectual camaraderie. Thanks to Celia Valiente, John Meyer, Nitza Berkovitch, Mary Fainsod Katzenstein, Yasemin Soysal, Conny Roggeband, Monica Threlfall, Petrea Kodre, Masumi Yoneda, Maria Teresa Gallego Mendez and Ratna Kapur for their helpful suggestions regarding various aspects of my research. Thanks to Julie Spencer for her translation work and to Mary-Louise Hickey for her invaluable editorial support. Thanks to the two anonymous reviewers at Routledge for their encouraging comments. A special thank-you to Jenny Dennis, Kathy Morton and Bina D'Costa for their inspirational friendship and intellectual vivacity.

There are a number of people and institutions that I would like to thank for their help on various research trips for this book. At the United

Nations Information Centre in Sydney, Toni Smith was most helpful, and suggested documents relevant to my research. At the United Nations Division for the Advancement of Women in New York, Koh Miyaoi and Alicia Gumapac were most generous with their assistance. At the International Labour Organization in Geneva, Lee Swepston, Constance Thomas and Katrine Landuyt were extremely generous with their knowledge and assistance, and made helpful suggestions regarding my research. At the European Women's Lobby in Brussels, Cecile Gravoval was most helpful. I would like, in addition, to acknowledge the indispensable help of librarians and staff at the International Labour Organization Central Library and Documentation Bureau in Geneva; the Universitätsbibliothek der Freien Universität Berlin; the European Union Central Library in Brussels; the Instituto Universitario de Estudios de la Mujer de la Universidad Autónoma de Madrid; the Lawyer's Collective in New Delhi; and the Centre for Women's Development Studies in New Delhi. I thank them for their patience and expertise. I owe a special debt of gratitude to the staff at the Centre for Feminist Legal Research in New Delhi for taking such good care of me during my research trip in 2000. I am particularly grateful to the director of the centre, Ratna Kapur, not only for her acute insight and generosity but also for her valued commitment to intellectual engagement and women's rights. I am also indebted to Dale and Conchetta Emerson for sharing their family home in Brussels in January 1997, and to Carroll and Heidi Valenzuela for sharing their fabulous apartment on West 58 Street in New York in October 1998. I thank them for taking a complete stranger in and for their warmth and laughter.

Parts of this book have appeared previously in 'Women's human rights and changing state practices: a critical realist analysis', *Journal of Critical Realism*, 4(2), 2005: 89–111, and 'On the ontology of international norm diffusion', in Clive Lawson, John Spiro Latsis and Nuno Miguel Ornelas Martins (eds), *Contributions to Social Ontology*, London: Routledge, 2006.

In completing this book, I owe a special debt of gratitude to my family for their boundless affection, constant support and, above all else, their patience. My parents, Harry and Eileen Savery, warrant particular thanks for their love and undying faith in their daughter's ability. Finally, I owe the deepest debt of gratitude to my darling husband and soulmate, David Hicks, for his unconditional love and warm snuggles, and to Ashleigh, Matthew, and Truly Scrumptious and Honeysuckle, the Shitzu girls, for lifting my spirits.

Abbreviations

AP	Popular Alliance (Spain)
ATCA	Alien Tort Claims Act (United States)
BDA	League of Employers Association (Germany)
BJP	Bharatiya Janata Party (India)
CAP	Common Agricultural Policy
CCOO	Worker's Commissions (Spain)
CEDAW	Convention on the Elimination of Discrimination Against Women (UN)
CERD	Committee on the Elimination of Racial Discrimination (UN)
CDU	Christian Democratic Union (Germany)
CSU	Christian Social Union (Germany)
CSWB	Central Social Welfare Board (India)
CSWI	Committee on the Status of Women in India
CWGL	Center for Women's Global Leadership
DEDAW	Declaration on the Elimination of Discrimination Against Women (UN)
DEVAW	Declaration on the Elimination of Violence Against Women (UN)
DGB	German Confederation of Trade Unions
DG V	Social Affairs Directorate (EU)
DIHT	German Chamber of Commerce
ECJ	European Court of Justice
ECOSOC	Economic and Social Council (UN)
EEOC	Equal Employment Opportunity Commission (United States)
EEOL	Equal Employment Opportunity Law (Japan)
EU	European Union
FDP	Free Democratic Party (Germany)
FSIA	Foreign Sovereign Immunities Act (United States)
GDR	German Democratic Republic
HRAW	Human Rights Action Watch
ICJ	International Commission of Jurists
ICSSR	Indian Council of Social Science Research
ILO	International Labour Organization

IM	Women's Institute (Spain)
IO	international organization
INAVAW	International Network Against Violence Against Women
INGO	international non-governmental organization
IWRAW	International Women's Rights Action Watch
IWTC	International Women's Tribune Centre
IWY	International Women's Year (UN)
JAIWR	Japanese Association of International Women's Rights
JSP	Japan Socialist Party
KCWS	Korean Council for Women Drafted for Military Sex Slavery by Japan
LDP	Liberal Democratic Party (Japan)
MDM	Democratic Movement of Women (Spain)
NGO	non-governmental organization
NOW	National Organization for Women (United States)
NPP	*National Perspective Plan for Women, 1988–2000* (India)
PCE	Communist Party (Spain)
PP	Popular Party (Spain)
PSOE	Socialist Spanish Worker's Party
SDP	Social Democratic Party (Germany)
TCCI	Tokyo Chamber of Commerce and Industry
UCD	Union of the Democratic Centre (Spain)
UFV	Independent Women's Association (Germany)
UGT	General Union of Workers (Spain)
UN	United Nations
WWIN	Working Women's International Network (Japan)
YWCA	Young Women's Christian Association

Introduction

Despite the post-war existence of an international women's human rights regime, it is only since the 1970s, when there was a significant expansion and strengthening of this regime, that norms of sexual non-discrimination have had any effect, and even then, states have been slower to integrate these norms domestically than other human rights norms. Moreover, the record of diffusion varies greatly from one state to another. This book seeks to explain why international norms of sexual non-discrimination have diffused unevenly and why their overall impact on state behaviour has been relatively limited at a time when international human rights norms in general have increasingly defined what constitutes a legitimate state (Risse 1999: 530). It does so by tracing the diffusion of various norms relating to women's civil, political and labour rights, and the issue of violence against women into Germany, Spain, Japan and India. The book's central thesis is that the gender-biased corporate identity of many states represents the most significant barrier to diffusion. However, it also demonstrates the way in which particular norms have been incorporated into particular states at particular points in time as a consequence of articulated international and domestic pressure. For instance, the European Commission's threat to initiate infringement proceedings against Germany in May 1979 for failing to implement the European Union (EU) equal pay and equal treatment directives by their designated deadlines induced a noticeable, albeit minimal, change to national legal practice.[1] If we are to fully comprehend the dynamic relationship between international norms of sexual non-discrimination and state behaviour, not only do such conditions conducive to diffusion have to be identified but, because of the relatively limited impact of these norms on the whole, so too do conditions unconducive to diffusion.

The observation that international norms of sexual non-discrimination have had a limited influence on state behaviour is likely to come as no great surprise to feminist international legal scholars, who have long questioned the importance and efficacy of international law in general. Hilary Charlesworth and Christine Chinkin claim that the international legal system has historically failed to respond appropriately to questions of gender equity, and that international law has simply 'brushed aside the injustices of women's situations around the world' (2000: xi). Shelley Wright laments that mainstream international human rights regimes and bodies have 'consistently failed to deal with human rights violations against women' (1993: 78–9). Charlotte Bunch maintains that the international legal classification of human rights 'perpetuates the idea that the rights of women are of a lesser order than the rights of man' and serves to justify discriminatory practices (1993a: 971–2). Fiona Beveridge and Siobhan Mullally argue that the international legal system treats gender-based human rights violations as a 'cultural, private, or individual issue, not a political matter requiring state action' (1995: 240). Frances Olson claims that international law is gender-blind not through simple oversight but because it is structured on and represents the interests of men as the 'embodied subordinators of women' (1993: 164–5).

The feminist international legal critique focuses primarily on the conceptual and procedural underpinnings of international law and maintains that the international legal system as a whole is thoroughly gender biased. Feminist international legal scholars argue that international law rests on a series of deeply gendered public–private distinctions that quarantine many practices of sexual discrimination from international legal regulation (Charlesworth 1995: 245, 254). In particular, they maintain that the traditional legal doctrine of state responsibility fails to extend state responsibility to the private domain of the family – a domain in which discriminatory practices commonly occur (see Chinkin 1999). They also maintain that the creation of an international legal regime designed specifically to eliminate sexual discrimination has done little to reduce the defining influence of the public–private dichotomy because it has allowed mainstream human rights bodies to disregard gender issues. Moreover, feminist international legal scholars assume that the regime is irrelevant and inconsequential because it lacks strong enforcement mechanisms. Yet since their assumption is reached in the absence of empirical inquiry, feminist international legal scholars are less than ideally positioned to explain why international norms of sexual non-discrimination diffuse into states at different rates and with different behavioural consequences, and this study addresses that lacuna.

In contrast to feminist international legalism, the question of how and under what conditions international norms matter has been the subject of keen debate within the discipline of international relations in recent years. From this debate, several distinct and sometimes competing theories of international norms have emerged. Yet, as Chapter 1 explains, neither neoliberal, liberal intergovernmental, sociological institutionalist nor constructivist accounts of international norms adequately explain the diffusion of international norms of sexual non-discrimination into domestic state practices. Neoliberalism assumes that international norms exist and function as a tool of utility-maximizing states. States, neoliberals claim, create and comply with international norms in order to realize their material and economic self-interests, which are predetermined and fixed. Like neoliberalism, liberal intergovernmentalism provides a utility-maximizing explanation of norms but assumes that norms and compliance are fundamentally determined by the utility-optimizing behaviour of individuals in domestic society. Intergovernmentalists argue that international norms result from interstate bargains based on the domestic power and preferences of individuals or groups. They also assume that states have an interest in complying with international norms because they are endogenous. However, as we shall see, the existence and diffusion of international norms of sexual non-discrimination is not necessarily contingent on either state or individual utility maximization. Sociological institutionalism attributes the existence and efficacy of international norms to the global culture or world polity that envelops the interstate system. Sociological institutionalists argue that international norms are institutionalized in an ever-expanding and deepening world polity, which has a constitutive and directive effect on state identity, preferences and behaviour. As a component of the world polity, international norms are said to diffuse in an ongoing and ubiquitous process that results in far-reaching isomorphism across states. This approach fails to explain resistance by states to incorporating international norms of sexual non-discrimination, or the persistent heterogeneity among state practices. Constructivism views the relationship between international norms and states as mutually constitutive. Constructivists argue that international norms and state practices constitute and reconstitute each other in a dynamic process of iteration. They also argue that states are socialized into incorporating patterns of behaviour and role expectations subscribed by international norms. This perspective struggles to explain domestically determined change to or continuity in state practices in the presence of international norms of sexual non-discrimination, as it tends to overestimate the process of socialization and efficacy of international norms.

Since neither feminist international legal analysis nor existing international relations theory adequately explains the dynamic between international norms of sexual non-discrimination and state behaviour, Chapter 2 sets out to articulate a more sufficient explanation by drawing on some of the core ideas associated with critical realism. It must be stressed at the outset that my aim here is not to develop a general theory of norm diffusion but rather to develop a specific explanation of the diffusion and efficacy of international norms of sexual non-discrimination. In fact, I argue that it is neither possible nor desirable to look for universal laws or develop a single general theory or explanation for norm diffusion, because diffusion is not a predetermined process. There is no single essential mechanism, principle or conduit that predetermines the diffusion of international norms. On the contrary, varying factors interact with one another to either inhibit or enhance the international diffusion of various norms. Critical realism offers us the means by which to get a firm analytical grip on the particular triggering conditions and operative mechanisms that facilitate or block the diffusion and efficacy of particular norms. The critical realist explanation of the diffusion of international norms of sexual non-discrimination advanced in this book consists of three interrelated components: structural–agential interaction, contentious discursive interaction and power relations.

The central argument of this study is that, while the gender-biased corporate identity of the state is a prime obstacle to diffusion, there are particular conditions conducive to the diffusion of particular norms of sexual non-discrimination, and these preconditions emerge as a consequence of historically and locationally specific structural–agential interaction. Social interaction resulting in a change to state practices may occur within and/or between the international and domestic spheres. For example, Germany's enactment of the Employment Law to Comply with the European Community Provisions in 1980 was the result of changing regional conditions in which the European Commission found the political will to enforce implementation of European equality legislation through the infringements procedure established under Article 169 of the 1957 Treaty of Rome. Before the mid-1970s, the European Commission rarely tried to force state compliance through infringement proceedings for fear of jeopardizing its relationship with member governments. However, as a consequence of a series of landmark decisions by the European Court of Justice establishing the direct effect of European equality legislation and the court's admonishment of the commission for failing to pursue breaches of said legislation, the European Commission began bringing infringement proceedings against member states for defaulting on their obligations under the European equality directives. On 10 May 1979, the European Commission began infringement proceedings against Germany for failing to implement the European equal pay and equal treatment directives, and served notice that the state should take specific measures to implement the directives. Germany only narrowly avoided the infringement proceedings by making the minimum changes to national legislation necessary to comply with the directives. While Germany's compliance on this occasion originated in regional pressure, it is more common for state compliance to originate in a combination of external and internal pressure – the internal pressure emanating from feminist activism and private individual litigation.

Domestic feminist activism and private individual or group litigation are often critical in bringing about changes in state behaviour both in the presence and in the absence of international norms of sexual non-discrimination. In other words, they frequently play an important role not only in ensuring the state's internalization of international norms of sexual non-discrimination but also in effecting changes in state practices that pre-date or coincide with the emergence of particular systemic norms. Where diffusion is concerned, feminist advocates and litigants empowered by domestic and/or external political and legal conditions pursue changes to national legislation and public policies and, in the process, directly or indirectly ensure the state's incorporation of international norms of sexual non-discrimination. Successful feminist activism necessarily involves the effective discursive articulation of grievances, justice claims, and means of redress and change, which is produced in reaction to the exigencies of a particular situation and in conflict with dominant domestic discourses of masculine privilege. For instance, after a considerable period of repression in which the Spanish authoritarian regime revoked women's civil and political rights and enforced a highly discriminatory legal and public policy system, and, at a time when it was cracking down on political dissent, the regime's recognition of the United Nations International Women's Year (IWY) in 1975 opened the way for Spanish feminists to mobilize and discursively dispute the state's legal and public policy positions on women. Following a period of democratic transition, continuing internal pressure from Spanish feminists and external pressure from the European Union (EU) imposing conditions of membership combined to produce changes in Spanish employment policies.

A critical realist argument can also be used to identify and explain conditions unconducive to the diffusion of international norms of sexual non-discrimination. In this situation, the gender-biased corporate identity of the state is virtually impervious to internationally derived change. Dominant domestic agents such as the state and the Church endorse an inherently discriminatory set of ideas about gender relations and successfully pursue their vested interests in reproducing gender-biased legal and public policy practices. Adverse domestic political conditions constrain the emergence and crystallization of effective feminist opposition and thus prevent the discursive repudiation of dominant understandings of the gendered social order and family–state relations. For instance, upon winning the Civil War in 1939, Spain's authoritarian regime and the Catholic Church united to develop a familialist and pronatalist legal and public policy system based on orthodox Catholic principles of gender relations. Pre-existing Republican civil and political laws were repealed and restrictive labour regulations were enacted that rewarded and compensated for paternity. Church and state together fashioned an official discourse on the role of women in Spanish society around Catholic integrationist doctrine and notions of nationalism and imperial expansionism. The authoritarian regime brutally repressed political dissent and stifled any form of domestic feminist opposition, and, in doing so, prevented any discursive resistance to or questioning of its legislation and policies. Therefore, although the Franquist regime ratified a number of important conventions, international norms of sexual non-discrimination had no influence on state behaviour during the period of authoritarianism in Spain.

The gender-biased corporate identity of the state, though by no means the only aspect to the modern state, presents a major impediment to the diffusion of international norms of sexual non-discrimination because it is politically constituted and reconstituted within the state and, thus, highly compelling. The term 'the gender-biased corporate identity of the state' refers to a particular aspect of the state's preconceived sense of self, which, in turn, political elites play a crucial, although by no means exclusive, role in producing and reproducing. They do so by pursuing, more or less consciously, policies that uphold certain social values and beliefs about the gendered social order and family–state relations. The gender-biased corporate identity of the Japanese state is a case in point. With the departure of Allied occupation forces in 1952, the Japanese state determined to reinstitute the traditional family system (*ie*) and pre-war notions of hierarchy between spouses, with the express purpose of restoring the family-community of the nation and a patrilineal corporate identity. Vestiges of the family system established in the Meiji period (1868–1912) remained in the Criminal Code, the Nationality Law and the family registration system, which reinforced the notion of a male-dominated family structure (Mackie 2003: 130). The Japanese state made moves to overturn constitutional revisions to the family system imposed by Allied occupation forces, and although such moves were thwarted by Japanese feminists, the state continued to promote ideas of the patrilineal family and of 'good wives and wise mothers' (*ryosai kenbo*) through legal and public policy initiatives. It introduced a series of employment, social security and taxation measures designed specifically to instil within the family a 'strong consciousness of hierarchical order vital for sustaining the state, the economy and society' (Toshitani 1980: 144). These measures were also designed to ensure that women fulfilled their destiny as homemakers and child-rearers (Marfording 1997: 441). This highly gender-biased corporate state identity proved decidedly resilient and continues to present a formidable obstacle to internationally derived change.

International norms of sexual non-discrimination have evidently prompted different responses from states in international society, and by comparing a number of states we can evaluate precisely how different their behavioural responses are. The challenge is to explain these differences and the on the whole relatively limited efficacy of systemic norms of sexual non-discrimination. How do we account for the observable cross-national variation in the incorporation of international norms of sexual non-discrimination? Through what processes, and promoted by which agents, do states come under pressure to comply with these norms? Why are some states more responsive to and exert more effort than others to comply with these norms? Why do particular norms diffuse more readily than others and why do certain norms fail to diffuse into domestic state practices? By attending to the relationship between states and the international society in which they are embedded, we can begin to identify the various factors affecting diffusion and ascertain why certain norms diffuse differently, having a greater impact in some states than others. A crucial issue within this is to determine why some states are more open to international norms of sexual non-discrimination and more diligent in their application. This requires tracing of the various pressures exerted on the state by certain agents both within the state and in the international sphere. It also demands that the various factors underpinning state motivations and intentions be identified.

In particular, I trace the diffusion and efficacy of a distinct range of international norms of sexual non-discrimination that span the public–private divide. These include norms relating to women's civil, political and labour rights, and the issue of violence against women. To determine the extent to which these norms diffuse and influence state behaviour, I conduct a cross-national and cross-regional comparative study between Germany, Spain, Japan and India. This research is important because it may well provide the means for gauging the extent to which international norms of sexual non-discrimination matter and for evaluating whether international law is an appropriate tool for effecting changes in state behaviour and empowering women's lives. If we are able to identify the conditions under which international norms of sexual non-discrimination are most likely to diffuse into state practices, then the expected outcomes of state behaviour will be easier to determine. Such a study also contributes to our understanding of the relationship between international norms and state behaviour by broadening the analysis of norm diffusion to include an examination of norms that have relatively little influence on state behaviour. It also demonstrates the importance of opening up the state and analysing the political processes of corporate state identity formation. Further, it highlights the importance of analysing the dynamic interaction between state elites and other actors inside and outside the state.

Although this research is primarily driven by the analytical questions I have chosen to try to answer, I am also motivated to test the explanatory powers of existing theories in international relations. Hence, I have selected the comparative method to test the competing hypotheses of choice-theoretic and interpretive perspectives regarding the diffusion and influence of systemic norms on state behaviour. Peter Katzenstein, who has frequently employed the comparative method, defines it as 'a focus on analytical relationships among variables validated by social science, a focus that is modified by the differences in context in which we observe and measure those variables' (1995: 11). In the case of examining the explanatory potential of international norms of sexual non-discrimination, such contextual differences can only be provided by selecting a number of states, since states are the entities these norms are designed to influence. A single case study could not adequately measure the extent to which the source of state behavioural change is defined by systemic norms of sexual non-discrimination. Furthermore, as Sheri Berman points out, 'the comparative method, like counterfactual analysis, helps uncover the most important factors shaping political outcomes and is particularly good at eliminating variables from the pool of potential causes' (2001: 243). By conducting a cross-national comparative analysis, I am able to determine the impact of international norms of sexual non-discrimination on state behaviour and why these norms diffuse unevenly. The additional cross-regional dimension exists to assess the effects of institutional embeddedness and issue linkage on diffusion.

Rather than working deductively from a given theoretical model, as choice-theoretic perspectives do, this comparative analysis works inductively in its search to identify the conditions under which international norms of sexual non-discrimination diffuse into states. The cases selected have not been plucked at random; but rather, they have been chosen to control for certain variables. Germany and Japan have been selected because they operate in different regional contexts and yet both are considered major regional powers and international economic powerhouses – irrespective of Japan's recent economic difficulties. Both are considered stable democracies, having had their constitutions remodelled under the direction of the United States at the end of the Second World War, and both have had their sovereignty constrained (Katzenstein 1993a: 266). While Germany is deeply embedded in the sophisticated human rights system of Europe and is an influential member of the EU, the region of Asia in which Japan operates has not developed a similar human rights system. Like Germany, Spain is embedded in the European human rights system, where the potential for issue linkage is high. However, whereas Germany is one of the original members of the EU, Spain only joined in 1986 after making the transition from an authoritarian regime to a democracy. India shares Japan's Asian locale and, therefore, is not subject to any strong regional human rights institutions. From this cross-regional comparison we can assess the effect of issue linkage on the diffusion of international norms of sexual non-discrimination, thereby controlling for this variable. We can expect to find that if issue linkage is important, then diffusion is more likely to occur if a state is embedded in international institutions.

While Spain and India reside in the same respective regional neighbourhoods as Germany and Japan, they share neither the same level of industrial development nor a similar position in the world economy. Spain and India are both developing economies and are in the process of industrialization. By looking at states with different material and economic interests we can ascertain the extent to which preferences determine diffusion. All four states also present distinct social identities in the international community, which controls for the systemic constructivist notion that state social identities mediate between international norms and state behaviour. For example, Germany has enjoyed a reputation as a paragon of European integration and has been actively involved in the evolution of international legal norms since the Second World War. Japan, in contrast, has historically adopted a passive stance towards the international community, viewing it as something that has to somehow be tolerated. Since independence, India has been a prominent and active participant in the United Nations (UN), while Spain has recently emerged to join the EU in 1986, after years of anonymity under the rule of General Francisco Franco, to become one of its keenest supporters. Although this is certainly not a large-*N* study, the detailed cross-examination of four states does provide a broad enough range of cases to test sociological institutionalism's claim that international norms have an isomorphic effect on states.

The outcome of diffusion is measured in terms of substantive state legislative amendments and government public policies, which are extensive in their scope and are implemented, as opposed to cosmetic or superficial legislation and policies that merely pay lip service to the elimination of sexual discrimination. Diffusion is also measured in terms of whether or not state gender-rectifying changes are offset or neutralized by other state gender-reinforcing legislation or policies.[2] This not only overcomes the problem of trying to measure diffusion in terms of the changed social experiences of women but also provides a means for collecting comparable data. Identifying the reasons for substantive changes to national legislation and the initiation of concrete government public policies requires tracing of the processes by which international norms diffuse. In tracing the legal and policy formation process in the four states selected, we are able to discern the various factors responsible for the internalization of norms of sexual non-discrimination, whether these be external, internal or interaction between the two. It is important, Katzenstein reminds us, that the data collected for measuring the dependent variable – state behaviour – are different from the data collected for measuring the independent variable – state motivations (Katzenstein 1990: 174). Here, state behaviour is measured in terms of substantive changes to national legislation and concrete government public policy initiatives. Information about state legislation and policy responses is principally gathered from the UN, the International Labour Organization (ILO) and the EU. The methods for collecting the necessary data about state motivations, or the reasons why states make changes to national legislation and public policies when they do, are qualitative and consist predominantly of contemporary historical archival sources, email correspondence, interviews and extensive secondary documentary sources.

Before we immerse ourselves in the comparative analysis of norm diffusion that follows, a context for the norms selected for investigation is necessary. Hence, Chapter 3 traces the emergence of salient international norms of sexual non-discrimination within the UN and European international legal systems. It considers the development of international norms of sexual non-discrimination since the UN adoption of the Universal Declaration of Human Rights in 1948 and argues that, while there is currently a vast array of such norms in place, certain issue-specific areas of norm elaboration stand out as historically and substantively significant: women's civil, political and labour rights, and the issue-area of violence against women. Moreover, these issue-areas combined straddle the public sphere of citizenship and employment and the private sphere of home and family. However, whereas key international norms of sexual non-discrimination relating to civil, political and labour rights began being elaborated by the UN and European legal systems as early as 1951, the issue of gender-based violence was considered exclusively the province of states until the early 1990s, when it finally became part of the UN and EU agendas.

The reasons why these international norms of sexual non-discrimination emerged when they did, although not strictly the province of this study, are nonetheless important and can be explained, interestingly enough, using the same argument as that used to explain norm diffusion. Drawing on insights from critical realism, we can trace the development of systemic norms of sexual non-discrimination through historical phases of social and contentious discursive interaction in both the international and regional spheres in which the actions of various agents are mediated by power. In particular, we can examine how international feminist activism, which is the principal catalyst for norm elaboration, is enabled and constrained by changing international and the regional political conditions. The rebuilding of international institutions in the aftermath of the Second World War, for example, provided international feminists with the opportunity to organize and agitate for the creation of an international regime embodying norms of sexual non-discrimination. Drawing on the liberal individual rights discourse of the period, feminists negotiated the establishment of a series of international conventions aimed at recognizing and protecting the civil and political rights of women, as well as equal opportunity in employment. However, securing the codification of equality in these international conventions was not easy, with the international community disagreeing on the legal definition of equal rights, and state delegations and parties objecting to many provisions and their potential challenge to state sovereignty (United Nations 1998: 11, 18, 20).

Turning finally to the comparative analysis of norm diffusion, Chapters 4–7 investigate the diffusion and effects of salient international norms of sexual non-discrimination on the domestic practices of Germany, Spain, Japan and India respectively. Drawing on insights from critical realism, we can distinguish historical phases of social interaction in each case that lead to the state in question either incorporating or not incorporating particular international norms of sexual non-discrimination. Where social interaction leads to the state incorporating a particular norm, the change in state behaviour may originate from either within or outside the state, or it may emerge as a result of a combination of endogenous and exogenous factors. The change in state behaviour, for instance, may be induced by a regional body imposing conditions of membership or threatening to initiate infringement proceedings; it may be induced by criticism from an international body; it may be induced by domestic feminist activists and private individual litigants challenging state gender-biased practices; or it may even be generated by a combination of international and domestic pressures. Either way, states only make changes to national legislation and policies if they are under considerable pressure to do so. In the event that the changes are engendered by domestic feminist activism and litigation, we can trace the specific political processes by which feminists and litigants discursively express and enact dissent against discriminatory state practices.

In the period from 1945 to the mid-1970s, when the international legal regime was expanded and strengthened, international norms of sexual non-discrimination remained virtually dead letters.[3] In the mid-1970s, states came under mounting external and internal pressure to incorporate systemic norms of sexual non-discrimination, but their responses varied. Beginning with the case of Germany, Chapter 4 argues that, despite post-war constitutional guarantees of equality and its long-standing reputation as an exemplary member of the international and European communities, the German state was until 1998 relatively reluctant to incorporate systemic norms of sexual non-discrimination. The profoundly paternalistic corporate state identity reforged after the war, in reaction against the Nazi period and embodying Catholic ideals and principles of gender relations, had a lasting inhibiting effect on the diffusion of systemic norms of sexual non-discrimination. Despite constant international and domestic pressure since the mid-1970s to modify its behaviour, the state remained committed to an ecclesiastical regime of gender relations that privileged the male breadwinner until the late 1990s. Any changes to national legislation and public policy across the issue-areas studied were minimal and piecemeal. Moreover, with the exception of the amendments to national employment law in 1980 and 1994, the principal determinants of these changes were domestic feminist activism and private individual litigation at the *Land* (state) and local levels. In the 1970s, for example, it was German feminists who established shelters for battered women, whereas in its 1996 report to the UN Committee on the Elimination of Discrimination Against Women the state claimed that they were a government policy initiative to eliminate violence against women. Between 1998 and 2004, the state became less resistant to incorporating international norms of sexual non-discrimination.

The Spanish case, Chapter 5 argues, is one in which the state's receptiveness to systemic norms of sexual non-discrimination fluctuates over time. For thirty years, between 1945 and 1975, the authoritarian state remained vehemently opposed to incorporating international and

European norms of sexual non-discrimination. After the re-establishment of democracy in 1976, the state began to incorporate systemic norms of sexual non-discrimination and continued to do so throughout the 1980s. Between 1996 and 2004, the state became increasingly resistant to internalizing such norms. At the end of the Civil War in 1939, the authoritarian regime's official commitment to communal Catholic values led to the creation of an extremely gender-biased corporate state identity embodying pronatalist and familialist principles – the residual impact of which remained an important constituent of post-democratic reforms. The transition to democracy in 1976 marked the beginning of vertiginous political changes that involved the Spanish state withdrawing all legal and political privileges of the Catholic Church to administer family law and influence public policy-making. The state also made certain changes to civil law and labour legislation in accordance with international and European norms of sexual non-discrimination. These substantive legislative changes, while primarily induced by the state's desire for international and regional recognition, were only ensured by the intervention of Spanish feminists, whose demands for legislative amendments were articulated predominantly in reaction to the policies of the Franquist regime. Following these initial post-democratic reforms, various external and internal pressures induced further state legislative amendments and public policy initiatives across the three issue-areas studied. However, certain gender-rectifying changes were compromised by the state's inability to rescind family policies inherited from the Franquist regime. Between 1996 and 2004, the state showed a marked reluctance to incorporate systemic norms of sexual non-discrimination.

In the case of Japan, Chapter 6 argues that, despite extensive liberal reforms introduced by Allied occupation forces between 1945 and 1952, the Japanese state has been extremely reluctant to incorporate international norms of sexual non-discrimination. In the post-occupation period, the Japanese state implemented a broad range of policies designed to re-establish the traditional family system and, in doing so, reconstructed a patrilineal corporate state identity. With the exception of the 1951 ILO Equal Remuneration Convention and the 1952 UN Convention on the Political Rights of Women,[4] the state steadfastly refused to ratify or comply with any international conventions of sexual non-discrimination until 1985, when it ratified the United Nations Convention on the Elimination of Discrimination Against Women (CEDAW) and enacted the Equal Employment Opportunity Law (EEOL). Even then, the state only took these steps in order to 'save face' in the international community and to defuse the efforts of Japanese feminists and private individual litigants to obtain legislative and public policy reform. Moreover, the state introduced gender-reinforcing social security policies during the same period that effectively neutralized the gender-rectifying changes to employment legislation (Mikanagi 1998: 184). Incensed by the

restrictive changes to the social security system and by the apparent ineffectiveness of the EEOL, Japanese feminists intensified their campaign for
reform during the early 1990s. Their efforts, in conjunction with the pressure of private group litigation and international criticism, finally compelled the state to enact legislative amendments to the EEOL in 1997.
However, even the small gains made with these legislative amendments
were offset by further gender-reinforcing social security measures introduced by the state to ameliorate the effects of a rapidly ageing society and
falling birth rate. In the 1990s, the state also resisted enormous international and domestic pressure to admit direct responsibility for and offer
compensation to victims of state-sponsored violence in the form of
enforced military prostitution during the Second World War.

In the case of India, Chapter 7 argues that, despite its self-proclaimed
commitment to gender equity, the Indian state has been and continues to
be unwilling to incorporate international norms of sexual non-discrimination. In fact, in the late 1990s, the state became increasingly loath to ratify
or comply with international conventions enshrining norms of sexual non-
discrimination. At the root of this increased recalcitrance was the resurgence of religious communal politics and reinforcement of an already
communalist corporate state identity embodying highly discriminatory
religious principles of gender differentiation. The state always responded
to any internal or external criticism of its discriminatory laws and practices
with empty promises and cosmetic legislative changes, but in the late
1990s it tried to silence its critics and divert attention from its highly
conservative agenda by appropriating and championing the domestic
feminist political cause. Furthermore, the state tried to curtail the activities of Indian feminists by, among other restrictive measures, limiting
their access to information about government plans and policies. This did
not go unnoticed by the international community, but, despite considerable international pressure, the Indian state continued to refuse to modify
its behaviour in accordance with international norms of sexual non-
discrimination.

Thus, as this comparative study shows, international norms of sexual
non-discrimination have diffused unevenly and their overall impact on
state behaviour has been relatively limited. State behavioural responses to
international norms of sexual non-discrimination offer, on the one hand,
evidence of the inhibiting effects of the gender-biased corporate identity
of the state, which is politically constituted and reconstituted within the
state, and, on the other hand, evidence of the enhancing effects of international pressure and domestic pressure from feminist activism and
private individual litigation. As Chapter 8 concludes, it requires a new
argument drawing on insights from critical realism to explain the nature of
the relationship between international norms of sexual non-discrimination
and state behaviour. This argument, in turn, has several theoretical
implications, the most significant of these being that an analysis of the

construction of the corporate aspect of state identities and of the relation-ship between this aspect of state identities and various international and domestic agents pressing for state behavioural change, may produce more incisive analysis of the diffusion of a variety of norms.

As well as the theoretical implications of the argument advanced in this study, there are several practical implications for those operating in the field. First, international and domestic agents trying to promote state behavioural change need to pay close attention to how state elites create and maintain the gender-biased corporate aspect of state identities. Second, international and regional bodies need to find ways to generate positive attitudinal change among state elites and other dominant actors within states, such as the Church, religious communities and the judiciary. Third, these bodies need to create positive incentives to encourage state compliance and support those fighting for progress from within states. Fourth, these bodies need to strengthen enforcement mechanisms and, more importantly, develop the political will to apply such mechanisms and hold states accountable to their agreements. Finally, advocates struggling for change at the domestic level need to be aware that discursively chal-lenging political elites' ideas of *proper* and *appropriate* gender roles and relations in society contributes to generating state behavioural change.

1   Existing explanations of international norm diffusion

While considerable theoretical attention has been paid to the origins and substance of the international women's human rights regime in recent years, surprisingly little attention has been paid to the effectiveness of this regime. Feminist international legal scholars have examined the international law-making process in detail and highlighted conceptual and substantive deficiencies in the women's human rights regime but they have tended to neglect the significance of this regime for state behavioural change. This neglect raises several important questions: what are the implications of the regime regarding international norms of sexual non-discrimination for state legislation and public policies? Under what conditions do international norms of sexual non-discrimination diffuse or fail to diffuse into states? Why do certain norms diffuse more readily than others? Through what processes, promoted by which agents, do states come under pressure to incorporate international norms of sexual non-discrimination? In short, to what extent do international norms of sexual non-discrimination matter?

Although international relations scholars have recently paid a great deal of attention to questions concerning the relationship between international norms and state behaviour, they have paid scant attention to the diffusion and effectiveness of international norms of sexual non-discrimination. Furthermore, existing international relations theories of norm diffusion and efficacy fall short of providing a satisfactory explanation of the diffusion and effectiveness of international norms of sexual non-discrimination. As is noted in the Introduction, existing accounts of norm diffusion struggle to explain either the cross-national variation in the diffusion of international norms of sexual non-discrimination or why these norms on the whole have had a relatively limited influence on the behaviour of states. The purpose of this chapter is to critically evaluate the feminist international legal critique of international norms as well as alternative international relations theories of norm diffusion. It begins by critically evaluating the feminist international legal critique of the international legal system in general and the regime regarding international norms of sexual non-discrimination. It then critically evaluates several prominent international relations theories of norm diffusion, including two major variants of rational choice theory – neoliberalism and liberal intergovernmentalism – and two major variants of interpretive theory – sociological institutionalism and constructivism. Finally, it critically evaluates an emerging trend in international relations to fuse insights from rational choice and constructivism to explain international norm diffusion.

Feminist international legalism

Although the relationship between international norms of sexual non-discrimination and state behaviour is both theoretically and practically significant, it has been largely overlooked by feminist international legal scholars, who direct their analytical attention almost exclusively to the conception, substance and procedure of international law (Fellmeth 2000). Feminist international legal scholars are highly critical of the defining influence of liberal distinctions between the public and private spheres on international law, the traditional legal doctrine of state responsibility, the liberal definition of equality and the gender-biased procedures of international law-making. They also contend that the creation of an international regime designed specifically to eliminate sexual discrimination has led to the *ghettoization* of women's human rights at the international level, and question the relevance and efficacy of such a regime. Yet they assume that the various norms embodied in this regime are inconsequential because the regime lacks adequate enforcement mechanisms and because patriarchal interests restrain state actions. According to feminist international legal scholars, states universally pursue these patriarchal interests to the detriment of women, and unless enforcement mechanisms are attached to the international regime there is scant hope of altering the behaviour of states. Here, the correlation between international norms and state behaviour is framed purely in terms of problems of ensuring compliance, and the role of norms is seen only as an extension of state patriarchal interests. While the feminist international legal critique has added a gender dimension to the theoretical analysis of international law and highlighted the marginalization of women in the international law-making process, it tells us little about the formation and evident stabilization of international norms of sexual non-discrimination or the dynamic between these norms and state behaviour. Confined as it is to a conceptual, substantive and procedural analysis of international law, this critique provides no frame of reference for explaining why and how norms diffuse unevenly. Nor does it provide the means by which to distinguish the source of changing state practices.

Feminist international legal scholars question the conceptual underpinnings of international law, arguing that the accepted sources of international law and its liberal basis are inherently masculinist, and that the depiction and centrality of the state in international law implicitly ignores women's concerns, interests and 'special vulnerabilities' (Charlesworth and Chinkin 2000: x). Most fundamentally, they claim, the regulatory scope of international law is limited to interstate relations by the distinction drawn between the public international sphere and the private sphere of domestic jurisdiction. 'Even international human rights law, which is regarded as radically challenging the distinction between international and domestic concerns,' argue Hilary Charlesworth and Christine Chinkin, 'targets public, state sanctioned violations rather than those that have no apparent direct connection to the state' (ibid.: 31). Thus, they explain, domestic violence against women is 'typically not regarded as an international legal issue, even if the violence is tolerated by a legal and political system that provides inadequate remedies to the victims of violence', because under international law only states and not private individuals are held responsible for human rights violations (ibid.: 31). Furthermore, claims Donna Sullivan, the international legal upholding of the right to privacy, which calls on the state to protect the institution of the family, discourages direct state intervention in the personal domestic sphere (1995: 127). Feminist international legal scholars interpret international law's regulatory focus on interstate relations as protecting the patriarchal order within the state and the legal inviolability of the family as protecting the patriarchal order within the personal private space of the home and family.

While it is certainly true that the international community long neglected the issue of violence against women, feminist international legal scholars fail to recognize the recent progress of the international legal system in addressing the problem of gender-based violence. Since the early 1990s, the UN has adopted the Declaration on the Elimination of Violence Against Women (DEVAW), appointed a Special Rapporteur on Violence Against Women, and adopted the optional protocol to CEDAW. At the regional level, the EU has adopted binding legislation prohibiting sexual harassment in the workplace. While it is also undeniable that state legal and public policy systems produce and maintain gender inequities, the feminist international legal conception of patriarchy is essentialist and ahistorical, and thus unable to embody difference and change. It allows no room for variation and change in domestic legal and public policy systems, or for differences in state responses to international norms of sexual non-discrimination. The static and universalistic concept of patriarchy cannot explain, for instance, why Germany, Spain and Japan have all developed secular systems of civil or family law while India has retained a religious system of personal or family law. Nor is it able to explain the implications of this difference between state civil legal systems for the diffusion of international norms of sexual non-discrimination. The cases examined in this study show that states with secular systems of civil law tend to be less resistant to incorporating international norms of sexual non-discrimination pertaining to civil rights than those with religious systems of civil law.

The state, as depicted in international law, is problematic for feminist international legal scholars because, they argue, it is separated as an entity from individuals within it and shielded from internal scrutiny by the principle of non-intervention and the doctrines of immunity and non-justiciability (Charlesworth and Chinkin 2000: 125). At the international level, therefore, states Susan Boyd, 'only relations between states, or issues that states have agreed to submit to regulation through international treaty or contract, are legitimate subjects for international legal regulation' (1997: 11). The international legal system created by states is a fundamentally state-centred one of reciprocal rights and obligations between states, argues Andrew Byrnes, and, as such, struggles to deal with the question of state liability in relation to acts of discrimination by private individuals (1988–9: 226–7). By extension, therefore, it also fails to deal with sexual discrimination by private individual men. The state, as conceived in international law, is also attributed with a 'male' identity that, according to Charlesworth and Chinkin, 'makes it difficult to represent women's interests in international legal discourse' and 'naturalises beliefs about gender difference and relations, which then help sustain female subordination and oppression' (2000: 125). If sexual discrimination is to be eliminated, they argue, then the boundaries of international law have to be redrawn and the depiction and centrality of the state in international law simultaneously reconceived and undermined (ibid.: 21, 164, 169).

The weakness in this critique of the state is that it tends to conflate the international legal depiction of the state and the actual dynamics of international relations. Thus, it assumes that the dynamic of international relations is determined by rational unitary states seeking to maximize their patriarchal interests. It also assumes that reconceiving international law will automatically alter this dynamic. However, states are not unitary actors, and state behaviour in international relations is not necessarily governed by the instrumentally rational pursuit of interests, whether these are economic, material or patriarchal. Rather, while states establish various international norms of sexual non-discrimination primarily because of external feminist political pressure, they comply with these norms primarily because of internal feminist political pressure. Following the Second World War, for instance, sustained international feminist pressure led to the establishment of an international regime embodying norms of sexual non-discrimination relating to civil, political and labour rights. While the establishment of these norms has not been accompanied by the equivalent change in the behaviour of states, it is evident that certain norms have diffused and influenced the behaviour of a number of states. Much of this internationally derived change in state behaviour has crucially depended on domestic feminist pressure. As three of the four cases in this study demonstrate, domestic feminist activism, in combination with international and/or regional pressure, plays a critical role in generating state behavioural change in accordance with systemic norms of sexual non-discrimination.

The establishment of an international regime designed specifically to eliminate sexual discrimination provides little solace for many feminist international legal scholars, who see it as a means for placing gender issues outside the purview of general international human rights law, which itself is problematic because of its inherent androcentrism. Charlesworth and Chinkin argue that the substantive rules of international human rights law are gender-biased because they privilege male interests. Comparing the three generations of international human rights law, they observe that, 'despite their apparently different philosophical bases, the three generations are remarkably similar in their exclusion of women's perspectives' (2000: 231). They claim that the use of the masculine pronoun throughout international human rights law and the inviolability of the family are indicative of this exclusion. Even if the use of the masculine pronoun is intended to be generic, they argue, it implicitly reinforces gender-based hierarchies and is non-inclusive. The presumed sanctity of the family in international human rights law reinforces a distinction between the public and personal private spheres that, they declare, 'operates to muffle, and often completely silence, the voices of women' (ibid.: 232). Charlesworth and Chinkin conclude that this dichotomy between public (regulated) action and private (unregulated) action serves, among others, religious and commercial interests in the domestic arena, which 'benefit from a lack of international human rights scrutiny' (ibid.: 231–2).

The establishment of an international regime designed specifically to eliminate sexual discrimination fails to compensate for these failings of international human rights law, argue feminist international legal scholars, because it simply allows international human rights treaty bodies to continue to neglect the problem of sexual discrimination (Charlesworth and Chinkin 2000: xi). Moreover, they argue, international human rights law is ill-equipped to deal with problems of female subordination and oppression throughout the world because its understanding of equality and sexual non-discrimination tends to reinforce accepted gender relations, and to neglect underlying structural inequities. As Titia Loenen explains, the dominant, formal interpretation of equality as equal treatment 'hides in several ways a male bias by reflecting masculine norms and values under the guise of objectivity and neutrality and, thus, may help reproduce and enforce current gender positions and gender relations' (1993: 424). It also ignores fundamental social, economic and political disparities between men and women (ibid.: 424).

According to feminist international legal scholars, the definition of equality as equal treatment (with men), which provides the rationale for various international conventions, including CEDAW, also fails to consider 'whether existing male standards are appropriate' (Charlesworth and Chinkin 2000: 231). By taking (Western) men as the universal reference point, argues Elizabeth Jelin (1996: 178), international human rights law makes women different, which almost always implies inferior. As a consequence, argues Shelley Wright, the value of specifically female experiences such as maternity is indirectly subverted and marginalized as requiring 'special measures' (Wright 1993: 79). As key features of Western liberal thought, both the notion of equal treatment and the public–private dichotomy have long been the target of wider feminist debate in which liberalism has found its defenders as well as its detractors. So absorbing is this important debate that participants have yet to realize that it is, in part, responsible for the establishment and expansion of international norms of sexual non-discrimination. Participants also have yet to acknowledge the changing 'meaning' and normative content of liberalism, and the impact these changes have had on women (see Sawer 1993; Harrington 1992; Strang and Chang 1993). Such questions of norm formation and change are not addressed in the feminist international legal critique of international human rights law.

Feminist international legal scholars pay particular critical attention to CEDAW because it is the primary international instrument regarding sexual non-discrimination, but opinion is divided about its substantive value between those who dismiss the convention as an 'ambiguous offering' (see Charlesworth *et al.* 1991: 634; Donner 1993–4) and those who view it as a 'concise and comprehensive' contribution to international human rights law (Pietila and Vickers 1996: 126; Zoelle 2000: 35; Burrows 1985: 459). Despite this difference of opinion, feminist international legal scholars agree that CEDAW suffers from weak enforcement mechanisms and provisions for state responsibilities, and from a disproportionately high number of reservations. Comparing it with the 1965 UN Convention on the Elimination of All Forms of Racial Discrimination, on which CEDAW is closely modelled, Laura Donner concludes that CEDAW is the weaker instrument of the two because the UN has treated sexual discrimination with less concern and priority than racial discrimination. First, the committee established by CEDAW to supervise the implementation of the convention's provisions possesses weaker mandates than its counterpart, the Committee on the Elimination of Racial Discrimination (CERD), and, until recently, lacked CERD's authority to consider and investigate interstate or individual complaints. From its inception in 1982 to October 1999, when the UN General Assembly adopted an optional protocol to CEDAW containing complaints procedures, the CEDAW committee was only authorized to examine regular state reports and make suggestions and general recommendations (Donner 1993–4: 249). Second, from its inception to the early 1990s, when the General Assembly extended its sittings, the CEDAW committee met less frequently than CERD. Finally, the CEDAW committee lacks the formal means to receive information from non-governmental organizations. In terms of compliance, CEDAW does not contain the same strict enforceable restrictions on reservations as the racial convention. This lack of enforceable limits, Donner states, 'has resulted in CEDAW being one of the most reserved of all human rights instruments' (ibid.: 252). For feminist international legal scholars, susceptibility to reservations and inadequate enforcement mechanisms understandably raise questions about the capability of international human rights law to protect women's rights – the assumption being that without enforcement mechanisms, norms are inconsequential.

Rebecca Cook examines CEDAW's reservations in greater detail, making brief reference to the relationship between international human rights law and states. The international legal system, she claims, encourages tolerance of reservations to international human rights law on pragmatic grounds. Cook argues that international human rights law impinges on state sovereignty without, at the same time, offering any economic advantage that may render a compromise of sovereignty worthwhile. She also argues that reservations mitigate state apprehension about the possible consequences of accepting human rights conventions by reducing uncertainty and allowing states to fully protect their interests (1989–90: 650). Furthermore, she assumes that international human rights regimes regulate interstate relations and that reservations provide 'out clauses' and, hence, an incentive for states to agree to conventions and treaties. Here, the significance of international human rights regimes lies in their usefulness to states, which create and modify them to maximize their interests. Reservation regimes, meanwhile, are created by states to protect their interests. Reservation regimes and enforcement mechanisms indeed do have some bearing on state behaviour but so too do international reporting procedures, regional conditions of membership, the gender-biased corporate identity of the state, domestic feminist activism and private individual or group litigation – none of which is accounted for by feminist international legalism. As each of the four cases in this study demonstrates, it is the interaction between these various structures and agents that determines whether or not international norms of sexual non-discrimination diffuse into states and alter their behaviour. For example, changes in Spain's employment law in the late 1980s can be traced to a combination of EU conditions of membership and domestic feminist activism.

Feminist international legal scholars assert that the existing bias in the substance of international human rights law results from a procedural bias in the international law-making process (Fellmeth 2000: 699). Charlesworth and Chinkin argue that the under-representation of women in state delegations involved in treaty-making negotiations and in international law-making bodies ensures that international human rights law is defined and codified by men, and that this procedural bias acts as a barrier to the development of gender-sensitive international legal principles such as the prohibition of violence against women (2000: 70, 98, 99). However, they add, it will require more than simply adding women to the law-making process to alter the androcentric nature of the international legal system (ibid.: 70). Sandra Whitworth points to a similar procedural bias in the ILO's law-making process, revealing how male-dominated ideas about reproduction and the appropriate roles of women and men in society, the workforce and the family inform ILO law-making. The under-representation of women within the ILO, she contends, has contributed to the masculine interpretation of gender roles in society (1994: 405).

Although critically examining the procedures of international law-making is important when dealing with substantive issues in international human rights law, scholars need to take care not to underestimate the extent to which women have defined and redefined international law regarding sexual non-discrimination. Since the 1970s, for instance, international feminists have challenged and redefined international human rights law to include the norm of state responsibility within the private sphere of the family, and the prohibition of private actor violations (Thompson 2002: 97). They have also challenged and reconstituted international human rights law to include the prohibition of gender-based violence. Meanwhile, at the regional level, feminists have questioned and redefined European labour law to include the principle of equal opportunity in employment and social security schemes, and the prohibition of sexual harassment in the workplace. As part of the wider feminist international legal critique, this procedural analysis also leaves unexplained the relationship between international norms of sexual non-discrimination and state behaviour. International relations theories, in contrast, have dealt extensively with the relationship between international norms and state behaviour, and it is to these theories that we now turn.

Neoliberalism

Neoliberalism expresses a deductive account of the incentives, constraints and calculations confronting states, and operates on the basis of explaining the behaviour of states, not the formation of state preferences or identity. It contends that international regimes or institutions and the norms they embody are created by states to resolve certain problems and because of their intended effects. In other words, explain Lisa Martin and Beth Simmons, 'institutions are both the objects of state choice and consequential' (1998: 743). States are assumed to have predetermined economic and material interests, which, as rational actors, they will pursue by what they calculate to be the most effective means possible. When the interests of states overlap, co-operation is often judged the most effective means of facilitating agreements and ensuring the realization of those interests.

Operating as they are in an environment that lacks a central authoritative government, states overcome the associated problems of uncertainty, a lack of legal sanctions and information, and high transaction costs by establishing issue-specific international regimes or institutions. Specifically, institutions are tools created by states to reduce information and transaction costs through co-ordination. For that reason, neoliberals maintain, compliance with international norms is generally high and is a function of state interests or preferences.

Neoliberals consider state agents and preferences as unproblematic. States are seen as black boxes with fixed preferences that are taken as given, and the actions of states are perceived to be governed by the instrumentally rational pursuit of preferences. Thus, neoliberals offer no explanation of the socially contingent formation of preferences because preferences are assumed to be manifest in states' choices. States are viewed as intentional agents whose actions are directed by their interests, which are regarded as exogenously specified, and the only influence international norms have on the behaviour of states is as tools of co-ordination or facilitation (Finnemore 1996a: 3). Norms either constrain or regulate behaviour. For neoliberals, state agents are ontologically primitive, and behavioural outcomes are the result of states pursuing their predetermined preferences or interests. International institutional structures are treated as an epiphenomenon of the preferences of the constituent states and, as such, are considered to have no independent ontological status or generative powers. Instead of creating and constituting state actors and interests, institutions, according to neoliberals, are constituted by states (ibid.: 14). States, they argue, are intentional agents whose actions are directed by their preferences and who establish institutions, which are a dimension of the international systemic structure within which their activities are regulated and made coherent.

Once constructed, neoliberals argue, institutions provide a strategic context in which states evaluate their course of action. Therefore, any institutional changes tend to alter the structure of a situation, and thus the constraints and incentives facing states. The strategies adopted by states in this situation are based on reciprocity, with institutions acting as intermediaries by providing a framework of rules, norms, principles and procedures for negotiating agreements between states (Keohane 1982: 337). In other words, international institutions and the norms they embody operate as intervening variables between the assumed interests of states and their related behavioural outcomes. Represented by Robert Keohane (1984: 22) as standards of behaviour defined in terms of rights and obligations, norms act as regulators or constrainers of state actions and have no independent impact or effect on state behaviour. Since, according to neoliberals, institutions are created by states to realize their shared interests and to facilitate the making of mutually beneficial agreements, it is hardly surprising that they find there is generally a high level of compliance. As Keohane points out, 'most commitments are convenient most of the time; they were made on the basis of calculation of interests, the interests are maintained and, therefore, there is no particular reason to break them' (1992: 176). He adds that it is the anticipation of increased compliance that, to some extent, accounts for the willingness of states to enter into these agreements in the first place (1984: 22).

If for some reason of self-interest a state's international commitments prove inconvenient, it will nevertheless comply with them, says Keohane, either to avoid retaliation from other states; to minimize damage to its reputation; because it is enmeshed institutionally; because justifications of non-compliance are inconsistent with the normative views held by foreign-policy-making elites; or for the sake of maintaining a collective institution.[1] Since international regimes tend to be linked together hierarchically or by precedents, he contends, a state will think twice before reneging on any particular institutional commitment for fear of retaliation in other issue-areas or to avoid the risk of tarnishing its reputation or credibility in future commitments (1992: 178). Rather than risk the breakdown of an international regime, argues Keohane, states will comply with international rules or norms that conflict with their 'myopic self-interest' (1984: 100). If international norms ultimately prove incompatible with individual state interests, then compliance is more likely to occur if the state is deeply embedded in other institutions because of issue linkage. Keohane states:

> [S]ocial pressure, exercised through linkages among issues, provides the most compelling set of reasons for governments to comply with their commitments. That is, egoistic governments may comply with rules because if they fail to do so, other governments will observe their behaviour, evaluate it negatively, and perhaps take retaliatory action.
>
> (1984: 103)

So, in a heavily institutionalized environment such as the EU, issue linkage is more easily maintained than in a relatively non-institutionalized environment such as the Asian region, and thus the temptation for states to renege on agreements is reduced. In the dense web of EU institutions, a state is more likely to comply because of a desire to maintain its reputation or because of fears of retaliation from other member states. As Keohane explains, 'For reasons of reputation as well as fear of retaliation and concern about the effects of precedents, egoistic governments may follow the rules and principles of international regimes even when myopic self-interest counsels them not to' (1984: 106). States can also design institutions that create demands for linkage and cover issue-areas that can be profitably linked, thus enhancing the scope of co-operation (Martin 1995: 87).

Ultimately, according to neoliberals, international institutions and norms exist as a result of interstate interaction and serve to constrain or regulate state behaviour. Norm diffusion only occurs with the conscious consent of the state, even if it is under external pressure to comply or when the costs of compliance outweigh the benefits. In attributing the source of norm generation and compliance to state interests and interaction alone, however, neoliberalism is unable to account for the various sources of norm formation, or for the variance in or non-diffusion of international norms of sexual non-discrimination. Moreover, the anticipation and prediction by neoliberals that states will broadly comply with the institutions they have established not only explains why they concentrate most of their analytical energy on institution formation but it also leaves their explanation of non-compliance rather weak. The variance in state responses to international norms of sexual non-discrimination and the limited impact these norms have had on the whole clearly pose a challenge to neoliberal arguments of compliance. As the cases examined in this study demonstrate, states generally resist complying with international norms of sexual non-discrimination. When states do comply, it is not necessarily because it is in their economic interests to do so but rather because of pressure by international bodies and/or domestic feminist activists and private individual litigants. Such domestic pressure simply cannot be detected by neoliberalism because it black-boxes the state.

Liberal intergovernmentalism

Apart from problematizing state preference formation, liberal intergovernmentalism bears a striking resemblance to neoliberalism. Both subscribe to the view that state behaviour in international relations is interest driven, but whereas neoliberalism takes state interests or preferences as given, intergovernmentalism assumes that they are in fact derived from predominant domestic individual or group preferences. Intergovernmentalists speak of states as the ultimate locus of decision-making, pursuing policies that mirror the direct aggregation of domestic interest-group demands. Thus, they concede the intentionality of states to the interest-group baseline and then use this baseline to measure international institutional outcomes. The international institutional context itself, however, has no feedback effect on fundamental state–society relations. The pre-existing preferences of individuals and groups, from which state preferences are derived, are economic and material rather than ideational. Intergovernmentalists do not deny the presence of ideas in international relations but they do deny ideational factors any causal importance (Moravcsik 1999: 674–5). Adopting a managerial approach to compliance, intergovernmentalists argue that since states have a propensity to comply with their international commitments and obligations, ensuring that they do is less a matter of hard enforcement than of collective management.

The foremost exponent of intergovernmentalism, Andrew Moravcsik, lays out a three-step process of preference formation and bargaining:

preference formation, interstate bargaining and the institutional locking in of bargains (2000: 220), and concludes that all international regimes – whether they be trade, monetary or human rights regimes – exist as an instrumental calculation of how best to strengthen or protect democratic governance (ibid.: 248–9). Advocating a bottom-up approach to preference formation, Moravcsik emphasizes the derivation of state preferences from the interests of powerful individuals and groups in domestic society who, he says, apply pressure to government decision-makers to pursue policies consistent with their interests. In the first step of the three-step process of preference formation and bargaining, domestically located individuals and private groups rationally pursue their economic or material interests by what they calculate to be the most effective means possible, which is often through the state. State representative institutions and practices act as a transmission or conveyor belt for individual or group preferences, which are aggregated by varying government procedures to arrive at state preferences or interests (Moravcsik 1997: 518–19). In the second step of the process, government officials carry these preferences into international negotiations and bargain to achieve outcomes acceptable to both state government counterparts and domestic constituencies in all affected states (Choi and Caporaso 2002: 488). Once agreement is reached, international institutions are devised to lock in, monitor and enforce the agreements, and provide a buffer against defection. The locking in of interstate agreements through the establishment of international institutions is the end product of the three-step process. International institutions are not, however, designed or expected to affect or change state preferences. According to intergovernmentalists, while states delegate some authority to international institutions to monitor compliance with international obligations and to obviate the costly need to make exhaustive agreements that anticipate every dispute that might arise among states, the creation of institutions implies no loss of state autonomy or change in state preferences (Mattli and Slaughter 1998: 180). This is because individual preferences, from which state preferences are derived, are 'defined independently of politics' and exist prior to 'political exchange' (Moravscik 1997: 517). In short, preferences are assumed to be fixed and immutable at the individual level. The question for intergovernmentalists is who among societal agents will prevail in the race to influence state policy.

Given that intergovernmentalists presume that international regimes or institutions are established by interstate agreements based on converging or compatible interests, it is hardly surprising that they find levels of co-operation and compliance relatively high. They maintain that international co-operation is made easier, and the chances of compliance enhanced, by the fact that the preferences of states entering into agreements reflect the preferences of domestic societal agents. Since international institutions result from interstate bargaining derived from the preferences of domestic societal agents, the international solutions negotiated by states are unlikely to require drastic adjustments to their domestic institutional structures (Risse *et al.* 2001: 18). Intergovernmentalists see ensuring compliance and both regime effectiveness and robustness as simply a management process, explains Friedrich Kratochwil, involving

> not only the means of discovering a violation but also of ascertaining its significance, and justificatory arguments in which interested publics, international organizations, national bureaucracies, and even private parties interact and elaborate the concrete measures which the norms require in a specific instance.
>
> (2000b: 66)

Abram Chayes and Antonia Handler Chayes articulate intergovernmentalism's managerial approach to compliance, arguing that, because states possess a self-evident sense of obligation when entering into international agreements, sanctions and other hard enforcement measures are unnecessary to ensure compliance. Instead, they recommend a process of collective management of (non-)performance in which states are held not to a standard of strict compliance but to an appropriate or tolerable level of compliance set through negotiation, and sometimes tacitly (1993: 201–4). Managerialists presume that states have a propensity to comply with their international commitments because international legal institutions are largely endogenous, compliance is cost-efficient from an internal decision-making point of view, and an extant norm of international law – *pacta sunt servanda* (treaties are to be obeyed) – induces a sense of obligation in states to comply with agreements they have signed (ibid.: 178–87). Chayes and Chayes admit that instances of non-compliance may occur from time to time but they contend that such instances are rare and generally inadvertent. They argue that non-compliance is seldom premeditated or deliberate but more often the result of ambiguities within the international agreement, state incapacity or significant resources constraints, or unavoidable time lags between undertaking and performance (ibid.: 188–97). To improve compliance, they suggest reducing ambiguity through more specific rules; incorporating a transparent information system; introducing performance reviews; and offering technical and financial assistance to states that are having problems complying. While they acknowledge that many of these prescriptions are already common practice in international dispute resolution, they argue that managerialism provides theoretical justification of enforcement through assistance and persuasion as opposed to punitive sanctions (ibid.: 204–5). Unfortunately, as the cases examined in this study demonstrate, signatory states to international conventions regarding sexual non-discrimination are frequently reluctant to fulfil their international commitments and their non-compliance is often deliberate and sustained.

Although intergovernmentalism takes the important step of opening up the black box of the state to analyse preference formation, it neglects to question how individuals and private groups know what they want. Its exogenization of individual preferences fails to grasp the socially interactive process of preference formation, and its utility-maximizing foundation leaves no room for the ideational basis of individual preference formation. Thus, intergovernmentalism cannot explain why domestic feminist activists mobilize around both state corporate identity issues and issues that seldom reflect purely economic or material interests; for instance, issues of violence against women or civil rights issues. Moreover, since intergovernmentalism's upwards flow of causation peaks at the emergence of international institutions, it has virtually nothing to say about the effects these international institutions have on domestic state practices. There is no explicit treatment of how norms affect and influence agents' preferences or behaviour (Kratochwil 2000b: 62), and hence no real explanation of diffusion. Intergovernmentalism's assumption that the diffusion of norms is a linear process cannot account for the high degree of variance in state responses to international norms of sexual non-discrimination. Nor can it account for the relatively limited overall impact of these norms on domestic state practices.

Sociological institutionalism

Sociological institutionalism or world polity theory questions the limitations of choice-theoretic perspectives by challenging the assumptions that state preferences are either pre-given or derived from domestic societal actors. Instead, it locates the source of state interests in the ideational normative structure in which states are embedded. Sociological institutionalists begin their analysis at the international level and examine how 'the world polity context that envelops the competitive state system' has 'led to a remarkable degree of isomorphism among states and national societies' (Boli and Thomas 1999a: 1–2). In contrast to choice-theoretic perspectives, sociological institutionalism gives structure ontological primacy and derives state agents from it. In other words, institutions create states instead of states creating institutions. However, according to sociological institutionalists, states are not the only actors affected by international institutions or the world polity context. The world political culture impacts on all component actors, including states, sub-state organizations, private groups and individuals, and its effects are expected to be totalizing (Finnemore 1996a: 21). The world polity not only constitutes the identities and preferences of all component actors but also directs the goals and purposes actors adopt, 'the means they employ, and the causal logic they use to orient means to goals and purposes' (ibid.: 3). According to John Meyer and Ronald Jepperson, this culturally devolved 'authorized agentic capability' leads to isomorphism, standardization, internal decoupling, high structuration, and a capacity for prolific collect-ive action within and across types of actors, including individuals, organi-zations and states (2000: 100, 117). Sociological institutionalists thus promote a thoroughly top-down approach to international relations, proposing that changes in agent identities and preferences reflect pre-dominantly exogenous international institutional processes (McNeely 1998: 23).

The state and the international system derive from a wider world polity, which, according to sociological institutionalists, 'both provides a neces-sary legitimacy and defines appropriate and necessary arenas of jurisdic-tion and form for the state' (Meyer *et al.* 1987: 33). This expansive world political culture consists of a complex set of assumptions, generalized rules and standards that constitute the state and its understanding of legitimate goals and practices. Cultural values grounded in a Weberian rationality support and legitimate certain forms of organization and activ-ities over others. This underlying notion of rationality privileges the state as the primary organizational form and invests it with the authority and responsibility to pursue the goals of progress, development, freedom, justice and equality. Herein lies sociological institutionalism's explanation for the expansion and resilience of the states system, and for the converg-ing similarities in organizational structures and practices of states through-out the system. A set of worldwide rules provides states with rational goals and defines the social institutions by which these goals will be achieved (Finnemore 1996a: 19–20). As these rules and models of behaviour diffuse throughout the international system, states with very different cultures, histories and resources organize and structure their political and social institutions accordingly. For example, explains Martha Finnemore (1996b: 331–2), the pursuit of progress, defined in terms of increasing individual wealth and gross national product, and justice, defined in terms of equal access and opportunity, has led to the bureaucratization and marketiza-tion of states across the globe. The modern bureaucratic state, according to sociological institutionalists, has thus become the sole legitimate form of political organization in the world.

The most essential condition for the cross-national diffusion of inter-national norms, argue David Strang and John Meyer, is the intersubjective or shared understanding of what it means to be a state in the international system. They argue that states are socially constructed within the world polity as structurally similar units by virtue of their legal status as sover-eign, and legitimated as modern entities with similar purposes. Individuals within the state are constructed as autonomous, rational and purposive citizens, whose personal endeavours, combined with those of the state, are expected to contribute to the collective good of society as a whole (1993: 491, 501). The rapid spread of international norms only makes sense, they maintain, if we understand that the cognitive frames and functions of actors within the state and the state itself are derived from a global 'hegemonic cultural frame' (ibid.: 500). International institutions and norms, as constituents of this overarching cultural frame, go beyond affecting the strategic calculations of states to defining their most basic interests and identities. States may act in a rational, goal-oriented manner but such actions are themselves socially constructed or defined as appropriate by the world polity. States and individuals act according to a set of global templates, which determine and legitimate their behaviour.

One of the central legitimizing features of the modern state, argues John Boli, is its Constitution, which defines the formal political relationship between the state and individuals (Boli 1987: 137–8). The constitutional state establishes the individual as a citizen with various civil, political and social rights. Boli contends that the development of these three principal types of rights has proceeded in a co-ordinated fashion since the eighteenth century and has been institutionalized in state constitutions throughout the system (ibid.: 134–5). For instance, Francisco Ramirez *et al.* argue, the worldwide enfranchisement of women during the twentieth century is directly linked to the constitutional status of states and the development of an incorporative model of political citizenship. From the beginning, they explain, the movement for universal suffrage was an international one that carried with it a gender-neutral definition of political citizenship, which quickly became linked to national independence and development. As universal suffrage rights became institutionalized in the world polity, newly decolonized states and politically reforming states codified women's suffrage within their constitutions. In fact, they argue, universal suffrage has become such a deeply institutionalized feature of the modern state that when South Africa reformed its Constitution in 1994 on the basis of this principle, the enfranchisement of South African women went virtually unnoticed (Ramirez *et al.* 1997: 735–6).

One of the most significant carriers of universal rights, according to sociological institutionalists, has been the UN, whose activities and institutions account for the rapid post-war diffusion of international human rights norms. As a purveyor of Western cultural values of universalism, liberal individualism and world citizenship, the UN reflects the premise of sociological institutionalists that the functioning of international organizations (IOs) is akin to that of a courier. As the programmes and institutional principles of IOs course through the international system, they shape and redefine the identity and interests of states. The monitoring and reporting systems of these organizations further ensure that states pattern their behaviour on certain models of progressive policy (Strang and Meyer 1993: 492). The primary concern of IOs and international non-governmental organizations (INGOs), according to Boli and George Thomas, is 'enacting, codifying, modifying and propagating world cultural structures and principles' (1997: 173). These international organizations are the concrete or reified means through which Western cultural values such as universalism, individualism, rational voluntaristic authority, rational progress or development, and world citizenship are promoted (Boli and Thomas 1999b: 34–41). Rather than being measured in terms of the political, economic and social conditions within states, the diffusion of these principles is measured in terms of the determining strength of Western cultural values.

In addition to states, sub-state organizations, private groups, individuals and social movements are also seen by sociological institutionalists as entities constructed and motivated by world-cultural principles or institutional frames (Boli and Thomas 1999b: 13). In the case of the women's movement, the cross-national identification of feminists is explained as a matter of institutional equivalence, whereby feminists in a particular state come to regard their counterparts in other states as salient reference groups (McAdam and Rucht 1993: 64). During the campaign for the enfranchisement of women at the turn of the twentieth century, for instance, feminists in various Western states saw themselves in an equivalent position to each other and, increasingly, as part of a collective movement. Suffrage movements in Finland, Britain, France, Norway, Denmark, Germany, Australia, Canada and America were aware and appreciative of each other's efforts and based their campaigns on the same universalistic principles (Ramirez *et al.* 1997: 736–7). Appealing to a more inclusive model of political citizenship, the ideas and strategies of women's enfranchisement diffused cross-nationally and rapidly led to the formation of a transnational collective identity.

The resurgence of the women's movement that swept Western Europe and the United States during the late 1960s receives the same treatment by sociological institutionalists, who view the second wave of feminism as a social construct of the world polity and its cross-national campaign for equal rights as a further enactment of a privileged Western principle. In fact, according to Nitza Berkovitch, this feminist resurgence represents an ongoing expansion and transformation of the international women's movement that corresponds to the development and advancement of world polity culture and structure (1999a: 101). According to Ramirez and Elizabeth McEneaney, it is modernist notions embedded within this broader world cultural frame that provide the rationale for the 1970s campaign for equal rights. These modernist notions, they continue, also provide the rationale for more recent extensions of women's rights such as the elimination of violence against women. They state that

> models of progress and justice will foster expanded models of political citizenship and these, in turn, will provide more compelling rationales for further women's rights. Paradoxically, however, the expansion of the egalitarian yardstick generates the discovery of further inequalities culturally encoded as inequities.
>
> (1997: 20)

They also assert that it is through international social movements, IOs and groups of experts that the 'world culture unfolds as a series of blueprints for attaining authentic nation-statehood' (ibid.: 19). Moreover, Strang and Meyer argue, the diffusion of an issue such as women's equality will be greatly enhanced if it is linked to prevailing theories of the modern (1993: 502). Thus, sociological institutionalists claim they are able to account for the emergence and proliferation of various international regimes and norms of sexual non-discrimination, whether they are rights derivative from those already extended to men or rights that uniquely apply to women. All principles and norms can seemingly be attributed to, or their origins traced backed to, world cultural models of progress and justice.

However, for all their meticulously collected large-N empirical data, sociological institutionalists offer only a vague explanation of where this world culture comes from. They also make the mistake of assuming that the constituent components of the world polity are largely congruent. Apart from pointing to Western Christendom as the source of world culture, and to colonization, economic expansion and evangelization as the means by which it initially spread, sociological institutionalists have yet to give a detailed account of the origins of the world polity. Their assumption that the array of norms which make up the world polity are mutually reinforcing leads to what Finnemore describes as the obscuring of deep tensions and contradictions between elements of the world normative structures and the marginalization of politics and power (1996b: 340–1). Their picture of an ever-expanding Western cultural frame, which not only generates the organizational structure and interests of states but also defines and constructs the goals and functions of individuals within the state, is misleading. Not only does it overlook the inherent tension between world cultural norms such as development and equality, but also it ignores the tension that often exists between international and domestic institutional structures. Furthermore, because it holds that the source of all change can be found in the world cultural frame, domestic sources of change are marginalized.

The presumption that differing conditions within states are not significant predictors of diffusion blinkers sociological institutionalists to the possibility of domestic politics playing any part in the diffusion process. With its tendency to treat the effects of Western cultural values as totalizing, sociological institutionalism cannot explain the uneven diffusion of international norms of sexual non-discrimination. Moreover, while it offers insights into the profile of international legal regimes and norms most likely to diffuse, it provides no means for accounting for the formation and varying effectiveness of regional legal regimes and norms. Whether the EU, Inter-American and African human rights systems have any distinct influence on state behaviour, or whether Asia's lack of a regional body of human rights institutions has any significant impact, is of little interest to sociological institutionalists. It is also of no concern that a regional human rights system is unlikely to emerge in Asia, despite the best efforts of the UN and non-governmental organizations.[2] Yet the challenge of Asian states to a Western definition of human rights, including those of women, represents a significant contestation of the very values sociological institutionalists claim are diffusing in an orderly manner across the globe. The fact that international norms, including norms of sexual non-discrimination, are sometimes imposed upon states and subsequently compromised by local circumstances cannot be explained by sociological institutionalism. Nor is it able to account for any resistance or opposition from states to the domestic incorporation of systemic norms of sexual non-discrimination. The four cases examined in this study demonstrate that the diffusion of such norms does not resemble the smooth process implied by sociological institutionalism but, rather, is often subject to indifference or intense resistance by states.

Constructivism

While constructivists share the concern of sociological institutionalists about the a-priori manner in which rational choice theorists treat preferences, they part company with them over the content and effects of international institutions and norms. Whereas sociological institutionalists attribute the origins and effects of all international norms to the world polity, constructivists prefer to analyse state responses to specific norms because doing so allows for a more detailed examination of the process of identity and preference formation, and avoids the tendency to treat the effects of norms as totalizing. While united in their efforts to trace the sources of state identity and preference formation, constructivists diverge into three main camps in their theoretical approach to international relations. The first of these, third-image constructivism, is typified by the work of Alexander Wendt, who is committed to a systemic theory of state identity and preference formation. The second, second-image reversed constructivism, focuses on the process by which the external environment affects the internal nature of the state. The third, rational constructivism, uses a blend of rational choice and constructivist insights to explain the efficacy of international norms.

Third-image constructivism

Wendt disputes the central assertion of choice-theoretic perspectives that systemic interaction is determined by the rationally calculated self-interest of states. Against choice-theoretic perspectives, Wendt challenges the presumption that states are ontologically primitive units by posing the mutually constitutive and co-determined relationship between international normative or ideational structures and state practices. Also against choice-theoretic approaches, Wendt disputes the certainty that material factors are the defining element of international systemic structures by asserting the constitutive role of systemic ideational structures on the preferences and identities of states. Indeed, he argues that systemic ideational or intersubjective structures give meaning to material realities, and 'it is in terms of meanings that actors act' (quoted in Kratochwil 2000a: 74). The identity that Wendt is referring to in this systemic analysis of reciprocal interaction is the social identity of the state, and the diffusion of international norms is dependent on this identity. It is a state's social identity rather than its corporate identity that interacts with international norms, and whereas a state's corporate identity is singular in nature, a state may acquire multiple social identities through the socialization process.

According to Wendt, state identities are produced and reproduced through a mutually constitutive process of systemic interaction, and thus are relational. A state has an identity only to the extent that it is recognized by other states (Ringmar 1997: 281). The identities of states within the international system are constituted and reconstituted by practices and actions of mutual recognition among states. States are recognized as legitimate members of the international community by their adherence to international institutions and norms, and the legitimacy of international institutional structures are maintained or reproduced through the ongoing practices of states. As such, a state's social identities are 'primarily external: they describe the actions of governments in a society of states' (Katzenstein 1997d: 20). They interact with international institutional structures and mediate between them and state preferences and practices. A state's social identities vary in salience, argues Wendt, with the salience of a particular social identity depending on how deeply the social structure that this identity instantiates penetrates a state's conceptions of self (Wendt 1994: 386). However, how we assess or measure institutional salience remains undefined by Wendt.

The distinction between the state's corporate and social identities is central to Wendt's defence of his decision to theorize only the international system. He argues that it is necessary 'to bracket the internal processes that constitute the state, to temporarily reify it, in order to get on with systemic analysis' (2000: 175). Furthermore, he argues that the state's corporate and social identities correspond with the 'I' and 'me' in symbolic interactionism (1997: 50), a social theory 'that seeks to explain society – the whole – as an aggregate outcome of intersubjective interaction' (Palan 2000: 593). For Wendt, symbolic interactionism holds obvious attractions for analysing the dynamics of the states system, and he uses its premise that identities and interests are constituted in social interaction to explain the generation of state social identities through systemic interaction, and to justify treating the state as a pre-social corporate entity relative to other states. He argues that 'we can theorise about processes of social construction *at the level of the states system* only if such processes have exogenously given, relatively stable platforms' (1999: 198); these being states as corporate entities. According to Wendt, the corporate or individual identity of a state refers to 'the intrinsic, self-organizing qualities that constitute actor individuality ... and provide[s] motivational energy for engaging in action at all and, to that extent, [is] prior to interaction' (1994: 385). Wendt maintains that states, as the dominant agents in international relations, are ontologically emergent. Hence, he argues that the concept of the state as a corporate actor refers to a real but unobservable social structure that is not reducible to the properties and interaction of individuals who instantiate it. As such, he claims, states possess relatively stable properties of territorial boundaries, national interests, foreign policies, and so on (1999: 215–18).

The problem with attributing unitariness and intentionality to a corporate body such as the state is that it becomes reified – a problem that Wendt acknowledges but shrugs aside with the argument that 'even if a state has multiple personalities domestically they may manage to work together when dealing with outsiders' (1999: 222). However, as Heather Rae points out,

> the fact that the corporate identity of the state is just that – corporate – and not an individual identity, means that we need to look at how this identity is constructed, how the 'we' to which Wendt refers is constituted and maintained.
>
> (2002: 46)

By bracketing the domestic – corporate – sources of state identity and preferences, Wendt shuts out an important source of social change and state motivation. His restrictive systemic approach not only presents a narrow, mechanistic view of the process of mutual constitution between structure and agency but also renders his framework unable to explain the evident influence of interaction between domestic structures and agents on state motivations and actions regarding international norms of sexual non-discrimination. Third-image constructivism cannot explain why and how the gender-biased corporate identity of the state frequently acts as a barrier to the diffusion of systemic norms of sexual non-discrimination. Nor can it explain why and how the gender-biased corporate identity of the state is mitigated through the diffusion of such norms.

The idea of the gender-biased corporate identity of the state derives from the distinction Wendt makes between the social and corporate identities of the state but, in contrast to Wendt, who dismisses the corporate identity of the state as unimportant in explaining the relationship between international norms and state behaviour, I argue that it is crucial in explaining the diffusion of international norms of sexual non-discrimination. The domestically situated gender-biased corporate identity of the state gives rise to state motivations and affects a state's reactions to international norms of sexual non-discrimination. However, the gender-biased corporate identity of the state presents a formidable but not insurmountable obstacle to the diffusion of systemic norms. Through a combination of external and internal pressure exerted on the state by various actors, certain international norms of sexual non-discrimination diffuse into domestic state practices and, in the process, mitigate the gender-biased corporate identity of the state. For instance, as I demonstrate in Chapter 5, prior to the democratic transition in the late 1970s, Spain's extremely gender-biased corporate identity prevented the diffusion of systemic norms of sexual non-discrimination into domestic state practices. Following the democratic transition, during which the state came under considerable pressure from the European Commission and domestic feminist activists to comply with systemic norms of sexual non-discrimination, the Spanish government made rapid changes to national legal and public policy practices. In the process, the gender-biased corporate identity constructed by the Franquist regime was politically redefined.

Second-image reversed constructivism

Second-image reversed constructivists challenge the limitations imposed by third-image constructivism by paying attention to the domestic determinants of change. Unafraid of probing inside the state to explain social change, they accept the possibility of domestic or internal identity and preference formation. According to second-image reversed constructivists, however, state preference formation is not simply a matter of the aggregation of domestic interest-group demands – as liberal intergovernmentalists claim – but rather the incorporation and internalization of international norms of appropriate behaviour. Motivated to explain particular substantive problems, second-image reversed constructivists have conducted a wide range of empirical research, and because of this and their wariness of theoretical claims to universal laws of behaviour, we are compelled to review their theoretical concerns within the context of their empirical inquiries. Since we are interested primarily in the diffusion of international norms, I have limited this review to three prominent scholars – Kathryn Sikkink, Audie Klotz and Peter Katzenstein – who choose to examine the impact of international norms on state identity and preferences in distinct contemporary issue-areas.

Sikkink's early research on the diffusion of an international norm or idea of developmentalism into the Latin American states of Brazil and Argentina in the 1950s looks at the relationship between the international and domestic economies, and the ideas held by domestic policy-making elites and powerful business groups, to explain differing policy outcomes (1991: 2). In the post-war period, an international economic model of developmentalism emerged to redefine the legitimate social purpose of peripheral states away from that of import-supported economic growth towards that of state-supported domestic industrial growth (ibid.: 20). This idea, however, took different forms and was enacted with varying degrees of success in Brazil and Argentina because of its interaction with very different domestic institutional structures and ideas held by policy-making elites and business groups about economics and politics. Sikkink maintains that, while a strong political and social consensus emerged on development policies in Brazil during the 1950s and 1960s, no such consensus ever emerged in Argentina. This consensual variation occurred, she argues, because developmentalism came to take on different meanings in the two political contexts. Whereas developmentalism was adopted in Brazil into a context of understanding the idea as nationalist, it was adopted in Argentina into a context of understanding the idea as anti-nationalist and selling out to foreign interests (ibid.: 21–2). She describes how, unlike in Argentina, developmentalism was supported at all political levels in Brazil, stating that the idea was 'embraced by the industrial associations at the national level ... and became part of the institutional identity of the National Development Bank, the Development Council, and parts of the *Banco do Brasil* and the Foreign Ministry' (ibid.: 24). As a result, developmentalist ideas diffused and became domestically institutionalized more readily in Brazil. However, the ease with which such institutionalism occurred in Brazil was also partly the result of what she describes as an existing domestic institutional framework with a continuity and complexity that Argentina lacked (ibid.: 24). She adds that the degree of continuity in government policy-makers and administrative personnel also affects policy outcomes (ibid.: 24–5).

More recently, Sikkink has investigated the relationship between international human rights law and domestic state practices in the Latin American region. In partnership with Ellen Lutz, she measures the extent of compliance among Latin American states with international human rights law on torture, disappearance and democratic governance in terms of the degree of legalization in each of these three issue-areas. Legalization refers to the degree of obligation, precision and delegation that an international legal institution possesses, and when it is applied to the question of compliance, Lutz and Sikkink discover that, contrary to expectations, the level of compliance is lowest in the most legalized issue-area – torture – and highest in the least legalized area – democratic governance (Lutz and Sikkink 2000: 634–9). Apart from finding that legalization contributed little to human rights law effectiveness in Latin America between the mid-1970s and the mid-1990s, they also maintain that certain domestic factors, namely the severity of human rights violations and differences in domestic ratification of relevant treaties, played no role in state compliance (ibid.: 654–5).

Finding the explanatory power of legalization wanting, Lutz and Sikkink turn to the concept of norm cascade and to the degree of national decision-making centralization to explain the pattern of compliance witnessed in the Latin American region. They argue that the broad improvement in human rights practices in Latin America during the period under investigation can be attributed largely to the combination of a regional human rights norm cascade – a rapid shift towards recognizing the legitimacy of human rights norms and international and regional action on behalf of those norms – and a high degree of national decision-making centralization (2000: 638–9). Thus, they conclude, 'international norms and the pressures exercised to enforce them will be more effective in securing compliance when decisions are made by a handful of powerful, central political actors than when decision-making is decentralised' (ibid.: 639).

The application of a norm cascade concept to compliance represents for Sikkink a shift away from second-image reversed analysis towards systemic-level analysis of international norm diffusion. Although her earlier research does not extend beyond political elites and powerful interest groups to include other domestic agents in its analysis, it nonetheless takes domestic conditions seriously – something her research in partnership with Finnemore into international norm dynamics does not do. Finnemore and Sikkink's three-step process of diffusion – norm emergence, cascade and internalization – underscores the importance of state socialization in this process (1998: 895). They argue that socialization is the 'dominant mechanism' through which newly articulated norms cascade through the international system, aided by a combination of material sanctions and peer pressure. Ultimately, they assert, states want to be like other states and are motivated to respond to peer pressure by legitimation, conformity and esteem. Compliance brings international legitimation and a sense of social belonging, as well as enhanced national esteem and political leadership self-esteem, while non-compliance and violation are met with disapproval and social isolation. The internalization of norms depends on systemic state interaction, which, according to Finnemore and Sikkink, encourages iterated behaviour and habit. At some point, they conclude, international norms become so widely accepted throughout the international system that they assume a 'taken-for-granted' quality that renders conformance unconscious or automatic (ibid.: 902–4).

The problem is that Finnemore and Sikkink provide no measures of internalization, and their argument displays a systemic bias strong enough to rival that of sociological institutionalism. As a consequence, it suffers similar problems to sociological institutionalism of being largely correlative and able to capture only collective tendencies rather than the effects of international norms on particular states (Cortell and Davis 2000: 68, n. 12). Likewise, the concept of norm cascade is ill-equipped to deal with deviations or violations. If Finnemore and Sikkink were to take a detailed look at the legislative and public policy provisions enacted by states in the name of compliance with international norms of sexual non-discrimination, they would see that often these measures fall well short of international standards or requirements. For example, while no one would deny that the norm of suffrage has assumed a certain taken-for-granted quality, its internalization by most states in the international system belies the reality that other political rights of women have either been ignored by states, deliberately or otherwise undermined by related national policies, or received minimal or cosmetic treatment from states. Even the international principle of equal remuneration, which shares a similar historical pedigree to the norm of suffrage, has yet to be fully realized or internalized by a single state in the system (Clark 2001). This, of course, includes the four states examined in this study.

Klotz's research into the role played by an international norm of racial equality in the demise of the apartheid regime in South Africa verifies the necessity of examining domestic or internal conditions to explain diffusion. Using the notion of state socialization as her reference point, Klotz seeks to explain why the United States, Britain and Zimbabwe adopted sanctions against the South African apartheid regime, despite their having strong material and economic interests in maintaining current relations with South Africa. She shows that these states' adoption of sanctions does not make sense without appreciating the independent status of the international norm of racial equality, or how this norm penetrated states through domestic institutional and political contexts. In the case of the United States, sanctions were adopted because of widespread domestic demands to adopt them, generated by civil rights activists who linked national issues of race to the situation in South Africa. In response, states Klotz, 'Policy-makers accepted the importance of promoting racial equality in South Africa despite immediate economic costs and strategic uncertainties, reversing the longstanding assumption that strategic and economic interests outweighed any benefits from promoting majority rule' (1995: 11).

By contrast, a similar network of activists, employing a similar tactic of linking apartheid policies to national issues of race relations, was not so successful in pressuring the British government to adopt sanctions. This, claims Klotz, is because they 'lacked access to policy-making in the British Parliamentary system [and] the domestic discourse of race politics did not offer the same salient connections that activists in the United States stressed' (1995: 11). In the end, Britain's decision to adopt sanctions came out of a concern for its reputation within the EU and the Commonwealth. It could not be seen to tolerate or support racism. In its new-found independence from white majority Rhodesian rule in 1980, Zimbabwe made a commitment to implement racial equality policies that became the basis for its calls for international sanctions against South Africa. Thus, Klotz states, opposition to apartheid became Zimbabwe's marker for redefining domestic and regional interests, despite the risk of high material and economic costs (ibid.: 11).

On the other side of the equation, Klotz argues, South Africa's response to the sanctions adopted throughout the international community was not so much the result of coercion but rather the effects of both incentive and legitimation processes. Finally, after years of international isolation and pressure to eliminate apartheid, the South African government initiated legal reforms that dismantled the formal structures of apartheid and culminated in universal-suffrage elections in 1994 (1995: 12, 151). The government's capitulation was partly the result of what Klotz describes as external costs incurred through the loss of international membership in the UN, the Commonwealth and the Organization of African Unity, and partly the result of the external incentives of lifting sanctions (ibid.: 10, 151). Furthermore, she adds, international sanctions legitimized domestic political opposition to apartheid, enabling the African National Congress and Inkatha to negotiate 'the structure of post-apartheid South Africa based on racial equality' (ibid.: 162). Ultimately, she argues, South Africa's social identity was transformed in a process of socialization within the international community to become 'democratic' and 'non-racial' (ibid.: 170). Klotz clearly shows that rational choice explanations or purely systemic accounts of international relations cannot fully explain the behaviour of states or the definition and redefinition of state identities and interests. However, despite demonstrating the inadequacies of extant international relations theory, Klotz, by her own admission, over-emphasizes the importance of structure at the expense of agency (2001: 224). As Jeffrey Checkel points out, her ontology is not one of mutual constitution but rather 'a study of how social structures, a global norm of racial equality, reconstituted agents' (Checkel 1998: 337). Given the critical role played by various international and domestic agents in the diffusion of international norms of sexual non-discrimination, it is important to ensure agency is sufficiently explained.

Recently, Klotz has turned her attention away from norm diffusion processes and outcomes towards transnational social activism and its impact on international regimes or institutions, national governments and civil society. Drawing on her earlier research into apartheid, she compares the experiences of anti-apartheid activists with those of anti-slavery activists in the mid-nineteenth century to highlight the importance of transnational activism in international norm establishment and changing state policies. She argues that the experiences of both not only calls into question the novelty of contemporary transnational social activism but, more importantly, brings the question of agency in international relations into focus (2000: 56). Finding the explanatory power of international notions of epistemic communities and transnational advocacy networks wanting, she turns to social movement theory to explain the dynamic of transnational mobilization against slavery and apartheid.[3] However, while the application of social movement theory to transnational activism fills in certain gaps in both the epistemic communities and advocacy networks concepts, her analysis of the relationship between structure and agency is cast almost exclusively at the systemic level, rendering it of little use in explaining the diffusion of international norms of sexual non-discrimination and changing state practices.

In contrast to Sikkink and Klotz, whose research has gravitated towards systemic-level analysis, Katzenstein often begins his analysis inside the state or at the unit level. For instance, taking domestic institutional structures as his starting point, he conducts a comparative study of the effect of internal security policy on the international security conduct of Germany and Japan. He argues that the domestic institutional context of each state has shaped its responses to the formulation of international anti-terrorist policy in different ways (1993a: 266). Whereas Germany has taken an activist stance in the international arena by promoting internationally co-ordinated anti-terrorist policies to combat terrorist threats to internal security, he explains, Japan has resisted adding any international dimension to its security policy, preferring to rely on the traditionally close relationship between the public and police in solving internal security problems. He argues that Germany's impulse to view itself as part of an international community of states seeking to protect itself from terrorism through the formation of international laws owes its origins to a concept of universal sovereignty and a strong preference given to legal norms in domestic politics (ibid.: 273–4, 281).

Conversely, Japan's distinct lack of involvement in the formation and promotion of international anti-terrorist law is a reflection of the social embeddedness of Japanese law and the collectively held understanding of itself as unique in the international system. Although Japan endorses the human rights foundation that informs international anti-terrorist policies, Katzenstein says, its domestic institutional structures, which shape its identity and interests, hamper its active participation in the international community (1993a: 284). He states that

> The structure of state–society relations in these two cases corresponds clearly to the directive role of legal norms in Germany as contrasted with the social embeddedness of Japan's legal norms. And the links between the state and transnational structures, which are so much stronger in Germany than in Japan, correlate with the activist stance Germany has chosen in furthering the evolution of international norms in contrast to Japan's passivity.
>
> (ibid.: 289)

Furthermore, the projection of very different configurations of domestic social arrangements and norms into the international setting has seen Germany fit more easily into the international community than Japan. Germany's transference of a Groatian sense of belonging to the international community is more easily accommodated, he contends, than

Japan's Hobbesian engagement with the international community (1996a: 190).

Broadening the scope of his inquiry into security issues, Katzenstein looks at the implications of the end of the Cold War for regionalism and state identities. He argues that with the end of the Cold War, issues of collective identity and multilateralism have become increasingly important, changing how states identify themselves in the international community (1996b: 22–3). In two companion volumes, he examines the role of Asian and European regions in international politics (Katzenstein and Shiraishi 1997b; Katzenstein 1997b). Multilateralism, he maintains, is taking different forms in different regions, and in the case of Asia the weak formal institutionalism of Asian regionalism owes its profile to the contested definitions of Asian identity (Katzenstein 1997a: 10). The heterogeneity of Asia has inhibited the emergence of a common Asian identity and the establishment of formal regional institutions. Instead, he claims, Asian regionalism defines security largely in economic terms and has taken the form of multiple networks and centres of influence based on a combination of Japanese *keiretsu* systems of complex social connections and Chinese ethnic and familial ties (ibid.).

The weak institutionalism of Asian regionalism, according to Katzenstein, can be traced to two factors: power and norms in the international system, and the character of domestic structures. The United States, keen to maintain its independent decision-making on Asian policy after 1945, flexed its post-war hegemonic muscle and established the principle of bilateralism in the region. Combined with the various historical forces of colonialism, empires and kingdoms, which have shaped the network character of Asian states, bilateralism has made it very difficult for any formal multilateral institutions to emerge in the region. Apart from these external forces, he argues, the relatively weak institutionalism of Asia can be attributed to the nature of domestic state structures in the region. Whereas the Weberian bureaucratic and legal structures of European states lend themselves easily to regional integration, he explains, the network character of Asian states and the governance of relations between state and society by social norms rather than legal norms makes it difficult for the formation of any European style of formal institutions (1997a: 23, 27–30).

In particular, Katzenstein and co-author Takashi Shiraishi examine Japan's role in the region, arguing that Japanese colonialism and imperialism in North-East Asia have left a deep impression in the area and, combined with South-East Asia's marked ethnic, linguistic and religious differences, have inhibited the emergence of a common Asian identity, which, in turn, has made regional integration difficult (Katzenstein 1997a: 7). They argue that Japan's post-war experience under Allied occupation and the lack of far-reaching Asian regional institutions have left Japan relatively isolated. Furthermore, they argue, asymmetric economic dependence among Asian states and a lack of regionally institutionalized norms of collective identity have meant that ties between Japan and Asia are relatively weak (Katzenstein and Shiraishi 1997a: 365–6). However, despite its economic dominance in the region, Japan's leadership in Asia is likely to remain 'soft' (ibid.: 281). Katzenstein and Shiraishi attribute Japan's light hand to the state's weak regional institutional embeddedness and to the externalization of Japanese institutional forms of state–society relations – networks – and practices of reciprocity. They also state that 'Asia's network style of market integration has made it possible for Japan through economic instrumentalities such as trade, investment, resource diplomacy and aid to lead from behind' (ibid.: 371–2).

The structure of informal networks that characterize Asian regionalism contrasts sharply with the set of formal institutions that characterize multilateral arrangements in Europe. Focusing, in particular, on the relationship between Germany and European integration, Katzenstein attributes Germany's willingness to cede sovereignty gains made by unification to the EU primarily to its 'remarkably internationalised identity' (1997d: 5). Over the past decades, he states, 'European states and, in particular, Germany have acquired collective identities that are significantly more international than before' and, in this situation, states may act against their individual preferences to further the interests of European integration (ibid.: 3–4). However, he argues, the process of European integration is a mutually constitutive process in which regional institutions and state practices simultaneously shape and reshape one another. Germany is an ardent supporter of the Europeanization process because of its highly internationalized state identity, and, he claims, its political practices reinforce regional institutions (1997c: 261, 265). He states that

> Since 1945, Germany has been socialized into embracing multilateralism as the legitimate institution through which European states should conduct their business with one another. The internationalization of German state identity is a clear manifestation of this important political fact. The effects of German power are softened because of Germany's participation in European institutions. To a substantial degree, that participation has come to define Germany's identity and interests. Germany is the good European par excellence. It consistently advocates policies that support European integration, even if these policies reduce Germany's national power or run counter to its short-term interests.
>
> (ibid.: 260)

Like Japan in Asia, Germany exercises 'soft' power in Europe but does so through forging EU political conditions rather than leading from behind in markets (Katzenstein 1997d: 3, 4; Katzenstein and Shiraishi 1997a: 373). The softness of German power in Europe, states Katzenstein, is also the result of institutional similarities between the European system of 'associated sovereignty' and German 'semi-sovereignty' (1997d: 4).

While Katzenstein's regional comparative research underlines the importance of thick, unit-level analysis, its contention that the degree to which a state's identity is internationalized significantly conditions state preferences and behavioural outcomes does not help explain state responses to international norms of sexual non-discrimination. For instance, despite its highly internationalized identity, Germany has consistently resisted the incorporation of European and international norms of sexual non-discrimination. As I explain in Chapter 4, from 1957 to 1979, when the European Commission threatened it with infringement proceedings, Germany openly flouted its legal obligations to implement Article 119 of the Treaty of Rome and resisted complying with the EU equal pay and equal treatment directives. It also refused to comply with the ILO equal remuneration and equal treatment conventions. Since enacting the Employment Law to Comply with the European Community Provisions on 13 August 1980, the German government has made only modest amendments to employment legislation in accordance with international law. Hence, Katzenstein's argument tends to overestimate the effects of socialization on state interests and practices.

Rational constructivism

Recently, a trend has emerged to integrate or build a bridge between rationalism and constructivism. The effort to reconcile rationalism and constructivism is being led by Jeffrey Checkel, who brings scope conditions to bear on the socialization process and compliance, and Thomas Risse, who uses a blend of instrumental rationality and argumentative rationality to explain socialization dynamics and compliance. Concentrating much of their efforts at synthesis on the processes of European integration and international human rights diffusion, they firmly believe in burying the metatheoretical hatchet for the sake of what Checkel describes as 'empirically informed dialogue' (2001b: 581). The task, according to Checkel, is to identify and solve substantive puzzles using a combination of rationalist and constructivist methods (ibid.: 581). The question is whether or not rationalism and constructivism are theoretically compatible, and whether there is anything to be gained from their synthesis.

Beginning from the premise that it is time to move beyond a 'gladiator style of analysis' that pits rationalism and constructivism against one another, Checkel argues that both can be used to explain different aspects of the socialization process and compliance. He maintains that integrating the two theories is simply a question of scope: in certain situations, a rationalist explanation is called for; in other situations, a constructivist explanation is more appropriate (1997: 473; 2001b: 581). Criticizing constructivism for its failure to establish little more than a correlative relationship between international norms and preferential outcomes, he advances the proposition of instrumental choice and social learning as compliance mechanisms and specifies scope conditions under which states are more open to one or the other (2000). Examining the impact of European citizenship and membership norms, he argues that the structure of state–society relations predicts whether these collective understandings will have a constraining (rationalist) effect or a constitutive (constructivist) effect within states, and which diffusion mechanisms – cost/benefit calculations and social sanctioning (dynamics consistent with rationalism) or argumentative persuasion and social learning (dynamics consistent with constructivism) – will prevail (2001a: 180–3).

Checkel draws up a four-dimensional typology of state–society relations – liberal, corporatist, statist and state-above-society – from which he deduces and predicts cross-national variation in norm diffusion mechanisms and effects (2001a: 182). Applying this argument to two cases selected for their different historical contexts and institutional settings, he concludes that Germany's response to European citizenship norms is explained by a rationalist account of compliance dynamics. On the other hand, he argues, Ukraine's response to these same norms is explained by a constructivist account of diffusion (2001b: 553–4). The trouble is that when it comes to solving the substantive puzzle of the diffusion of systemic norms of sexual non-discrimination, Checkel's typology is of little use. As each of the four cases examined in this study demonstrate, whether a state has a liberal, corporatist, statist or state-above-society polity is of no real consequence in regard to the diffusion and efficacy of systemic norms of sexual non-discrimination.

Following Jürgen Habermas, Risse distinguishes between strategic rationality and argumentative rationality as alternative socialization mechanisms in the diffusion and internalization of international human rights norms into state practices (1999: 530–1). Risse characterizes strategic rationality as 'processes of forced imposition of norms, strategic bargaining, and instrumental adaptation' (a rational logic of action) and argumentative rationality as 'processes of moral consciousness-raising, argumentation, dialogue, and persuasion' (a constructivist logic of action). He contends that these modes of social interaction, along with a third mode of action marked by processes of institutionalization and habitualization (a sociological institutionalist logic of action), are necessary to achieve norm internalization. However, depending on the conditions, certain modes of interaction will dominate at certain phases in the process of international human rights norm internalization (ibid.: 530). Argumentative processes, according to Risse, are particularly crucial during the latter phases of the socialization process, when the repressive state in question starts 'talking the human rights talk' and begins justifying its actions to its international critics, and when the norm-violating state accepts the validity of international human rights norms and modifies its behaviour accordingly (Risse and Sikkink 1999: 25–31). In short, he argues, human-rights-abusing states succumb to a process of argumentative 'self-entrapment' whereby they move from 'rhetorical action and strategic adaptation to external pressure' to arguing and eventually matching 'words with deeds in terms of an improved human rights record' (Risse 2000: 32–3). Of course, he admits, not all norms-violating states are successfully socialized into international human rights norms.

While Risse's socialization argument is important because it emphasizes the processes by which international human rights norms diffuse and shape domestic outcomes, its focus on oppressive and very *bad* non-Western states overlooks the fact that Western liberal democratic states, while not necessarily systematic human rights violators or abusers, nevertheless resist the incorporation of certain international human rights norms, including norms of sexual non-discrimination. Since Risse's argument of international norm socialization is geared towards explaining human rights changes in repressive states, its ability to explain the behaviour of non-repressive *good* states – such as Germany – when it comes to norms of sexual non-discrimination is limited. As I explain in Chapter 4, although many regard Germany as a model international and European state, it has been relatively reluctant to incorporate systemic norms of sexual non-discrimination. There is no question that Germany 'talks the human rights talk' and accepts the validity of international human rights norms. Nor is there any question regarding Germany's post-Second World War human rights record. Yet the German state has, until recently, strongly resisted complying with a range of systemic norms of sexual non-discrimination. Thus, Risse's belief in the general applicability of his argument of international norm diffusion and internalization (Risse and Sikkink 1999: 2) is misplaced. Furthermore, his socialization argument tends to overemphasize the role of international compliance dynamics at the expense of national-level dynamics. It is also rather agent-centric and thus falls short of being able to explain the evident importance that national-level social interaction has in the diffusion of international norms of sexual non-discrimination.

Conclusion

Neither feminist international legalism nor existing international relations perspectives adequately explain the relationship between international norms of sexual non-discrimination and domestic state practices. Feminist international legal scholars are at a loss to explain variance in the efficacy of systemic norms of sexual non-discrimination because they presume that these norms are inconsequential. They presume that these norms have virtually no effect on the domestic practices of states because the international legal regime in which they are embodied lacks enforcement mechanisms, and because state patriarchal interests are profoundly inhibiting. When considering state motivations or reasons for acting in relation to international norms of sexual non-discrimination, neither neoliberals nor liberal intergovernmentalists are able to explain the evident non-economic or non-material sources of state or individual preferences. Moreover, because both claim that compliance is generally high, neither is able to account for the relative intransigence of states towards complying with or incorporating systemic norms of sexual non-discrimination. The expectations sociological institutionalists have that international norms diffuse expansively across the state system and have isomorphic effects on state behaviour is contradicted both by the varied efficacy of international norms of sexual non-discrimination and by the sustained heterogeneity in domestic state practices. Finally, the argument made by constructivists that states are socialized into adopting practices subscribed by international norms leaves unexplained the high degree of non-state socialization in relation to various systemic norms of sexual non-discrimination. Seeking to overcome the limitations of these perspectives, the following chapter develops an alternative, critical realist argument to identify and explain the conditions under which international norms of sexual non-discrimination diffuse or fail to diffuse into domestic state practices.

2 International norms of sexual non-discrimination and changing state practices

Between 1945 and the mid-1970s, international and European norms of sexual non-discrimination had virtually no impact on state behaviour, both because international and regional bodies had no expectations that states would comply with these or any other human rights norms, and because states refused to take the initiative to incorporate systemic norms in the absence of any external pressure. In a process apparent since about the mid-1970s, international and regional bodies have expanded and strengthened legal regimes regarding sexual non-discrimination and established concrete measures of implementation. They have also developed detailed 'how to' sets of instructions in the form of action plans or programmes specifying the requisite legislative and public policy action to be taken by states.[1] This international regime strengthening, in turn, has exerted pressure on states to modify their practices accordingly. Yet while regime strength is by itself a necessary condition for diffusion, it is not sufficient to explain either the variance in state responses to systemic norms of sexual non-discrimination or the limited overall impact these norms have had on state behaviour. Whether or not a state incorporates systemic norms of sexual non-discrimination depends also on the strength of the gender-biased corporate identity of the state, the degree of international political will to use existing monitoring and enforcement resources, and the effectiveness of domestic feminist activism and private individual litigation. The explanation for why states respond differently to systemic norms of sexual non-discrimination lies in the complex interplay between these various structures and agents, and the best way to capture this dynamic, I suggest, is to draw on some of the core ideas associated with critical realism.

The critical realist explanation of the diffusion of international norms of sexual non-discrimination advanced in this chapter consists of three interrelated components: structural–agential interaction, contentious discursive interaction and power relations. From a critical realist perspective, we can see that particular state actions – such as the Japanese state's elaboration of equal pay legislation in 1985 – are the outcome or result of a historical sequence of reciprocal structure–agent interaction involving changes in both international and domestic conditions. At any particular point in time, social interaction regarding systemic norms of sexual non-discrimination results either in the elaboration of state legislation and public policy or in the preservation of existing domestic legal and public policy practices. Critical realism also allows us to explain why and how external and internal legal and political conditions generate domestic feminist activism and private individual litigation, which, in turn, directly or indirectly influence the efficacy of systemic norms of sexual non-discrimination. Critical realism enables us to explain how discourse mediates contention between dominant corporate agents – such as the state, church, or religious communities – and dissident corporate agents – namely, feminist activists and litigants – over the accepted meaning of gender relations, and the consequences of this for systemic norm diffusion. It also helps us explain how contentious discursive interaction between states and international bodies affects diffusion. However, critical realism does not take us very far in analysing the operations of power in social interaction, because it tends to treat it simply as the property of agents or voluntary. Conceiving of power relations as relations in which *all* social actors are situated provides the remedy and allows us to examine how power impacts on the diffusion and efficacy of international norms of sexual non-discrimination.

Explaining state behavioural responses to international norms of sexual non-discrimination in critical realist terms entails a cyclical analysis of structural–agential interaction leading to state action or inaction. Change or stasis in domestic state practices may be the end result of an extensive sequence of reciprocal structural–agential interaction or the outcome of a short sequence of social interaction. Analysing state behaviour in terms of dynamic cycles of structural–agential interaction involves a temporal distinction that is merely implicit in the constructivist argument of mutual constitution. By incorporating time as an actual theoretical variable, we are able to explicitly ground structure–agency dialectics in historical time. The temporal dimension of social interaction is underpinned by a commitment to a dualism of structure and action whereby the two aspects are treated as distinct – they are neither co-extensive nor co-variant – and are linked in a non-reductive analysis of the interplay between the two aspects of social reality over time (Archer 1995: 66, 87). As Margaret Archer (1982: 458) explains, 'action of course is ceaseless and essential both to the continuation and further elaboration of the system, but subsequent interaction will be different from earlier action because it is conditioned by the structural consequences of that prior action.' Upholding the temporal distinction between structure and agency in order to examine their interplay depends, according to Archer, on the dual proposition that structure necessarily pre-dates the actions that reproduce or transform it, and that structural elaboration necessarily post-dates those actions. However, she adds, while structure is the elaborated outcome of interaction, it is simultaneously the conditioning medium of social action: agency is systematically transformed in the process of interaction (1995: 15, 247). Critical realism's inclusion of temporality as a variable factor in social interaction accounts for immediate social conduct (or the *durée* of day-to-day life) as well as social processes that may span decades (or the long *durée*). The short and long *durée* are treated not as separate entities but rather as interconnected time-frames (Sibeon 2004: 154).

Critical realism distinguishes between individual human actors or primary agents and supra-individual actors or corporate agents, which give rise to an individual's personal and social identity respectively and are dialectically related. As primary agents (the conditioned *me*), explains Archer, individuals are born into a socio-cultural context and are distinguished from corporate agents (the interactive *we*) at any given time by their atomistic or uncoordinated reactions to their inherited context (Sibeon 2004: 259). If, through self-reflection on their situation, primary agents seek and are able to realize collective action to either retain or reshape existing socio-cultural structures, they become corporate agents (Archer 2000: 11). As corporate agents, individuals pool their intra-personal deliberations about what they care about most and then subject these concerns to interpersonal scrutiny before acting (Archer 2003: 133). The capacity of primary agents to realize concerted action, however, is conditioned by structural enablements and constraints (Archer 2000: 269). Following this line of argument, the process by which systemic norms of sexual non-discrimination diffuse or fail to diffuse into domestic state practices involves social interaction in which the agents are corporate agents whose practices are intentionally designed to produce either societal continuity or societal change. Of course, Archer cautions, 'such intentions do not themselves determine the outcome and the result is rarely what anyone seeks' (2003: 356). Corporate agents intent on defending or transforming gender-biased social structures include, among others, domestically situated corporate agents such as the state, the Church and feminist activists, and internationally situated corporate agents such as the United Nations Committee on the Elimination of Discrimination Against Women, the European Commission and the European Court of Justice. While it is the collective action of corporate agents that is of prime importance in the process of systemic norm diffusion and state behavioural changes, the agency of small minorities and even individuals can sometimes be decisive; for instance, private individual or group sex discrimination litigation, or the actions of a single female lawyer or politician (see Barker and Lavalatte 2002: 155).

The gender-biased corporate identity of the state

In critical realist terms, the state as an agent is regarded not as a singular subject or entity analogous with an individual person *à la* Alexander

Wendt but, rather, as a corporate agent, defined as a group or collective with the capacity for articulating shared ideas or interests and organizing for their pursuit. As a corporate agent, the state is thus synonymous with political elites or government decision-making authorities capable of engaging in concerted action 'to maintain or re-model the socio-cultural system and its institutional parts' (Archer 1995: 265). It is reasonable, then, to speak in terms of the state possessing a corporate identity. The gender-biased corporate identity of the state, though by no means the only aspect to the modern state, is the most significant impediment to the diffusion of systemic norms of sexual non-discrimination.[2] The term 'the gender-biased corporate identity of the state' is used here to denote a particular aspect of the state's preconceived sense of self or state subject-ivity, which political elites play a crucial, although by no means exclusive, role in producing and reproducing. They do so via a process of narrative interpretation that is, explicitly or implicitly, founded upon certain situa-tional ideas, values and beliefs, and, therefore, variable from state to state. In other words, the development of narratives by political elites is the means by which the state establishes a sense of self distinct from that of others.

This knowledge of the self or self-interpretation, according to Paul Ricoeur, is mediated by the narrative function, which in turn borrows from history and fiction, making the life story or identity a historical fiction (1991: 73). In other words, he continues, an identity 'is not that of an immutable substance, nor that of a fixed structure but that, rather, of a recounted story' (1995: 7). In the case of the state, its corporate identity is constituted by an official history. Unfortunately, laments Ricoeur, official histories often 'claim not only to specify a community's essence but also to justify the community's having and clinging to its putative essence' (1996: 16). Such claims fail to acknowledge, however, that a political society con-structs as well as inherits its identities (Dauenhauer 1998: 129). Rather than being preserved in their history, the corporate identities of states are created, revised and reworked through a process of reflectivity exhibited as narrative, and, as such, are bound to be subject to competing pressures and tensions. States as reflective selves, therefore, can be said to acquire or possess corporate identities independent from both their physical or material and social or relational modes of self-existence. Such a *meaning-making* approach to state identity challenges the rational choice notion of states as rational agents in the making.

But ascribing a corporate identity to the state is to suggest that it pos-sesses a self-referential component or consciousness and intentionality. This is not to say that it has a consciousness in the same sense that indi-viduals do, but that it possesses shared knowledge or meaning (see Wendt 2006). The state's capacity for self-reflectivity or to turn a mirror on itself and establish order among its attitudes and beliefs, and give direction to its action (see Seigel 2005), finds expression in the form of the polis. The various figurations of the polis or body politic are more often than not gendered, inscribing the female in a gender-biased order. In the immediate post-war period, Germany's gender-biased corporate identity, for instance, was politically reconstituted in such a way that proved highly discriminatory. The state explicitly set out to re-establish the principle of German paternity as the foundation of national identity and redomesticate German women by implementing a gender-reinforcing regime with a firm Christian–occidental dimension. The Christian Democratic government of the time vehemently defended what it called the complete, i.e. Christian male-breadwinner, family, arguing that equality constituted an 'assault on divinely created human nature' and would ultimately destroy the individual bodies and souls of women, as well as the nation as a whole (Weitz 2001: 227). If women were to leave the home and enter employment, the government charged, they 'would be unable to nurture their charges properly, would be unable even to reproduce', and hence 'the nation itself threatened to disappear' (ibid.: 227). During the 1950s, the state emphasized the virtue of traditional gender ascriptions as a bulwark against totalitarianism and communism, sentiments echoed by the Catholic Church. The Minister of Family Affairs, Franz-Josef Wuermeling, a staunch supporter of the German state's programme of *normalizing* gender relations, argued that it was the responsibility of the state and society to assist women to stay at home and follow their 'true calling' as mothers and housewives (Schissler 2001: 364). The state's determination to return Germany to normality by restoring national security and stability in the *lebensraum* (living space) of the family was promoted by politicians, clergy, academics and the media, and was realized in the national security, industrial relations, taxation and employment systems. Traditional gender relations were also upheld in the German legal system. Despite the post-war reality of women with or without children seeking employment out of sheer financial necessity, the state, Church leaders and trade unions continued to discourage and discriminate against women in the workforce (ibid.: 366–7). Moreover, as Germany experienced an economic surge in the late 1950s, and with it a growing need for labour, the state adopted the policy of importing millions of foreign workers as *guest workers* rather than disturb the paterfamilias by integrating women in the labour force.

Germany's post-war struggle to return to normality also demonstrates how the gender-biased aspect of state corporate identities is established and sustained by political elites pursuing policies justified or legitimated in terms of broader social ideas and beliefs concerning the *proper* differentiation of gender relations in both the private and public spheres. However, establishing and sustaining credible legitimations is always difficult and, as such, offers means to resist it. In other words, the representation of political actions concerning state–society gender relations as legitimate involves an attempt to reconcile said actions with wider social values, not simply the assertion of their legitimacy, and failure to do so is likely to limit their effectiveness. Hence, explains Michael Braddick, 'the difficulty of establishing and sustaining credible legitimations shapes the exercise of political power and offers means to resist it' (2000: 70). As such, the legitimacy enjoyed by any political measure taken is not absolute but rather a matter of degree (ibid.: 89). Depending on the degree of success of particular strategies of legitimation, political elites may be forced to seek other justifications, or modify their political actions. In the case of state gender regimes, political elites have sought justifications for their actions in terms of a variety of diffuse ideas, values and beliefs. For instance, faced with formidable opposition to its plan to officially restore the pre-war patrilineal system and rescind reforms made during the Allied occupation, the Japanese government resorted to the notion of women balancing the necessity of employment with their domestic duties and responsibilities.

Ideas, values and beliefs of gender differentiation refer to aspects of the domestic cultural system, which, as an emergent entity, possesses emergent properties that are distinct from those of both the structural system and individual agents. An emergent system is one that, as a whole, has properties or powers that its component parts do not possess in isolation (Elder-Vass 2005: 320). According to Archer, cultural emergent properties, which are the ideational resultants of socio-cultural interaction, are distinguishable from structural emergent properties, which are the material resultants of interaction (1995: 176–80). Analysing the process by which socio-cultural structures and agency shape and reshape one another on the basis of a social ontology of emergentism allows for the recognition that socio-cultural structures are not reducible to individual agents even though these structures are still rooted in agential practices. Structural, cultural and agential properties, Archer explains, are 'relational', 'capable of reacting back' upon that from which they emerged, and possess their 'own causal powers', which are 'irreducible to the powers of [their] components' (ibid.: 9–10). As an emergent entity, the cultural system is a complex system composed of theories, beliefs, values, ideas and arguments that, while emerging from individuals in interaction, become autonomous and external to individuals, and exert causal power over those individuals. In other words, cultural phenomena have causal powers independent of individuals. Macro-cultural phenomena emerge from individual action and then, in turn, shape the future action and interactions of individuals. The different emergent outcomes of this interaction primarily result from differences in the metapragmatic properties of inter-agential discourse (Sawyer 2005: 182), which is discussed in greater depth later in the chapter, and interpenetrate the structural domain through the process of institutionalization.

Once certain ideas, values and beliefs of gender differentiation are institutionalized in the state legal and public policy systems, these aspects of the domestic cultural system, although often contested and historically

contingent, become relatively enduring. This is because institutionalization, which endows norms with endurance and political influence, occurs
more readily and forcefully in the domestic as opposed to the international sphere, and thus exerts a powerful pull on state behaviour
(Checkel 1999: 108). However, gender-biased corporate state identities
are not fixed or immutable but vary in complexion and strength according to the particular historical junctures at which distinctive ideas of
gender relations are institutionalized. This variance, in turn, results in different degrees of constraint on the diffusion of systemic norms of sexual
non-discrimination. Domestic ideas, values or beliefs of gender differentiation may permute through social interaction in different historical
periods but they always remain linked to earlier periods and have a residual effect on the institutionalization of successive norms. The fact that the
gender-biased corporate identity of the state is internally situated does not
obscure the dynamic nature of the relationship between the domestic and
international spheres and the potential, therefore, for the mitigation of
the gender-biased corporate state identity through the diffusion process.
Since particular or specific sequences of internal social interaction constitute the state as gender biased, the possibility of different gender-biased
corporate identities portends variance in state motivations and, hence,
variance in state responses to international norms of sexual non-
discrimination. Through a combination of external and internal pressure
exerted on the state by various actors, certain norms diffuse into domestic
state practices and, in the process, mitigate the gender-biased corporate
identity of the state.

Feminist political activism and private individual litigation

As far as internal pressure applied by feminist activism and private individual or group litigation is concerned, the international and domestic
socio-cultural contexts, which are produced by past agential actions, condition the actions of contemporary activists and litigants. For, as Archer
explains, socio-cultural structures do not determine the actions of agents
but rather 'supply reasons for actions' (1995: 209). Analysing the process
by which feminist activism and private individual litigation are generated
can explain why and how international and domestic political and legal
conditions produce opportunities for and constraints on contentious
action. Thus, we can chart the influence of specific historical constella-
tions of various opportunities and constraints that generate particular
forms of feminist activism at particular points in time in each state, and
examine how this activism then affects the diffusion of systemic norms of
sexual non-discrimination.

The international and domestic socio-cultural contexts condition the
actions of domestic feminist activists, in part, by shaping the values, beliefs
and preferences that activists hold – a constitutive effect that is missing in

liberal intergovernmental accounts of international politics. These collective values, beliefs and preferences then affect the strategic decisions of
feminists by determining which actions activists will evaluate as useful or,
alternatively, counter-productive. Activists may also value a particular strategy or tactic for reasons other than its effectiveness in achieving their goal.
It is also important to realize that political opportunities for activism are
not always recognized as such or seized on by feminists. Also, in the
process of social interaction, the state or other counter-agents – such as
the Catholic Church or religious communities – may react against feminist
activism to protect their vested interests in maintaining gender-biased
national practices, thus creating a contracting political situation for
activists. At the extreme, argues Lee Ann Banaszak, it is possible for the
state to so restrict the range of possible outcomes that activists cannot
realize any of their objectives no matter what strategy they utilize or how
many resources they expend (1996: 29, 33). For instance, the Japanese
state has, on occasion, been particularly effective at thwarting the efforts
of domestic feminists to effect substantive legislative and public policy
change. Since the end of occupation in 1952, the Japanese state has
repeatedly used a variety of stalling tactics to stave off feminist pressure,
including paralysis by analysis, concession-making and neutralization. On
numerous occasions the Japanese state has effectively silenced its domestic
and international critics by claiming that it needed more time to study or
analyse the compatibility between Japanese and international law. At other
times, the state has offered modest legislative or policy concessions in a
bid to avoid public scrutiny. It has also sometimes introduced gender-
reinforcing legislation or policies that not only neutralized small gains but
also strengthened the gender-biased corporate identity of the state. For
instance, small gains made with amendments to employment legislation in
1997 were offset by changes to the social security system that effectively
increased the burden of care for children, the elderly and disabled people
on women. These changes followed earlier measures introduced in the
1980s aimed at strengthening the patrilineal corporate identity of the state
by placing the family 'at the core of the nation' and reinforcing the traditional notion that care was a woman's responsibility.

Furthermore, Banaszak contends, while activists make strategic and tactical decisions based on their perceptions of political opportunities, their
perceptions will not always reflect reality. Activists view their society and
political system through particular lenses, which colour their perceptions
and, in turn, their actions (1996: 31–2). To an extent, this explains why
the timing, form and effectiveness of feminist activism may vary from state
to state. For instance, German feminists emerging out of the New Left in
the late 1960s were divided in their perceptions of the political system
between those who were sceptical of the state and those who sought political change through the state. At the time, this split left German feminism
as a whole in a considerably weakened and marginalized position, which,

as a consequence, meant that the state was less likely to initiate changes in accordance with international or European norms of sexual non-discrimination. Similarly, during the transition period of reunification, East and West German feminists were deeply divided over the identity-related issue regarding the relationship between motherhood and employment because of their different experiences in the post-war period. They also disagreed on a range of logistical issues such as organizational structure, relations to the state and political strategies. Consequently, Brigitte Young explains, 'facing a common *enemy* in the form of the West German state was not sufficient to unite the movement for the purpose of gaining access to the negotiations for German unity' (1999: 148). As a consequence, the state was able to achieve its objective of converting the German Democratic Republic to the West German model of gender relations with relative ease and, in the process, reinforce the paternalistic corporate identity of the state.

Critical realists tend to think of social interaction and its effects on the actions of agents such as feminist activists as an exclusive feature of the domestic sphere, but this comparative study shows that international, regional and national political and legal conditions interact to define the preferences of activists and create particular forms of mobilization. For instance, in mid-2000, under European and domestic pressure, the German state introduced a revision to national parental leave legislation that, although improving on previous policies, failed to comply fully with the EU's Parental Leave Directive, which had come into force in 1998. German feminists within the new political elite were somewhat disappointed because they had been pressing the state to implement comprehensive legislation that enabled both men and women to reconcile family and occupational responsibilities. They had done so by challenging the traditional model of the male-breadwinner family on the basis that women were no longer willing to choose between family and work.

Critical realists also tend to make the assumption of a relatively stable state in their examination of social interaction and its effects on agency, but this study demonstrates that domestic feminist activism is also shaped by fundamental changes in the nature of the state, such as India's transition from colonialism to independence or Spain's transition from authoritarianism to democracy, Japan's transition to post-occupation, and German reunification. International and regional political conditions influence both the emergence and the development of domestic feminist activism by legitimating and, in some cases, shaping activists' actions and claims. For instance, in 1975, international and domestic events coincided to mobilize Spanish feminists to pursue changes to highly discriminatory practices of the Spanish state. The United Nations International Women's Year not only lent legitimacy to Spanish feminist activism but also provided a protective shield for activists at a time when regime reprisals and imprisonment for any form of activism were all too real. Here, international conditions interacted with national political conditions – involving a crisis of the state and a dramatic shift in regime type from authoritarianism to democracy – to generate feminist activism, which, in turn, put pressure on the state to alter its behaviour and comply with systemic norms of sexual non-discrimination.

Legal conditions – especially regional and national – also enable feminist activists and private individual litigants to challenge discriminatory state legislation and practices and, in the process, deliberately or inadvertently put pressure on the state to comply with systemic norms of sexual non-discrimination. Usually, activism and litigation work in tandem because, while private individual litigation may occur in isolation, other forms of feminist activism in the political arena often accompany it (Shaw and More 1995: 267). Individual or group actions brought before national courts may even form part of a wider litigation strategy employed by feminists in their campaign to procure state legislative change. Of course, litigation is not always successful, but even when cases are lost, feminists sometimes use the loss to exert pressure on the state for legislative reform. For example, an Indian Supreme Court decision reversing a Bombay high court conviction of two policemen accused of rape provoked a written attack on the court in 1979 in the form of an open letter sent by four law professors. This was rapidly followed by demonstrations and rallies by feminists around the issues of rape, dowry deaths, battering and other issues of violence against women. Further litigation emanating from these campaigns put increasing pressure on the Indian state to modify its legal practices pertaining to violence against women – pressure that the state, unfortunately, was largely able to resist.

While the domestic legal environment on its own provides opportunities for litigation and feminist activism, regional and international legal conditions sometimes interact with national legal conditions to facilitate activism and generate change in state legal practices. This is particularly so in Europe, where violations of EU law are brought to the European Court of Justice (ECJ), and the court's decisions are used to force member states to respect their regional legal obligations. As Karen Alter explains, this makes 'European legal appeals a potent source of leverage for private litigants, groups, and the European Commission to influence national policy' (2001: 229). Just the threat of legal suits by these actors puts pressure on member states to comply with EU law (ibid.: 229). For example, as is noted in the Introduction, the European Commission's threat to initiate infringement proceedings against the German state in 1979 induced an amendment to national employment legislation. Private individual litigation at the German national level during the 1980s exerted additional pressure on the state to further modify its legal practices, as national labour courts invoked EU law in legal disputes and referred cases to the ECJ. Unfortunately, despite the growing internal pressure from litigation, the German state refused to amend national labour law.

The international legal system lacks the enforcement mechanisms of the EU, but, nevertheless, if national courts invoke international law regarding sexual non-discrimination in their decisions, it puts indirect pressure on states to comply. The success of plaintiffs and the invocation of international law in judicial decisions also facilitate domestic feminist activism, creating an additional internal pressure on states. For instance, a recent Indian Supreme Court judgment invoking the UN Convention on the Elimination of Discrimination Against Women (CEDAW) in a case involving sexual harassment and abuse in the workplace put considerable pressure on the state to respond accordingly. The Supreme Court's decision to issue guidelines in the absence of domestic legislation put further pressure on the state to act on the issue of sexual harassment. The *Vishaka* v. *the State of Rajasthan* judgment of 1997 also provoked considerable debate among Indian feminists and prompted demands for preventive national legislation (Kapur 2001c; Aruna Singh 1998). Aside from being invoked by domestic courts, the international women's human rights regime primarily relies on a periodic state reporting system to hold states accountable. While not as effective as EU measures, this reporting system still exerts pressure on states to comply with systemic norms of sexual non-discrimination. For instance, when states ratify CEDAW, they are expected to submit periodic reports for consideration by the CEDAW committee. After repeated admonishment by the committee for its tardiness in implementing the convention, the German state eventually introduced certain changes, albeit modest ones, in the areas of employment and violence against women in 2000 and 2002 respectively. The CEDAW committee has also exerted considerable pressure through the convention's reporting system on Japan over the years. In late January 1994, in its consideration of Japan's second and third periodic reports in New York, the committee chastised the state for submitting reports that were purely descriptive and lacked any critical analysis of the obstacles to full implementation of the convention in Japan. The committee also criticized the Japanese state for failing to recognize any specific problem areas or issues of sexual discrimination. Moreover, the committee demanded that the state take the appropriate legislative and policy steps.

Contentious discursive interaction and power

To fully explain state behavioural responses to international norms of sexual non-discrimination, we need to appreciate that discourse and power mediate social interaction, and therefore have behavioural consequences. The term 'discourse' is used here to denote clusters of statements that occur, not in isolation but in dialogue, in relation to or, more often than not, in opposition to other clusters of statements. In other words, explains Sarah Mills, each agent involved in a particular dialogue, whether they be an individual or collective agent, will have their discursive parameter defined for them in part by the other (2004: 10). Moreover, such contentious discursive interaction consists of statements that have meaning and effect, as well as the potential to be inclusive and exclusive. At the heart of this interaction lies the contest or struggle over particular ideas, be they social, political, religious or other. Discursive interaction can also have unintended effects on the social environment. For example, although protests against custodial rape by Indian feminists in early 1980 achieved their intended outcome of government legislative action, they also had the unintended consequence of political parties using the issue to attack their rivals. Indian feminists then found themselves in the unexpected and unwanted position of having to rescue the issue from becoming a political football for politicians.

The notion of contentious discursive interaction helps us understand how the ongoing discursive tug of war between dominant corporate agents – such as the state, Church and religious communities – and dissident corporate agents – namely feminist activists and litigants – over the accepted meaning of gender relations indirectly affects the diffusion and efficacy of international norms of sexual non-discrimination. Such contentious discursive interaction commonly occurs within a discursive field generated by dominant corporate agents who attempt to inhibit the development of meanings antagonistic to their own and devalue, ridicule and marginalize hostile meanings where they do develop (Chik Collins 1996: 76). Such discursive domination can never be total, though, explains Marc Steinberg, with new discursive practices or genres emerging through resistance. However, he continues, as dissident corporate agents 'seek to transform existing meanings in discursive practices to articulate senses of injustice, make claims and establish alternative visions, they also remain bounded by the fields and the genres within which they struggle' (2002: 213). Moreover, he concludes, 'since discursive resistance is always a dialogue with domination, for the latter can always talk back[,] even the successful appropriation and reworking of discourse in one context contains the potential for resurgent dominant meanings in another' (ibid.: 213). This is certainly evident in India in the late 1990s, where the state appropriated the discourse of Indian feminists in an attempt to silence both its international and its domestic critics.

However, discursive dynamics are not the exclusive province of domestic politics. International and regional discourses of human rights occasionally become incorporated in domestic contentious discursive interaction. For instance, prior to 1990, when Japanese feminists imported the concept directly from the United States, sexual harassment simply did not exist as an issue in Japan because there was no term in the Japanese language for sexual harassment other than the vague and rarely used phrase *seiteki iyagarase* (sex-related unpleasantness). Japanese feminists and lawyers imported the term from the United States by taking advantage of sexual harassment lawsuits against American affiliates of Japanese corporations to raise the issue discursively at the domestic level. Soon, the media entered the debate surrounding the issue, and leading Japanese law journals and periodicals began publishing articles and even special editions dedicated to the issue of sexual harassment. Feminists demanded that the state take legislative action, but the state initially adopted its oft-used tactic of trying to outlast domestic pressure by claiming that it needed time to study the issue.

Contentious discursive interaction contributes not only to the processes of feminist political mobilization and action but also to the constitution and reconstitution of the state gender-biased corporate identity, because it is through discourse that both dominant and dissident corporate agents articulate ideational notions of appropriate gender relations. However, since discourse involves dialogue situated in particular historical and political contexts, the impact of this process on systemic norm diffusion varies from state to state. For instance, recent contentious discursive interaction between the German state and German feminists over the definition and meaning of accepted relations is quite different from that between the Japanese state and Japanese feminists. It is also distinct from earlier contentious discursive interaction between the post-war German state and German feminists, and this has different effects on the diffusion of systemic norms of sexual non-discrimination. In the post-war period, German feminists were divided over strategies and objectives and, discursively, did not deviate substantially from conservatively held ideas of gender relations built into the German social security system and related employment policies. Activists were reluctant to identify independence with employment or to fully embrace the egalitarian idea of women's full-time employment. Consequently, there was little chance of the state initiating progressive changes to employment legislation. More recently, German feminists have discursively challenged traditional ideas of gender relations and articulated their demands for substantial revisions to labour legislation by drawing on the European discourse of equality. Despite domestic and international pressure, however, comprehensive legislative change in the last five years has been slow. Evidently, inherent in the social and contentious discursive interaction surrounding norms of sexual non-discrimination is an interplay or struggle between domination and resistance that involves both pernicious and non-pernicious forms of power. To understand how social interaction is mediated by power requires a conception of power that is able to account for the interplay between domination and resistance, constraint and enablement.

Power, of course, is a fiercely contested concept in contemporary social and political theory, with an agreement on its definition yet to be reached. Stephen Lukes argues that 'the very search for such a definition is a mistake', however, for 'what unites the various views of power is too thin and formal to provide a generally satisfying definition, applicable to all cases' (1986: 4–5). In the light of this, it is important to emphasize the relational dimension of power. Power is an emergent outcome of social relations; it is not something that can be procured or possessed. Agents become more or less powerful in the process of social relations and as a result of changing socio-cultural conditions. In other words, power is to some extent an effect rather than a cause of social interaction. This is not to deny that there are asymmetries in power relations between various agents but, rather, to say that these asymmetries are contingently produced and reproduced through social interaction. Thus, while there is the potential at any point in history for asymmetric power relations, with certain actors exercising domination or *power-over* others, there also exists the potential for the distribution of power to shift. To argue that power is, in part, an effect of social relations is also not to deny that power is embodied or cumulated in social structures. On the contrary, structures such as international and domestic legal and policy structures hold the power to shape social action. At any given point in time, socio-legal structures define and delimit the actions not only of those who seem relatively powerless but also of those who appear powerful. The question is, how and why does power shift? How and why do agents resist or challenge domination? What makes resistance effective, what legitimates it, what motivates it?[3]

Resistance, or *power-to*, is a socially generated form of concerted action that is neither instrumental nor strategic but rather is situational, in that it is conditioned by what Archer terms *vested* or *positional* interests (1995: 203). The motivation for resistance is derived from vested interests, which emerge within any given social situation or context and provide *strategic guidance* for agents, guidance that is not determinant but rather predisposing or conditioning (ibid.: 210). It is plausible, then, to talk in terms of agents having 'reasons for their commitments' or actions to resist and change their social disadvantages. Actors do not have calculated interests or take 'emotive leaps in the dark' (ibid.: 210–11). The fundamental point to remember about motivation, Archer argues, is that it depends neither upon zero-sum relations nor upon maximizing strategies but, rather, is relationally constituted and reconstituted (ibid.: 204). Of course, vested interests also provide those in a dominant position with the motivation to defend or maintain their social advantages. Positional or vested interests are neither fixed nor predetermined but, rather, shift through social interaction and are often multiple and sometimes conflicting or contradictory. Even when they do not conflict, there is usually room for agents to interpret or act upon positional interests in a number of ways, some of which may be contrary to each other. As Roger Sibeon explains, on occasion, certain positional interests are forsaken in order to satisfy other interests, needs or wants (2004: 143–4). For instance, during their legal campaign against discriminatory employment practices in the 1960s, Japanese plaintiffs and lawyers forsook their initial interest in creating a new moral and political consensus for a greater interest in securing specific legislative change. Of course, forsaking one set of positional interests for another does not necessarily result in the desired change, nor does the capacity of individuals to act in solidarity, or exercise *power-with*, in the face of domination of other agents. However, the ability of individuals to act together or collectively to achieve an agreed-upon end certainly heightens the possibility of generating change. For instance, in their struggle to secure revisions to national employment legislation, Japanese feminists worked together to attain the common goal of passing an amendment to the Equal Employment Opportunity Law that included a provision prohibiting sexual harassment in the workplace, a provision that, once passed in 1997, ensured that employers could no longer safely ignore the problem.

Conclusion

To explain the diffusion or non-diffusion of international norms of sexual non-discrimination into domestic state practices, we need to fully comprehend the dynamic relationship between international and domestic structures and agents. Using a critical realist argument, we can trace the process by which systemic norms of sexual non-discrimination diffuse or fail to diffuse through carefully analysing historical sequences of social interaction and the mediating role power plays in contentious discursive interaction between dominant and dissident agents. We can also trace the effects of social and contentious discursive interaction between states and international or regional bodies on the diffusion of systemic norms of sexual non-discrimination. Following the overview of the emergence and development of salient international and regional norms of sexual non-discrimination, this argument is used in Chapters 4–7 to identify and explain the conditions under which these norms diffuse or fail to diffuse into the domestic state practices of Germany, Spain, Japan and India respectively. These cases illustrate how social interaction between international and domestic structures and agents creates conditions that are either conducive or unconducive to the diffusion of systemic norms of sexual non-discrimination. Where social interaction creates conditions that are conducive to the diffusion of systemic norms of sexual non-discrimination, the cases examined in this study illustrate the importance of contentious discursive interaction between the state and various international and domestic agents in the diffusion process. They also illustrate the importance of domestic feminist practices and strategies of resistance to gendered power effects, such as questioning dominant understandings of masculine privilege and undermining dominant forms of knowledge regarding gender relations.

3 Origins and development of international norms of sexual non-discrimination

Since the end of the Second World War, international and regional human rights regimes have been established that have shaped both the behaviour of individual states and relations between states in international society. From the outset, both the UN and European human rights systems have upheld the principle of equality. Along with its broad human rights instruments, the UN and its special agency the International Labour Organization (ILO) have developed a range of instruments enshrining norms of sexual non-discrimination. The most important of these is the UN Convention on the Elimination of Discrimination Against Women (CEDAW), which, since its adoption in 1979, has been recognized at both the international and the regional level as the primary instrument regarding sexual non-discrimination. At the regional level, a number of human rights systems have been created, including the European, Inter-American and African systems. Asia is the only region without a regional system of human rights. The most long-standing and comprehensive of the established regional human rights systems is the European system. However, the European Council has not created a regime designed specifically to eliminate sexual discrimination. Instead, the European Council upholds CEDAW as the pre-eminent instrument regarding sexual non-discrimination in the regional context. The council's reliance on the European Convention on Human Rights (1950) and the European Social Charter (1961) has attracted growing criticism, and the council has been accused of failing to take seriously the problem of sexual discrimination in Europe (Council of Europe Press 1995: 41). This has seen the EU, which has adopted a number of legally binding directives prohibiting sexual discrimination in employment, become central to the furthering of European women's rights.

While the international and European legal regimes currently enshrine a broad spectrum of norms of sexual non-discrimination, certain issue-specific areas of norm elaboration stand out as historically and substantively significant: civil, political and labour rights, and violence against women. Moreover, these issue-areas span the public sphere of citizenship and employment and the private sphere of home and family. The driving force behind the development of these norms is international feminist activism, which is enabled or constrained by changes in international political and legal conditions. Applying the argument developed in the previous chapter, we can identify three historical periods of norm elaboration in which international feminist activism plays a key role in the establishment and expansion of international norms of sexual non-discrimination. We can also identify two interim periods of norm continuity in which adverse international political conditions constrain international feminist activism and thus restrict the development of new norms of sexual non-discrimination. In each of the three periods of norm elaboration, activists take advantage of certain international political and legal conditions to campaign for normative changes to the international regime. In their pursuit of norm elaboration, activists draw on the dominant international political discourse of the time to articulate their demands and claims. Their demands for normative change are frequently contested by state delegations, however, and achieving such change is difficult. In each of the two interim periods of norm continuity, adverse international political and legal conditions limit the opportunities for international feminists to articulate gender-based claims and generate further normative change.

The first period of norm elaboration, from 1948 to 1962, saw the emergence of an international women's human rights regime. In particular, it saw the UN and the ILO adopt a series of conventions related to women's civil, political and labour rights. It also saw six European states agree to include an equal pay clause in the 1957 Treaty of Rome, under which the European Economic Community was established. In this period, international feminists exploited the post-war reconstruction of international institutions to pursue and negotiate the creation of an international women's human rights regime. In particular, they sought the creation of a series of international conventions enshrining the principle of equality in relation to women's civil, political and labour rights. Activists developed a well-articulated form of justification for their demand for the legal codification of the principle of equality by drawing on the dominant international political discourse of the period, which centred on notions of individual liberal rights. The international community, however, disputed their equality claims, and consequently the conventions adopted were relatively narrow in scope and lacked adequate enforcement mechanisms. Partly as a result of these international developments and partly as a result of pressure from France during treaty negotiations, six European states agreed to include an equal pay clause in the 1957 Treaty of Rome, which provided the legal basis for the future elaboration of EU norms of sexual non-discrimination.

The second period of norm elaboration, from 1975 to 1980, saw the UN General Assembly adopt CEDAW and subsume under it all norms elaborated earlier. It also saw the EU adopt a series of legally binding employment directives. In this period, the international community's growing recognition and support of international human rights enabled international feminists to pursue a significant expansion in the international women's human rights regime. In particular, activists insisted on the creation of a comprehensive international convention establishing the principle of state responsibility to intervene in both the public and private spheres. Drawing on the dominant international political discourse of the period, which focused on the eradication of discrimination – particularly racial discrimination – activists articulated their demands for the creation of such a convention in terms of eliminating sexual discrimination. Negotiating CEDAW proved a lengthy and difficult process, however, with state delegations insisting on extensive revisions to the convention and weak enforcement mechanisms. Shortly after the UN adopted CEDAW, an international feminist-led debate on parental leave in employment resulted in the ILO adopting the 1981 Convention on Workers with Family Responsibilities. At the regional level, a decision by the European Council of Ministers in 1974 to establish a social action programme created an opportunity for European feminists to seek the expansion of EU employment measures. Two ECJ decisions in the mid-1970s also spurred activists to press for these changes and for the scope of EU competences to be extended beyond the confines of employment policy. However, while the European Council of Ministers adopted a series of *strong* employment directives, it refused to extend the scope of EU competences.

The third and final period of norm elaboration, from 1990 to 2004, saw norms prohibiting violence against women begin to be established at both the international and the regional level. In this period, preparations for the UN Vienna Conference on Human Rights in 1993 and the conference itself created an opportunity for international feminists to demand the inclusion of violence against women on the international agenda. Drawing on the international human rights-based discourse of the time, activists made a significant impact on the Vienna Conference. At the conference, activists effectively placed the issue of gender-based violence on the international agenda. Moreover, in the wake of the conference, activists achieved their objective of securing an international commitment to eliminate gender-based violence in the form of a UN declaration and the appointment of a Special Rapporteur on Violence Against Women. In response to further campaigning by international feminists, the UN also adopted an optional protocol to CEDAW establishing an individual and interstate complaints procedure. At the regional level, however, the European Council of Ministers resisted pressure from European feminists to adopt a range of measures to eliminate gender-based violence on the grounds that the issue fell outside the scope or competence of the EU. Finally, after sustained pressure from European feminists, the European Parliament and the European Commission, the European Council of Ministers adopted legally binding measures to eliminate sexual harassment in the workplace.

The first period of norm elaboration: 1948–62

The rebuilding of international institutional structures in the aftermath of the Second World War provided international feminists with the opportunity to organize and press for the establishment of an international regime enshrining norms of sexual non-discrimination. Activists outside and inside the newly established UN Commission on the Status of Women (1947) drew on the dominant international political discourse of the period concerning liberal individual rights to negotiate the creation of such a regime. At the time, international feminists were concerned about the failure of many states to grant women suffrage. They were also concerned about the discriminatory effects of existing state nationality laws and marriage practices. Furthermore, they were deeply concerned about the discriminatory effects of existing ILO protective labour laws and state practices of restricting women's right to work that had become prevalent during the 1930s depression. Hence, their campaign to establish an international regime embodying norms of sexual non-discrimination was centred specifically on norms pertaining to women's civil, political and labour rights. Seizing on and refashioning the liberal individual rights discourse of the period, advocates negotiated the establishment of a series of international conventions aimed at recognizing and protecting the civil and political rights of women, as well as establishing equal opportunity in employment (Prugl and Meyer 1999: 15; Lycklama a Nijeholt *et al.* 1998: 26; Hevener 1986: 75). These include the ILO Equal Remuneration Convention (1951), the UN Convention on the Political Rights of Women (1952), the UN Convention on the Nationality of Married Women (1957), the ILO Discrimination (Employment and Occupation) Convention (1958) and the UN Convention on Consent to Marriage, Minimum Age of Marriage, and Registration of Marriage (1962). However, securing the codification of equality in these international conventions was not easy, with international bodies disagreeing on the legal definition of equal rights, and state delegations objecting to many provisions and their potential challenge to state sovereignty (United Nations 1998: 11, 18, 20). Consequently, most of these international measures are relatively narrow in scope and contain either very weak or no implementation provisions.

Despite problems of a narrow mandate, significant budgetary and procedural constraints and a relative lack of organizational weight within the UN, the Commission on the Status of Women was instrumental in the initial elaboration of international norms of sexual non-discrimination in the areas of women's civil, political and labour rights. In the late 1940s, the commission placed a high priority on the question of political rights and urged the UN Economic and Social Council (ECOSOC) to press for an international convention on the political rights of women. The commission argued that such a convention was essential, given that many member states continued to deny women political rights. In response,

ECOSOC assigned the commission the task of drafting a convention on the political rights of women. Drafting began in 1949 but proved a difficult process, with ECOSOC repeatedly referring drafts back to the commission for further consideration (Reanda 1995: 282). The convention was finally adopted in 1952 and was designed not only to ensure the enfranchisement of women but also to prevent the disenfranchisement of women who already had the right to vote. Under the convention, ratifying states are obliged to grant women, on equal terms with men and without discrimination, the right to vote, to stand for election and to hold public office. The terms of equality relate to all aspects of employment, including salary, retirement benefits, promotion opportunities and the employment of married women. However, the convention was adopted without any implementation provisions. After the convention came into force in 1954, the commission submitted a proposal for the establishment of a reporting system, which was duly adopted by ECOSOC. The reporting system was purely voluntary, however. Consequently, despite repeated requests made by the commission throughout the 1960s for reports, very few states obliged, and those that did provided only scant and selective information (Burrows 1984: 337–41). In 1979, the convention and its reporting system were subsumed by CEDAW.

As well as placing a high priority on the question of political rights, the Commission on the Status of Women also viewed the question of women's rights of nationality in marriage as extremely important. As Laura Reanda explains, the commission first proposed a convention establishing the right of married women to retain their own nationality in 1947, in a bid to 'resolve conflicts of nationality law between [states] which had resulted in hardships for many women' (1995: 283). However, she continues, the commission did not begin drafting the convention until 1953, as it spent several years debating 'whether this matter should be the object of an international treaty and, if so, whether the commission was the most appropriate body for undertaking the exercise' (ibid.: 283). When the commission finally began drafting the Convention on the Nationality of Married Women, it decided to abandon its objective of creating a convention based on the principle of equality, 'for fear that it would not be widely ratified' (ibid.: 283). Many member states indicated that they would not ratify the convention if they felt that their 'sovereign interests' were threatened in any way by its provisions (United Nations 1998: 20). As a result, Reanda explains, the commission limited the convention's scope to 'protecting women against the automatic loss or acquisition of nationality as a consequence of marriage' (1995: 283). Aside from its narrow scope, the convention contains no compliance measures, and, according to Reanda, the commission has never 'specifically considered its implementation' (ibid.: 283). Similar problems plagued the 1962 Convention on Consent to Marriage, Minimum Age of Marriage, and Registration of Marriage, which was the final convention drafted by the commission in the initial period of norm elaboration.

The Commission on the Status of Women was also instrumental in the establishment of two major international employment conventions. By the late 1940s, commission members and other international feminists had begun to question the discriminatory effects of international protective labour measures – particularly those pertaining to wages – and in early 1948 the commission adopted a resolution calling for the ILO to take legal action with respect to equal pay (Lubin and Winslow 1990: 94). The following year, the commission pressed the ILO to include in such action the rate for the job irrespective of sex, equal opportunity for jobs and promotion, the abolition of legal or customary restrictions on the pay of female employees, and technical training and guidance (ibid.: 94). As a result of this international feminist pressure, the ILO initiated a study on the issue of equal remuneration and, after considerable debate, adopted two conventions: the 1951 Equal Remuneration Convention and the 1958 Discrimination (Employment and Occupation) Convention. However, both are purely *promotional conventions* (see Leary 1997: 214) in that, rather than laying down precise and substantive objectives, they expect states merely to 'promote' and to ensure implementation by 'means appropriate to national methods, conditions and practice' (International Labour Conference 1986: 12, 1988: 243). Such vague expectations make it difficult to measure and monitor compliance.

The international feminist-led debate on equal pay and the subsequent adoption of the ILO Equal Remuneration Convention played a crucial role in the decision of six European states to include an equal pay provision in the 1957 Treaty of Rome, under which the European Economic Community was established. The equal pay clause – Article 119 – of the treaty also owes its existence, in part, to a-priori French equal pay legislation, the existence of which prompted France to successfully demand that such a clause be included in the treaty (Hoskyns 1996: 52–3). During treaty negotiations, France insisted on the inclusion of an equal pay clause and on its short period of implementation because it feared that its industries would suffer a competitive disadvantage in a common market where tariff barriers were lowered (Neilson 1998: 65). French negotiators argued that France's existing equal pay law would put it at a disadvantage since it would incur higher social costs than the five other states because domestic industries were likely to move to areas with lower social costs and more flexible labour markets (a practice called *social dumping*). Germany disagreed and, despite having ratified the ILO Equal Remuneration Convention, opposed the inclusion of an equal pay clause in the treaty on the grounds that it was impractical and unnecessary. German negotiators argued that industrial competitiveness was dependent on a range of factors beyond indirect labour, including taxation and productivity, and that they therefore saw no reason to focus particularly on harmonizing social policy in Europe (Ostner and Lewis 1995: 162). They also maintained that social costs would inevitably align across member states as a result of market competitiveness.

Concerned by the rising tension in treaty negotiations, the ILO asked Bertil Ohlin, a former Swedish Minister of Commerce, to chair a study by an expert group of economists into the social aspects of European economic integration that addressed the various concerns of the French and German negotiators. The Ohlin Report, published in 1956, concluded that, while European Community intervention in national social affairs should be minimal, it was nonetheless necessary in specific industrial sectors to correct certain distortions to competition such as pay inequities. The report's recognition of the potential distortion to economic competition of pay inequities not only strengthened the French position but also provided the rationale for the other states to agree to the inclusion of Article 119 in the Treaty of Rome (Ellina 1999: 55–6). By autumn 1956, a draft for an article on equal pay had been prepared that mirrored the provisions of the ILO Equal Remuneration Convention, and in November that year, treaty negotiators approved it, with a reservation on the phrase 'work of equal value' (ibid.: 60–1). Consequently, when the Treaty of Rome was signed in 1957, Article 119 only guaranteed 'equal pay for equal work', which could be interpreted by states to mean that they had only to provide equal pay for work identical in nature rather than work of equivalent worth (McKean 1983: 169).

The initial momentum of the immediate post-war years, however, was not sustained. As international human rights issues in general became sidelined by the Cold War and by the European Community's determination to concentrate on the creation of its internal economic market, it became increasingly difficult for international feminists to bring about further normative change. Despite numerous requests from activists and the Commission on the Status of Women for a comprehensive international convention combating sexual discrimination, the UN General Assembly refused to act until 1963, when it took the tentative step of adopting a resolution inviting member states and appropriate non-governmental organizations (NGOs) to submit comments and proposals on principles that might be included in a legally non-binding declaration on the elimination of discrimination against women (Fraser 2001: 45–6; Tinker and Jaquette 1987: 419). Two years later – after thirty states, fifteen NGOs and four UN specialized agencies had submitted comments – the Commission on the Status of Women began drafting the declaration. However, Reanda explains, the drafting process, once again, proved difficult because of a lack of agreement within the commission itself over both the form and the substance of the declaration (Fraser 2001: 47; Reanda 1995: 284–5). Furthermore, member states disagreed over the content of such a statement.

According to Reanda, the main disagreement among member states was between East European states, which argued for a declaration setting forth state responsibilities for implementation, and Western democratic states, which viewed the proposed declaration 'as a statement of fundamental rights, similar to the Universal Declaration, without reference to obligations by states' (1995: 285). Member states also disagreed over the specific rights to be included, she continues, with East European states calling for a broad instrument that included protective measures and Western states arguing for a narrow instrument without protective measures. Eventually, she concludes, a compromise was reached whereby sexual discrimination was not specifically defined and 'each substantive article was drafted to refer to measures to be taken without spelling out who should take such measures' (ibid.: 285). Thirteen years were to elapse between the adoption of the Declaration on the Elimination of Discrimination Against Women (DEDAW) in 1967 and the corresponding convention, primarily because Western member states opposed the adoption of a convention. They argued that a convention was likely to undermine or conflict with existing human rights measures, including ILO labour standards, and hinder ratification of other UN treaties, particularly the two international covenants of 1966 (namely the International Covenant on Civil and Political Rights, and the International Covenant on Economic, Social and Cultural Rights).

At the regional level, Article 119 of the Treaty of Rome remained a dead letter for almost twenty years until 1976, when the European Court of Justice ruled that it had direct effect, which meant that national courts had to protect individual rights whether or not the state concerned had adopted equal remuneration legislation (Rossilli 1999: 173). Prior to the European Court of Justice's (ECJ) ruling, member states simply ignored a series of implementation deadlines set by the European Commission. Attempts by the European Commission to define equal pay more precisely and to establish a special Article 119 Group in 1961, with the purpose of facilitating implementation, also had no impact on state behaviour (Ellina 1999: 119–20). As every new deadline came and passed, the European Commission reported that member states delayed or failed to comply with the timetable (Warner 1984: 144). At the time, the European Community was racked by an internal dispute between France and its five European partners over European fiscal policies (Ruttley 2002: 238). At the height of the dispute, France boycotted Council meetings for seven months from June 1965 to January 1966, and although a compromise was eventually reached, the internal political crisis meant there was little chance of new European norms of sexual non-discrimination being developed.

The second period of norm elaboration: 1975–80

In the mid-1970s, changing international and European political conditions gave rise to a wave of intense international feminist activism, which in turn engendered a significant expansion in the international and EU women's human rights regimes. At the time, the international community was beginning to pay greater attention to international human rights in general and the European community was beginning to focus its attention on the development of social policy. Within the UN, a new human rights monitoring body – the Human Rights Committee – was established, and, for the first time in its history, the UN subjected a state engaging in gross human rights violations – Chile – to an intensive and detailed investigation. Outside the UN, Jimmy Carter's administration in the United States instituted an external human rights policy that lent legitimacy to the work of international human rights advocates, including that of international feminists (see Sikkink 1993; Donnelly 1999). In Europe during the same period, the European Council of Ministers realized that political and social integration was as important to the survival of the European Community as economic integration, and in 1974 adopted a social action programme with gender equality policies featuring prominently in the programme. At the same time, the ECJ became extremely active, in response to private individual petitions, in redefining the reach of European employment law.

As the UN began to pay closer attention to international human rights, international feminists stepped up their campaign for an international conference dedicated to women's human rights. In 1972, the Commission on the Status of Women submitted a recommendation to ECOSOC and the UN General Assembly that 1975 be designated International Women's Year (IWY) and that an international conference be held to crown the year. The UN General Assembly agreed to the commission's recommendation, provided that funding for the international conference came from voluntary contributions and not the regular UN budget. At the time it agreed to an IWY conference, according to Irene Tinker and Jane Jaquette, the General Assembly 'anticipated just another world conference along the lines of the issue-oriented conferences on environment in Stockholm (1972) and population in Budapest (1974)' (1987: 419). That same year, the Commission on the Status of Women, disappointed by the lukewarm response of states to DEDAW and other UN conventions, began pressing for the adoption of a comprehensive international convention on the elimination of discrimination against women. Finally, ECOSOC appointed a special working group to begin work on the new convention, and after the group's first meeting in January 1974, a draft text was prepared and, along with three other drafts from Benin, Indonesia and the All African Women's Conference, submitted to the Commission on the Status of Women, which was only expecting to discuss a single draft convention at its twenty-sixth session in 1976 (Jacobson 1995: 445). During the session an additional draft was presented by Belgium, further complicating the drafting process (Tinker and Jaquette 1987: 419).

Also during the session, a number of commission members argued that, for the convention to be effective, it had to go beyond the accepted goal of redressing legal inequalities to eliminating sexual discrimination. They argued that sexual discrimination was a deep and pervasive problem

throughout international society because it was based on negative stereo-
typing and rooted in cultural assumptions. Consequently, the commission
redrafted the convention to include a legal definition of discrimination
that was to be applied and enforced. Numerous commission members also
argued that the convention needed to address discrimination under marriage and family or civil law while, at the same time, acknowledging the
phenomena of single mothers and female-headed households. As a result,
explains Arvonne Fraser, the phrase 'married and unmarried women' was
included in numerous articles (1995: 86). Knowing that these civil rights
provisions were potentially divisive and contentious, she continues, the
commission decided to place them at the end of the draft convention so
that 'the readers and potential ratifying states would see the less controversial provisions first, building up to the logical conclusion that law,
including marriage and family law, institutionalized inequality' (ibid.: 86).
Furthermore, the commission agreed on a unifying convention that
addressed discrimination in as many aspects of public and family life as
possible. Thus, the draft text incorporated the civil and political rights
provisions of earlier instruments and included a substantive article outlining state responsibilities in eliminating discrimination in employment.
Finally, the commission decided to include a provision endorsing affirmative action as a temporary measure to accelerate de facto equality.

With agreement reached on the substantive articles, the commission
proceeded to the questions of implementation, monitoring and the
number of ratifying states needed to make the convention an international treaty. After considerable debate, the commission proposed an
ad hoc group of ten to fifteen individuals elected by the commission as
the monitoring body, and twenty ratifying states (Fraser 1995: 86). Buoyed
by the unprecedented response of domestic and international feminists,
IWY and the proclamation of the period from 1976 to 1985 as the UN
Decade for Women, the commission was confident that the draft convention would be promptly approved by the General Assembly. However, a
complex and lengthy debate began in 1977 in the Third Committee of the
Assembly, and a working group was established to negotiate the text. This
group adjourned after twelve meetings, having failed to reach a consensus
on a number of substantive articles. The Third Committee did not meet
again until March 1979, when it discussed extensive revisions made to the
draft convention by a second General Assembly negotiating group in 1978
(United Nations 1998: 41). The most difficult substantive articles to reach
agreement on were Articles 15 and 16, which gave women equal legal
capacity and equality under marriage and family law. According to Fraser,
this was because the specific provisions of these articles threatened virtually every state legal system (1995: 87). A debate ensued over interpretations of both private and public law, with the draft text being re-examined
in minute detail. Difficulties also arose over the definition of equal treatment, with committee members confused over whether it meant 'the

same' or 'identical' treatment, or whether the term 'equality' should be used in a normative sense. Similarly, committee members debated whether or not the definition of discrimination meant unjustifiable or unreasonable differentiations (McKean 1983: 191). Finally, a near-consensus was reached on the substantive articles of the convention, leaving the provisions on reporting and implementation to be discussed.

However, the committee could not reach agreement on these provisions, and another meeting was held in early December 1979 to discuss four different proposals for a monitoring body. The committee finally settled on the Swedish proposal, explains Fraser (1995: 87), which called for a committee composed of twenty-three members selected by ratifying states, who would serve in their private capacity in four-year terms. The Mexican delegate, concerned by the lack of complete consensus on substantive articles, proposed that the draft convention be recirculated for state comments and that the committee reconvene to consider state replies in late 1980. However, the committee chair appealed strongly for an immediate resolution sending the new convention to the General Assembly for adoption in time for the mid-decade world conference in Copenhagen in July 1980. The resolution was adopted, the General Assembly finally adopted CEDAW on 18 December 1979, and the first signatory states acceded to the convention's terms at the Copenhagen conference on 17 July 1980. Sixty-four states signed at the time and two states ratified the convention, which went into effect on 3 September 1981 after twenty ratifications had been received. In April 1982, ratifying state parties met to elect the twenty-three members of the CEDAW committee, which first met in October 1982 at the UN International Centre in Vienna.

From the outset, the CEDAW committee met annually for no more than two weeks to consider state reports submitted within one year of ratification, and thereafter every four years or whenever the committee requested. Unlike other core international human rights conventions, however, the General Assembly refused to grant CEDAW a procedure for reviewing complaints made against a state by either another state or an individual. The General Assembly also refused to grant the convention a procedure for receiving information from non-governmental sources. The General Assembly's decisions followed ardent opposition to such procedures from East European and developing states, which, according to Reanda, 'could not agree that violations of women's rights should be placed on the same footing as those occurring under repressive and racist regimes' (1995: 288). Moreover, in comparison with other UN human rights treaty bodies, the committee was allocated considerably less time and resources, resulting in a backlog of state reports awaiting review. Also, unlike other treaty bodies, the committee's sessions were not held at the UN Centre for Human Rights in Geneva. Rather, they were held in Vienna and New York on alternate occasions until 1993, when the committee's servicing body, the Division for the Advancement of Women, was permanently relocated to New York from Vienna. Before this relocation, according to Mara Bustelo, the committee and its work went virtually unnoticed by the mainstream UN bodies and by international human rights advocates in general (2000: 81).

By the 1985 Nairobi world conference marking the end of the UN Decade for Women, the CEDAW committee's work had gained little recognition among international and domestic feminist activists, who had focused their attention on the conference and ratification of the convention rather than its reporting and review process. Nonetheless, the drafting and adoption of the convention had created a new awareness within the mainstream UN human rights system of issues of gender inequalities and of the influence of law and custom on the status of women. At the Nairobi NGO forum, a series of workshops were held to generate greater awareness among feminists of the committee's work, and out of this the International Women's Rights Action Watch (IWRAW) network was formed to publicize the convention and monitor its national implementation (Fraser 1995: 90). The rationale behind the setting up of IWRAW was that it would serve to maintain independent pressure on states to comply with CEDAW, provide a focal point for domestic feminist activism and research, and provide support for the CEDAW committee by informally supplying it with information and parallel reports on state behaviour. The Nairobi NGO forum also produced the International Network Against Violence Against Women (INAVAW) and a number of new regional networks that, along with IWRAW, began pressuring the CEDAW committee to include a general recommendation on violence against women in the convention (Connors 1996: 163–5; Keck and Sikkink 1998: 169, 179).

In the meantime, the ILO had finally adopted a convention to supersede the 1965 Employment (Women Workers with Family Responsibilities) Recommendation. Adopted in 1981, the same year that CEDAW came into effect, the Convention on Workers with Family Responsibilities was the outcome of an international feminist-led campaign to replace the traditional domestic division of labour with a gender-neutral understanding of parental responsibility. Based on the Scandinavian model, the convention's parental leave provision – according to which either parent can obtain leave of absence or paid leave in the case of illness of a child or other member(s) of the immediate family – represented a radical international ideational shift in the understanding of gender relations. As Nitza Berkovitch explains, for the first time 'linking men to child-care – that is, incorporating men into the domestic sphere alongside women – was recognised as an essential step for equal incorporation of women into the public sphere'. It was also seen as an essential step for achieving economic equity (1999b: 134).

At the regional level, meanwhile, European feminists both inside and outside the European Commission pressed for an expansion of EU employment law, and for the scope of EU competences to be extended beyond the confines of employment policy. Activists were spurred to press for these changes by two critical ECJ judgments resulting from private individual litigation, and by the European Council of Ministers' adoption of a social action programme in 1974. European feminists were also encouraged by the UN General Assembly's decision to designate 1975 as International Women's Year. At the time, the EU decision-making process was particularly vulnerable to feminist activism because of its 'pluralist and open' nature, and because the European Commission, European judges and members of the European Parliament were committed to consolidating and expanding the social policies and legal authority of the EU (Mazey 1998: 138). Thus, there was a constituency of ready support for intervention in the policy area of gender equity. Moreover, having decided to try to shore up the political legitimacy of the EU through a social action programme, the European Council of Ministers was also sympathetic to the issue of gender equality. The Council of Ministers entrusted the European Commission with the task of drawing up a social action programme following the 1972 Paris Summit, at which the heads of state and commission representatives pondered the worrying lack of popular support for the EU and sought a solution to the problem. At the summit it became clear that the general public, seeing the EU as an economic power-brokerage uninterested in social justice issues, was questioning its political legitimacy. With this in mind, the commission drew up a social policy action programme aimed at giving the EU 'a more human face' (Hoskyns 1985: 79). The programme included practical measures and time-frames for the implementation of these measures. Thus, the social action programme adopted by the Council of Ministers on 21 January 1974 recognized the need to focus on employment-equity policies and, in particular, policies addressing the issue of wage disparity. It also anticipated a series of directives aimed at eliminating sexual discrimination in employment (Vogel-Polsky 1985: 104). It is clear that this programme appeared to be an attractive way of legitimizing the EU, and because the Social Affairs Directorate (DG V) had already begun to campaign for more effective regional equality laws, women's rights were a core part of the proposal.

A French official who had been with the European Commission since 1958, Jacqueline Nonon, led this campaign (Hoskyns 1996: 100). Nonen drew on a seminal report on the problems of women's employment in member states, which had been commissioned by the DG V in 1970, to press for European legislation extending beyond the confines of equal pay. In consultation with the French sociologist and author of the report, Evelyne Sullerot, Nonon advocated that the principle of equality be extended to all conditions of employment, and that action be taken to make easier reconciling family and occupational responsibilities. Although the reference to family responsibilities went beyond the EU's existing definition of employment policy, it was nonetheless incorporated into the 1974 Social Action Programme as Action II(4), which required that 'immediate priority be given to the problems of providing facilities to enable women to reconcile family responsibilities and job aspirations' (Hoskyns 1985: 79). Despite the assumption that it was only women who had family responsibilities, the action nevertheless represented a signific-ant ideational advance in the European Commission's thinking (ibid.: 79). Following the adoption of the social action programme, the Euro-pean Commission established an ad hoc group, led by Nonon, to draw up drafts for two new equality directives. Drafting the directives also gained a sense of urgency from the designation by the UN of 1975 as IWY and the desire for the EU to have something substantive to present at the inau-gural world conference in Mexico.

Parallel to these events, the ECJ made a ruling that was to play a crucial role in the expansion and strengthening of the European regime of sexual non-discrimination during the 1970s. In 1971, a case was referred through the Belgian courts to the ECJ that called for an interpretation of Article 119 of the Treaty of Rome for the first time since its inception. A feminist lawyer, Professor Elaine Vogel-Polsky, brought a series of actions against the Belgian airline Sabena on behalf of a former flight attendant, Gabrielle Defrenne. Instituting two actions simultaneously in the Belgian Conseil d'État, the litigant, Defrenne, complained in the first action that Sabena Airlines' policy of insisting on different retirement ages and occu-pational pension schemes for men and women was contrary to Article 119 (*Defrenne I*). In her second action, Defrenne claimed that the airline's dif-ferential rate of pay between male and female flight attendants was dis-criminatory (*Defrenne II*). The first action was dealt with by the ECJ in 1971, and, although it ruled pension schemes to be technically outside the scope of Article 119, the court's judgment did imply that in other cases relating directly to equal pay, the article should be read as giving women direct rights (Vallance and Davies 1986: 75). This is evident in the opinion delivered by the Advocate-General of the ECJ, who stated that

> [a]lthough the difficulties of application encountered by certain countries were great and although in particular, a conference of Member States extended until 31 December 1964 the period initially laid down, it appears to me that at least as from this date Article 119 created subjective rights which the workers of the Member States can invoke and respect for which national courts must ensure.
>
> (ECR 1971: 456)

This point became central to the second *Defrenne* case addressed by the ECJ in 1975, which dealt directly with the question of equal remuneration.

The ECJ's ruling in *Defrenne II* was ambitious and far-reaching. It ruled that Article 119 was capable of creating both horizontal and vertical direct effects in national courts, and that it was the duty of national courts to scrutinize discrimination (Nielsen and Szyszczak 1991: 83, 85). In other words, it could be invoked for claims against both the state and private employers before the national courts,

> in particular as regards those types of discrimination arising directly from legislative provisions or collective labour agreements, as well as in cases in which men and women receive unequal pay for equal work which is carried out in the same establishment or service, whether private or public.
>
> (ECR 1976: 476)

Thus, it appeared that state legislation and labour policy were no longer immune from judicial scrutiny in determining whether Article 119 had been infringed (Nielsen and Szyszczak 1991: 85). Also, the binding nature of European social law on relations between individuals was made clear for the first time (Hoskyns 1996: 93). In its ruling, moreover, the court also chided the European Commission for failing to initiate proceedings under Article 169 of the Treaty of Rome, arguing that the commission's inaction was likely to consolidate the incorrect impression as to the effects of Article 119 (Forman 1982: 21). The court's criticism and its reference to the private sector in *Defrenne II* caught the European Commission by surprise. Prior to the ruling, the commission had assumed that Article 119 imposed directly enforceable duties only upon states (Landau 1985: 25). The implications of the *Defrenne* rulings also unsettled member states as they realized they could no longer simply ignore Article 119. Both regional and domestic feminist activists also recognized the implications of the ECJ judgments. Following the 1971 ruling, activists realized that, while private individual litigation had drawn attention to Article 119, it had also highlighted the limited applications of the existing legislation. Hence, they began pressing the ECJ for a broader interpretation of EU legislation, which the court clearly responded to in *Defrenne II*, as well as working towards further secondary EU legislation to clarify, specify and tighten Article 119 (Vallance and Davies 1986: 75).

The *Defrenne* cases attracted considerable media attention (Hoskyns 1986: 305), and this, combined with the external and internal pressure exercised by feminist advocates, persuaded the European Commission to give the go-ahead for an equal remuneration directive that extended the scope of Article 119, and another directive that dealt with broader issues of equal treatment and opportunity in employment. The commission entrusted Nonon of the DG V with the responsibility of preparing the two directives. Using her considerable influence and contacts, Nonon was able to sidestep consulting government 'independent experts' and civil servants and secure the services of advocates actively involved in women's employment issues for the ad hoc drafting group. At the third of four meetings held by the group between February and November 1974, the lawyer representing Defrenne, Professor Vogel-Polsky, submitted a draft for a directive that gave equal weight to the notions of *égalité de traitement* and *égalité de chances*. While the group agreed on the need for the second directive to extend beyond the workplace to ensuring that women were able to reconcile domestic responsibilities with occupational aspirations, it was decided, on the advice of the European Commission's legal service, that the draft directive should restrict itself to conditions within the employment situation (Hoskyns 1985: 81). Thus, the draft directive dealt with equal treatment in access to employment, vocational training, promotion and working conditions.

The European Commission approved the draft before it was examined and substantially revised by the Social Affairs Working Group of the Council of Ministers, which consisted, in the main, of the social affairs attachés from state delegations to Brussels (Hoskyns 1985: 82). The working group deleted all mention of positive discrimination or affirmative action and, with the use of exceptions, limited the scope of the directive as much as possible. For instance, one exception to the principle of equal treatment allowed states to differentiate between men and women if gender was a determining factor in ability to perform work, while a second permitted states to retain protective legislation. Furthermore, the working group insisted on removing all social security provisions, but when the European Commission intervened, it agreed to a separate directive dealing with the issue of social security. Finally, as with the directive on equal remuneration, it was left to national authorities to decide the choice of form and methods of implementation. While the Council of Ministers adopted the Equal Pay Directive on 10 February 1975, in time for the UN conference in Mexico, adoption of the Equal Treatment Directive was delayed by these and further council deliberations until 9 February 1976.

Commonly described as the last of the *strong* directives adopted in the 1970s – when the EU was still committed to the idea of extending its competence in the social field (Hoskyns and Luckhaus 1989: 321) – the Social Security Directive of 19 December 1978 extended the principle of equal treatment to the sphere of state statutory social security schemes, which provide protection against the risk of sickness, invalidity, accidents at work and unemployment. Eager to realize the commitment made by the council's social affairs working group during negotiations of the Equal Treatment Directive, and to 'fill in the gaps left by the *Defrenne* decisions' (Hoskyns 1996: 107), the European Commission began preparing the third directive as soon as the Equal Treatment Directive had been adopted. However, no consultative ad hoc group was created to draft the directive. Instead, responsibility for its preparation was given to a commission official working on the EU's Poverty Programme, who consulted government experts and representatives on social security issues rather than equal treatment (ibid.: 107). Consequently, the meaning of equal treatment in social security was narrowly interpreted and, rather than

benefits being individualized or 'decoupled', as feminists desired, aggregation and dependency would be allowed to continue.[1]

Although an initial draft was ready for negotiation in January 1977,
nearly another two years passed before it was finally adopted with several
amendments. In the intervening period, the Social Affairs Working Group
of the Council of Ministers met on several occasions to discuss the draft
directive. These discussions proved difficult because of the complexity and
diversity of existing domestic social security schemes, and, as a result, the
working group decided to limit the directive's scope to statutory social
security schemes and postpone occupational or employer schemes to a
further directive (Hoskyns and Luckhaus 1989: 322). This amendment,
according to Catherine Hoskyns, 'followed anxiety about the complica-
tions of renegotiating the terms of occupational schemes' (1996: 110).
Other problems raised by the working group concerned the appropriate-
ness of EU intervention in the area of social security, the EU extending its
powers, and the effect of the directive on the breadwinner/dependent
model of entitlement (Hoskyns and Luckhaus 1989: 324). As negotiations
neared conclusion, Hoskyns argues, state representatives began to panic
about the implications of the directive, but the ECJ's ruling in the third
Defrenne case in June 1978, affirming that the elimination of sexual discrimination was a fundamental human right, strengthened the commission's resolve (Hoskyns 1996: 111). To secure the directive's adoption,
however, the commission conceded to an unprecedented period of six
years for national implementation (Neilson 1998: 68).

In the period immediately following the adoption of the Social Security
Directive, the Council of Ministers did a complete U-turn on social policy
and generated a stand-off between itself and the European Commission
over further social regulation and the extension of EU competence in
matters of social legislation (Rossilli 1999: 175). Despite enjoying the
support of the European Parliament, which in February 1981 adopted a
wide-ranging resolution on equality measures, attempts by the European
Commission to strengthen EU sexual non-discrimination legislation
largely failed (Vallance and Davies 1986: 79). The Council of Ministers
refused to entertain the commission's proposal for a series of directives on
parental leave and leave for family reasons, part-time employment, and
burden of proof in cases of sexual discrimination (Vogel-Polsky 1991: 22;
Ellina 1999: 82). It also refused to approve a proposal for a non-binding
resolution on reconciling family and occupational responsibilities.[2] Furthermore, the Council of Ministers enacted the promised directive on
equal treatment in occupational social security schemes only on 24 July
1986, after much deliberation and dilution of the directive's provisions
(Neilson 1998: 71). During negotiations of the directive, the Social Affairs
Working Group excluded a range of measures from the scope of the
directive, including individual insurance contracts, retirement and surviving spouse pensions, and the optional provisions of occupational schemes

offered to participating individuals. The regulation of these social security problems was deferred to a future directive (Laurent 1986: 679). Also, once again, the directive was adopted with a six-year period of national implementation.

Despite the cold political and economic climate of the 1980s, however, European policy-makers, convinced of the need to deregulate, found it impossible to roll back existing regional equal treatment legislation, particularly as the ECJ continued its judicial activism as far as core employment rights were concerned and the European Parliament gained greater control over EU spending on social programmes. The strong presence of feminists within EU bodies also helped prevent any regressive measures and, in fact, maintained non-discriminatory policy initiatives (Hoskyns 1996: 142). As well as a fifth directive on equal treatment for the self-employed being adopted on 11 December 1986, a series of action programmes or detailed 'how to' sets of instructions for states were initiated. The fifth directive, according to Hoskyns, 'broke new ground in that it focused, in part, on the overlap between domestic and productive work which takes place in a family business' (ibid.: 148). The first Community Action Programme on the Promotion of Equal Opportunity for Women (1982–5), which was co-ordinated by the European Commission's Women's Bureau,[3] incorporated many of the provisions of the 1981 European Parliament's resolution and was funded by a budget line protected by the Parliament's Committee on Women's Rights (ibid.: 142). The primary objectives of this and subsequent action programmes were twofold. The first objective was to achieve equal treatment by legally strengthening individual rights and by encouraging positive or affirmative action programmes. The second objective was to monitor outcomes and to make sure that there was close co-operation between national equality agencies and the EU (Vallance and Davies 1986: 80). To this latter end, the European Commission established an Advisory Committee on Equal Opportunities for Women and Men consisting of national equality agency representatives, which continues to meet regularly to exchange ideas and discuss progress. The commission also established a network of independent experts drawn from member states to monitor the implementation of EU directives (ibid.: 81).

The third period of norm elaboration: 1990–2004

By the late 1980s, it had become evident to international feminist activists that the establishment of separate organizational bodies to deal with women's rights had contributed to the marginalization and isolation of issues of sexual discrimination within the international human rights system. It had also become evident, in the face of disturbing accounts of the use of rape as a weapon of war in Bosnia-Herzegovina, that states should be held responsible for violence and human rights violations directed at women. Preparations for the second UN World Conference on Human Rights in Vienna in 1993 created a political opportunity for international feminists to pursue the integration of gender issues into the mainstream of UN system-wide activities and policy-making, and to draw attention to the issue of gender-based violence (Reanda 1999: 58). Indeed, in the run-up to the Vienna Conference, the issues of mainstreaming and gender-based violence became linked in the international feminist-led campaign to ensure that women's rights were included on the conference's agenda. No mention of discrimination or women's human rights violations had been made in the advance preparatory documents of the conference and, angered by this, the Center for Women's Global Leadership (CWGL) at Rutgers University, New Jersey, convened a strategic planning meeting in February 1993 to prepare for the conference. Participants at the meeting agreed that the issue of gender-based violence demonstrated 'most clearly and urgently what it means to expand human rights to incorporate women' (Bunch 1993b: 148). The centre then joined with the International Women's Tribune Centre (IWTC) and the International Young Women's Christian Association (YWCA) to initiate an international petition 'calling on the 1993 conference to comprehensively address women's human rights at every level of the proceedings and demanding that gender-based violence be recognized as a violation of human rights requiring immediate action' (Keck and Sikkink 1998: 185–6). Together with the IWTC, the CWGL also planned an international tribunal on violations of women's human rights to be convened during the conference. The idea of convening a tribunal was derived principally from the 1976 International Tribunal on Crimes against Women. The CWGL asked local grassroots organizations to hold hearings in the six months leading up to the Vienna Conference, with the intention that some of the complainants would then testify at the tribunal (Chen 1995: 484–5; Keck and Sikkink 1998: 187).

Prior to the conference, international discussion in the Commission on the Status of Women and other forums treated the question of violence against women as a social or crime prevention problem involving either specific forms of violence such as domestic battery, genital mutilation, sexual slavery, trafficking in women, dowry deaths and honour killings, or specific categories of women such as refugees, migrant workers or political prisoners (United Nations 1998: 55; Reanda 1999: 57). Moreover, international bodies and many state delegations regarded gender-based violence as 'a private matter between individuals, not a public human rights issue requiring government or international action' (United Nations 1998: 55). Pressured by an international feminist network advocating a *human rights-based* approach – as opposed to an *equal treatment* approach – to the question of gender-based violence, the Commission on the Status of Women and the CEDAW committee began to speak and act in terms of violence against women being a single, unified human rights issue. In

November 1991, the commission convened an expert meeting to discuss a range of possible measures to eliminate gender-based violence, including the strengthening of the general recommendations of the CEDAW committee, the appointment of a special rapporteur on violence against women, a declaration on violence against women, an optional protocol on violence to the 1979 convention, and even a convention dedicated to gender-based violence (Joachim 1999: 152).

However, the last two measures were dismissed as too time-consuming to negotiate, and likely to undermine the work of the CEDAW committee by implying that gender-based violence was not prohibited by the terms of the 1979 convention (Charlesworth and Chinkin 1994: 22). Instead, the experts prepared a draft declaration for presentation to the Commission on the Status of Women at its thirty-sixth session in 1992. At the session, it was decided that the definition of violence needed further elaboration, and the commission convened an inter-sessional working group to complete the task. The commission also invited international feminists as observers and advisers to the working group. That year, the CEDAW committee issued a general recommendation affirming that although gender-based violence was not explicitly mentioned by the convention, it nevertheless constituted a form of sexual discrimination. As such, states were obliged to take legal and other measures to eliminate violence against women, 'including acts which inflict physical, mental or sexual harm or suffering, threats of such acts, coercion and other deprivations of liberty' (United Nations Secretary General 1994: chapter 1, paragraph 466). Furthermore, the committee asserted that 'states may also be held responsible for private acts (of violence) if they fail to act with due diligence to prevent violations of rights, to investigate and punish acts of violence, or to provide compensation' (United Nations 1998: 56).

In preparation for the Vienna Conference, the United Nations held four sessions of the Preparatory Committee and three regional preparatory meetings – Africa, Latin America and the Caribbean, and Asia – at which NGOs held satellite meetings and drafted recommendations for inclusion in the regional documents and in the draft of the Vienna Declaration. As a result, in large part, of NGO efforts, all the regional preparatory meetings produced at least one document dedicated to women's human rights concerns. However, official UN reports on the regional meetings barely mentioned such concerns (Mertus and Goldberg 1994: 205, n 14). In addition to the UN regional preparatory meetings, the Council of Europe organized a satellite interregional meeting in advance of the Vienna Conference. Among the recommendations made in the report from this meeting were the appointment by the UN Human Rights Commission of a special rapporteur on sexual discrimination and violence against women; an optional protocol establishing an individual and inter-state complaints procedure under CEDAW; and the consideration of reservations to CEDAW (Sullivan 1994: 154, n 8). At the fourth and final session of the UN Preparatory Committee held in Geneva from 19 April to 7 May 1993, the draft Vienna Declaration and Program of Action were prepared. However, state delegations disagreed on many points. To complete the draft declaration, the session had to be extended by a week, thereby precluding participation and lobbying by many NGOs during the final drafting phase. Consequently, the committee not only failed to integrate gender-based human rights issues throughout the draft declaration but, because the purpose of the draft was to minimize drafting time at the Vienna conference itself, also used 'the most expansive language possible'. At the conference in June 1993, the issue thus 'became not one of attempting to include new items but, rather, of preserving what was contained in the draft' (Mertus and Goldberg 1994: 206, n 16). Consequently, this made it difficult for advocates to influence the final declaration.

Nevertheless, with the help of influential non-governmental allies such as Amnesty International and Human Rights Action Watch (HRAW), activists were able to convince international policy-makers at the Vienna Conference of the universality of women's human rights. They were also able to convince international policy-makers that gender-based violence was not beyond the responsibilities of states (Joachim 1999: 155, 159). Amnesty International and HRAW, under pressure from international feminists, had begun to take an interest in women's rights in the 1990s and, despite the fact that they investigated only acts of gender-based violence perpetrated or condoned by the state, their findings submitted at the conference provided vital evidence of the political and international nature of the issue and enhanced its legitimacy. According to Jutta Joachim, the findings of Amnesty International and HRAW were influential because 'these organisations had a reputation for presenting reliable and well-researched information' (ibid.: 156–7). International policy-makers also responded to the rights-based discourse used by international feminists, in part because of their acute sensitivity to the systematic rape and human rights abuse of women in the conflict in the former Yugoslavia, which had been widely publicized and the subject of numerous NGO submissions to the UN Commission on Human Rights at its forty-ninth session in Geneva from 1 February to 12 March 1993. Highlighting the issue of gender-based violence further, the day-long Global Tribunal on Violations of Women's Human Rights organized by CWGL and IWTC was transmitted live on television monitors throughout the Vienna Conference hall (Fraser 2001: 57). Organizers of the tribunal then negotiated time on the official conference agenda for a report of the tribunal and its recommendations to be presented, and for thousands of signed petitions demanding women's human rights to be delivered to the conference floor beforehand (Bunch and Reilly 1994: 103).

In the wake of the Vienna Conference, the UN General Assembly adopted the Declaration on the Elimination of Violence Against Women

(DEVAW), without amendment, on 20 December 1993. In March the following year, the UN Commission on Human Rights appointed a Special Rapporteur on Violence Against Women, Radhika Coomaraswamy, to investigate and report on the causes and consequences of gender-based violence, and to make recommendations on actions to be taken to ensure the elimination of violence against women. While DEVAW is not legally binding, explains Donna Sullivan, it does represent 'the first international instrument to express international political consensus that states have human rights obligations to prevent gender-based violence and to redress the harm caused' (1995: 131). DEVAW, according to Coomaraswamy, also 'provides the normative framework for all international action in the field of gender-based violence' (Coomaraswamy 1999: 173). The declaration is formulated on rights-based language, citing the UN Convention on Torture and the International Covenants, and its definition of violence is broad and all-inclusive. The declaration demands the elimination of gender-based violence in the private sphere of the family and in the community. It also demands the elimination of violence against women perpetrated or condoned by the state (ibid.: 173; Ashworth 1999: 267). In her preliminary report to the UN Commission on Human Rights in November 1994, the special rapporteur recommended the inclusion of an optional protocol to CEDAW, placing the convention on the same footing as other human rights conventions. In the annual reports that have followed, the special rapporteur has defined a vast array of causes and sites of violence against women, and made a range of recommendations on actions to be taken by states to eliminate gender-based violence. The special rapporteur has also undertaken a number of on-site fact-finding missions to various states and produced corresponding reports that are striking for both their breadth and their outspoken criticism of state behaviour and the failings of international human rights law.[4] Following each of these missions, the special rapporteur monitors state responses to her recommendations and, if necessary, conducts a return visit.

The campaign for an optional protocol to CEDAW gathered momentum with a preliminary draft optional protocol being drawn up by an independent expert group which met at the Maastricht Centre for Human Rights at the University of Limburg in the Netherlands from 29 September to 1 October 1994 (Byrnes 1997). The Maastricht meeting was organized by the NGO International Human Rights Law Group after the UN Commission on the Status of Women, at its thirty-eighth session in March 1994, declined to endorse a proposal by the CEDAW committee for the convening of an expert meeting by the Secretary-General to prepare a draft optional protocol (UNDAW 2000: 3). Financed by the Australian and Dutch state governments and other sponsors, the Maastricht meeting was attended by members of the CEDAW committee and the UN Committee on the Elimination of Racial Discrimination, and other international human rights experts. Following the Maastricht meeting, the preliminary draft was presented to the CEDAW committee at its fourteenth session in early 1995 in a paper presented by Justice Silvia Cartwright, and, after an intense debate, the committee adopted suggestion 7, endorsing most aspects of the Maastricht draft (Bijnsdorp 2000: 330). Suggestion 7 was then submitted to the Commission on the Status of Women for consideration at its thirty-ninth session in March 1995, but, preoccupied with preparations for the fourth World Conference on Women later that year in Beijing, the commission decided not to discuss the suggestion. Instead, the commission recommended that the Secretary-General circulate the suggestion to states, intergovernmental bodies and NGOs for comment (UNDAW 2000: 3).

The commission also recommended that a working group be established by ECOSOC to meet in parallel to the commission's fortieth session in March 1996 to consider the comments received and to discuss the feasibility of an optional protocol (UNDAW 2000: 3). At its forty-second session in March 1998, the commission deleted the broader standing provisions of the Maastricht draft optional protocol because of strong resistance by states. These included a provision allowing complaints of systemic discrimination rather than just individual complaints, and a provision binding states to remedy violations identified through the complaints mechanisms. A provision allowing the CEDAW committee to inquire into allegations of grave violations of the convention without a specific complaint survived in the diluted form of an 'opt-out' provision (Charlesworth and Chinkin 2000: 245). This meant that ratifying states could choose not to accept the inquiry procedure. After another two years of extensive discussions in the open-ended working group of the commission, the optional protocol to CEDAW was finally adopted by the General Assembly on 6 October 1999, in time to celebrate the twentieth anniversary of the adoption of the convention. Despite the problems finalizing its scope, the protocol brought the convention's enforcement mechanisms in line with those of existing international treaties, and on 22 December 2000 it entered into force following ratification by the tenth state party to the convention.[5]

At the regional level, the European Council of Ministers has, with the sole exception of sexual harassment, resisted intervening substantively on issues of gender-based violence. On 27 November 1991, the European Commission adopted a recommendation on the protection of the dignity of women and men at work. Annexed to the recommendation was a code of practice on measures to combat sexual harassment. The adoption of these measures was the culmination of a process that had begun in March 1986 when, under mounting pressure from the European Parliament's Committee on Women's Rights and European feminists, an informal meeting of the Council of Ministers requested the European Commission to conduct an investigation into the problem of protecting the dignity of women in the workplace (Beveridge and Nott 1998: 297; Evelyn Collins

1996: 25).[6] As a consequence, a report was prepared that evaluated existing national legislation relating to sexual harassment and made recommendations for action by the commission. The report, entitled *The Dignity of Women at Work: A Report on the Problem of Sexual Harassment in the Member States of the European Community*, was published in October 1987 and concluded that states were doing little to tackle the widespread problem of sexual harassment (Beveridge and Nott 1998: 297). It argued that existing national legal remedies were inadequate and that few meaningful voluntary initiatives, such as collective agreements or research studies, had been taken (Rubenstein 1992: 70). It also strongly recommended that the European Commission adopt a directive on the prevention of sexual harassment at work, which, in conjunction with a code of practice, would require employers to adopt policies and practices that would establish and maintain a working environment that was free of the risk of sexual harassment. Employers would be legally liable for sexual harassment in the workplace unless it could be demonstrated that all such reasonably practicable steps had been taken (Beveridge and Nott 1998: 298).

However, despite the report's recommendation, the Council of Ministers opted instead to pass a resolution on 29 May 1990 on the protection of the dignity of women and men at work. The resolution, which did not explicitly use the term 'sexual harassment', called on the European Commission to simply draw up a code of practice in 1991 (Bakirci 1998: 10). However, in a bid to enhance its legal standing in the European Union, the commission decided to annex the code to a recommendation supplementing the Equal Treatment Directive – a decision taken bearing in mind a recent ECJ ruling establishing the legal effectiveness of recommendations (Rubenstein 1992: 71). In the case of *Grimaldi* v. *Fonds des Maladies Professionelles*, the ECJ held that recommendations, though not legally binding in themselves, were nonetheless capable of giving rise to legal effect. National courts, the ECJ stated, were bound to take recommendations into consideration in disputes, particularly where they were designed to supplement binding Community measures (ECR 1990: 4407). The European Commission reiterated the need for a legally binding directive on sexual harassment, but such a measure continued to cause controversy among state delegations, and employers and employee representatives. Finally, as a result largely of the persistence of the European Commission, the Council of Ministers adopted a directive in September 2002 revising the Equal Treatment Directive of 1976 and providing binding legislation on sexual harassment in the workplace. Apart from recognizing that sexual harassment constitutes sexual discrimination, this directive holds that employers are financially liable for cases of misconduct and grants courts the right to award financial compensation with no upper limit to victims of sexual harassment.[7] The directive came into effect in 2005, by which time member states were expected to bring into force legislation, regulations and administrative provisions to comply with the directive.

Conclusion

Since 1945, there have been three distinct periods of international and regional regime formation in which systemic norms of sexual non-discrimination spanning the public and private spheres have been elaborated. In each of these periods, certain political and legal conditions gave rise to international and regional feminist activism that was effective in generating regime change. This successful feminist activism necessarily involved the effective discursive articulation of grievances, justice claims and means of change, which was produced in reaction to the exigencies of the particular situation and in contentious interaction with the dominant discourse of the period. There have also been two interim periods of stasis in which little progress was made in the development of international and regional norms of sexual non-discrimination. In each of these periods, adverse political conditions constrained international and regional feminist activism, and thus hampered the negotiation of further non-discriminatory legal provisions. The question is, what effect, if any, have salient systemic norms of sexual non-discrimination had on the domestic practices of states? It is to this question that we turn in the following four chapters, which trace the diffusion of various systemic norms of sexual non-discrimination into the domestic practices of Germany, Spain, Japan and India respectively. In each of the four cases, I investigate the specific conditions under which international norms of sexual non-discrimination diffuse or fail to diffuse and affect state behaviour.

4 Germany

Despite its long-standing reputation as an exemplary international and European state, Germany, until recently, has been relatively reluctant to incorporate international norms of sexual non-discrimination. The single most significant impediment to norm diffusion has been the gender-biased corporate identity of the state, which has been described as a needle's eye through which norms must pass (see Ostner and Lewis 1995). The corporate aspect of German state identity was politically reconstituted in the aftermath of the Second World War as a Christian-occidental (*Christlich-abendlandische*) nation in which the family is the fundamental ordering principle of social life. During the 1950s, the state discursively emphasized the virtue of the so-called complete Christian male-breadwinner family as a bulwark against totalitarianism and communism, sentiments that were echoed by the Catholic Church. This vision of restoring national security and stability in the *lebensraum* (living space) of the family was embedded in the national social security, industrial relations, taxation and employment policy systems. The highly paternalistic corporate state identity constructed in the immediate post-war period survived the social and political upheavals of the late 1960s and German reunification largely intact, and, to a large extent, explains why international and regional norms of sexual non-discrimination had a relatively limited impact on domestic state practices prior to 1998.

This chapter examines why the German state, until recent years, was a laggard in terms of incorporating international and regional norms of sexual non-discrimination. It also examines why domestic feminist activism, which emerged in the politically conducive conditions of the late 1960s and again with the collapse of the East German state in 1989, had virtually no influence on state behaviour. It examines why changing regional conditions induced a noticeable, albeit minimal, change to state employment legislation in 1980, and why changing domestic conditions preceding German reunification induced a further minor change to state employment legislation in 1994. Further, it examines why, between 1998 and 2004, the state became more receptive to incorporating international norms of sexual non-discrimination. The chapter begins by tracing the political reconstitution of the paternalistic corporate identity of the state after the Second World War before examining how this identity construction has affected the diffusion of international norms of sexual non-discrimination. Using the argument outlined in Chapter 2, I investigate how the German state actively resisted incorporating these norms prior to 1998 and how, despite this resistance, international and domestic pressure did induce some modest changes in domestic state practices. I argue that, while the state's reaction to these norms between 1945 and 1997 is generally one of behavioural continuity, occasionally the state responds to regional or domestic pressure and changes its behaviour in accordance with particular norms. We can identify three periods of state behavioural continuity, between 1945 and 1997, in which social interaction tends to result in the reproduction of discriminatory state practices. Both the first and the last of these periods are interrupted by instances of either regionally or domestically derived state behavioural change. We can also identify a period of state behavioural change, from 1998 to 2004, in which social interaction results in the adoption of particular non-discriminatory state practices.

The first period of state behavioural continuity, from 1945 to 1984, saw Germany become a signatory member of the European Union (EU) and ratify a number of key international conventions but decline to meet its European and international legal obligations. It also saw domestic feminist activism emerge in the politically conducive conditions of the late 1960s but fail to influence state behaviour. There are several factors that might account for this. In the 1970s, the state cracked down on reactionary politics, which, in turn, limited the opportunity for activism. Feminists disagreed on strategies and objectives. Finally, discursively, they did not deviate substantially from conservatively held ideas of gender relations. Thus, there was no contentious discursive interaction between feminists and the state. This first period of stasis was punctuated by an instance of state behavioural change induced by changing regional conditions in which the European Commission developed the political will to use infringement suits to ensure compliance with European equality directives. The second period of state behavioural continuity, from 1985 to 1989, saw the state finally ratify the United Nations Convention on the Elimination of Discrimination Against Women (CEDAW) but fail to take any initiative to implement the convention or submit its initial periodic report on time. It also saw the consolidation of the paternalistic corporate identity of the state. It was a period in which the state introduced new gender-reinforcing measures, created conditions unconducive to feminist activism at the federal level, and laid claim to initiatives of private individual litigants and feminists within the Green Party and progressive *Länder* (state) governments as evidence of its compliance.

The third period of state behavioural continuity, from 1990 to 1997, witnessed German reunification and saw the state impose gender-reinforcing reforms in the German Democratic Republic (GDR) that were at odds with international and regional requirements. It also saw feminist activism emerge with the collapse of socialism but have virtually no influence on the unification process or state behaviour. There are two major factors that might account for this. First, the West German state excluded all opposition groups, including feminists, from the treaty negotiations for German unity. Second, East and West German feminists were deeply divided over strategies, objectives and the identity-related issue concerning the relationship between motherhood and full-time employment. Thus, once again, feminists failed to create an oppositional discourse to that of the state's concerning gender relations. This last period of stasis was punctuated by an instance of state behavioural change induced by changing domestic conditions. Faced with high female unemployment in the former GDR and waning electoral support, the conservative federal government decided to amend national employment legislation in 1994.

The year 1998 marks the start of a period of state behavioural change. This period of change, from 1998 to 2004, saw a 'dramatic changeover at the elite level' (Checkel 2001a: 193) and a distinct shift in the state's attitude towards incorporating international norms of sexual non-discrimination. It also saw feminists within the new Social Democratic Party (SDP)–Green coalition government pursue a range of legally binding measures designed to bring state practices into alignment with international and regional standards (Tons and Young 2001: 145). Feminists discursively challenged traditional notions of gender relations and articulated many of their demands for legislative change by drawing on the European discourse of equal opportunity. Despite domestic and international pressure, however, comprehensive legislative and public policy change was slow.

Post-Second World War reconstruction of the gender-biased corporate identity of the state

Following the first post-war elections in 1949, the conservative Christian Democratic Union (CDU)–Christian Social Union (CSU) coalition government was strongly committed to Catholic social ideas and embarked on a series of programmes and actions that restored the traditional family at the head of society and as 'the natural origin and source of state order' (Minister of Family Affairs Franz-Josef Wuermeling quoted in Frevert 1989: 282). Central to the coalition government's reconstructive policies lay the notion of the 'complete' male-breadwinner family, existing predominantly free from state interference and discursively positioned as a stronghold against totalitarianism and communism. Invoking visions of families being destabilized and destroyed by communist policies in East Germany, which encouraged women to go out to work for the benefit of the state, the coalition government pursued a public policy programme of *normalization* and self-identification with the West. The notion of actively promoting paid employment as an individual or social objective for women was anathema to a government intent on resurrecting and preserving the housewife-marriage as the social norm (ibid.: 284). East Germany's policy of fully integrating women into the labour force was portrayed as forced emancipation by the coalition government and used as a counterpoint for justifying the implementation of conservative family-oriented policies.

Supported by a vocal Catholic Church, the coalition government also used East Germany's rejection of Christian family values to dismiss feminist claims for equality and to discredit the main opposition party's support for family law reform, labelling it as communist. Quick to distance itself from the allegation that it advocated a 'socialist ideal of equality' that eliminated 'pre-given differences' between men and women, the SDP insisted on the importance of conserving the unified domain of the family (Moeller 1993: 107). Having brought the political opposition into line, the ruling coalition was able to transform a Christian-occidental view of gender relations into a set of public policies that emphasized the importance of the male breadwinner in the economic recovery of Germany and the primacy of the paterfamilias in both the domestic and the political spheres (Ostner 1993: 100). The coalition government mounted a public campaign against two wage-earners and revealed its policy blueprints for reconstructing traditional patterns of familial solidarity and a gendered division of labour. Every social and employment policy was geared towards the male-breadwinner model of the family.

After being delivered an overwhelming mandate in the 1953 general election, the CDU–CSU coalition government established the Ministry of Family Affairs under the direction of the militant Catholic Wuermeling, who denounced any notion of equality that threatened 'the Christian foundations of the family authority exercised by the father' (Moeller 1993: 102). Adopting a 'defensive position' against any misconception of equality, Wuermeling championed government measures that protected and promoted large families, measures modelled on an ecclesiastical regime of gender relations (ibid.: 102). Such families, he claimed, represented a defence not only against the intrusions of totalitarianism and communism but also against the destructive influences of liberal-inspired individualism and materialism (Heineman 1996: 30). Although the ministry lacked the power to initiate legislation, it was able to influence those government departments responsible for drafting and guiding legislation through the parliamentary process (Moeller 1997: 122). With the backing of the Catholic Church, which had just created its own family association – the Family Federation of German Catholics – to increase its influence on family policy, the ministry ensured the passage of a child benefit law in 1954 that provided monthly state-administered payments to wage-earners with three or more children, as well as tax concessions for large families.

The Catholic Church was determined to ensure that revisions to the 1896 Civil Code necessitated by the new constitutional guarantee of equality would not threaten the preordained hierarchical order of the Christian marriage and family.[1] It exhorted the state to defend a legally grounded paterfamilias, arguing that, where civil law was concerned, constitutional protection of the family took precedence over the constitutional guarantee of equality. The CDU–CSU coalition government was happy to oblige, but, because the SDP refused to extend the 1 April 1953 deadline for revisions, it was forced to suspend the Civil Code, leaving it to courts to give rulings in marital disputes solely on the basis of constitutional law (Frevert 1989: 281). Despite considerable anger from the Social Democrats at the Catholic Church's aggressive intervention on the issue, the coalition government continued to delay revising the Civil Code. Finally, after a heated and controversial parliamentary debate, the Bundestag passed the Act on Equal Rights for Men and Women in 1957, repealing the most discriminatory aspects of the Civil Code but upholding the housewife-marriage. The Act repealed a husband's right to determine whether or not his wife entered or remained in paid employment, as well as his right of disposal over family property and income. Articles 1256 and 1360 of the Civil Code permitted women to take paid employment provided this decision did not interfere with their primary duties as mothers and wives. These revisions thus served to define the housewife-marriage as the social norm and to maintain the Christian ideal of a 'natural functional division' between men and women.

The conservative coalition government also incorporated Christian ideals of the male breadwinner and female homemaker into its reorganization of the social welfare system. The system that emerged during the 1950s was a dual system of social security and social assistance based on the Catholic principles of status maintenance and subsidiarity. According to the principle of status maintenance, social policy should alleviate the suffering produced by industrialization without altering traditional status or class relations in society. Therefore, the social security scheme established by the government was generous but did not disturb status differences because it based eligibility on occupational status – assuming men to have occupational status and women to have dependency status. In other words, women were dependent on benefits derived from their husband's contributions. However, because benefits and contributions were earnings-related, the occupational status of the male breadwinner varied in relation to that of others. Those who made higher social insurance contributions, courtesy of higher salaries, received more generous benefits than those in low-paying occupations. The stress on prior activity in the labour market to establish a contribution discriminated against women entering the paid labour force. According to the principle of subsidiarity, social problems and needs should be addressed and met at the lowest level in society – the family. State intervention is justified only after all other groups in the community, including voluntary and religious organizations, and employers, have failed to solve social problems or meet the welfare needs of individuals. Hence, the social assistance scheme established by the government relied on means-tested supplementary assistance and social transfer payments – in the form of pensions and unemployment benefits – but was lean on public services such as childcare and care for elderly people (Morgan 2001: 113). This meant that the burden of care fell largely on women within the family.

Furthermore, the CDU–CSU coalition government incorporated the principle of subsidiarity into its industrial relations system by handing responsibility for the labour sector to employers and employees (the *social partners*). During the initial post-war period, a complex system of collective bargaining between employer associations and trade unions emerged to negotiate agreements on pay and conditions of employment. This system was protected from state intervention by the constitutional guarantee of freedom of contract (*tarifautonomie*), which was included in the Constitution in reaction against the state control of the labour market in the National Socialist period. With the autonomy of wage relations guaranteed, management and unions negotiated a job evaluation system and six-step wage scale based on the premise of continuous employment and built around a cornerstone wage set at the amount paid an average skilled employee (Cook 1980: 59). Special women's wage scales were negotiated, but, because employers and unions uncritically accepted the idea of the paterfamilias, they were set well below those of men. They were initially set at between 60 and 75 per cent of the male scale and were designed to protect the male breadwinner's wage, which was supposed to be sufficient to support the family (Ostner and Lewis 1995: 187). Although the Supreme Labour Court declared the special women's wage scales unconstitutional in 1955, employers and unions continued to discriminate against women by replacing these scales with the light-work categories. Set at the bottom of the normal six-step wage scale, the light-work categories, while apparently gender neutral, were defined in such a way as to reserve them almost exclusively for women.

Even though its corporate identity-related ideas of restoring national security and stability in the *lebensraum* (living space) of the family conflicted with the post-war reality of many thousands of women having to provide for themselves and their families financially, the CDU–CSU coalition government continued to target the *complete* and legitimate family both discursively and through policy measures. It maintained that in introducing 'a legal social order that is one of the most protective of the family', it had made the right and proper decision (Thomas 2003: 225). In 1958, the government instituted a tax system, called *Ehegattensplitting* (tax-splitting), which favoured married couples by adding the income of both partners together before dividing the total by two and taxing this as two separate incomes. Such a system is advantageous only to married couples with one high income and one low income, and discriminates against cohabiting couples and lone parents (Hantrais 1994: 147). If women are to seek employment, this taxation system encourages them to seek only part-time work in the low-income bracket. The conservative coalition government also reintroduced protective labour legislation restricting women's access to certain occupations, which, according to Robert Moeller, had been 'suspended first by the Nazis to meet the needs of the war economy and held in abeyance by the allied occupation forces to respond to the shortage of adult men after the war.'[2] The government justified enforcing such legislation on the basis of ensuring that economic growth did not drive women into jobs for which they were physiologically unsuited, as it had in the Nazi period (Moeller 1993: 154).

The coalition government and Church leaders saw those women who did enter into paid employment as a serious social problem and publicly accused them of neglecting the long-term well-being of their children for the sake of short-term pecuniary gain (Sharp and Flinspach 1995: 176; Frevert 1989: 269). Women in the workforce were blamed for all manner of societal ills and the term *'Schlüsselkinder'* (latchkey children) was coined to describe the neglected and potentially delinquent children of these women. The government, referring to the opinions of prominent social theorists such as Helmut Schelsky and paediatricians, discursively emphasized the importance of the family as a fundamental social institution and warned of the detrimental effects on children of women working outside the home (Moeller 1993: 117). Schelsky, who was director of the newly founded Hamburg Academy for Communal Economics and an adviser to the Ministry of the Family, argued that women's entry into paid employment threatened to draw them into the contradictions between 'primary and abstract social relationships that consumed men's lives', and thus 'undermine social order' (Moeller 1997: 118). Despite the growing need for labour during the economic surge that began in the late 1950s, the CDU–CSU coalition government adopted the policy of importing millions of foreign workers as 'guest workers' rather than disturb this social order by integrating women into the labour force. As Alice Cook (1984: 66) explains, mobilizing the potential resource represented by women was not countenanced or even discussed by the government, employers, economists or business leaders.

Under the guise of protecting democratic stability and order, successive conservative coalition governments denounced and stifled any political discussion of their family policy and related social security and employment measures. They were aided in this endeavour by the Catholic Church, which exerted its considerable political influence to oppose the integration of women into the formal economy and the polity. Through its extensive network of women's associations and from the pulpit, the Church steered women away from participating in the public sphere by praising their return to domesticity and extolling the virtues of family unity. At the same time, it directed its congregation to vote for the CDU and CSU parties. The government also resisted integrating women into the political sphere, confining its acknowledgement of women's political rights to the vote. Moreover, the government viewed remnants of the pre-war women's movement as politically suspect. These highly conservative political conditions diminished the possibilities for any feminist critique of the identity-related idea of the *complete*, normal family and its implications for social security and employment policy measures.

By the mid-1960s, however, a shortage of qualified and flexible workers forced the state to moderate its attitude towards women working. In 1966, the CDU–SDP coalition government published a report, entitled 'The Situation of Women at Work, in the Family, and in Society', in which it laid out a three-phase model of a woman's working life designed to provide a much-needed skilled and flexible labour force without compromising the responsibility of motherhood. This model divided a woman's working life into three stages. The first stage saw a woman being trained and educated for a period of employment before marriage. The second stage saw a woman's career being suspended for the period of child-rearing and household maintenance. The third saw a woman re-entering the labour force when her children were older, but still retaining the primary responsibility for lightened household duties (*Bericht der Bundesregierung über die Situation der Frauen in Beruf, Familie und Gesellschaft* 1966). Educational reforms based on this model not only encouraged women to remain at secondary school but also provided them with increased access to tertiary education. Prior to these educational reforms, almost 80 per cent of girls had left school at fourteen and only about 2 per cent of young women attended grammar school and qualified to go to university. However, access to employment remained restricted because discrimination at the point of recruitment made it difficult for women to enter their chosen fields. Access also remained restricted because many women were employed in the light-work categories of the wage scale (Kolinsky 1996a: 271).

The first period of state behavioural continuity: 1945–84

The deeply paternalistic corporate state identity reconstituted in the post-war period had an immediate and lasting inhibiting effect on the diffusion of international norms of sexual non-discrimination. The German state initially refused to ratify the 1952 UN Convention on the Political Rights of Women, and even after finally ratifying the convention in 1970, it continued to marginalize women in the political sphere. It was also extremely slow to ratify the 1957 UN Convention on the Nationality of Married Women and the 1962 UN Convention on Consent to Marriage, Minimum Age for Marriage, and Registration of Marriages.[3] Despite ratifying the ILO Equal Remuneration Convention in 1956 and the ILO Discrimination

(Employment and Occupation) Convention in 1961, the state failed to implement either convention. In the interim, the state became a signatory member of the EU but, after reluctantly agreeing to the inclusion of the principle of equal pay in the founding Treaty, openly flouted its legal obligation to comply with Article 119. In the late 1970s, the German state refused to implement the newly adopted European equal pay and equal treatment directives, claiming that the constitutional guarantee of equality provided adequate legal compliance (Harvey 1990: 54). By this time, however, the state was under mounting internal and external pressure to meet its international legal obligations. Remaining recalcitrant, the state was eventually compelled to take legislative action to avoid infringement proceedings raised against it by the European Commission in 1979 for failing to comply with the European equality directives. The question is, why did internal pressure from feminists fail to induce the change in state behaviour?

Towards the end of the 1960s, many young women who had benefited from improved educational opportunities but were angered by discriminatory employment conditions joined the student protest movement known as the Extra-parliamentary Opposition (*Außerparlamentarische Opposition*), which dominated alternative politics from the violent protests of 1968 to the mid-1970s (Schmid 1990: 227). However, most feminists quickly became estranged from the New Left after protesting against their 'second-class status in the political struggle of the Extra-Parliamentary Opposition' (ibid.: 229). Divided in their views of the political system, between those who were sceptical of the state and those who sought change through the state, feminists either became part of the radical autonomous movement or joined established political parties and organizations – in particular, the SDP and Free Democratic Party (FDP). At the time, this split left German feminism as a whole in a relatively weak and marginalized position. It also meant that, despite the protests of activists within established political parties and the German Confederation of Trade Unions (DGB) against discriminatory employment practices, feminist activism had little influence on state behaviour.

Feminist activism was also constrained by the state's declaration of a state of emergency and enactment of the 1972 Decree against Radicals (*Radikalenerlaß*), the implementation of which affected liberals, leftists, pacifists and feminists alike, and 'led to the erosion of constitutional rights such as freedom of expression, of affiliation and choice of political organisation' (Jacobs 1978: 166).[4] Gisela Kaplan (1992: 121) describes how the secret police and Office for the Protection of the Constitution searched and investigated individuals and organizations on the faintest suspicion of left-wing sympathies and anti-constitutional activities, creating a climate of fear and repression. Feminists were regarded as suspect and were frequently screened and black-banned from public occupations by the Office for the Protection of the Constitution. In this hostile environment, feminists feared signing petitions or attending demonstrations, activities commonly regarded by the police as suspicious, and were intimidated by attempts by the state and Catholic Church to link their actions to terrorism. In particular, the Catholic Church accused feminists fighting to legalize abortion of being sympathizers of terrorism (Jacobs 1978: 171). It was under these extremely trying conditions that feminists within the SDP, the FDP and the DGB mobilized to press the state to comply with the European equality directives by eliminating discriminatory national employment practices. However, they could not agree on the necessary corrective legislative measures, and this had detrimental political consequences.

Having observed the responses of other European member states to the directives, feminists within the SDP and FDP debated whether or not a comprehensive anti-discrimination law with an equality agency to enforce it should be adopted by Germany (Hoskyns 1988: 41). While those within the FDP favoured a comprehensive anti-discrimination law, feminists within the SDP wanted to follow the Swedish model of an active public labour market policy, which involved affirmative action combined with a high degree of autonomy for employers and unions to settle matters concerning pay and employment conditions (Nielsen 1983: 115). The Women's Division of the DGB was also doubtful about a comprehensive law, preferring that gender-related issues be given a higher priority within the collective bargaining process. The DGB itself and employer associations objected to a comprehensive law and monitoring agency on the grounds that it interfered with the freedom of contract. The DGB also feared that a special agency would erode its bargaining position. Employers, meanwhile, feared that any new legislation would increase their costs. Moreover, many feminists viewed the EU with scepticism and shared the opinion of state officials that it was '*inappropriate* to receive gender equality provisions from external sources' (Hoskyns 1988: 41). Furthermore, discursively, feminists did not deviate substantially from the conservative ideas built into the German welfare system and the related policies of combining paid employment and family responsibilities sequentially. As Ilona Ostner explains, feminists were reluctant to identify independence with employment or to fully embrace the egalitarian idea of women's full-time employment (1993: 95). While many felt that the invisible unpaid work of women in the home should be financially compensated, argue Andrea Vogt and Susanne Zwingel (2003: 463), there were those who even thought gainful employment was simply another form of dependency. With feminists divided over the objectives of legislative changes, and employers and unions united in opposition to a comprehensive anti-discrimination law, there was little chance of the state initiating changes in accordance with the directives.

Hence, the state's decision to enact the Employment Law to Comply with the European Community Provisions (Adaptation Act) in 1980 was induced not by changing domestic conditions but rather by changing regional conditions in which the European Commission developed the political will to enforce implementation of European equality legislation through the infringements procedure established under Article 169 of the 1957 Treaty of Rome. Prior to the mid-1970s, the European Commission rarely initiated infringement proceedings against states for non-implementation of European law because it feared such action would 'aggravate its fragile relationship with member governments' (Stein 1981: 6). However, as a consequence of a series of landmark decisions by the European Court of Justice (ECJ) establishing the direct effect of European equality legislation, and the court's admonishment of the commission for failing to pursue breaches of said legislation, the European Commission began bringing infringement proceedings against member states for defaulting on their obligations under the European equality directives.[5] In May 1979, the European Commission began proceedings against Germany for failing to implement the European equal pay and equal treatment directives. Following a series of fruitless discussions with the German government, throughout which state representatives argued that the German Constitution gave adequate effect to the directives, the European Commission issued Germany with a deadline for compliance. Keen to avoid the judicial stage of the infringement proceedings, the German government finally made amendments to national legislation.

However, the amendments made by the state were minimal and piece-meal (Hoskyns 1996: 119). Rather than implement a new piece of legislation, the 1980 Adaptation Act inserted the barest of clauses into the pre-existing Civil Code of 1896.[6] The amendments were also a compromise, with evident problems. First, to protect the freedom of contract between employers and employees, the amendments applied only to individual employers and not to the parties of collective bargaining, for which Article 3 of the Constitution applied (Ostner and Lewis 1995: 188). This constraint applied to both the principles of equal pay and equal treatment embodied respectively in Articles 612 and 611 of the Civil Code. With over 80 per cent of German employees covered by collective agreements, this meant that a significant proportion of the labour force remained excluded from these provisions (Bercusson and Dickens 1997: 22). The self-employed were also excluded from the equal treatment provisions, which related exclusively to employees bound by a contract of employment. Second, the amendments failed to eliminate discrimination produced by the light-work categories in collective agreements. Third, the equal treatment provision allowed an employer to justify direct discrimination if sex were an indispensable condition for the job, which employers often interpreted loosely both in the recruitment process and in the drawing up of contracts, or in employment practices (Bertelsmann and Rust 1995: 41–2, 44). Fourth, the amendments failed to provide adequate sanctions for breach of its provisions (Hervey 1993: 112). This was particularly evident in the absence of any penalty for discriminatory notices of or advertisement for job vacancies (Bertelsmann and Rust 1995: 45–6). Fifth, the amendments made no mention of indirect discrimination or positive action (Hervey 1993: 118). Sixth, the burden of proof, at least in prima facie evidence, rested with the person discriminated against. Thus, it was left to the individual to enforce equality in the workplace by taking legal recourse (Rhoodie 1989: 222). Finally, no administrative provisions were made to ensure implementation.

The European Commission was highly critical of the Adaptation Act. In its 1981 review of Germany's implementation of the European equality directives, the European Commission faulted the legislation in several ways. As Hoskyns explains, the commission criticized the legislation for its use of the concept of *indispensable condition* to justify occupational exceptions to the principle of equal treatment, and for failing to protect self-employed and public employees adequately. The commission also criticized the German state for failing to provide a list of occupations that were exempt from the principle of equal treatment, and for failing to make any provision to review exempted occupations (Hoskyns 1996: 133). However, the state refused to discuss these criticisms with the commission, and, as a result, the commission delivered a reasoned opinion in October 1982. The state continued to ignore the commission, and in 1984 the commission issued infringement proceedings against Germany. The German state failed to respond and the case progressed to the judicial stage of the infringement proceedings. On 21 May 1985, the ECJ ruled that the situation in Germany ran counter to the provisions of the European equal treatment directive. The ECJ also held that the state was in derogation of its duties to provide a list of exemptions and to periodically review said exemptions. Although it did not define which occupations could be exempted from the principle of equal treatment, the ECJ held that states must regularly engage in a thorough review of any exemptions and forward the results of their reviews to the commission (Hoskyns 1996: 62).

The second period of state behavioural continuity: 1985–9

Paradoxically, a couple of months after the ECJ's ruling, the German state finally ratified CEDAW on 10 July 1985. However, it took no initiative to implement the convention, and its initial periodic report was submitted two years late. The state also delayed responding to the ECJ's May ruling until 1987. Moreover, when it forwarded the requested list of exempted occupations to the European Commission, the state emphasized that the list was not binding on domestic labour courts. The only requirement binding the courts, according to the state, was to interpret the relevant general provisions of the Civil Code (Bertelsmann and Rust 1995: 42). The government's non-binding interpretation of the ECJ's binding decision was criticized by the European Commission's Network of Experts on the Implementation of the Equality Directives, which also expressed concern that considerable scope for discrimination remained within the state's list of exceptions. Nevertheless, the state resisted making further changes to domestic employment practices. Furthermore, the federal government introduced a series of policy measures that reinforced the paternalistic corporate identity of the state and discriminated against women in full-time employment. These gender-reinforcing measures reflected the government's deeply held belief in the importance of the family as the fundamental ordering principle of social life. The measures also reflected the government's intention to create what it called a new motherliness among German women. Furthermore, the measures were aimed at reversing the declining birth rate and rising unemployment by returning women from the labour force to the home (Chamberlayne 1991: 203). As Prue Chamberlayne explains, the government's keynote document on family policy 'focused equal rights and disadvantage on the differential position of working women and housewives, and suggested that emancipation lay in *self-fulfilment* in motherhood' (ibid.: 204).

Policy measures introduced following the release of this document included the 1986 'DM 10 billion family package', which provided universal child-rearing allowances and parental leave – the conditions of which favoured women leaving full-time employment (Chamberlayne 1994: 180–1). As Elisabeth Vogelheim explains (1988: 115–16), the Parental Allowances Law discriminated against women in full-time employment because it allocated a monthly allowance after the birth of a child on the basis of the parent having no income or working less than twenty hours a week. Since the industrial relations system, with its light-work categories and indirectly discriminatory job-grading system, still favoured a male earning a higher income, it was more likely that a woman would take advantage of the allowance. The allowance, combined with parental leave of up to thirty-six months, also relieved the state of the need to provide childcare facilities. The government also introduced a labour policy that discouraged women from entering full-time employment by permitting temporary contracts between employers and employees, which were not subject to the usual constraints governing permanent contracts. This policy allowed employers to circumvent the existing protection against dismissal for pregnancy because the Maternity Protection Law applied only to permanent employees. Moreover, temporary staff did not have the same access to social security benefits that permanent employees had (ibid.: 115–16).

Needless to say, the state neglected to mention these problems in its initial CEDAW report submitted on 15 September 1988. Moreover, the state laid claim to a number of legal and policy measures that had, in fact, first been initiated either by feminists within the Green Party and SDP at the state (*Land*) and local levels, by feminists within the Green Party at the federal level, or by private individual litigants fighting sexual discrimination in employment. First, the state claimed that it had established government equality agencies at all levels – federal, state and local – to improve the situation of women. Second, it claimed that it had broadened the legal concept of discrimination to include indirect discrimination. Third, the state claimed that, in the political sphere, 'a number of political parties had established quotas or targets to increase the percentage of women' (United Nations General Assembly 1990: 13). Despite government claims to the contrary, equality agencies actually originated at the state and local level courtesy of feminist political intervention, the concept of indirect discrimination found its way into the national legal framework via litigation, and the Green Party first introduced quotas.

During the 1980s, confronted by the reactionary politics of the conservative federal government, many feminists gravitated to the newly formed Green Party and exploited its open structure to demand and obtain increased political representation within the party through the introduction of an affirmative action policy. The Greens' initiative to introduce a 50 per cent quota for all ballot lists to internal party and parliamentary elections triggered debate and change within the major parties. Feminists within the Greens, alongside activists within the SDP and trade unions, also turned to those state or city governments with Green–SDP coalitions to press for legislative and policy change at the state and local levels (Ferree and Gamson 1999: 45–6). These changes included the establishment of government equality agencies or units (*Frauenbeauftragte*), affirmative action legislation, anti-discrimination in employment legislation, and funding for women's refuges and rape counselling centres. At the same time, private individual litigants exploited the legal opportunity provided by the establishment of the direct effect of European equality legislation to challenge discriminatory employment practices. The pressure emanating from feminist activism within political parties and private individual litigation led to legislative and public policy changes that were then claimed by the federal government as evidence of Germany's compliance with and implementation of various international and regional norms of sexual non-discrimination.

Founded in January 1980, the Green Party entered the federal parliament in March 1983 as 'the self-styled voice of extra-parliamentary issues and movements at the parliamentary level' (Kolinsky 1988: 139). From the outset, feminists were attracted to the Greens, with the expectation that the party would protest against gender-based discrimination and influence public policy-making. With its emphasis on rotation and against professionalization, the Green Party was more open and accessible than the mainstream political parties to women holding office, but, despite the party's apparent approval of equal opportunities, feminists complained that their standing remained lower than that of male party members and insisted on the introduction of a quota system across all party offices and candidate lists at the federal, state and local levels (Kolinsky 1989: 198). In

September 1986, the Greens adopted a 50 per cent quota regulation based on the 'zip principle', whereby candidates' lists for party and public office are put together by alternating male and female candidates (Paterson 1989: 357). In the party organizations, according to Eva Kolinsky, 'positions were to be filled in such a way that equal responsibilities and equal seniority for women was ensured' (1989: 200). The Green Party's radical approach to increasing the political representation of women had an immediate impact on the major political parties, which, faced with a considerable swinging female vote, promised recommendations to increase female parliamentary candidates in the run-up to the 1987 election. Feminists within the SDP pressured the party to increase the number of women at decision-making levels, and in 1988 the party introduced a 40 per cent quota for women for all party offices and a 33 per cent quota for ballot lists (Peters 1999: 222). That same year, the CDU, which rejected a quota system on principle, adopted a so-called flexible goal that women be represented proportionate to their party membership (Lemke 1993: 157). The FDP also rejected quotas, preferring a system of representation based on membership proportion. However, the CDU-led government made it clear that it had no intention of legislating for affirmative action or quotas in political decision-making bodies or in employment (Schoepp-Schilling 2000: 62, n 17).

At the federal level, feminists within the Greens also intervened on the question of discrimination in employment but, because of internal divisions over the corporate identity-related issue of motherhood, were ineffective in challenging national labour policies. In 1987, a newly formed Mothers' Faction within the Greens opposed the anti-discrimination legislation proposed by mainstream feminists within the party. The Mothers' Faction produced a manifesto in which members proclaimed that 'the future depends on mothers' and that 'mothers create the psychological and physical well-being of the whole of society' (Kolinsky 1989: 201). Members of the Mothers' Faction demanded the rights of mothers to choose their own priorities and to be rewarded for their caring work within the family through the provision of pay and pensions for home-carers, childcare facilities and flexible employment (Chamberlayne 1993: 180). They also demanded that the proposed anti-discrimination legislation be amended before being resubmitted to the new Bundestag. Mainstream feminists within the Greens and the SDP condemned the manifesto as a 'return to Nazi-style glorification of motherhood' (Kolinsky 1989: 201), but, despite their protests, the Mothers' Faction gained a recognized foothold in the Greens and amendments were made to the proposed anti-discrimination legislation. As a consequence, the power of feminists within the Greens to discursively challenge the gender-biased corporate identity of the state and influence national labour policies was diminished.

However, despite this setback, feminists within the Greens were making their presence felt at the state and local levels. Exploiting those state or city governments with Green–SDP coalitions, activists within the Greens, SDP and trade unions pressured for the establishment of public equality agencies mandated to enact and implement legislation and public policies. Activists justified the need for such agencies on the basis of the affirmative action programmes required under the EU's First Community Programme on the Promotion of Equal Opportunities for Women (1982–5), and by 1986 the number of state and local equality agencies had expanded to such an extent that the federal government and those state governments with conservative coalitions were compelled to establish similar agencies. However, rather than set up an autonomous body akin to those established by progressive state and local governments, the federal government simply extended the scope of the Ministry for Health, Family and Youth to include women's issues. Equality agencies established by progressive Green–SDP state and local governments were well resourced, and feminists working within them initiated ambitious affirmative action programmes and laws, anti-discrimination in employment legislation, and funding for women's refuges and rape support centres.[7]

Feminists working within the more progressive state equality units and trade unions also supported and assisted private individual litigants fighting sexual discrimination in the workplace. In the 1980s, a series of employment discrimination cases decided by labour courts cast doubt upon the compatibility of specific provisions of the 1980 Adaptation Act with European equality law and put pressure on the federal government to amend national employment legislation (Shaw 1991: 27–8). The first two cases concerned discriminatory hiring practices whereby the plaintiffs had applied for positions for which they were suitably qualified but had been rejected because of their gender. In both *Von Colson & Kamann* v. *Nordrhein-Westfalen* and *Harz* v. *deutsche Tradax, GmbH*, the plaintiffs argued that, as a result of Article 6 of the European Equal Treatment Directive, they had the right to be offered the positions for which they had applied or, alternatively, damages amounting to six months' salary (Ellis 1988: 207). The *Von Colson* court in Hamm and the *Harz* court in Hamburg both referred the cases to the ECJ for a determination of whether the European Equal Treatment Directive conferred a right to be offered a contract of employment or, if not, whether the directive required them to impose a sanction greater than that provided by the national Adaptation Act. The ECJ decided both cases simultaneously in April 1984, finding in favour of the plaintiffs. On the basis of the ECJ's ruling, which indicated that Article 611(aII) of the Adaptation Act was in breach of the European Equal Treatment Directive, both courts awarded damages of six months' pay plus interest (Harvey 1990: 59–60).

Following these highly publicized decisions, other private individual litigants began to challenge discriminatory employment practices before the courts. The case of *Bilka-Kaufhaus GmbH* v. *Weber Von Hartz* is particularly significant because it addressed a major area of wage discrimination against women in Germany, discrimination against part-time employees, and led to the expansion of the national legal concept of discrimination to include indirect discrimination (Harvey 1990: 67). The case concerned the exclusion of part-time employees from an occupational pension scheme provided by Bilka, a large department store chain. In the case, the plaintiff claimed that the company's practice of requiring that part-time employees work full time for at least fifteen years over a total of twenty years in order to receive a pension indirectly discriminated against women in breach of Article 119 of the European Treaty of Rome (ibid.: 68; Ellis 1988: 193). The Federal Labour Court referred the case to the ECJ for a determination of whether Article 119 of the Treaty of Rome was directly applicable in this situation; whether the company's defence that the purpose of its policy was not to discriminate against women but to discourage its employees from choosing to work part time was valid; and whether employers were required to take affirmative action in their occupational pension schemes to compensate women for their family responsibilities (Harvey 1990: 68).

The ECJ decided the case in May 1986, finding in favour of the plaintiff on the first two questions but for the employer on the last question. The ECJ ruled that pension schemes constituted pay and were, therefore, covered by Article 119, and that a scheme that effectively denies pensions to a far greater number of women than men is indirectly discriminatory unless the employer can establish that the policy is necessary and appropriate. The *Bilka* case subsequently became a model for a series of lower labour-court cases dealing with indirect discrimination in national statutes and collective agreements. The resulting body of constructive case law redefined the national legal concept of discrimination to include indirect discrimination and put pressure on the federal government to amend employment laws. However, the conservative coalition government resisted making any immediate legislative changes and was soon distracted by the momentous events accompanying the fall of the Berlin Wall on 9 November 1989.

The third period of state behavioural continuity: 1990–7

Reunification was rapid, occurring very much on West Germany's terms and characterized by what Peter Katzenstein describes as 'an inexorable extension of West German institutions, norms, and practices into East Germany' (1993b: 69). Preoccupied with the politics of reunification, the federal government resisted mounting external pressure from the ILO Committee of Experts and the UN CEDAW committee to address a range of discriminatory domestic practices. During the 1990s, the ILO Committee of Experts repeatedly questioned the compatibility of the light-work categories in industrial collective agreements with the principle of equal remuneration, and by 1997 was admonishing the state for lack of change in the situation (International Labour Conference 1997: 248). The federal government consistently maintained that it was constitutionally bound to refrain from directly intervening in the collective bargaining process and argued that 'the mere presence of light wage groups in collective agreements does not indicate whether or not the work of women is in fact undervalued in the respective occupational sphere' (International Labour Conference 1995: 256). Consequently, the federal government refused to force the social partners (employers and unions) to take action to eliminate the light wage groups in collective agreements. The CEDAW committee also demanded that the state take steps to eliminate gender-based discrimination in collective bargaining agreements, but to no effect.

In its consideration of Germany's initial report in January 1990, the CEDAW committee chastised the state for its minimalist approach to the incorporation of the convention and raised substantial questions about the lack of state measures to promote women's political and labour rights. The committee expressed 'astonishment' at the state's failure to take action to eliminate discrimination produced by the light-work categories in collective agreements despite having ratified the ILO Equal Remuneration Convention. In particular, the committee criticized the state's refusal to 'interfere' with collective agreements. It also criticized the state's readiness to leave it to individuals to implement and enforce the principle of equal pay by taking legal recourse. The committee raised questions about the issue of part-time employment and the gap in coverage by social security schemes. It also criticized the lack of publicly funded crèches and measures making it easier for women (and men) to combine work and family responsibilities (UNCEDAW 1990). Not only did the federal government fail to act on these criticisms, but it also failed to submit Germany's second periodic report, which was due in August 1990. Moreover, as part of its annexation of the GDR, the government imposed gender-reinforcing legislative and policy reforms that conflicted with international and regional requirements.

In 1990, the federal government removed state support for employees with family responsibilities and abolished affirmative action in education and employment in the GDR. It also began rapidly phasing out state subsidies for housing and childcare. Federal support for childcare centres and kindergartens was cut off in June 1991, resulting in the disintegration of the extensive network of childcare centres that had enabled East German women to combine employment and family responsibilities. A few were maintained through limited communal funds or moved to the private sector, like centres in the West, but at full cost their services often became unaffordable (Adler 1996: 293). In 1993, job protection and payment for single mothers unable to find childcare for children under the age of three (if born before January 1990) was repealed, further compounding the problem (Shaeffer-Hegel 1992: 106). The federal government also revoked a monthly housework day, leave for parents to nurse sick children, and lengthy fully paid maternity leave – six weeks before and twenty weeks after the birth (Berghahn 1995: 39). In place of these provisions, the West German social welfare and industrial relations systems were extended into the East, along with their assumption of a male-breadwinner family. Furthermore, West German regulations and laws concerning the tax system, family allowances and employment conditions were also imposed upon the East with the intention of 'financially persuading' East German women to stay at home with their children (Rudolph, Appelbaum and Maier 1994: 24, 26).

Rather than considering which, if any, entitlements and legal guarantees of the GDR were worth preserving and incorporating in the new united Germany, the federal government's objective was to convert the GDR to the West German model of gender relations and, in the process, reinforce the paternalistic corporate identity of the state. The loss of many important economic and social rights confirmed the fears of East German feminists, who, in the politically opportune pre-unification period, had fought against the impending dismantling of social and childcare services, and the wholesale installation of West German legal and public policy systems. During the transition period, activists in the Independent Women's Association (Unabhangiger Frauenverband, UFV) worked hard to save beneficial legislation and public policy measures, and to secure the civil and political rights that had been denied by the communist regime.[8] In March 1990, activists representing the UFV at the round-table talks between the Hans Modrow government and non-parliamentary groups succeeded in persuading the round table to include anti-discrimination clauses in drafts of the new Constitution, the law on political party and action groups, and the new election laws. They also succeeded in persuading the round table to adopt two documents outlining a comprehensive programme for achieving gender equality and protecting women from the repercussions of economic and monetary union with West Germany (Young 1999: 101, 104–11). However, Brigitte Young explains, neither the Social Charter nor the 'Essential Features for the Equality of Women and Men' had any political influence, because by the time the documents were adopted by the round table on 5 March 1990, 'the economy was close to collapse, the Modrow government had virtually lost all credibility, and the people had decided that they wanted to be *one Volk* with the more prosperous West Germans' (ibid.: 105). Yet activists in the UFV continued to believe that the GDR would remain an independent state; that the basic principles of the socialist state such as the right to employment would be retained; and that most of the public administrative bodies would continue to operate (Ferree 1993: 99).

These beliefs were shattered on 18 March 1990 with the GDR's first and last independent election, which was dominated by the affiliates of the West German CDU party campaigning on a platform of rapid unification. The newly elected conservative coalition led by the East German Christian

Democrats ditched the UFV's social charter on the basis that it was unwilling to fight for reforms that the West German federal government was likely to object to (Shaeffer-Hegel 1992: 107). The East German Christian Democratic Party was also keen to distance itself from its communist-affiliated past, and, since equality had been a central plank of communist policy, the party withdrew its support for the charter. The West German federal government, according to Young, simply 'disregarded the document' (1999: 112). Confronted by the inevitable dissolution of the East German state, members of the UFV decided to redirect their attention to the West German political system and to try to form an alliance with their West German counterparts against the impending reality of *Germany – unified fatherland* (ibid.: 143). However, hopes of creating a united feminist political movement were dashed as misunderstanding turned to open hostility at the first East–West feminist Congress at the Technical University in West Berlin in April 1990. Despite sharing ambivalence towards reunification, East and West German feminists were deeply divided over the identity-related issue concerning the relationship between motherhood and full-time employment. In contrast to their West German counterparts, East German feminists believed that women's independence was linked to the availability of full-time employment and the economic benefits and independence that came from having a salary (Vogt and Zwingel 2003: 463). They also disagreed on a range of logistical issues such as organizational structure, relations to the state, and political strategies (Young 1999: 146, 149). Consequently, 'facing a common *enemy* in the form of the West German state was not sufficient to unite the movement for the purpose of gaining access to the negotiations for German unity' (ibid.: 148).

Nevertheless, East and West German feminists tried separately to intervene in the reunification negotiations but were thwarted by the Western German state, which systematically excluded feminist concerns from the unification treaty agenda.[9] Consequently, the treaty establishing political unity between the Federal Republic of Germany and the German Democratic Republic, which took effect on 2 October 1990, made no reference to the many demands made by feminists (Young 1999: 163). Bitterly disappointed by its inability to influence reunification negotiations and preserve the entitlements and legal guarantees bestowed by the GDR, the UFV began to splinter. At its first major meeting after unification in Leipzig in March 1991, UFV members heatedly debated the value of parliamentary politics, with the sharpest division being between those who preferred to ignore the state and those who continued to see value in pursuing change through the state (Ferree 1993: 102). Despite these internal divisions and a significant decline in membership and staff, the UFV continued to protest against discriminatory practices and to press the state for legislative and public policy reforms. Realizing the need to revive East–West feminist political co-operation, the UFV organized its fifth congress in 1993 specifically as an East–West Women's Congress. The meeting was well attended by feminists from both sides of the former border, according to Young, and the congress passed a resolution to establish a working forum to 'prepare a programmatic foundation for national feminist co-operation capable of political action' (1999: 204). The working forum held its first meeting in Kassel on 23 June 1993.

An immediate result of this new national feminist co-operation was the organization of a women's strike to coincide with International Women's Day, 8 March 1994 (Young 1999: 204). Women's Strike Day was designed to draw public and political attention to the 'dismantling of civil and employment rights, the reduction of social services and increasing feminisation of poverty, and the backlash against women's rights' (ibid.: 195). The UFV office in Berlin served as one of two national co-ordination headquarters for Women's Strike Day, with staff carrying out the planning and publicity for the strike action. One of the aims of Women's Strike Day was to bring together autonomous activists and feminists within political parties and trade unions. Yet, as Young explains, the major labour unions and the umbrella organization for all German unions – the DGB – objected to the use of the term 'strike'. Invoking the letter of the law, the unions maintained that the term 'strike' could not be used for a protest event. Despite the efforts of the Women's Division of the DGB to persuade the organization's hierarchy 'to endorse the protest event and support a political strike of women', the DGB refused. Consequently, there was little collective action at work sites to support the strike action on 8 March (ibid.: 195). Nevertheless, over one million women participated in strike events throughout unified Germany, putting pressure on the federal government to adopt more progressive policies.

The CDU-led coalition government was already under increasing electoral pressure to introduce measures to alleviate the high level of female unemployment in the former GDR. In the lead-up to the October 1994 general election, CDU female moderates expressed their disaffection with the party, and it also became clear that women's electoral preferences were diversifying. In a bid to bolster its credibility among female voters and party moderates, the CDU government introduced legislation extending the 1980 Adaptation Act to all public employees. The legislation, entitled the Act to Establish Equality for Men and Women (Second Equality Act), also established three-year plans to promote and hire more public service employees, offered protection against sexual harassment in the workplace, and included measures to increase the number of female representatives in government departments and labour councils. The amended legislation came into force a month before the general election, on 1 September 1994. However, the legislation was vague in relation to its practical application, lacked sanctions for non-compliance and offered little improvement in employment conditions for women in the private sector (Schoepp-Schilling 1995: 35–6). Although the CDU was returned to office in the election, the party suffered overall losses and, because of its opposition to quotas, very few female parliamentary candidates were elected.

The electoral debacle compelled the CDU to reconsider its position on quotas and to address the issue of female unemployment in the former GDR. Despite its long-standing opposition to positive discrimination measures and quotas, the CDU promised to introduce affirmative action measures aimed at improving female representation in its ranks – but not before the 1996 party congress (Kolinsky 1996b: 283–4). The CDU coalition government also introduced quotas in training, retraining and public job creation schemes to try to improve women's employment situation in the former GDR. The federal government began formulating legislation and public policy in terms of affirmative action because the political discourse surrounding sexual discrimination had been redefined in these terms by progressive state governments and the Green Party through the course of the 1980s. Without the equality agencies and the work of feminists within the Greens and SDP to establish them, it is unlikely that these affirmative action measures and quotas would ever have been adopted.

However, despite these changes and the increasing domestic pressure to further modify its behaviour, the federal government neglected to submit Germany's third CEDAW report by the due date of August 1994. Having already failed to submit Germany's second CEDAW report in 1990, the federal government finally submitted a combined second and third report to the CEDAW committee in October 1996. The content of this combined report indicates that, aside from the aforementioned labour initiatives, the situation on the nature, scope and outcome of government action in the areas of civil and political rights and labour had not changed substantially since 1990, when the CEDAW committee admonished the state for its tardiness in implementing the convention. In an annexe to the combined report, however, the federal government laid claim to the implementation of a number of measures related to violence against women that had, in fact, first been initiated at the local level by radical feminists in the 1970s. The federal government claimed that it had established and funded shelters for battered women across Germany, along with counselling centres and emergency hotlines for victims of sexual abuse. However, at the time it was preparing the state's combined report to CEDAW, the federal government was doing its best to legally and politically minimize the state's obligation to act on the issue of violence against women. According to Sabine Berghahn, there was tremendous resistance among conservative politicians against legislative reform in the field of gender-based violence. She concludes that, in spite of Germany's regional reputation as a 'taillight of legal reform' with regard to violence against women, political discussion on the issue remained stagnant (1995: 47).

Autonomous feminists in Berlin opened the first women's refuge on 1 November 1976, and by 1979 women's refuges offered support, legal advice and counselling to victims of domestic violence in fourteen cities. Radical activists also demonstrated against rape and domestic violence, and in the spring of 1977 the first rape-crisis hotline appeared in Berlin (Markovits and Gorski 1996: 143). During the 1980s, an uneasy alliance began to form between autonomous feminists in need of government funding to sustain the refuges and feminists working within progressive state equality units looking to increase their political leverage (Ferree 1995: 100). As the number of state and local units expanded during the late 1980s, so too did the number of women's refuges. However, in a bid to maintain control of the refuges, autonomous feminists accepted government funding only to the extent that the autonomy of the organization was not compromised. Of course, Myra Marx Ferree states, the price of autonomy was low-level funding, a precarious financial status and a heavy reliance on volunteers to keep a refuge open (1987: 187). Ulrike Pallmert testifies to this as she chronicles the ongoing struggle with the state government to obtain funding for the first two Berlin refuges without abdicating control to the state. The state government's conditions for funding were highly discriminatory, she claims, because only women 'unable to help themselves out of a socially undesirable position' qualified for financial assistance, and because 'we were required to keep a file on each woman granted shelter' (1984: 179). 'We decided to deny the Senate this avenue of control', she states,

> whereupon it threatened to deny us any public funding if we turned down the terms of financing. Following extensive bargaining with the Senate, low-level public funding was granted for six paid positions per annum, which left the refuges heavily dependent on volunteers and struggling to provide effective services.
>
> (ibid.: 179)

State behavioural change: 1998–2004

Before the CEDAW committee was able to examine Germany's combined second and third report, the federal government submitted Germany's fourth periodic report on 27 October 1998, immediately following a federal election in which an SDP–Green coalition government replaced the conservative CDU-led government. The fourth report was introduced to the CEDAW committee for consideration in New York on 1 February 2000 by a representative of the new federal government, who emphasized that the change in government 'had led to new priorities in the country's equal rights policy', the most important of which included the Women and Work action programme and the Action Plan to Combat Violence Against Women (United Nations General Assembly 2000: 29). While the committee welcomed these initiatives, it questioned the state's commitment to eliminating the persistent wage gap between men and women. It also questioned the state's commitment to eliminating other discriminatory labour and labour-related practices related to recruitment and promotion, social security, taxation and childcare. The committee urged the state to introduce legislation ensuring equal opportunity in the private sector of the labour market, review its taxation system of jointly taxing married couples (*Ehegattensplitting*), introduce non-transferable parental leave for fathers, take steps to eliminate wage discrimination in collective bargaining agreements, and provide legal protection against and redress for gender-based violence. In response, the state promised it would 'implement the convention more effectively than in the past' (ibid.: 30). Despite its promise, however, the state was slow to introduce comprehensive legislative and public policy changes.

The Women and Work action programme referred to by the state representative at the CEDAW meeting in New York in February 2000 was allocated a very small budget and failed to address taxation, social security and gender wage gap issues (European Commission's Expert Group on Gender and Employment 2001: 55). Proposed changes to the tax-splitting system were cancelled, plans to invest in childcare facilities for children under the age of three were shelved because of resistance among the *Länder* and among political parties (Maier 2001: 8, 20), and, despite intense pressure from the ILO Committee of Experts, the government refused to legislate against light-work categories in collective agreements (see ILO Committee of Experts on the Application of Conventions and Recommendations 1999, 2000, 2001). Furthermore, an initiative included in the Women and Work action programme to enact a law ensuring equal opportunities in the private sector failed to eventuate. In September 2000, the German federal government presented a draft bill on equal opportunities in the private sector, but German employers' associations strongly opposed any such legislation. The main employers' association, the League of Employers Association (Bundesvereinigung der Deutschen Arbeitgeberverbände, BDA), argued that state intervention in the private sector was unnecessary on the grounds that existing pay differentials were the result of different personal employment histories rather than discrimination in collective agreements. The BDA insisted that it supported the incorporation of the principle of equal opportunity in the private sector but only through voluntary employer initiatives (Schulten 1997).

The draft bill also lacked the support of the SDP hierarchy, which, according to Angelika Koch, 'decided to focus on corporatist regulation attempting to achieve gender equality in the workplace by a neocorporatist arrangement between the state, business and organised labour' (2003: 443). In line with this, Chancellor Gerhard Schröder promised the BDA and the German Chamber of Commerce (Deutscher Industrie und Handelstag, or DIHT) that the bill would not be tabled in parliament if private employers issued a declaration of self-obligation to realize equal opportunity in the private sector. Feminist advocates within the government, trade unions, and the German Women Lawyers' Association lobbied in vain to save the bill, articulating their demand for legislative change in terms of bringing German labour law into line with international and regional standards (Schiek 2001: 20; Tons and Young 2001: 145). In July 2001, the government and employers' associations signed an agreement in which the employers' associations declared their intention to develop and implement their own measures to promote equal opportunities and family-friendly conditions in the private sector (Scheele 2001). And, with that, the draft bill on equal opportunity in the private sector, which had formed part of the SDP–Green coalition pact, was shelved indefinitely.

On 7 July 2000, under regional and domestic pressure, the SDP–Green coalition government adopted a revision of the Federal Childcare Payment and Parental Leave Act (*Bundeserziehungsgeldgesetz*). The European Parental Leave Directive had come into force in 1998 and the government was under pressure to enact legislation to comply with the directive. The government was also under internal pressure from feminists to implement legislation that enabled both men and women to reconcile family and occupational responsibilities. Demanding legislative change, feminists discursively challenged the traditional model of the male-breadwinner family on the basis that women were no longer willing to choose between family and work (see Tons and Young 2001: 153). Although this legislative revision improved on previous government policies, it did not comply fully with the European directive, nor did it introduce non-transferable parental leave for fathers as recommended by the CEDAW committee (Schiek 2000: 35). Given the significant income differentials between men and women, it remained unlikely that men would take parental leave unless it was non-transferable.[10] Furthermore, the state failed to ratify the 1981 ILO Convention on Workers with Family Responsibilities.

The action plan on violence against women referred to by the state representative at the CEDAW meeting in New York in February 2000 consisted largely of crime prevention measures, public and professional awareness campaigns, and nationwide surveys. The federal government proposed to examine the degree to which women were protected against violence by existing criminal and civil law but hesitated to enact new civil legislation on the basis that it would not put an end to violence against women. The government argued that intervention in domestic violence situations was a matter for the police, and police law was the responsibility of the *Länder* (Heinrich Boll Foundation 1999; Ministry for Family, Senior Citizens, Women and Youth 1999). The action plan made no mention of the problem of sexual harassment, which is unsurprising given that, according to Kathrina Zippel, it was generally not recognized as a serious issue (2002: 7). Eventually, the government adopted a law on the protection of women from domestic violence, which came into effect on 1 January 2002, and several progressive *Länder* legislated to give police the power and obligation to evict a violent person from the home for a period of approximately ten days (Hageman-White 2003). The federal government also agreed to ratify the optional protocol to CEDAW on 15 January 2002. Within a few months of ratifying the optional protocol to CEDAW, the SDP–Green coalition government was once again under considerable electoral pressure to confront the issue of reconciling family and employment responsibilities. The government pledged, if re-elected on 22 September 2002, to convert 25 per cent of schools into all-day institutions, expand the number of childcare centres and increase child support payments, but this pledge was only partially fulfilled.[11] The Alliance 90/Greens had proposed that the expanded childcare system be funded predominantly by revising the tax credit, the *Ehegattensplitting*, which had long privileged married couples. They argued that such a move would not only redistribute wealth but also promote a new family paradigm. However, the Christian Democrat opposition accused the government of threatening the constitutional protection of marriage and family, and vowed to take the issue to the Federal Constitutional Court. Fearing 'nothing but trouble', the Social Democrats retreated from the proposal (Vogt and Zwingel 2003: 474–5). Thus, the German gender-biased corporate identity remained intact.

Conclusion

Germany's unwillingness, prior to 1998, to incorporate international and European norms of sexual non-discrimination stands in sharp contrast to its reputation as a highly internationalized state and 'good European par excellence' (Katzenstein 1997c: 260). The history of Germany's response to these norms since 1945 has been dominated, as we have seen, by three periods of state behavioural continuity in which the state created and consolidated an extremely paternalistic corporate identity and resisted international and domestic pressure to incorporate international and European norms of sexual non-discrimination. Domestic feminist activism, which emerged in the politically conducive conditions of the late 1960s and again with the collapse of the Berlin Wall in 1989, had virtually no influence on state behaviour, primarily because of internal divisions over objectives, tactics and the corporate identity-related issue of the relationship between motherhood and work. Also, feminists failed to discursively challenge traditional assumptions embedded in the legislative and public policy systems about gender relations and the family. Hence, there was virtually no contentious discursive interaction between activists and the state to generate change and assist in the diffusion of international norms of sexual non-discrimination. However, the periods of stasis were interrupted on occasion by a change to state employment practices compelled by either changing regional or internal conditions. After 1998, and a dramatic change in the political elite, the state became more receptive to incorporating international norms of sexual non-discrimination, but state behavioural change was slow. Feminists within the new political elite discursively challenged the male-breadwinner model of gender relations and pursued a range of legislative and public policy changes designed to bring state practices into line with international and regional standards. Also, international bodies continued to pressure for state behavioural change.

5   Spain

Spain's response to international norms of sexual non-discrimination has varied over time. Prior to 1975, Spain was governed by an authoritarian regime that fiercely resisted incorporating international norms of sexual non-discrimination. In 1976, democracy was re-established and the state began to accept and internalize these norms, particularly European norms of sexual non-discrimination. Spain continued to incorporate international norms of sexual non-discrimination throughout the 1980s – a response that can be explained partly by international and regional pressure and partly by domestic feminist intervention. Between 1996 and 2004, the state became less receptive to incorporating international norms of sexual non-discrimination.

As an authoritarian state intent on resurrecting a traditional Catholic Spain, the Franquist regime constructed a profoundly gender-biased corporate state identity that was impervious to internationally or domestically derived change. At the end of the Spanish Civil War in 1939, the authoritarian regime revoked women's civil and political rights, and dictated that women were to serve the National–Catholic agenda by producing and maintaining a model Christian family, which was the principal social unit on which the state was built. This vision of restoring stability and social order to the nation through true Catholic womanhood (Gomez 1999: 51) was embedded in the legislative and public policy systems and remained intact until the democratic transition following General Francisco Franco's death on 20 November 1975. As a democratic state, Spain reinstated the civil and political rights of women and, under regional and domestic pressure, introduced reforms in accordance with certain international and European norms of sexual non-discrimination. Following these initial post-democratic reforms, various external and internal pressures induced further changes to domestic state practices. However, certain gender-rectifying changes were compromised by the state's inability to rescind family policies inherited from the Franquist regime. Between 1996 and 2004, the Spanish state showed a marked reluctance to incorporate international norms of sexual non-discrimination.

This chapter examines why Spain's response to international and

European norms of sexual non-discrimination has fluctuated so. It also examines why domestic feminist activism, which emerged as part of the pro-democracy movement in the early 1970s, was able, in conjunction with the imposition of European membership conditions, to ensure a degree of state compliance with EU law in the late 1970s and early 1980s. It investigates how and why the profoundly gender-biased corporate state identity of the Franquist era remained a fetter on state behavioural change during this period. It examines how and why intense domestic feminist pressure throughout the 1980s induced significant changes to state practices. Further, it examines why the state, between 1996 and 2004, resisted incorporating international norms of sexual non-discrimination. The chapter begins by tracing the political construction of the neoconservative corporate identity of the state after the Spanish Civil War before examining how this identity construction affected the diffusion of international norms of sexual non-discrimination both prior to and following the dramatic shift in regime type from authoritarianism to democracy in the late 1970s.

Using the argument developed in Chapter 2, I investigate how, prior to 1975, the state ratified several key international conventions but refused to comply with its international legal obligations. I argue that the state's response to international norms of sexual non-discrimination between 1945 and 1975 is one of behavioural continuity, whereby structural–agential interaction results in the preservation of discriminatory state practices. I also discuss how, following the re-establishment of democracy in 1976, state practices underwent considerable change. This change, I maintain, is the outcome of social interaction between various structures and agents. We can identify two periods of state behavioural change following the transition. We can also identify a second period of state behavioural continuity, from 1996 to 2004, in which social interaction fails to produce progressive change.

The first period of state behavioural continuity, from 1945 to 1975, saw the authoritarian state ratify a number of key international conventions but fail to comply with any of them. It also saw the authoritarian state brutally repress political dissent and stifle any form of feminist opposition to or discursive repudiation of its discriminatory practices. The first period of state behavioural change, from 1976 to 1981, saw the authoritarian regime transform itself into a democratic regime and start to incorporate international norms of sexual non-discrimination. It also saw domestic feminist activism emerge as part of the pro-democracy movement and begin to affect state behaviour. Spanish feminists discursively challenged the neoconservative corporate state identity constructed by the authoritarian regime and demanded sweeping legal reforms. However, securing such change was not easy, with the state distracted by what it considered were more pressing political and economic concerns, and the Catholic Church objecting strongly to civil law reform. In this period, Spanish feminists appropriated and reworked the politically popular discourses of secularism and progressive politics to defend their claims for equality in civil law.

The second period of state behavioural change, from 1982 to 1995, saw a combination of regional pressure in the form of European conditions of membership and domestic feminist pressure induce further state behavioural change. It saw Spanish feminists exploit the state's desire for international and regional recognition to push for the creation of a national equality agency, the ratification of international conventions, and the incorporation of international norms of sexual non-discrimination into ministerial policy-making. It also saw activists capitalize on the Spanish EU presidency and political consensus on European integration to successfully persuade the state to enact sexual harassment in the workplace legislation. Feminists used the discourse of European integration to advance their claims and demands, which was effective because of its powerful resonance among the Spanish political elite. The year 1996 marks the beginning of a second period of state behavioural continuity. This period of stasis, from 1996 to 2004, saw a changeover to a conservative political elite and the state aspire to re-establish a more traditional corporate state identity based on the male-breadwinner family. It also saw the state disregard criticism of its gender-reinforcing policies by the UN Committee on the Elimination of Discrimination Against Women and Spanish feminists alike. Interestingly, private individual litigation has played virtually no part in the diffusion of international norms of sexual non-discrimination into Spanish state practices because very few sex discrimination cases have been brought before the Spanish courts (Valiente 1997a: 210).

Post-Civil War reconstruction of the gender-biased corporate identity of the state

At the end of the Spanish Civil War in 1939, the dictatorship of Franco quickly set about constructing a 'new state' founded on traditional Catholic and National Syndicalist principles, the most fundamental of which was that the family constituted the principal base of the state. Thus, while every branch of the economy was organized in vertical syndicates or compulsory unions incorporating male workers, women were indoctrinated to fulfil their Christian responsibility to the state as mothers (Cousins 1995: 179). Women were indoctrinated by the *Sección Femenina* (Women's Section), which, as the female branch of the Franquist regime, was entrusted with the task of defending the 'authentic Spanish national spirit' by re-establishing what was referred to as true Catholic womanhood (Enders 1992: 674). The authoritarian regime revoked the Republican legislation on civil matrimony and divorce, as well as female suffrage, and heeded the Catholic Church's call for the return of the administration of family law to the Church. Together, the regime and the Catholic Church regulated all aspects of women's lives in accordance with a vision of the perfect *casada* – the dedicated and submissive spouse and mother – by introducing a range of inducements and coercive measures designed to ensure that women fulfilled their 'biological destiny as forgers of the nation's future generations' (Nash 1991: 167).

Deliberately blending Falangist[1] and Catholic doctrine, the Franquist regime rightly assumed that the Church would support the regime and act as a legitimizing authority to ameliorate the international ostracism that followed the Second World War (Cooper 1976: 48). At a time when Spain was reviled as a pro-fascist power, Catholics within the regime forged links with foreign Catholic groups in a systematic attempt to improve Spain's international standing, and these efforts culminated in unreserved Vatican support for the regime in the 1953 Concordat. The Concordat's recognition of Spain as a truly Catholic nation and 'spiritual reserve of the West' was also an endorsement of the regime's twin policies of pronatalism and familialism, upon which the state constructed a neoconservative corporate identity. These twin policies were discursively justified by the regime in terms of Catholic integrationism, imperial expansionism and restoring Spain to world power status. In a speech addressed to the *Sección Femenina*, Ramón Serrano Súñer, a key ideologue of the Franquist regime, stressed the importance of the state adopting a serious demographic policy of producing a numerous and vigorous people if Spain were to be a powerful nation. The regime also discursively emphasized the virtue of the strong Christian family as an antidote to the moral degeneracy of the Second Republic (Nash 1991: 161–2). Amid claims by the regime that the social upheaval, economic disorder and nationalist tensions of the 1930s could all be attributed to the moral decadence of the Second Republic, a set of pronatalist and familialist policies were implemented that conformed to orthodox Catholic teachings. Church and state worked together to install a legislative and public policy system that promoted pronatalist ideals of motherhood and procreation.

The authoritarian regime portrayed the Civil War as a crusade to liberate Spain from the chaos of liberal democracy – with its attendant evils of atheism and communism – and as an opportunity to 'pathologically remake the physical stock of the *Patria* (Fatherland) and its morality' (Richards 1998: 47). The authoritarian regime asserted that the Christian family was the key to establishing social stability because it 'functioned to reproduce the nation as a source of morality and a barrier to deviance and illicit passions of all kinds' (Grugel and Rees 1997: 134). As such, the family needed special protective legislation on the indissolubility of marriage and the reinforcement of male authority within the family. Hence, the regime granted legal status to the male head of the household (*cabeza de la familia*) by reintroducing the 1889 Civil Code and the 1870 Criminal Code. The Civil Code gave a man complete control over all personal property and his wife's right to work, while the Criminal Code entitled him to kill his wife or daughter if she committed adultery. The Civil Code was later incorporated into the *Fuero de los Españoles* of 1945 – a major legal statement of the New State – in which the family was declared 'a natural institution with specific prerogatives and rights which went beyond the boundaries of human law' (Nash 1991: 170). Here, Church doctrine on the sacred institution of the family became directly incorporated into state legislation.

According to Catholic doctrine, which was central to the political construction of the neoconservative corporate state identity, women played a pivotal role in the family as the 'angel of the home' and were destined to serve the family and the state, not only through domestic duties but also by 'imparting religious values, love of nation and respect for (male) authority' (Grugel and Rees 1997: 134). In her natural sphere, a woman's primary task was to produce children, followed by a dedicated effort to ensure moral piety in her family and the wider society. Spanish women were exhorted by the Church and state to create Christian families by fostering vocations among sons and reinstating traditional pious practices, and the regime used certain religious figures to exemplify this ideal vision of Catholic womanhood, including the Virgin Mary, Isabel la Católica and Saint Teresa of Ávila – the so-called Saint of the Race (Vincent 1996: 122; Graham 1995: 184). Saint Teresa of Ávila featured prominently in Catholic-Franquist discourse because she represented the ideal model of pure Spanish womanhood, untainted by 'any strain (*raza*) or blemish (*macula*) of Moors or of Jews' (Richards 1998: 50). Saint Teresa not only exemplified true Spanish womanhood but, because of her immaculate Christian lineage, also represented a model of racial purity (Richards 1998: 50–1). In addition, explains Helen Graham,

> Church teaching on the irreducible nature of male and female, and the latter's exclusive fitness for the home, received tendentious justification via pronouncements of the medical establishment which presented women as weak and emotional creatures, a miry mess of hormonally inspired conditions.
>
> (1995: 184)

Moreover, the medical establishment maintained that there were natural biologically determined differences between men and women that were absolute and irreducible. Psychiatrists also lent their support to the institution of the Christian family by recommending a kind of psychological autarky or self-sufficiency for women to prevent a premature awakening of female sexuality and to create spiritual cleanliness and purity (Richards 1998: 52, 65). This psychological autarky consisted of women cultivating a 'sacred space within the home' in which to contemplate the 'interior manifestations of life' (ibid.: 65). Thus, a dominant religious, political and medical discourse combined with Church iconography to sacralize motherhood and confine women to the domestic, private sphere.

The authoritarian state's obsession with constructing a neoconservative corporate identity based on the ideal Christian family led to the imposition of highly restrictive labour regulations on married women, inducements for single working women to marry, and family subsidies and bonuses. As early as 1938, the Labour Charter (*Fuero del Trabajo*) stipulated that married women were to be 'freed from the workplace and the factory' in order to fulfil their domestic duties and undertake a six-month stint of social service to the state (Enders and Radcliff 1999: 127–8). The Labour Charter, which was later converted into a fundamental law of the state, was intended only to provide secure employment for men, and prohibited a woman from working without the permission of her husband.[2] Also in 1938, family allowances were introduced which were paid directly to the head of the family (*jefe de familia*) and were considered as supplementary to his income, as well as being intended to discourage his wife from working (Cousins 1995: 184). These family benefits were only available to those in legitimate marriages, and by 1946, under the Family Subsidy Law, men were deprived of the benefits if their wives continued to work.

The coercive measures embodied in the Labour Charter and family benefits scheme were followed by an inducement for women to leave the labour force and marry. In 1942, the state introduced a compensatory dowry grant (*la dote*), which was awarded to female employees who left their jobs to marry. In 1948, nuptiality prizes were awarded to marriage unions formed by a woman under thirty and a man under thirty-five, and loans with a 25 per cent repayment reduction were offered to families on the birth of up to four children (Nash 1991: 171). Large families were given numerous fringe benefits in the form of an extra month's salary, transport subsidies and special credit terms, and prizes were awarded to the largest family (usually over fourteen children) (Cousins 1995: 184). These family allowance schemes, prizes and inducements served a dual purpose of driving women from the labour force and encouraging procreation. Thus, the state's programme of familialism, which was based on a male-breadwinner model of the family, was intimately linked with the regime's pursuit of pronatalism.

The implementation of the state's twin policies of pronatalism and familialism were aided by the activities of the *Sección Femenina*, whose purpose, according to the regime's Interior Minister, was to exercise vigilance over women and act as a moral prophylactic throughout society. The *Sección Femenina* also played a part in the authoritarian regime's constant surveillance of society for any signs of a 'campaign against the state' (Richards 1998: 53). The official mandate of the *Sección Femenina* was to integrate women into the state by way of compulsory social service (the female version of national service). Over a six-month period, single women between the ages of seventeen and thirty-five were subject to three months of social training (*formación*) and three months of unpaid welfare work. Underpinning the social training was the central belief that Spanish women were the custodians of honour and their nation-state's paramount values (Enders 1992: 675). As such, according to Pilar Primo de Rivera, the national spokesperson for the *Sección Femenina*,

[t]he true duty of women to the Patria is to form families in which they foster all that is traditional ... these women, formed thus with Christian doctrine and National Syndicalist style, will be useful to the family, the Municipality and to the syndicate ... these women will know how to give – as they are giving now with their entire will – their fiancées, their husbands, their sons and brothers to the Patria.

(ibid.: 674)

Social training consisted of courses conducted at the School of the Home (*Escuela del Hogar*) on religion, family and social formation, sewing, domestic science and economy, childcare and cooking (Shubert 1990: 215).

The three months of unpaid welfare or free labour (*prestación*) in schools, hospitals, orphanages, food kitchens and homes for the elderly not only indoctrinated women into Falangist values but also provided the state with a rudimentary welfare system on the cheap (Grugel and Rees 1997: 136). Indeed, a decree issued by the state on 9 February 1944 stipulated that 'social service was created with the aim of mobilizing Spanish women to serve the Nation' (Kenyon 1995: 53). As part of these welfare duties, women also made up clothes and baby baskets for the poor in the workshops run by the *Sección Femenina* or assisted literacy teachers and rural health visitors (Graham 1995: 187). The primary goal of these health visitors, according to Jean Grugel and Tim Rees, was to reverse the high infant mortality rate among the agrarian poor by checking that couples were not using birth control, as well as checking on their general health (1997: 136). From the outset, social service was a prerequisite for women sitting state examinations and government employment, and until 1945, when it became compulsory for women seeking a passport, a driving licence or membership of cultural and sports organizations, the only means of gaining exemption from social service was marriage (Shubert 1990: 215).

The authoritarian state did establish a basic social welfare system consisting of social security benefits in the form of pensions, invalid benefits and unemployment benefits, but these payments were only indirectly available to women. The benefits were extended directly to the male breadwinner through employment-related insurance schemes and indirectly to women as dependants. Since the Franquist regime made it almost impossible for women to work, they were unable to qualify as contributors or direct beneficiaries of social security payments. The regime's social welfare system was also based on the Catholic principle of subsidiarity, according to which social problems should be addressed and met at the lowest level in society – the family. Hence, the regime relied on the family to act as the primary provider of social services such as childcare, and caring for elderly, and mentally or physically handicapped, people. This meant that the burden of care inevitably fell on women within the family.

However, social reality failed to reflect the Franquist regime's assumption of a male-breadwinner family. In the 1940s and 1950s, at least 500,000 families were without a male breadwinner, and harsh socio-economic conditions led many women to resort to desperate and illegal measures, such as abortion, to ensure the survival of their families (Graham 1995: 184; Nash 1991: 173–4).

Yet the Franquist regime continued to impose its corporate identity-related idea of reinforcing the unity and power of the state through the divinely ordained family. The authoritarian state enlisted the help of demographers and sociologists to justify and legitimize its vigorous dual programme of familialism and pronatalism. Prominent demographers, such as Severino Aznar and Javier Ruiz Almansa, defended the state's twin policies on the basis that they were the foundation on which the national economy, political stability, military power and cultural imperialism were built. The authoritarian state even established a research centre in 1944, the Instituto Balmes de Sociología, with the express purpose of producing scientific data and arguments to support and sustain its dual policy programme. The research centre published the influential journal *Revista Internacional de Sociología*, in which the declining birth rate was lamented and pronatalist doctrine was heavily promoted (Nash 1991: 163–4). It was on the basis of the centre's published findings that the authoritarian state implemented many of its legislative and policy measures encouraging natalism, familialism, and female subordination in both the public and private spheres.

However, while the guiding religious principles of the Franquist regime remained intact, a volte-face on domestic economic policy in 1959 led to a period of intense industrialization and the need to employ women to meet national labour demands. This need, in turn, led to the revision of legislation barring married women from the paid labour force. Prior to the 1959 Stabilization Plan (*Plan de Estabilización*), the authoritarian regime imposed a policy of economic autarky and import substitution in a so-called bid to protect Spain against the nefarious influence of the powerful *internacionales* – communists, socialists and freemasons – and liberal economics (Vinas 1999: 305, 308). In fact, as Michael Richards points out, economic autarky in practice was always relative, with the authoritarian state continuing to trade in commodities with the United States and Britain. The Franquist regime even signed an Anglo-Spanish trade agreement in March 1940 and, after the Second World War, negotiated trade and payment agreements with several other European states (Richards 1998: 102; MacLennan 2000: 19). Nevertheless, by mid-1959 the Spanish economy was in crisis after a number of years of severe balance of payments deficits and rampant inflation. With the government facing bankruptcy, the regime's economic ministers persuaded a reluctant Franco that the implementation of a programme of economic stabilization and liberalization could no longer be delayed (Payne 1987: 468–70).

The initial period of stabilization, in 1960, resulted in a temporary decline in real income and the emigration of a sizable proportion of the labour force to other European states, including France, Germany, Belgium and Switzerland. While the Franquist regime initially resisted this loss as a 'loss of blood', it quickly began promoting it as a deliberate policy for alleviating unemployment and providing foreign exchange (Carr and Aizpurua 1979: 54). As employment expanded, the regime was forced to overturn its restrictions on married women working. Confronted with the reality of increasing female employment, the regime introduced the Women's Political, Professional, and Employment Rights Law (*Ley de Derechos Políticos, Profesionales y de Trabajo de Mujer*) in 1961, in an attempt to ensure that women were employed only in positions that were deemed appropriate and that did not interfere with their domestic commitments (Jones 1995: 386). The legislation precluded women from several professions, including the judiciary and the armed forces, on the grounds that these professions 'involved activities that might offend or brutalise women's delicate sensibilities' (Jones 1997: 77). Although the legislation acknowledged the principle of equal pay for equal work, the principle was not implemented in practice. Moreover, because the Civil Code remained unchanged, women remained subordinate to their husbands in labour matters. A married woman still required her husband's permission before she could take up a contract of employment or receive her salary directly. The intention of the regime in introducing the legislation was certainly not to eliminate discrimination but, rather, to control the direction and nature of female employment. This was made patently clear by the head of the *Sección Femenina*, Primo de Rivera, when she introduced the law to the Franquist Cortes (Parliament). She assured the Cortes that

> in no way do we want to make man and woman two equal beings; not by nature nor by ends to gain in life could they ever be equal . . . what we ask with this law is that the woman forced to work out of necessity do it in the best possible conditions.
>
> (Enders 1992: 675)

Legislators included these sentiments in the preamble of the law, and, with this, the neoconservative corporate identity of the state was preserved.

The first period of state behavioural continuity: 1945–75

The neoconservative corporate state identity constructed after the Spanish Civil War had a totally inhibiting effect on the diffusion of international norms of sexual non-discrimination between 1945 and 1975. Despite its admittance to the United Nations in 1955, the Spanish state initially refused to ratify the 1952 UN Convention on the Political Rights of Women, the 1957 UN Convention on the Nationality of Married Women and the 1962 UN Convention on Consent to Marriage, Minimum Age for Marriage, and Registration of Marriages. The state eventually ratified the Convention on Consent to Marriage in 1969 and the Convention on the Political Rights of Women in 1974 but failed to comply with either. As of 2004, Spain had yet to ratify the UN Convention on the Nationality of Married Women. After being admitted to the International Labour Organization in 1953, the state eventually ratified both the ILO Equal Remuneration Convention and the ILO Discrimination (Employment and Occupation) Convention in 1967, but, once again, failed to comply with either convention. Unlike the ILO and the UN, the EU consistently refused to allow Spain to join while the Franquist regime was in power, and therefore whether or not the Spanish state complied with European equality law was a non-issue.

After its initial post-Second World War exclusion from international organizations, Spain was admitted to the UN and its special agency the ILO at the insistence of the United States, which, with the onset of the Cold War and the outbreak of war in Korea, recognized Spain's strategic importance in the Mediterranean defence against communism and in winning an 'imminent third world war' (Portero 1999: 225). The Spanish state persistently exploited the deterioration of relations between the United States and the Soviet Union by lobbying in Washington against the 1946 UN resolution condemning the authoritarian regime, and for military and economic assistance (Liedtke 1999a: 269). It did so, explains Paul Preston, because it knew that it 'could not survive on repression alone if the international situation was adverse' (1999: 12). Spanish–American relations culminated in the 1953 Pact of Madrid, under which the Spanish state agreed to the United States establishing military bases in its territory in exchange for a loan of $26 million and US support for its admission to the UN, which occurred in 1955 (MacLennan 2000: 16–17). From the perspective of the Franquist regime, the Pact of Madrid and admission to the UN, on the one hand, ameliorated international ostracism and, on the other hand, 'eliminated any chances of success for a democratic opposition movement to introduce democratic reforms' (Liedtke 1999b: 239). When the European Economic Community was established on 25 March 1957, the Franquist regime promptly established an interministerial committee three months later, entitled the *Comisión Interministerial para el Estudio de las Comunidades Europeas*, to study the effects of the Treaty of Rome and advise on Spain's prospective entry to the common market (MacLennan 2000: 39). It quickly became clear to the regime that European integration was both politically and economically vital for Spain, and on 9 February 1962 the Spanish government submitted its application to join the EU. However, the application was rejected because the Spanish state failed to meet the political requirements established by the European Parliament's Birkelbach Report of 15 January 1962, which stipulated that: 'states whose governments do not have democratic legitimization and whose peoples do not participate in government decisions, either directly or through fully elected representatives, cannot aspire to be admitted into the circle of peoples that forms the European communities' (Pollack 1987: 134). The EU's rejection was, according to Grugel and Rees, a 'considerable slap in the face for the regime' (1997: 170).

The partial readmission of the Spanish state into the international system fuelled the Franquist regime's desire to win wider acceptance from the international community, and, as part of its bid to gain further international recognition, the regime ratified both the ILO Equal Remuneration Convention and the ILO Discrimination (Employment and Occupation) Convention on 6 November 1967, and the UN Convention on Consent to Marriage on 15 April 1969. At the time of ratifying, the Franquist regime believed that ratification posed little risk to state sovereignty or to the continuation of its current discriminatory policies. Thus, the regime felt it could gain a significant public relations tool in being a party to the conventions. As Monica Threlfall explains, the international conventions were ratified by the Spanish state 'in order for it to be part of the international community on paper if not in practice' (1999). The existing state legislation upon which ratification was based, the 1961 Women's Political, Professional and Employment Rights Law, complied with the international conventions in name only. As we have seen, state legislators made it very clear in the preamble to this law that the last thing they intended to do was grant equality between men and women. This applied to civil and political rights as well as employment rights. The law itself was discriminatory because it allowed types of work 'exclusively performed by women' to be rated as of less value than other, similar work performed by men, and consequently provided justification for paying them less (Butragueno 1982: 190). Since the incorporation of women into the Spanish labour force during the 1960s and early 1970s was restricted largely to the service industries and unskilled factory work, which were deemed appropriate occupations for women, female wages remained considerably lower than male wages. Furthermore, the legislation severely restricted the promotion and access of women to positions of responsibility, thus maintaining women's status in 'low-paid' jobs.

In between ratifying the ILO conventions and the UN convention, the Spanish state brutally repressed a wave of dissent and resistance, which began in the spring of 1968 as a consequence of social changes wrought by the rapid industrialization accompanying the economic stabilization and liberalization measures introduced in 1959. Industrialization had transformed the demographics of Spanish society from being largely rural based to predominantly urban based and, in the process, undermined the authoritarian regime's control over society. As Grugel and Rees explain,

> The cultural and social institutions of the regime had been constructed largely to meet the need to control a rural population.

Suddenly, the established party structures, youth groups, the *Seccion Femenina*, the clergy, Catholic organizations and churches themselves, lost their clientele. Local patterns of supervision and control that were built into village life disappeared with the population or simply became irrelevant.

(1997: 147)

As urban areas rapidly expanded, they lacked these in-built mechanisms of social control, and the regime found it increasingly difficult to monitor a mobile urban population (ibid.: 147). This social mobilization created conditions conducive to protest and resistance from political opposition groups such as the Communist Party (Partido Comunista de España, or PCE), other left-wing organizations and trade unions. In alliance with the PCE, feminists within the Democratic Movement of Women (Movimiento Democrático de Mujeres, MDM) also participated in the resistance to the authoritarian regime by criticizing the neoconservative corporate identity of the state.

The MDM, which was formed in 1965, began by infiltrating chapters of the National Organization of Housewives (which was created by the *Sección Femenina* in 1963), and by 1968 had a head office and local chapters in working-class neighbourhoods of the major cities. In 1968, the MDM started publishing a clandestine monthly bulletin entitled *La Mujer y la Lucha* (Women and Struggle), and organized a petition demanding a series of rights and reforms which was sent to the deputy Prime Minister (Threlfall 1986: 10–11). However, the *Sección Femenina* soon uncovered the MDM's infiltration of the National Organization of Housewives and, with the help of the police, had it expelled. Also, in reaction to wider social unrest, the authoritarian regime reverted to a hardline approach, and in 1969 the police razed the headquarters of opposition groups, including that of the MDM, and imprisoned their leaders (Astelarra 1992: 43–5). The regime also declared a state of exception, forbidding any meetings from being held; suspended reforms under a series of states of emergency; tightened censorship; and placed universities under virtual occupation by the police (Grugel and Rees 1997: 152). The MDM did not survive this repression (Threlfall 1986: 11).

Reasserting its authoritarian rule, the Franquist regime determined to reinforce the neoconservative corporate state identity by continuing to offer rewards and financial incentives for women to produce children and discursively re-emphasizing the importance of the Christian family. At the International Congress of the *Sección Femenina* in 1970, members discussed the problems associated with changing societal values, the fear of divorce, and the danger of women 'dedicated only to extra-familial tasks ... becoming physically and psychologically a dry human product with no plenitude' (Carbayo-Abengozar 2000: 118). These sentiments were echoed by the regime in official statements, which condemned the social

trend away from large traditional families towards modern nuclear families (Ussel 1991: 285). Despite the reality of changing social behaviour, the
state upheld the ecclesiastical control of family and matrimonial legislation, and enforced the legal framework within which the family operated.
It also retained a highly conservative attitude towards female employment,
and legally ensured that women's place in the labour force remained
insecure.

Paradoxically, at the same time that it became increasingly repressive
and reinforced the neoconservative corporate identity of the state, the
Franquist regime reapplied for admission to the EU, and in 1974 recognized the UN International Women's Year (IWY) and ratified the 1952
UN Convention on the Political Rights of Women. However, the state's
acknowledgement of IWY and ratification of the convention had less to do
with a genuine respect for women's rights than it did with the authoritarian regime's continuing search for respectability and recognition in the
international community. The state had no intention of implementing the
convention, and this was pointed out to the UN in an unofficial report
prepared and submitted by Spanish feminists affiliated with the clandestine pro-democracy movement. The report, which was sent to the UN
ahead of the official state delegation headed by the *Sección Femenina*
attending the UN IWY conference in Mexico, also pointed out the
regime's failure to comply with other international conventions it had ratified (Threlfall 1986: 13). Meanwhile, the EU again rejected the state's
application for admission, with the European Council of Ministers adopting a resolution on Spain expressing 'disappointment that Spain was a
long way from meeting the conditions necessary for membership ... as
she had no democratic institutions' (MacLennan 2000: 102). In addition,
the European Parliament declared that 'the Spanish government's
repeated violations of basic human and civil rights ... in a Europe that is
seeking its free and democratic way to unity, prevent Spain's admission to
the European Community' (Preston 1986: 60).

The first period of state behavioural change: 1976–81

In 1975, international conditions interacted with national political conditions – involving a crisis of the Spanish state and a dramatic shift in
regime type from authoritarianism to democracy – to generate domestic
feminist activism and put pressure on the state to comply with international norms of sexual non-discrimination. Not only did the UN IWY
lend legitimacy to the actions of Spanish feminists, but its recognition by
the authoritarian regime also provided protection for activists at a time
when regime reprisals for dissent and resistance of any kind were all too
real. Throughout 1975, Spain endured a tense period of confrontation in
which the brutality of the regime was matched by the consolidation of the
prestige of the opposition pro-democracy movement. Yet in the midst of

this confrontation, the Franquist regime inaugurated the UN IWY in Spain on 20 February 1975 and organized a series of events to mark the year. However, attendance of these events was restricted to members of the *Sección Femenina*, and feminists, who had arranged a series of events and meetings paralleling those organized by the regime's IWY Committee, ran the risk of a government backlash. Fortunately, the backlash did not eventuate and, in the last months before Franco's death on 20 November 1975, it became increasingly evident to progressives (*tácitos*) within the regime that political reform was the only means of ensuring the regime's survival. Immediately after Franco's death, therefore, the progressives descended upon Zarzuela Palace – the residence of Franco's appointed successor, Prince Juan Carlos – to persuade the prince of the need for a transition to democracy (Preston 1986: 74–5).

After being sworn in as King of Spain and the new head of state on 22 November 1975, Juan Carlos managed the installation of democracy. He did so, however, only after many months of social unrest and political uncertainty, and only after replacing the intransigent Prime Minister, Carlos Arias Navarro, with the politically astute Adolfo Suárez. When Suárez became Prime Minister in July 1976, he confronted mass demonstrations demanding an amnesty for political prisoners from an increasingly restless democratic opposition buoyed by international support (Preston 1986: 70). Feminists struggling for political legitimacy within left-wing opposition parties used the opposition's appeal for a general amnesty for political prisoners to make a particular demand for amnesty for women imprisoned for committing adultery, using contraceptives, having an abortion or leaving home. They argued that women condemned on the basis of such archaic laws should be considered political prisoners and released forthwith. They attracted attention to their cause by developing a campaign that tapped into the sensitization of public opinion to the plight of other political prisoners (Astelarra 1992: 45). However, further attempts by feminists to draw attention to women's rights within the opposition parties were resisted with arguments about political priorities 'backed up by dogmatic analyses that women's liberation was a deviation from the more urgent task of building democracy and socialism' (Threlfall 1985: 46). Thus, Threlfall concludes, feminists within left-wing opposition parties became an 'opposition within an opposition', endeavouring to displace deeply held paternalistic attitudes with the idea that a complete restructuring of the Spanish legal and public policy systems was needed if sexual discrimination were to be eliminated (ibid.: 46). Disappointed that, despite their contribution to the struggle for democracy, the opposition parties did not immediately take up the rights and justice claims of women, feminists nonetheless believed they could alter state behaviour through conventional politics (Duran and Gallego 1986: 209).

However, feminists within the left-wing opposition soon confronted criticism from newly emerging independent or autonomous feminists, who argued that change could only be achieved outside the political system. At a series of nationwide meetings held in Madrid and Barcelona between January 1976 and the first post-Franco general election on 15 June 1977, the tactical debate between activists within the Left and autonomous feminists heated up. While they shared a common agenda of the immediate restoration of women's civil and political rights, equal remuneration, and the provision of important social services such as child-care, activists could not agree on whether to adopt a strategy of *double militancy* or *single militancy*. Those affiliated with the PCE and the Socialist Spanish Workers' Party (Partido Socialista Obrero Español, PSOE) insisted on joint action or double militancy with political opposition parties in support of the demand for democracy. They argued that Spanish women could achieve their goals only 'through the active presence of women in structures and programmes devoted to guiding social demands' (Mendez 1994: 665). Doubting the effectiveness of such a strategy, and deeply suspicious of conventional politics, autonomous feminists advocated a strategy of single militancy strictly focused on women's rights. Autonomous activists argued that the belief that equality would be assured with the securing of democracy was short-sighted because, as they announced to the press, 'women's oppression does not end with the establishment of a democratic regime' (ibid.: 665). Although autonomous feminists attracted significant media attention with their radical demand for a revolutionary Spanish women's movement, the majority of feminists attending these early meetings agreed on a strategy of double militancy.

While feminists debated tactics, Prime Minister Suárez and opposition representatives negotiated the terms and conditions of democratic reform. The negotiations, according to Preston, dwelled on the power of the military and the continuing strength and obstinacy of the bunker (regime ultra-conservatives) (Preston 1986: 120). In order to avoid the potential threat that the military and ultra-conservatives represented to crucial political reform, the Left quietly abandoned its hope of overthrowing the government and forming a provisional government in a clear democratic break (*ruptura democrática*) for a negotiated break (*ruptura pactada*). The negotiations, according to Juan Linz, were also infused with a genuine desire on both sides to create a political culture based on mutual respect between political forces and devoid of the bitter conflict, distrust and imposition of the past. It is in this context, Linz continues, that the idea of consensus (*consenso*) and its expression in the form of pacts became central to the democratic transition (1993: 160). The first of these pacts saw the government make legal and political concessions to the Left, in exchange for its support of the government's programme of political reform (Diaz-Ambrona 1984: 28). These concessions included a general amnesty for political prisoners (except terrorists), the legalization of trade unions and political parties (except the Spanish Communist Party),[3] and ratification of both the UN International Covenants. The fundamental task of the government's programme of political reform, argues Linz, was to dismantle the authoritarian system within the framework of its legality so as to neutralize opposition in the armed forces and Cortes. This was the function of the Law for Political Reform, he continues, which served to give legitimacy of legality to the democratic reform process because it had been approved according to the government's constitutional procedures (Linz 1993: 148, 159). Passed by the Cortes in November 1976, the legislation provided for the holding of the first post-Franco general election and the formation of Parliament, which in turn represented a significant step towards the consolidation of a democratic constitutional system (Diaz-Ambrona 1984: 30).

In the months leading up to the general election, Spanish feminists traded on the media coverage that they had received throughout 1976 and early 1977 to put pressure on the contesting political parties to take note of gender issues (Kaplan 1992: 201). For their part, the media were keen to publicize the actions and demands of feminists because they represented the idea of a liberalized Spanish society, a society as free as any of its European counterparts (Mendez 1994: 666). Feminists realized that the pre-election period was the time to state their claims forcefully and have their demands incorporated into the programmes of political parties (Duran and Gallego 1986: 201). Of course, explain Maria Angeles Duran and Maria Teresa Gallego,

> the political parties, eager for recognition and for votes, were quick to see the potential in the women's issue. Even if it were a mere formality or pure demagogy, every party, from left to right, paid some attention to women's interests.
>
> (1986: 209)

The major demand of feminists was the dismantling of the authoritarian regime's discriminatory legal system. Their primary concern was reform in the areas of civil and criminal law, and in the pre-election period to June 1977 they pressed political parties for a commitment to extensive changes to both the Civil Code and the Criminal Code. Both the centre-right Union of the Democratic Centre (Union de Centro Democrático, UCD) and parties of the Left incorporated civil and criminal law reform into their party programmes. However, the UCD's social policy of protecting the family created an inherent tension between the two areas of reform. Nevertheless, even though the UCD won the first general election, the chance for these reforms looked promising because Suárez, the UCD's leader, was committed to a programme of democratic reform and because the PSOE did unexpectedly well at the polls (Threlfall 1985: 48).

Unfortunately, the issue of civil and criminal law reform was pushed into the background somewhat in the new parliament, as constitutional negotiations and economic stabilization took precedence. Both the UCD and the formalized opposition were acutely aware that the elaboration of a constitution was an essential but complex task of democratic consolidation, requiring political compromise and co-operation. They approached the task of drafting the Constitution with mixed feelings of hope and apprehension, states Paul Heywood, aware that political divisiveness over constitutional clauses had undermined Spain's previous democracy, the Second Republic. As Heywood explains,

> It had been precisely around constitutional issues that various forces of the right coalesced in their opposition to all the Second Republic represented. In particular, the constitutional provisions dealing with the Catholic Church and Spain's territorial organisation had provoked intense right-wing resistance.
>
> (1995: 37)

Thus, the UCD government and opposition parties formed a constitutional pact (*pacto constitucional*) to try to prevent a repeat of the past and ensure long-lasting democratic stability. Political consensus was essential in order to reach approval of a constitution acceptable to all the major parties from the PCE to the right-wing Popular Alliance (Alianza Popular, AP), and to the Catalan Nationalists (Linz 1993: 160). To this end, an all-party drafting committee consisting of seven parliamentary deputies was formed in August 1977 to produce a draft constitutional text (Preston 1986: 138). However, neither of the two committed feminist deputies, one from the PSOE and one from the PCE, was selected for this committee. Despite their non-selection, the two deputies made their presence felt in Parliament and voiced their demands during constitutional debates. Also, feminists within the PSOE had already persuaded the party to set up an advisory committee, Women and Socialism (*Mujer y Socialismo*), in the Federal Executive Commission's Secretariat for Political Education, whose recommendations filtered into constitutional negotiations. The advisory committee used its connections with a network of legal and public policy advocates to develop a comprehensive set of constitutional demands – certain of which were included in the final constitutional draft.

The final constitutional draft also reflected the Spanish state's desire to join the EU. The government had lodged yet another application for admission to the EU in July 1977, and all political parties were conscious of the need for a constitutionally consolidated democracy to meet the conditions of EU membership. For the majority of the Spanish political elite, full European integration was of fundamental importance to securing political stability, as well as social, economic and legal modernization. As Julio Crespo MacLennan explains, European integration not only 'symbolised the end of an intolerable period of isolation' but also 'guaranteed the practice of liberties', provided economic and social benefits, and enabled the replacement of the obsolete Spanish judicial system with the modern and efficient legislative system of the EU (2000: 150–1). In the case of the latter, it was assumed that modernizing the Spanish legal system would be difficult in a fledgling democracy and that membership of the EU would enable the introduction of European law. It was also assumed that modernizing the Spanish legal system would be 'tacitly accepted by Spaniards as the price to be paid for EU membership' (ibid.: 151). Furthermore, the Spanish political elite saw European membership as a form of insurance against 'military adventurism' (Graham 1984: 270). Thus, the final Spanish constitutional text responded to European post-war constitutionalism, incorporating elements modelled on the French, Italian and German Constitutions, and established the precedence of international human rights treaties over national law (Guerra 1998: 1945; Buergenthal 1997: 212, 217).

The passing of the Constitution on 3 January 1979 marked the beginning of vertiginous political changes in Spain, which involved the state withdrawing all legal and political privileges of the Catholic Church to administer family law and influence public policy-making, and amending civil law and labour legislation in accordance with international and European norms of sexual non-discrimination. These substantive legislative changes, while induced by the state's desire for international and regional recognition, were only ensured by the intervention of Spanish feminists, particularly those affiliated with the PSOE, whose demands for legislative amendments were articulated predominantly in reaction to the policies of the authoritarian regime. The promulgation of the Constitution also marked the beginning of a lengthy period of negotiation for EU membership, which frustrated the Spanish government because it had believed that once constitutional democracy was achieved, Spain would immediately be granted accession (Share 1986: 51–2). However, the EU declared that it was not prepared for further enlargement because of the serious financial costs involved and because of problems concerning the European Common Agricultural Policy (CAP) (MacLennan 2000: 161–2). In response, the Spanish state argued that by delaying its entry, the EU was 'damaging the cause of democracy in Spain, since in times of political instability the [state] could not afford to wait indefinitely for negotiations to finish' (ibid.: 163). As negotiations with the EU stalled, the Spanish state focused on improving relations with the UN by, among other initiatives, meeting its legal obligations under international conventions already ratified.

The first major set of reforms concerned the establishment of equal rights in the national Worker's Statute (1980) and the Basic Employment Law (1980). Although the Worker's Statute was considered the principal labour legislation of the new democratic state and formed the basis of the industrial relations system, the state included equality provisions in the statute only because of pressure from feminists affiliated with the PSOE and trade unions. Reacting against the discriminatory employment

practices of the authoritarian regime, activists demanded the incorporation of the principle of equality in employment legislation on the basis of
complying with international and European law. They also advocated
equality in employment on the grounds that economic independence was
an essential ingredient for women's emancipation (Valiente 2001: 118).
The Worker's Statute, which was passed by the UCD government on 10
March 1980, prohibited sexual discrimination in employment by rendering null and void any collective agreements between employers and trade
unions that ran counter to the legislation's provisions regarding the
demarcation of job classifications, promotion and pay (Threlfall 1985:
68). It also provided for individual recourse to labour courts – or administrative courts in the case of public servants – through trade union or staff
committee representation, as well as the right of appeal to the Constitutional Court (European Parliament 1989: 12). However, to the disappointment of feminist activists, the state only incorporated the principle of
equal pay for equal work – as opposed to the principle of *equal pay for work of
equal value* – and therefore the statute failed to comply fully with either the
ILO Equal Remuneration Convention or the European Equal Pay Directive.[4]

On 8 October 1980, the UCD government passed the Basic Employment Law, establishing the principle of equal opportunity and treatment
in employment. Shortly afterwards, the government promised to establish
special training programmes for workers facing difficulties gaining access
to the labour market, 'especially women with family responsibilities'
(Butragueno 1982: 192). However, the gender-rectifying provisions of the
Basic Employment Law and Worker's Statute were offset by gender-
reinforcing social policies that displayed a high degree of continuity with
those of the Franquist regime and restricted women's access to full-time
paid employment. Furthermore, the state failed to implement the special
training programmes aimed at improving women's access to the labour
force (ibid.: 192). Spanish feminists protested at the state's failure to
implement the training programmes, and advocates associated with
the trade unions were quick to point out to government policy-makers the
inherent tension between employment legislation and social policies. The
views of trade union feminists were represented in Parliament by both
the PCE, which had strong ties with the Worker's Commissions (*Comisiones
Obreras*, CCOO), and the PSOE, which had close ties with the General
Union of Workers (Unión General de Trabajadores, UGT).

The second major set of government reforms completely transformed
civil or family law. Again, these legislative changes were only ensured by
feminist political intervention, particularly from activists within the PSOE
and independent female lawyers (Cousins 1995: 185). However, while legislation abolishing the subordination of a wife to her husband was introduced with relatively little political controversy,[5] the introduction of
divorce legislation was accompanied by a bitter public dispute between

feminists and the Catholic Church, and sparked a crisis in the UCD government (Boetsch 1985: 165). Divorce was a highly contentious issue, and the Catholic Church was pitted against feminists and lawyers determined to see the introduction of legislation establishing divorce by mutual consent and protecting women from financial hardship after divorce (Threlfall 1985: 62). Feminists discursively condemned what they claimed were discriminatory assumptions and prejudices inherent in the existing Civil Code, and demanded both the legalization of divorce and the secularization of civil law in general. In retaliation, the Catholic Church discursively accused feminists of attacking Christian values and principles, and of trying to destroy the Spanish family. Yet despite a statement issued in February 1981 by the Permanent Commission of the Episcopate opposing divorce by mutual consent and an attempt by Christian Democrats within the ruling UCD coalition to block the legislation, the Minister of Justice, Francisco Fernández Ordóñez, was able to steer the divorce law through parliament on 7 July 1981 (Ussel 1991: 290; Moxon-Browne 1989: 75).

However, the civil divorce bill was limited by the requirements of a five-year period of judicial separation before divorce and of filing separately for separation and divorce (Rina Singh 1998: 123). This meant that filing for divorce involved two court appearances, making the process lengthy and expensive. Moreover, feminist demands for measures to protect women financially after divorce were not included in the Law on Secularization and Dissolution of Marriage (Threlfall 1985: 62). Following the passage of the divorce law, the Permanent Commission of the Episcopate issued a second statement declaring that it regretted the legislation because of the 'serious damage that would be inflicted on the stability of marriage and because the decision on dissolution was left to the will of the partners' (Ussel 1991: 290). The divorce law, according to Laurent Boetsch, represented a significant defeat for the Catholic Church as a political broker because it demonstrated that, 'despite its tradition, its influence and its resources, the Church was no longer the most important determining factor in the organization of Spanish society' (1985: 161). Boetsch concludes that 'parliament bore the pressures of the Church's strong opposition and approved a law that was an accurate reflection of the will of the majority of Spaniards' (ibid.: 161). However, the divorce law not only irrevocably altered Church–society relations, but also split the UCD government, eventually leading to its downfall.

The internal division over the divorce law marked the beginning of the end for the UCD government, which had already been destabilized by its failure to solve a series of problems, including the economic crisis facing Spain, a resurgence of separatist terrorism, the sudden resignation of Suárez in January 1981, and an attempted military coup a month later on 23 February 1981. The attempted *coup d'état* occurred at a time of delay in Spanish–EU entry negotiations and caught the European Community by surprise. The European Parliament immediately issued a resolution expressing support for the Spanish democratic regime, and several European leaders warned against a return to authoritarianism. The Vice-President of the European Commission issued a statement declaring that any state that was not democratic could not join the EU but denied that Spanish–EU entry negotiations would be further delayed by the coup (Pridham 1991: 235). In fact, the European Council of Ministers realized the political significance of Spain's accession to the EU and attempted to expedite negotiations, but France raised a series of objections to Spain's integration into Europe and negotiations came to a virtual standstill. In the meantime, the Spanish UCD government collapsed and the PSOE was swept into government in a landslide in the general election of 28 October 1982. The PSOE's electoral success raised hopes of solving the differences with France regarding Spain's integration into Europe and finalizing negotiations with the EU. It also raised hopes among Spanish feminists of greater legislative and public policy reforms.

The second period of state behavioural change: 1982–95

Finally, negotiations with the EU resolved Spanish–French differences and Spain was granted accession in 1984. On 12 June 1985, Spain ratified the treaty by which it became a member of the EU at the Royal Palace in Madrid. The treaty entered effect on 1 January 1986. The EU imposed exacting economic conditions of membership upon the Spanish state (Heywood 1995: 271), as well as the condition of compliance with European equality law (Warner 1984: 153). However, the Spanish state found it difficult to meet EU economic conditions *and* comply with the European equality directives. The Spanish socialist government realized that if it were to meet EU economic conditions of membership, it would have to sacrifice the economic and social policy reforms that it had promised in its pre-election platform. These promised social policy reforms were essential to the effective implementation of the EU equality directives. The economic policies pursued by the socialist government were based on neo-liberal principles and were aimed at reducing public-sector deficit and limiting expenditure on social security benefits and services. The policies included strong monetary controls, selling state-owned assets, lowering taxes, controlling wages, providing incentives for investments and containing non-wage labour costs (Marks 1997: 96). Initially, the government's programme of directing public resources to industrial restructuring rather than improving social services had the backing of the General Union of Workers (Almeda and Sarasa 1996: 163). As a result of the government's programme, access to social benefits remained based on labour market status, and the state continued to rely on the family – women – to provide social services. In other words, the family acted as a functional substitute for a comprehensive social welfare system by filling important social protection gaps such as the lack of income maintenance for job-seekers and extremely low minimum benefits for the elderly and those with a disability (Rhodes 1997: 10). The responsibility of caring for children, elderly people and disabled people continued to fall largely on women, restricting their access to employment and thus their independent entitlement to earnings-related social benefits.

To complicate matters, Spanish feminists were reluctant to intervene on questions of social policy because they associated such policies with the authoritarian regime's programme of familialism and pronatalism. Activists within the socialist government argued that social policy should be directed towards individuals and not families, and, as a result, the effects of social policy changes on families were not considered. Consequently, the socialist government, as well as failing to establish social policy initiatives, was hesitant to rescind social policies inherited from the Franquist regime. Only the most discriminatory social measures inherited from the authoritarian regime were rescinded. These included abolishing the monthly contributory benefit for a dependent spouse and terminating the one-off payments for marriage and the birth of each child (Valiente 1996c: 103). In essence, the influence of the gender-biased corporate state identity constructed by the authoritarian regime remained a fetter on state social policy initiatives and, indirectly, on the implementation of non-discriminatory employment measures.

Although feminists within the socialist government avoided questions of social policy, they campaigned vociferously for the establishment of an authoritative national equality agency to deal with a range of legislative and public policy issues. Prior to the 1982 general election, the PSOE had no intention of establishing such an agency, and feminists within the socialist government discursively traded on the government's pursuit of European membership to push for the creation of an equality agency. They sought the creation of an equality agency, having been advised by the *Chef de Cabinet* of the French Ministry of Women's Rights (*Ministère des Droits de la Femme*) on the effectiveness of an independent administrative body in generating state behavioural change in France (Threlfall 1998: 84). Perceiving the French Ministry to be highly successful, Spanish feminists pressed the socialist government for the establishment of a comparable body in Spain. As well as using the French Ministry in their campaign for an equality agency, activists pointed to examples of similar bodies in other European states. According to Celia Valiente, this discursive strategy was particularly compelling in the context of the strong political support for integrating Spain into Europe because the European states the socialist government was keen to emulate had, for the most part, some form of administrative apparatus for women's affairs. She adds that UN pressure also contributed to the government's decision to create national policy machinery charged with promoting gender equality for the state (1995: 224, 2001: 112).

The socialist government established the Women's Institute (Instituto de la Mujer, IM) in October 1983 as an autonomous body (*organismo autónomo*) within the Ministry of Culture. This meant that although the IM was not a fully fledged ministerial office, it was autonomous from the usual ministerial hierarchy. In other words, the director of the IM was directly responsible to the minister. However, being placed within a ministry, the IM was given neither the power nor the budget to formulate and implement legislation and public policy, but, rather, had to convince other government ministries of the need to elaborate equality measures. Moreover, the Ministry of Culture and the Ministry of Social Affairs, to which the IM was relocated in 1988, were both relatively minor ministries, and this meant that gender issues tended to be marginalized. Initially, the IM focused on convincing various ministries to incorporate gender issues into their policy-making through the periodic meetings of the IM's Governing Council (*Consejo Rector*) and on persuading the government to ratify international conventions (Valiente 1995: 225, 227; Real 1996: 45). Advocates within the IM and PSOE discursively traded on the socialist government's ongoing quest for international recognition in order to persuade it to ratify the Convention on the Elimination of Discrimination Against Women (CEDAW) in time for the final conference of the UN Decade for Women in Nairobi in mid-1985. As a result, the Spanish government ratified CEDAW on 5 January 1984. On 11 September 1985, it also ratified the ILO Convention on Workers with Family Responsibilities.

However, the socialist government was slow to comply with its international and European legal obligations, and by 1987 the IM realized that, as far as convincing government ministries to incorporate non-discriminatory norms in their policy-making was concerned, a new strategy was needed. It was evident that ministerial departments were either diluting or evading objectives agreed to at meetings of the IM's Governing Council, and, as a consequence, states Valiente, the IM developed the first in a series of equality plans designed to pressure the ministries to take substantial action within a specific time-frame (Valiente 1997b: 131). The First Equal Opportunities for Women Plan of Action 1988–1990 (*Primer Plan para la Igualdad de Oportunidades de las Mujeres 1988–1990*, Plan I) and subsequent plans were modelled on the EU action programmes (Astelarra 1995: 168). Negotiations with ministerial representatives over the content of Plan I proved difficult, however, with the IM's Governing Council rejecting several key measures (Jones 1997: 42). Eventually, the IM's Governing Council approved a plan that, with the exception of specific legislative amendments, was vague and gave no 'indication of how the stated aims were to be achieved or financed in practice' (ibid.: 43). Also, Cabinet refused to approve the plan, on the basis that it 'did not regard [this] as a task for the government', and therefore failed to commit itself to implementing the plan (Valiente 1996a: 184). Aside from these difficulties, the IM faced the distrust of independent feminists, who questioned both its autonomy and its intentions.

The tension between the IM and autonomous activists left Spanish feminist activism as a whole in a weakened position, which, as a consequence, meant that the state was less likely to initiate changes in accordance with international norms of sexual non-discrimination. Aware of this, the IM invited representatives of independent feminist organizations to form a commission to monitor the implementation of the first equality plan and to make recommendations regarding future policy directions (Valiente 1997b: 135). However, the deliberations of the commission were racked by 'numerous disagreements' between the members. Commission members also raised objections to having been excluded from the preparation of the original plan and were sceptical that the IM would adopt their recommendations (ibid.: 136). As a result, several representatives left the commission before it had compiled its findings, and the socialist government did not invite the commission to participate in formulating the second equality plan (Valiente 1995: 232). Also, divisions between the IM and independent feminists deepened, and consequently both 'lost crucial opportunities' to influence state policy-making (Valiente 1997b: 139).

In the meantime, the director of the IM had presented Spain's initial CEDAW report for consideration by the UN CEDAW committee in New York in April 1987. In its concluding comments, the CEDAW committee acknowledged the 'significant progress' made by the Spanish state since the democratic transition but expressed concern at its failure to eliminate discrimination in the area of political representation. The committee also raised substantial questions about job segregation, the high rate of female unemployment and the scarcity of childcare facilities. Furthermore, the committee raised questions about state policies on equal remuneration and on the reconciliation of employment and family responsibilities. Moreover, it expressed concern that the Worker's Statute of 1980 discriminated against mothers (United Nations General Assembly 1987). The Spanish government responded cautiously to the CEDAW committee's findings but, under internal pressure from feminists and due to assume the EU Presidency in January 1989, it introduced new measures in the areas of political representation and employment.

In January 1988, the thirtieth PSOE Congress approved a 25 per cent quota of women for all internal and public posts. Although the quota fell well short of party feminists' expectations, the appointment of Matilde Fernández to Cabinet as Minister of Social Affairs meant that, for the first time, an experienced feminist had direct oversight of government public policies on women's issues. On 7 April 1988, the socialist government adopted the Act on Infringements of and Sanctions under Labour Law, which was designed to safeguard the principle of equal treatment in access to employment. This legislation established that discriminatory job advertisements and infringement of the official recruitment policy were serious offences punishable by the imposition of heavy fines (Rollin 1995: 45–6).

It also established that those employers' actions that infringed upon privacy or personal dignity, or discriminated on the basis of sex in relation to conditions of employment, constituted serious infringements of the labour law (Arranz *et al.* 2000: 117). During its six-month tenure of the EU presidency, the Spanish government supported the European Commission's proposal for directives on parental leave, sexual harassment and reversing the burden of proof, and amended Spanish law in anticipation of the directives being adopted by the European Council of Ministers.[6]

Feminists within the IM and trade unions had been campaigning for legislation on sexual harassment since the mid-1980s and capitalized on the Spanish EU presidency to convince the government of the need for such legislation. The campaign began with advocates in two of the major trade unions conducting studies to establish the extent of the problem of sexual harassment in the workplace. The studies showed that sexual harassment was as widespread in Spain as in other European states, and the UGT–Madrid study of 1986 concluded that, along with awareness and support programmes, state legislation prohibiting sexual harassment was imperative. Using a guide published by the International Confederation of Free Trade Unions as a template, the women's secretariat of the Unión General de Trabajadores published and distributed a guidebook in 1987 on how trade unionists should deal with sexual harassment situations. In addition, states Valiente, the women's secretariat of the *Comisiones Obreras* published a brochure explaining the nature of sexual harassment and offered its support to female employees wanting to press charges. At the same time, she continues, representatives of the IM attended a series of international meetings at which the issue of sexual harassment was discussed. As a result of attending these meetings, the IM prepared and distributed information about sexual harassment and how female employees should best deal with it (Valiente 1997c: 184–5). Also, when the IM began preparing Plan I in 1987, it drew on studies carried out in other European states to lend credibility and legitimacy to its demand for government intervention (Ministry of Social Affairs: Women's Institute 1988: 76).

At the time Plan I went into effect, the Spanish government failed to recognize that sexual harassment was a serious problem or a public policy issue. Moreover, although Plan I and trade union publications helped to define sexual harassment as a problem requiring state intervention, feminists soon realized that in order to persuade the government to incorporate the issue into law, a co-ordinated lobbying campaign was required. To this end, advocates within the IM worked closely with trade union representatives in a strategic alliance. Together they were able to gain government support for prohibiting sexual harassment by capitalizing on the political consensus on European integration and Spain's EU presidency, and arguing that other European states had already adopted policies on sexual harassment (Valiente 1997c: 186–7, 193). Discursively, feminists were careful to clearly distinguish sexual harassment reform from the repressive authoritarian policies of the former regime by insisting that sexual harassment legislation 'was not an intrusion of the state in the sexual privacy of citizens but an official treatment of unequal power relations unrelated to sex' (Valiente 1998: 172). In 1988, feminists decided to take advantage of the government's drafting of a bill reforming labour legislation on maternity and parental leave to press for the inclusion of measures regulating sexual harassment (ibid.: 172).

When the bill was debated in Parliament, the main opposition party – the conservative Popular Party (Partido Popular, PP) – objected to any state intervention on the issue of sexual harassment. The PP argued that sexual harassment measures were the responsibility not of the state but of employers and trade unions negotiating collective agreements. It also maintained that the specific regulation of sexual harassment was unnecessary because women were already protected against 'unwanted sexual advances' under criminal law (Valiente 1998: 173). The socialist government defended the bill by using the same argument that feminists had used to convince it of the need for sexual harassment legislation in the first place. As Valiente explains, the government maintained that, in the context of the political consensus for Spain's integration into the EU, sexual harassment legislation was necessary because the European states Spain sought to emulate already regulated the matter (ibid.: 173). Finally, on 3 March 1989, the government passed Act 3/89 amending the Workers' Statute of 1980 and introducing measures to prevent sexual harassment. The Act established that those employers' actions that infringed upon the intimacy and dignity of workers (sexual harassment included) constituted serious infractions of the labour law, punishable by the imposition of substantial fines (Valiente 1997c: 188–9). However, feminists were concerned that this legal definition of sexual harassment was too vague to be effective – a concern that was soon vindicated.

In the early 1990s, the Act gave rise to a spate of sexual harassment cases across the state in which the labour courts consistently found in the complainant's favour, only to have the appeal courts frequently overturn the decision or reduce the amount of compensation awarded. For instance, in 1995, the Galicia Appeal Court made three decisions either overturning or significantly reducing the amount of compensation awarded by labour courts. The first decision reduced what the Appeal Court described as a 'disproportionate' award for moral damages and cancelled the physical damages award. The second decision reduced the initial award to the complainant when the complainant appealed for an increase in damages. The third decision overturned an award because, according to the Appeal Court, the harassment did not produce the mental upset and disturbance alleged by the complainant. The frequent overturning of labour court decisions and reductions of compensation raised fears among feminists that the labour courts might cease ruling against individuals and employers, knowing that their judgments were likely to be overturned on appeal (Aeberhard-Hodges 1996: 516–18, 531). Therefore, they lobbied the socialist government to tighten the law on sexual harassment, but the government initially resisted. Eventually, under intense pressure from the women's secretariat of the CCOO, the government reluctantly agreed to make sexual harassment a clearly defined offence (Threlfall 1997: 21). Act 10/1995 of 23 November reformed the Criminal Code, Article 184 of which defined sexual harassment as occurring when a person

> demands favours of a sexual nature for his/her benefit or for the benefit of someone else; taking advantage of a situation of superiority of professional, educational or similar nature; announcing to the other person explicitly or tacitly some harm to his/her expectations in his/her professional, educational or similar situation.
>
> (Valiente 1998: 174)

Under the Act, sexual harassment is punishable by a prison sentence of twelve to twenty-four weekends, or by the imposition of a heavy fine (ibid.: 174).

As well as bringing pressure to bear on the government to introduce sexual harassment legislation, feminists within the IM and trade unions joined forces with independent legal advocates in the mid-1980s to tackle the issue of domestic violence and convince the government that it was an issue for which the state should take legal and public responsibility. It is important to realize that Spanish feminists taking up the issue of domestic violence when they did pre-empted any move by the international community to recognize and elaborate measures to eliminate gender-based violence. The problem of domestic violence against women emerged as an issue in Spain almost by chance, when women's advisory centres and legal advocates discovered that a significant number of women coming to them for counselling and legal advice were initiating separation or divorce proceedings because they wanted to escape from domestic violence (Valiente 1996b: 175). Threlfall describes how legal advocates at one particular women's advisory centre in a suburb of Madrid 'became appalled at the number of cases of domestic violence' in the early 1980s (1985: 62). At the same time, says Valiente, doctors and psychologists working in health centres were dismayed by the large number of female victims of domestic violence coming to them for help. They also suspected that there were many more victims of domestic violence who were too frightened or unaware of their rights to come forward and report the abuse (Valiente 1996b: 175). Furthermore, lawyers representing victims of domestic violence became increasingly frustrated with the attitude of the police and judiciary, who treated them as 'revolutionaries trying to overthrow the system, rather than agents of the law seeking to have it enforced' (Threlfall 1996: 133).

As a result of their experiences, a group of legal advocates, social workers and psychologists formed the Commission to Investigate the Ill-Treatment of Women (*Comisión para la Investigación de los Malos Tratos a las Mujeres*) in 1982, and began pressing the socialist government to take action on the issue of domestic violence. Based in Madrid, the commission's principal aim was to effect a change in police, judicial and social attitudes towards abused women by 'breaking the conspiracy of silence' surrounding the problem of domestic violence. It also demanded that the Minister of the Interior ensure that police agents and the judiciary treated the issue of domestic violence appropriately. The Interior Minister responded by issuing a special order in 1983 to police stations throughout the state, instructing them to register all cases of domestic violence and report them to the judiciary, and to prepare monthly statistics (Threlfall 1996: 133). Meanwhile, the General Directorate of Police created a service whereby victims of abuse could file their charges with a policewoman (Ministry of Social Affairs: Women's Institute 1995: 99). Feminists within the IM and trade unions soon joined legal advocates in their battle to convert the private issue of domestic violence into a public concern, and the problem of domestic violence quickly became a priority of the IM.

Between 1983 and 1986, the IM ran a series of media campaigns to inform women of their rights and encourage them to seek help (Ministry of Social Affairs: Women's Institute 1995: 44). It also set up shelters for abused women run by local and regional governments, and subsidized independent refuges and agencies researching the extent of the problem. It subsidized the Commission on the Ill-Treatment of Women, which provided important statistical data on the number of incidents of domestic violence, and on the response of the police and judiciary to cases of abuse. The IM provided a toll-free hotline to advise women on where to go for shelter or other aid if maltreated (United States Department of Justice 1993: 15). At the same time, the IM began pressing the socialist government to establish a unit to research, analyse and make recommendations on legal and policy measures regarding domestic violence. As a result, on 5 November 1986, the government established a unit (*ponencia del Senado de investigación de malos tratos a mujeres*) of the Senate liaison with the Ombudsman and human rights committee (*Comisión de relaciones con el Defensor del Pueblo y de los derechos humanos del Senado*) to undertake this task and advise the Ministries of Interior, Justice and Education on potential measures to be taken (Valiente 1996b: 177). In 1989, the unit finished its work and published a report in which it referred to various studies by the UN and the European Parliament to support its recommendations, which aligned with those of the IM (Roggeband 1999).

By the time the government unit's report was published, the IM had already begun to address the question of legal reforms and ministerial actions on domestic violence. In preparing the first equality plan, the IM included legislative and public policy objectives designed to prevent domestic violence. The objectives included 'reforming emergency punitive machineries to prevent and curb spousal abuse' and 'furnishing due assistance and police protection to women who press such charges in police courts' (Ministry of Social Affairs: Women's Institute 1995: 98). Although these objectives were extremely vague, they nonetheless led to the establishment of a Women's Services division in police headquarters, and training courses to sensitize law enforcement agencies. The first in a series of educational courses organized by the Women's Institute for the Guardia Civil – the national and local police – was run in 1990. Feminists found it difficult, however, to persuade the government to initiate and implement legal reforms on gender-based violence (Valiente 1996b: 177). Eventually, the government enacted Law 3/1989 of 21 June amending the Criminal Code, Article 425 of which established that repeated physical violence in the domestic sphere by a husband or cohabiting partner was an offence punishable by a one- to six-month period of imprisonment. Feminists also found it difficult to persuade the government to ensure adequate services for victims of domestic violence, and as the new millennium approached, the number of refuges per number of battered women was proportionally considerably lower than that recommended by a resolution of the European Parliament in 1997: a shelter for every 100,000 inhabitants (Valiente 2001: 114).

During its tenure of the EU presidency, the socialist government prepared and submitted Spain's second CEDAW report on 9 February 1989, which was based almost entirely on the IM's first equality plan – Plan I. In considering Spain's second periodic report on 28 January 1992, the CEDAW committee expressed dissatisfaction with the Spanish government's decision to submit a report that 'consisted mainly of the 1988–1990 Plan for Equal Opportunities', because 'it did not always show what changes had occurred, [and] some of the figures were out of date and did not permit up-to-date comparisons' (United Nations General Assembly 1993). The socialist government's dependency on action plans as the sole means of defining state policy and the IM's close connection to the PSOE caused concern among Spanish analysts, who feared that should the PSOE lose power, the future of the IM and its ability to shape government policy would be uncertain. Analysts were certain that in the event of a conservative party's electoral victory, the IM's close ties to the ruling socialist party threatened its long-term future (Valiente 1995: 234). In 1996, the conservative PP did win the general election and, while it maintained the IM, it was certainly far less eager to pursue equality objectives.

State behavioural continuity: 1996–2004

The new conservative government harboured ambitions to re-establish a more traditional corporate state identity based on the male-breadwinner family. In a bid to reverse the decline in fertility rates and restore the family as the cornerstone of society, the government introduced legislation aimed explicitly at encouraging women to have, and care for, children. Law 39/99 of 7 November to Promote the Reconciliation of Work and Family Life of Employed Persons was conceived not in terms of parity or eliminating discrimination, but in terms of a traditional gendered division of labour between the private and public spheres. As Maria Luisa Molto and Valiente explain, the conservative government's solution to the problem of reconciling work and family responsibilities was not to increase the availability of publicly funded childcare facilities and care services for elderly and disabled people but to develop leave arrangements and promote part-time employment (2001: 5). Also, the unpaid parental leave and family leave schemes established under the law were available only to employees with a permanent employment contract and civil servants (Escobedo 1999: 3). Furthermore, the conservative government implemented gender-reinforcing social policies that placed a greater burden of welfare on non-governmental and voluntary associations, and the family (Guillen and Matsaganis 2000: 139). The legislation and gender-reinforcing social policies were criticized by feminist advocates within the PSOE and trade unions, who argued that they perpetuated the gendered division of labour between men and women, and reinforced discrimination against women in employment (see Comas 2001: 2).

As this legislation was being drafted, the director of the IM presented Spain's combined third and fourth periodic report for consideration by the CEDAW committee in New York in June 1999. The committee criticized the Spanish state for failing to introduce measures that promoted 'greater balance in the roles and responsibilities of women and men – particularly in the sharing of family responsibilities' (UNCEDAW 1999). The committee also criticized the state for failing to introduce measures that eradicated 'traditional stereotypes that perpetuate direct and indirect discrimination against women' (ibid.). Moreover, it criticized the state for failing to address the issue of women's 'double burden of paid and unpaid work' and expressed concern that certain state employment policies might actually reinforce 'stereotypical attitudes about women's family responsibilities, rather than increasing their participation in the labour market' (ibid.). The committee also expressed concern at the apparent increase in domestic violence and urged the state to pay 'rigorous attention' to implementing and enforcing measures aimed at eliminating gender-based violence (ibid.). Yet in spite of the committee's criticisms, the Spanish conservative government decided to introduce the aforementioned gender-reinforcing labour legislation and social policies. Not only did the government disregard the committee's concerns, but it also ignored calls by domestic feminists to tackle the problems of horizontal segregation, discrimination in promotion, and gender pay differentials in employment. In fact, rather than introducing measures that mitigated these problems, the government introduced part-time and parental leave legislation that exacerbated them (Molto and Valiente 2000: 10).

Furthermore, the conservative government rejected calls by feminists affiliated with left-wing opposition parties to reform the national electoral law to include a 40 per cent quota for female political candidates. In May 1999, the Spanish Co-ordination for the European Women's Lobby (*Coordinadora Española para el Lobby Europeo de Mujeres*) organized a conference on the issue of quotas, and invited politicians and academics from other EU member states to attend. The conference attracted considerable media attention and put pressure on the government to address the issue of gender parity in political decision-making (Jenson and Valiente 2003: 69, 88). Activists then seized on the upcoming general election of March 2000 as an opportunity to draw public attention to the issue of political representation and put further pressure on the government to introduce mandatory quotas for all electoral lists. A heated public debate ensued, involving the Spanish political elite, legal and academic experts, and feminists. Feminists argued that, in the context of European integration, the legal regulation of quotas was necessary because the European states Spain sought to emulate already had quota systems. However, the government strongly opposed quotas and resisted amending the electoral law. The General Secretariat of Social Affairs ridiculed such an amendment, calling it 'the wonderbra quota' (ibid.: 86). After winning the March 2000 general election, the conservative government refused to discuss the matter of quotas further, and continued to resist international and domestic pressure to incorporate international norms of sexual non-discrimination.

Conclusion

The story of the diffusion of international norms of sexual non-discrimination into Spanish state practices is one of fluctuating fortunes. As we have seen, there have been two periods of state behavioural change that have been flanked by periods of state behavioural continuity. Throughout the first period of state behavioural continuity, from 1945 to 1975, international norms of sexual non-discrimination were prevented from diffusing into Spain by the profoundly gender-biased corporate state identity created by the authoritarian regime in partnership with the Catholic Church. The authoritarian state abrogated women's civil and political rights, and effectively silenced any opposition to its policies through coercion. Hence, Spanish feminists were prevented from articulating their social grievances and mobilizing to demand change. Thus, there was no contentious discursive interaction between feminists and the state. The two periods of state behavioural change that followed saw Spain become increasingly receptive to incorporating international norms of sexual non-discrimination. However, state behavioural change was only guaranteed by a combination of international, regional and domestic pressure generated respectively by UN CEDAW committee reports, EU conditions of membership and

Spanish feminist activism. Activists exploited the state's craving for international and regional recognition to push for various changes to domestic state practices. They seized on the notion of European integration to justify their demands, which resonated well with the political elite's enthusiasm for integrating Spain into the EU. In 1996, however, Spain entered a period of stasis. This second period of state behavioural continuity, from 1996 to 2004, witnessed a changeover to a conservative political elite, and the state resisted international and domestic pressure to incorporate international norms of sexual non-discrimination. The state not only made light of international criticism of its policy direction, but also spurned calls by Spanish feminists for progressive change.

6 Japan

Despite the fact that legislative changes imposed by the occupation of 1945–52 swept away the juridical foundations of sexual discrimination in Japan, the Japanese state has since been extremely reluctant to incorporate international norms of sexual non-discrimination. The most significant impediment to norm diffusion has been the gender-biased corporate identity of the state, which was politically reconstituted in the post-occupation period as a traditional patrilineal nation in which the Japanese family system (*ie*) is the locus of social stability and strength. Vestiges of the family system established in the Meiji period (1868–1912) survived the Allied occupation, and during the 1950s and 1960s the Japanese state introduced a series of gender-reinforcing policies explicitly aimed at eroding occupation reforms and reviving traditional social gender divisions. Discursively, the state revived the pre-Second World War mantra 'a woman's place is in the home' and waxed lyrical about the proper traditional authority of the paterfamilias. This vision of restoring the traditional Japanese family system was embedded in the national security, taxation and employment policy systems. The deeply patrilineal corporate state identity constructed in the immediate post-occupation period proved decidedly resilient and continues to present a formidable obstacle to the diffusion of international norms of sexual non-discrimination.

This chapter examines why the Japanese state has been averse to incorporating international norms of sexual non-discrimination. It also examines why a combination of domestic feminist activism, private individual and group litigation, and international pressure induced a long-delayed citizenship revision and a noticeable if albeit ultimately ineffective change to state employment legislation in 1985. It examines the reasons why the Equal Employment Opportunity Law of 1985 failed and why a combination of domestic feminist activism, private group litigation and international pressure finally engendered amendments to this legislation in 1997. It also examines why, despite intense internal and external pressure, the Japanese state refused to admit direct responsibility or offer compensation in a case of past state-sponsored violence against women.

The chapter begins by tracing the political reconstitution of the patrilineal corporate identity of the state after the Allied occupation before examining how this identity construction has affected the diffusion of international norms of sexual non-discrimination. Using the argument advanced in previous chapters, I investigate how and why the state has resisted incorporating international norms of sexual non-discrimination and how, despite this resistance, international and domestic pressure has induced modest changes in domestic state practices. I argue that, while the state's response to international norms of sexual non-discrimination is generally one of behavioural continuity, occasionally the state responds to international and domestic pressure and modifies its behaviour. We can identify three periods of state behavioural continuity between 1952 and 2004 in which structural–agential interaction has tended to result in the reproduction of discriminatory state practices. The second and third of these periods are punctuated by instances of state behavioural change, but in each instance the change is minimal and commonly undermined by other, gender-reinforcing state policies.

The first period of state behavioural continuity, from 1952 to 1974, saw the state ratify two major international conventions but fail to comply fully with either, and steadfastly refuse to ratify any other international conventions. It saw international bodies exert pressure on the state to ratify and comply with international conventions. It also saw domestic feminist activists and private individual litigants exert pressure on the state to modify its behaviour in accordance with international norms of sexual non-discrimination. However, the state repeatedly deflected international and domestic criticism by reverting to a practice of paralysis by analysis. In other words, the state effectively silenced its critics by claiming that it needed time to study the compatibility between Japanese and international law. The second period of state behavioural continuity, from 1975 to 1989, saw the state ratify the UN Convention on the Elimination of Discrimination Against Women (CEDAW) but fail to comply fully with the convention. It also saw Japanese feminists protest against the state's inaction, and private individual litigants challenge discriminatory employment practices. Further, it saw activists discursively oppose the dominant understanding of Japanese women as subservient to society and the state. After a period of stonewalling, the state made modest legislative concessions aimed at saving face in the international community and heading off future conflict with Japanese feminists and litigants. However, the state also introduced gender-reinforcing social security measures that effectively neutralized the modest changes to employment legislation. Furthermore, the state's gender-reinforcing social security measures acted to consolidate the patrilineal corporate identity of the state.

The third period of state behavioural continuity, from 1990 to 2004, saw the state steadfastly resist intense international and domestic pressure to admit legal responsibility for and pay compensation to victims of state-sponsored violence against women in the form of military enforced prostitution during the Second World War. It also saw Japanese feminists and private group litigants campaign against sexual harassment in the workplace and ineffectual employment laws. Further, it saw international bodies exert pressure on the state to incorporate international norms of sexual non-discrimination across all the issue-areas studied by discursively challenging the state's understanding of gender relations. The Japanese government reluctantly made legislative concessions in the areas of employment and violence against women. However, these legislative changes were minimal and, in the case of amendments to employment legislation, were offset by further gender-reinforcing changes to the social security system.

Post-occupation reconstruction of the gender-biased corporate identity of the state

After the occupation of 1945–52, the conservative Japanese government openly began a campaign to resurrect a strong patrilineal corporate identity based on the traditional family system (*ie*), and to rescind all progressive reforms made during the Allied occupation. In particular, the government wanted to revive the traditional authority of the paterfamilias, thus restoring a male-dominated state and society (Kawashima 1983: 58). Vestiges of the family system established in the Meiji period (1868–1912) remained in the Criminal Code, the Nationality Law and the family registration system, and the government, buoyed by two Supreme Court decisions, made moves to overturn constitutional revisions to the family system imposed by Allied occupation forces. In 1950, the Supreme Court had made two separate decisions upholding the constitutionality of Article 205(2) and Article 200 of the Criminal Code respectively, articles referring to the principle of lineal ascendancy. These Supreme Court decisions gave the government confidence that its campaign to restore the family system had the support of the judiciary. The first case, the Fukuoka Patricide Case, was a *cause célèbre*, arousing widespread debate both inside and outside Japanese legal circles (Steiner 1956: 106).

On 21 October 1949, Toyoni Yamato severely beat his father about the head during a family quarrel over a missing coat. The father died the following day due to a brain haemorrhage and Yamato was indicted under Article 205(2) of the Criminal Code for the crime of inflicting bodily injury on a lineal ascendant, resulting in death (Maki 1964: 129). The court of the first instance, the Iizuka Branch of the Fukuoka District Court, found the accused guilty and sentenced him to three years' imprisonment but with a three-year stay of execution. In the course of the verdict, the lower court found that Article 205(2), in providing for a heavier penalty in cases where the victim is a lineal ascendant than in other cases, was unconstitutional because it violated the principle of equality embodied in Article 14 of the new Constitution. The public prosecutor then appealed the case directly to the Supreme Court, which quashed the original decision by a vote of thirteen to two and returned the case to the Fukuoka District Court (Steiner 1956: 108). The Supreme Court rejected the lower court's argument that the code governing family relationships was feudalistic and anti-democratic, ruling that Article 205(2) reflected a moral postulate that should not be confused with the artificial social system known as the family system. It asserted that

> [t]he morality governing the relations among husband and wife, parent and child, brothers and sisters is the foundation of ethics, a universal moral principle, recognized by mankind without regard to past or present or to East and West – in other words, it is a principle which, from the viewpoint of theory, belongs to the field of so-called natural law.
>
> (ibid.: 109–10)

In other words, according to the Japanese Supreme Court, a universal moral principle constituted the basis for Article 205(2) rather than the family system. Thus, the court could find no fault with a law that 'is based on the demands of morality' and upheld the constitutionality of the Article.[1] Two weeks after this decision, the Supreme Court upheld the constitutionality of Article 200 of the Criminal Court on the basis of the reasoning in the Fukuoka Patricide Case.[2]

Encouraged by these Supreme Court decisions, the government established the Constitutional Committee in 1954, with a view to amending the Constitution imposed by Allied occupation forces and restoring the Japanese family system. The chair of the Constitutional Committee stated:

> I think it is absolutely necessary that we foster the kind of family in Japan that will support our traditions, customs, and love of country. Based on the spirit of the *ie*, our nation will assume its own definitions and can move ahead on that foundation.
>
> (Kaji 1984: 16)

However, the government was at pains not to admit this publicly. The government's attempt to officially restore the family system was eventually thwarted by Japanese feminist political advocates, who formed a liaison council to oppose the reinstatement of the family system. The liaison council attracted activists, lawyers and ordinary Japanese women, who took to the streets in large numbers to protest against any constitutional revisions. Activists and lawyers produced pamphlets and gave speeches at various protest rallies. The more enthusiastically the government spoke about the *ie*, the more determined Japanese feminists became to prevent its restitution. After considerable public debate in newspapers, magazines and academic journals, the government abandoned its plan to legally restore the traditional family system. Nevertheless, it refused to abandon the idea of the family system and continued to promote the notion of the patrilineal family through legal and public policy initiatives.

Building on the existing family registration system and the associated resident card system, the conservative government reinforced the patrilineal corporate identity of the state by introducing a series of employment, social security and taxation measures designed to instil within the family a 'strong consciousness of hierarchical order vital for sustaining the state, the economy and society' (Toshitani 1980: 144). These measures were also designed to ensure that women fulfilled their destiny as homemakers and child-rearers (Marfording 1997: 441). Under the family registration system, which was used for census purposes, the family was designated the basic unit of registration. While most states in the international community had some system of registration such as electoral rolls, social security numbers and birth and marriage certificates, Japan's family registration system differed from others in using the household rather than the individual as the unit of identification. A range of information was packaged into each family register (*koseki*), explains Yoshio Sugimoto, 'socially ostracising those who did not fit into the male-dominated conventional family structure promoted by the *koseki* system' (1997: 142). By requiring each household to nominate its head (*honseki*), he continues, *koseki* schemes perpetuated the *ie* system and preserved the patrilineal family order because those nominated were nearly always male (ibid.: 137). It was the household head's personal details of surname and address that were registered as that of all individual members of the household. The government maintained that the family registry was a value-neutral system, but, as Taimie Bryant argues, it was actually value-laden because individuals were 'excluded or restricted' from participating in Japanese society 'on the basis of others' knowledge of negatively valued elements of their family register' (1991: 112).

Moreover, by exposing children of divorced parents to the possibility of being socially ostracized, the family registration system served as a deterrent to divorce and thus reinforced the traditional family system and patrilineal corporate identity of the state. As Sugimoto explains, the registration system required that two separate family registers be established on divorce and that any children be reassigned to one of the new registers, in most instances the mother's. Further, because copies of these papers were often required for the purposes of employment and marriage, the risk of stigmatization for children of divorced parents was high. Fearful of tarnishing their children's register, Sugimoto continues, many married couples, particularly the wives, decided against divorce. This fear of tarnishing a child's register emanated from the notion of *seki* – the belief that 'unless one is formally registered as belonging to an organization or institution, one has no proper station in society' (1997: 141). *Seki* caused individuals to be greatly concerned about which family register they were registered in and the form their entry (*nyuseki*) took (ibid.: 140–2).

The family registration system was supported by the resident card system, which required each household to register its address with the local municipal office. Established under the Residents Registration Act of June 1951, the resident card system served as an index for matters of local taxation, election registration, education, health and pension schemes, and other social security benefits. Like the family registration system, it defined individual family members in accordance with their relationship with the household head. More importantly, claims Masako Kamiya, the head of the household was the basic qualification for many social welfare benefits, including fringe benefits such as housing or lay-off priority, family allowances and tax benefits. Furthermore, she argues, both the resident card system and the family registration system, to which it was linked, reflected and reinforced the notion of a gendered division of labour (1986: 456). This notion also permeated employment, social security and taxation policies introduced by the government in the early 1960s. However, the government found it necessary to modify its neoconservative conception of the family system to suit the changing social and economic realities of the period. As Kathleen Uno explains, the government's belief in the duty of what it called the good wife, wise mother evolved from the 'duty to do reproductive and productive work at home into the obligation to manage household affairs while, if necessary, engaging in paid work that did not prevent fulfilment of domestic responsibilities' (1993: 304–5).

Japan was entering a period of rapid economic growth in the early 1960s and, faced with an acute labour shortage, the government implemented a series of employment and taxation policies that promoted full-time work for unmarried women and part-time work for married women because of their family and child-bearing responsibilities (Uno 1993: 305). A 1963 report of the Economic Deliberative Council, entitled 'Tasks and Measures for Development of Human Resources for Economic Growth', emphasized the need to encourage married women to enter the workforce while safeguarding the family structure (Buckley 1993: 367). As an advisory agency to the Prime Minister, the influential Economic Deliberative Council recommended that Japanese business and government policy-makers adopt the following strategies to deal with the future needs of the economy: use extensively young, unmarried female workers in simple jobs; use only a small number of educated women in supervisory positions; return to their families women of a suitable age for marriage; and rehire women of middle age. The council's recommendations allowed the government to address the problem of an imminent labour shortfall without compromising its vision of a traditional Japanese family headed by the male breadwinner. In fact, the government's vision served to legitimate the use of women as a 'flexible army of peripheral workers' subject to the disadvantages of low wages and job insecurity (Carney and O'Kelly 1990: 142–3).

At the same time, the government introduced tax incentives designed to discourage women from working full time by maintaining an income tax threshold under which the wife's income was not taxed and her husband could take advantage of a spouse deduction allowance. If the wife's income exceeded the threshold, she had to earn a significantly higher income in order to offset the tax increase (Cherry 1987: 104). Thus, the government's taxation policy virtually guaranteed that married women became a source of low-wage, part-time labour. Moreover, as temporary or part-time employees, women were generally excluded from unions, did not receive wage increases based on seniority and were not entitled to any of the employment security or fringe benefits of full-time employees (Upham 1993: 333). Parallel to the tax incentives, the government established a social security system embodying the ideal of the *ie* and designed to ensure that the family (i.e. women) bore the primary responsibility for care of the elderly, children and the disabled.

The social security system incorporated the principle of the *ie* by treating the household as a unit in administering medical insurance, and by treating a married couple as a unit in administering employee pensions. It ensured that the family bore the burden of care by deeming a person eligible to receive public assistance only when he or she had no relative to turn to for support. However, because the social security system presupposed a gendered division of labour between 'the husband as the breadwinner and the wife as the caretaker of domestic affairs' and thus rendered the female economically dependent on the male, this meant that the burden of care fell largely on women within the family. For instance, social insurance schemes assumed the male to be the 'standard' insured person, and, as a dependant of the insured, the wife was able to share in the benefits of the scheme only indirectly. As an individual, she did not qualify to receive health insurance or pension benefits. Employees' pension plans treated a couple as one unit in the payment of a pension, which was payable only to the husband as the insured (Osawa 1993: 166). Furthermore, the government allowed companies within the corporate sector to operate their own employees' pension insurance schemes as quasi-public programmes with various tax incentives attached to them, which they operated often to their own advantage.

The government also tacitly allowed the corporate sector to circumvent the equal pay provision of the 1947 Labour Standards Law imposed by the occupation authorities. Companies employed several strategies to avoid direct wage discrimination, including structuring their wage and promotion systems to stress continuity and duration of tenure, and drawing a distinction between permanent employees and part-time and temporary employees. The simplest way to accomplish the latter was to reserve managerial and supervisory positions for permanent employees. Another ploy used by management to avoid direct wage discrimination was to introduce policies that forced women to resign and then refuse to assign newly hired women for anything but subordinate jobs (Upham 1993: 333–4). For instance, explains Yoko Kawashima, companies offered special allowances to women to resign upon marriage, or even forced them to quit by applying overt or covert pressure (1995: 281). Many companies also adopted earlier mandatory retirement for women, setting the retirement age as low as 45. Companies even retired women and then rehired them as part-time employees to avoid giving the usual salary increases and fringe benefits. Furthermore, as part-time employees, women were entitled to a much smaller retirement bonus (Naftulin 1980: 14). Not only did the government fail to challenge these measures in the corporate sector, where their legality was questionable, argues Frank Upham, it actively discriminated against women in employment itself. Furthermore, trade unions rarely questioned the exclusion of women from permanent employment in the private sector (1993: 334).

The first period of state behavioural continuity: 1952–74

The deeply patrilineal corporate state identity constructed after the occupation of 1945–52 had an immediate and lasting inhibiting effect on the diffusion of international norms of sexual non-discrimination. Initially, the Japanese state was extremely reluctant to ratify any international conventions, and between 1952 and 1974 it ratified only two major international conventions: the 1952 UN Convention on the Political Rights of Women (in 1955) and the 1951 ILO Equal Remuneration Convention (in 1967). However, it failed to comply fully with either of these conventions and resolutely refused to ratify any others. In both cases, the state ratified the convention on the basis of legislative provisions introduced under the Allied occupation administration, provisions that did not fully comply with the convention in question. Eager to be readmitted to the UN, the Japanese state ratified the UN Convention on the Political Rights of Women on the basis of the new national Constitution, which guaranteed women political enfranchisement. The state saw ratification as an opportunity to demonstrate its commitment to the international community without having to take any further legislative or policy action. After being readmitted to the ILO in 1951, the Japanese state eventually ratified the ILO Equal Remuneration Convention in 1967 on the basis of the national Labour Standards Law, which prohibited employers from discriminating against female employees in respect of wages. Once again, the state saw ratification as an opportunity to enhance its international reputation without having to take any further action or effort to implement existing national legislation.

Furthermore, in both cases the impetus for ratification came not from the initiative of the state but from domestic or international pressure. In the case of the UN Convention on the Political Rights of Women, the impetus for ratification came from domestic pressure applied by the

Japanese Women and Minors Bureau, which was established under the Allied occupation administration in 1947. The Women and Minors Bureau had sent unofficial and then official observers to sessions of the UN Commission on the Status of Women since 1950 and, capitalizing on the state's desire to be readmitted to the UN, convinced it of the importance of ratification. In the case of the ILO Equal Remuneration Convention, the impetus for ratification came from international pressure applied by the ILO. In 1966, at the International Labour Conference, the ILO adopted a resolution concerning the contribution of the organization to the upcoming UN International Year of Human Rights. The resolution invited member states to ratify various ILO conventions, and, in response to a direct request from the Director-General of the ILO in January 1967, the Japanese government agreed to ratify the Equal Remuneration Convention in July 1967 (Hanami 1981: 768). However, the state steadfastly refused to ratify other key international conventions, including the 1957 UN Convention on the Nationality of Married Women, the 1962 UN Convention on Consent to Marriage, Minimum Age for Marriage, and Registration of Marriage, and the 1958 ILO Discrimination (Employment and Occupation) Convention.

Despite considerable international pressure to ratify these conventions and change its behaviour accordingly, the Japanese state resolutely refused, on the grounds that it needed time to study the compatibility between Japanese and international law. For instance, in 1967 and periodically thereafter, when the ILO Committee of Experts asked about the prospect of it ratifying the ILO Discrimination (Employment and Occupation) Convention, the state repeatedly replied that it needed to examine the convention's compatibility with national legislation and to conduct ongoing studies (International Labour Conference 1996a: 52). The Japanese government argued that because the convention embodied provisions that were closely related to employers' freedom of contracting, it was necessary to 'give consideration to the harmony between domestic law and the convention' (International Labour Conference 1988: 11). These so-called studies continued for over thirty years without conclusion, and as of 2004 the Japanese state had yet to ratify the convention. The state employed the same stalling tactic to avoid ratifying the UN Convention on the Nationality of Married Women and the UN Convention on Consent to Marriage. Again, as of 2004 the Japanese state had yet to ratify either of these conventions.

Apart from its reluctance to ratify international conventions, Japan's participation on various UN human rights commissions during this period, including the Commission on the Status of Women, was highly circumspect. In a bid to ward off international and domestic criticism of the secondary status accorded to Japanese women, the Japanese state had sought and gained a seat on the Commission on the Status of Women in 1960, after which it showed little willingness to follow the commission's guidelines and recommendations. In particular, the Japanese state was keen to ward off criticism from domestic feminist activists concerning the 1950 Nationality Law. Activists were issuing pleas for the government to amend the citizenship law because it discriminated against Japanese women who married foreigners by denying their children Japanese citizenship. Under the Nationality Law, Japanese nationality could be passed to a child only through the father, and as a result, even if the child was born in Japan to a Japanese mother, the child was denied all the rights and entitlements granted to Japanese citizens. The government's resistance to revising the citizenship law stemmed from its determination to protect the patrilineal corporate identity of the state by safeguarding the centrality of the male head of the household. The government's resistance also arose from its opposition to mixed marriages (see Peek 1992: 220–1, 224–5).

In 1967, Japanese feminists took advantage of the UN General Assembly's adoption of the Declaration on the Elimination of Discrimination Against Women to put further pressure on the government to address the issue of sexual discrimination in Japan and amend the Nationality Law. Once again, however, the government adopted the tactic of trying to outlast domestic and international pressure by claiming that it required time to study the compatibility between Japanese and international law. Several years later, the government used a similar stalling technique to fend off mounting domestic pressure generated by private individual litigation to address the issue of sexual discrimination in employment. The employment discrimination litigation first began in the mid-1960s and challenged discriminatory wage, retirement and reduction-in-force practices (Upham 1987: 129). The most significant litigation was that of the *Sumitomo Cement* line of cases, which began with the Tokyo Court decision in 1966. Initially, both the plaintiffs and the lawyers involved in the *Sumitomo* cases viewed their actions as contributing to broad social change by 'helping to create a new moral and political consensus', but as the litigation campaign progressed, the lawyers became more interested in 'the evolution of legal doctrine' and securing specific legislative change (ibid.: 156–7). Thus, the *Sumitomo* cases put considerable legal pressure on the government, in particular the Ministry of Labour, to legislate against sexual discrimination in employment.

The first of the *Sumitomo* cases concerned a discriminatory marriage retirement system. The plaintiff, Setsuko Suziki, had joined Sumitomo Cement in July 1960, two years after the company had adopted a series of new and highly discriminatory policies, including not hiring women with more or less than a high school education; assigning women to the status of lowest-grade employee (*hirashaiin*) until they retired; and requiring women to resign on marriage or, if unmarried, at the age of 30 (Krauss 2000: 3; Brown 1988: 198–9). Three years later, Suziki married, refused to resign, and was fired on 17 March 1964. With the backing of her labour union, Suziki filed a complaint, and after a long and intense court battle the Tokyo District Court declared null and void a contract between the complainant and the Sumitomo Cement Company requiring her to retire upon marriage. It did so despite a recent government announcement that early retirement systems were not illegal even though the constitutional guarantee of equality made them undesirable (Hanami 1984: 227). The court also made its decision despite the absence of national statutory legislation explicitly prohibiting such treatment of women by employers (Brown 1988: 192). Instead, it relied solely on the vague provision of Article 90 of the Civil Code, which stated that 'a juristic act whose object is such to be contrary to public policy or good morals is null and void'. Applying this standard to Sumitomo's retirement system and its effect on women, the court invalidated the provision in the plaintiff's contract of employment (ibid.: 197–8).

In making its decision, the court rejected Sumitomo's argument that Japanese companies commonly employed early retirement systems and that these systems were 'expected and accepted as natural and fair by workers, unions and employers, and that they were consistent with Japanese values and traditions' (Upham 1987: 132). It also rejected Sumitomo's argument that women were inherently inefficient and that discrimination was, thus, fair and reasonable. The court concluded, instead, that any alleged inefficiency was caused by the company's own practices rather than any intrinsic quality of women. On the specific question of a reduced productivity upon marriage, the court argued that it could find no valid reason for Sumitomo requiring female employees to be single. As Upham explains,

> the fact that the seniority-based wage scale meant the company lost progressively more money on female employees as they grew older was to the court simply a problem of the company's own making and could not be resolved by discriminatorily burdening its female workers.
>
> (1987: 133)

The *Sumitomo Cement* decision of 20 December 1966 formed the basis upon which a whole series of cases were subsequently built. Further, according to Upham, despite daunting doctrinal problems, litigants successfully attacked progressively more subtle and indirect forms of discrimination in employment (ibid.: 19).

The *Sumitomo* line of cases attracted considerable media attention and exposed both the government and the corporate sector to unwanted public scrutiny. Female employees familiar with the *Sumitomo* decision frequently took their employment contracts to the media in a bid to expose those companies continuing to maintain discriminatory retirement systems. According to Alice Cook and Hiroko Hayashi, the resulting adverse publicity often made it impossible for companies to implement their mandatory retirement policies (1980: 50). The adverse publicity surrounding the *Sumitomo* cases, combined with the threat of lawsuits and sustained lobbying by the Women and Minors Bureau, also placed the government under considerable pressure to eliminate discriminatory early retirement systems. Having almost been abolished by the government in the mid-1950s and again in 1965, the Women and Minors Bureau was not held in high regard by policy-makers, who initially ignored the bureau's complaints regarding early retirement systems.[3] Eventually, the bureau took matters into its own hands by approaching employers directly to modify their practices rather than going through the standard enforcement procedures of the Labour Standards Bureau. Finally, the Ministry of Labour issued administrative guidance urging the corporate sector to replace mandatory early retirement schemes. Unconvinced by this token gesture by the government, the Women and Minors Bureau continued to approach companies directly about their discriminatory practices.

However, the corporate sector simply ignored the bureau and rearranged its employment practices in such a way as to enable it to 'retain the economic and psychological benefits of discrimination without incurring social or legal criticism' (Cook and Hayashi 1980: 39). These rearrangements took various forms, including replacing compensation systems based on seniority with systems based on performance and function while simultaneously restricting women to low-paying jobs; hiring women only as part-time or temporary employees; and promoting women at a slower rate than men or using other discretionary measures to discourage long tenure. The government either chose to ignore these legally questionable practices or, in the case of employing women only on a part-time or temporary basis, issued enlightenment guidance – a diluted form of administrative guidance – asking the corporate sector to reconsider its position on part-time employment. Enlightenment guidance consisted of nothing more than the Ministry of Labour talking to companies about the desirability of hiring women as regular, full-time employees (ibid.: 147). Disillusioned by the government's superficial response and its failure to implement the ILO Equal Remuneration Convention, Japanese feminists continued to lobby the government throughout 1968 and 1969 to address the issue of discrimination in employment. In 1969, under mounting domestic pressure, the government established a private, non-statutory research body to the Ministry of Labour – the Labour Standards Law Study Committee – to investigate gender-based inequities in employment and make recommendations for legislative reform (Buckley 1994: 162). By setting up a study group, however, the government was once more reverting to its strategy of paralysis by analysis to avoid change and head off further conflict with feminists (Peek 1992: 227).

As well as taking purely cosmetic action on discriminatory early retirement schemes, the government planned to rescind protective provisions included in the 1947 Labour Standards Law introduced under the occupation administration. This government initiative, which was supported by the Tokyo Chamber of Commerce and Industry (TCCI), attracted the attention of feminists, who were suspicious of the motivation behind such a move. In 1970, the TCCI declared that it believed protection regulations were simply an excuse for discrimination, and thus obsolete. However, activists suspected that the chamber's real interest in the withdrawal of protective measures was to exploit a growing pool of cheap, part-time female labour (Buckley 1994: 161; Robins-Mowry 1983: 181–2). Activists were no less suspicious of the motivation of unions in mounting a comprehensive campaign not only to retain the existing protective measures but also to expand them (Buckley 1994: 161). For their part, argues Sandra Buckley, 'unions were not unaware of the risk to the status of their full-time male members should industry find itself free to employ larger numbers of women on all shifts and across the whole range of job functions' (ibid.: 161). Activists not only found themselves caught between the corporate sector and the unions but disagreed among themselves about whether protective labour measures should be retained or not. While some held that equality demanded the abolition of protective measures – except with respect to maternity – others felt that the pursuit of equality should be combined with the retention of existing protective legislation (Nakanishi 1983: 615).

The controversy over corporate Japan's campaign to remove protectionist legislation was further inflamed when the local media pounced on a report released by the ILO in 1974, which claimed that Japanese women workers were overprotected. A popular Japanese weekly magazine with a large circulation of educated readers remarked on the fact that the ILO, the 'patron saint of labour', had condemned protective labour legislation. The magazine went on to state that protective measures discriminated against men because 'having children or not was the woman's choice', and accused women of shirking their employment responsibilities (Jones 1976–7: 599). The article concluded that although women acted as if oppressed, in reality they were oppressing men by pushing them to work for women's own profit (ibid.: 599). The article caused enormous problems for Japanese feminists lobbying for the removal of protectionist measures because it provided those activists calling for the retention of such measures with ammunition to undermine their campaign by accusing it of being elitist. At the time, this deep division between activists over protectionist legislation left Japanese feminist activism as a whole in a considerably weakened and marginalized position. The lack of consensus among activists also meant that private individual litigants and their lawyers inevitably became less focused on litigation as a means of effecting social reform for Japanese women as a whole than on the evolution of legal doctrine (Upham 1987: 258).

The second period of state behavioural continuity: 1975–89

The Japanese government's recognition of UN International Women's Year (IWY) in 1975 provided Japanese feminists with a new political opportunity to press for state behavioural change. The government's acknowledgement of IWY owed much to increasing external criticism of its discriminatory employment practices and its desire to prevent the further alienation of female voters, who now outnumbered male voters at the polls (Peek 1992: 227). Japan's high economic growth in the first three decades following the end of the Second World War had attracted the attention of Western industrialized states and, with it, criticism of the Japanese state's discriminatory employment practices (Fujimura-Fanselow 1995: xxviii). In particular, the United States and a number of European states criticized the disparity between men's and women's wages in Japan (Hayashi 1988: 21). External pressure (*gaiatsu*) had already begun to affect Japanese economic policy (see Katzenstein 1996a: 38), and, taking advantage of the government's sensitivity to international criticism, feminists within the Women and Minors Bureau put pressure on the state to recognize IWY and modify its employment practices in accordance with international labour conventions. The government was also aware of its declining public support and of the increasingly large numbers of women attending nationwide employment protest rallies (Buckley 1994: 162).

The International Women's Year Action Group (*Kokusai Fujin Nen o Kikkake toshite Kodosuru omnatachi no kai*), which was established by the prominent Japanese feminists Ichikawa Fusae and Tanaka Sumiko in 1975, in partnership with the group *Tsukuru Kai* and a loose coalition of other feminist organizations, exploited the government's recognition of the UN IWY to press for equality in employment and to influence the outcome of the ongoing deliberations of the Labour Standards Law Study Committee. As part of their campaign, they also referred to the newly adopted British Sex Discrimination Act as a model. The Ministry of Labour had released the committee's preliminary findings in 1970 but its final recommendations were not released until November 1978. The International Women's Year Action Group also joined activists within political opposition parties to put pressure on the government to address the issue of women's political under-representation, to amend the Nationality Law and the Civil Code, and to establish an administrative body within the Prime Minister's Office. Interestingly, unlike their European counterparts, Japanese feminists argued for the retention of protection measures in employment. However, according to Vera Mackie, they argued that such measures should be extended to cover all Japanese workers, including male employees, who worked the longest hours of any industrialized nation. They reasoned that the gender-biased division of labour in the private sphere would be addressed only if men and women both worked reasonable hours. Employers' representatives countered that women's employment conditions should simply be bought into line with the masculine standard. Feminists argued that equality of opportunity under existing conditions would simply mean equality of exploitation. Rather than emphasize the idea of state protection, however, feminists talked in terms of *guaranteeing* the rights of women in employment (Mackie 2003: 180, 182–4). The use of this discursive strategy on the part of feminists was an attempt to undermine the state's historical positioning of women 'as weak supplicants, in need of [its] protection' (ibid.: 183–4).

In 1976, the Liberal Democratic Party (LDP) government lost its majority in the Lower Diet for the first time since 1955 and a reinvigorated opposition controlled almost all the major urban areas of Japan after effectively championing a number of public causes, including women's rights, during the civic activism of the late 1960s and early 1970s (Muramatsu and Krauss 1990: 301). However, the LDP government managed to cling to power and even reassert itself. It did so not by resisting the pressure for new policies but by appropriating the causes championed by the opposition, including gender equality. By doing so, the government effectively silenced the political opposition. The government promised to take a serious look at revising the Civil Code and the Nationality Law, and at amending national employment legislation. The government set up numerous committees to examine the role and status of women in Japan, and in January 1977 it released the National Plan of Action for the Promotion of Measures Relating to Women. However, as a government policy statement, the ten-year plan was criticized by feminists for being superficial and ambiguous. In reply, the government argued that the plan was only in the initial stages of preparation and that specific legislative and public policy measures would be forthcoming (Yoko, Mitsuko and Kimoko 1994: 401). This was followed by an announcement by the Ministry of Labour on 13 June 1977 that, rather than introduce new legislation prohibiting discrimination in employment, it would try to achieve equality through the process of administrative guidance. Infuriated by the government's apparent stonewalling, activists decided to intensify their efforts to influence the outcome of the Labour Standards Law Committee. Following the final report of the committee, which was submitted to the Minister of Labour in November 1978, formal government policy debates regarding the introduction of new labour legislation began. The committee recommended the enactment of an equal opportunity in employment law and the abolition of existing statutory protective measures – apart from those concerning maternity. This recommendation reignited the controversy between the corporate sector, trade unions and feminists over equality versus protective labour measures – a controversy that played into the hands of government policy-makers reluctant to act on the Labour Standards Law Committee's recommendations (Hanami 1984: 228).

However, the government soon came under renewed pressure to enact new employment legislation with the UN adoption of CEDAW in December

1979. Despite voting for the adoption of CEDAW in the General Assembly, the Japanese state strongly opposed the international convention because it conflicted with Japanese law in many areas, including citizenship or nationality law and employment law. During the drafting stage of the convention, the Japanese state raised numerous objections and proposed amendments to the convention wherever it conflicted with Japanese law. For instance, Japan proposed that the nationality clause of the convention be deleted entirely, and proposed amendments to Article 11 of the convention referring to employment. The Japanese state also attempted to ensure that the convention in general was 'toned down' (Iwasawa 1998: 207–8). For instance, it proposed that the phrase 'policy of eliminating discrimination' be replaced with the phrase 'policy of *promoting* the elimination of discrimination'. Further, Japan proposed that either sanctions attached to legislative measures be deleted or incentives be added as an alternative method of ensuring compliance (ibid.: 208). However, the majority of the Japanese proposals were rejected, and consequently the government decided against signing the convention (ibid.: 208–9). Another reason why government decided against signing the convention was that it knew that if it did so, it would be committed to working towards ratification and compliance, a course that government policy-makers saw as causing serious problems for Japan (Yoko, Mitsuko and Kimoko 1994: 403).

A month before the signing ceremony of CEDAW was held at the UN World Conference for Women in Copenhagen in July 1980, Japanese newspapers reported the government's decision not to sign the convention (Iwasawa 1998: 209). Japanese feminists, who had been pressing for early ratification of the convention, were shocked. The IWY Action Group and activists within the political opposition parties urged the government to reconsider its position. Activists openly criticized the government's plan to send a delegation to the Copenhagen conference when it had no intention of signing CEDAW and argued that to do so would seriously embarrass the Japanese delegates and the state (Yoko *et al.* 1994: 403). Eventually the government bowed to the domestic pressure and, keen to avoid being a target of international criticism at the Copenhagen conference, agreed to sign the convention on 17 July 1980 (Peek 1992: 227–8). Two days prior to signing, the government also decided at a cabinet meeting, under acting Prime Minister Masayoshi Ito, that it would ratify the convention by the end of the UN Decade for Women in July 1985. Once Japan became a signatory to the convention, Japanese feminists intensified their campaign for early ratification and rallied public support for their cause through the media (Yoko *et al.* 1994: 404). Activists also campaigned tirelessly for sweeping changes to national legislation in accordance with the international convention, but the government refused to consider comprehensive revisions of Japanese law.

Despite considerable international and domestic pressure, the Japanese government resisted revising the Civil Code before ratifying CEDAW on the grounds that the family law guaranteed equality (Hayashi 1995: 44). The government also resisted revising the Nationality Law and introducing new employment measures on the basis that it needed time to consider and study the issues (Lam 1992: 100). The Ministry of Justice repeatedly insisted that the law of nationality's principle of *jus sanguinis a patre* – that a child acquires Japanese nationality if the father is a Japanese national – was constitutional and did not contravene the principle of equality stipulated in international law (Iwasawa 1998: 226–7). However, under the added pressure of knowing that the UN Human Rights Committee condemned the Nationality Law as discriminatory, the Ministry of Justice began drafting an amendment to the law of nationality in October 1981 and in February 1983 released an interim progress report.[4] The IWY Action Group expressed its concern at the delay to the legislative amendment and submitted a position paper to the Ministry of Justice in May 1983. Finally, the Diet passed a revised Nationality Law in May 1984 (effective 1 January 1985), which granted citizenship to children born of a Japanese mother and a foreign father (Mikanagi 1998: 183). However, the Ministry of Justice continued to insist that the previous citizenship provisions were constitutional and that the amendment to the citizenship law should not be interpreted as the Ministry's admission of their unconstitutionality (Iwasawa 1998: 228).

Meanwhile, the formal political debate regarding the enactment of new employment legislation continued. In December 1979, the Tripartite Advisory Council on Women's and Young Workers' Problems (an advisory body to the Minister of Labour) appointed an ad hoc committee of experts to research and develop standards for determining and ensuring gender-based equality in employment. The committee, the Experts Group on Equality between the Sexes, consisted of fifteen representatives from labour and management, and neutral members selected from among women's organizations, academics and lawyers. Over the next six years, the committee of experts attempted repeatedly to draw up concrete guidelines for the legislation, but because of fundamental disagreements among the committee representatives, it proved impossible to reach a consensus. The major controversy centred on whether or not to retain statutory protective labour measures and on the scope of legislative provisions. With regard to the protective labour measures provided by the Labour Standards Law, management representatives maintained that retaining special protective measures for women was both discriminatory against men and inconsistent with the aim of gender-based equality in employment (Lam 1992: 95–6). Trade union and neutral representatives opposed any weakening of existing protective measures and accused management representatives of using the issue of discrimination to cut back on necessary protections (Upham 1987: 149). They were convinced that the removal of protective labour measures would lead to deteriorating working conditions in general and argued that equality was achievable only if protective measures were retained (Lam 1992: 96).

With regard to the scope of legislative employment-equity provisions, trade union and neutral representatives insisted on the prohibition of sexual discrimination in all aspects of employment and on punitive measures for violations. Management representatives strongly objected to the idea that the corporate sector should be legally bound to provide equal treatment and opportunity in employment. According to Alice Lam, management representatives argued that

> [w]hile legal prohibition of discrimination with regard to age limits, retirement, and dismissal would be inevitable (as these were ruled illegal by the courts in the past), other personnel procedures such as recruitment, job assignment and promotion were directly related to companies' assessment systems, which should not be subjected to legal intervention.
>
> (1992: 96)

This argument was based on the belief that the proposed legislation would destroy the two pillars of Japan's post-war economic success: lifetime employment and seniority-based compensation (Iwasawa 1998: 215). Management representatives recommended that rather than legally prohibit sexual discrimination, the proposed legislation should *morally oblige* employers not to discriminate against women in the areas of recruitment, job assignment, training and promotion. Trade union and neutral representatives doubted the effectiveness of moral obligation and demanded more effective legal enforcement procedures. Unable to reach agreement on the scope of the legislation, the committee of experts finally submitted its report to the Ministry of Labour in May 1982 without including concrete guidelines for the proposed law (Lam 1992: 97). The task of reaching an agreement on the scope of the proposed legislation then fell to the standing Tripartite Advisory Council, which presided over a further series of stormy sessions among management, union and neutral representatives. A group of representatives were even sent to Europe to research the current situation in the region, particularly in the Scandinavian states, and collect data to expedite the council's deliberations (Naftulin 1980: 14).

In December 1983, the Ministry of Labour released a progress report on the discussions of the Tripartite Advisory Council, which indicated that all three parties had reached agreement that new employment legislation was needed and that protective measures needed to be reviewed. However, the report indicated that the three parties were divided over the concrete measures to be included in the new legislation. Once again, opinion was split along management–labour lines, with both sides rejecting a compromise solution offered by neutral representatives. Management and union representatives disagreed on three aspects of the proposed legislation, including the practices to be prohibited, sanctions and protective measures. While management representatives were willing to include a prohibition against unreasonable discrimination in retirement and lay-offs, they refused to agree to the demand of union representatives that recruitment, hiring, placement and promotion also be covered. With regard to sanctions, union and neutral representatives insisted on explicit penalties for all violations, and the establishment of an administrative agency within the Ministry of Labour with the power to issue legally binding directives to offending employers. Management representatives, on the other hand, preferred a voluntary conciliation system to handle disputes (Upham 1987: 149). The third, and most contentious, issue remained that of protective legislation. While management representatives continued to insist on the repeal of protective measures, labour representatives demanded their retention. In the end, the Tripartite Advisory Council submitted its final report to the Ministry of Labour in March 1984 without having agreed on protective labour measures or sanctions for compliance. As a result, it was left to the Ministry of Labour to reconcile the disparate views of management and labour (Lam 1992: 98).

With the deadline for ratifying CEDAW rapidly approaching, the Ministry of Labour took what it described as a 'strong administrative initiative' and drafted legislation sympathetic to management's position, thus betraying the LDP government's close ties to the corporate sector (Lam 1992: 98; Mikanagi 1998: 189). The draft bill – the Equal Employment Opportunity Law (EEOL) – was submitted to the 101st Extraordinary Session of the Diet for approval in May 1984, but a lengthy, heated debate prevented the immediate passage of the legislation. During the final Diet debate on the legislation a year later, the Minister of Labour was challenged by a member of the opposition on whether the proposed legislation promised any real change for female workers. The minister replied:

> Until the present day lifetime employment has been a male-centred system. The individual is of course important but one cannot ignore the average difference between men and women. Companies' personnel management systems have been operating on this assumption. Up to the present, women's length of service has been relatively short, and one cannot say for sure that their length of service will increase. The future improvement of this will have to rely mainly on administrative guidance.
>
> (Lam 1992: 99)

The minister's statement, according to Lam, confirmed that management had won a significant victory in the long-running controversy regarding the new legislation and that the government preferred an incremental approach to implementing the law, taking into account the employment practices peculiar to Japan (ibid.: 99). In fact, according to Upham, management was quietly convinced that the proposed legislation strengthened rather than weakened its prerogatives *vis-à-vis* female employees (1987: 153).

Finally, on 17 May 1985, the Diet passed the bill with just the support of the ruling Liberal Democratic Party (LDP). The bill was passed in the last possible parliamentary session before the 17 July 1985 deadline for ratifying CEDAW. Following the passage of the EEOL, Japan ratified CEDAW on 25 June 1985 amid expressions of doubt on the part of many Japanese feminists and lawyers that the new legislation was sufficient to fulfil the state's legal obligations under the convention (Parkinson 1989: 618). The EEOL, which came into effect on 1 April 1986, was not, in fact, a new, self-contained piece of legislation but rather consisted of amendments to thirteen existing labour laws, including the 1947 Labour Standards Law and the 1972 Working Women's Welfare Law. According to the Ministry of Labour, the express purpose and ultimate objective of the EEOL was to improve the welfare of female employees, because this was the main pillar for guaranteeing equality in employment. In other words, according to Lam, the government defined equality as *welfare* handed down from the state to female employees rather than as an individual right (1992: 101). The EEOL divided employment into five separate areas and prohibited discrimination in the areas of training, employee benefits, and retirement and dismissals, but the prohibition was without penalty. According to Upham, the prohibition of discrimination in retirement and dismissals did little more than confirm legal doctrine developed in the employment litigation of the 1960s and 1970s (1987: 154). In regard to the remaining two areas of recruitment and hiring, and job assignment and promotion, the EEOL merely required that employers *endeavour* to treat female employees equally with male employees (*tsutome-nakereba-naranai*). Thus, explains Lam, these legislative provisions were purely hortatory, as opposed to comprehensive and substantive (1992: 101).

Furthermore, the legislation was passed with no significant punitive measures and did not provide for enforcement by means of a private right to legal action. In lieu of litigation, the EEOL provided a three-step process for resolving disputes arising between employers and employees. The first step of the process involved the voluntary resolution of employee discrimination complaints utilizing grievance procedures established by the employer. The second step entailed assistance in the resolution of a dispute given by the director of the prefectural Office of Women and Young Workers' Affairs when the two parties were unable to reach a settlement. The third and final step involved mediation by an Equal Opportunity Mediation Commission – established in each prefecture under the auspices of the prefectural Office of Women and Young Workers' Affairs – *if* both parties agreed to the mediation (Parkinson 1989: 607). However, there were several inherent problems with the mediation procedure. Equal Opportunity Mediation Commissions were not permanent bodies but were established on a case-by-case basis by the director of the prefectural Office of Women and Young Workers' Affairs. As government representatives of the Ministry of Labour temporarily assigned to prefectures, directors were reluctant to initiate mediation proceedings, because they were answerable to the ministry. Moreover, while directors were given the power to decide whether a complaint was worthy of mediation before any substantial fact-finding was conducted, they were not given the necessary powers to investigate complaints independently. Closely supervised by the Ministry of Labour, directors were, thus, extremely careful in selecting cases to refer to mediation because their positions were at stake (Kamiya 1995: 78–9).

Japanese feminists were appalled at the legislation's lack of stringent punitive measures for violations and accused the government of deliberately trying to deter private sexual discrimination litigation and prevent judicial intervention. The government retaliated by arguing that the establishment of mediation commissions in all the major prefectures reflected the Japanese preference for conciliation instead of confrontation with employers, and litigation (Eccleston 1989: 213; Upham 1987: 163). However, according to Upham, there is little doubt that the EEOL and its dispute resolution provisions actually reflected the Japanese government's preference for dealing with social conflict by 'simultaneously ameliorating its causes and incorporating the antagonists into government-controlled mediation machinery' (1987: 163). Moreover, argues Patricia Boling,

> [i]nchoate policies with a large degree of administrative discretion have several advantages: they leave it to the bureaucracy to decide how and whether to enforce laws or make exceptions; they avoid litigious, individualistic enforcement strategies; and they respond to domestic and international pressure with an apparent commitment to ending discrimination against women without actually requiring business to change their employment practices.
>
> (1998: 184)

On the domestic front, many feminists were certainly convinced that the EEOL reflected nothing more than the government's desire to defuse their efforts to obtain significant legislative reform. Their suspicions were confirmed when prefectural offices began minimizing their participation in dispute resolutions under the EEOL by strongly encouraging voluntary in-house dispute resolution. This severely restricted the opportunities for female employees to seek redress for discrimination, because many women felt too intimidated to confront their employers, and because in-house grievance procedures were often biased or inadequate (Knapp 1995: 129).

The government's lack of commitment to gender equality is also reflected in the fact that during the same period that it was drafting and enacting the EEOL, the government attempted to strengthen the patrilineal corporate identity of the state through a policy announced in 1979, entitled *Perfecting the Foundation of the Family* (Reiko 1986: 15). The aim of this policy was to 'place the family at the core of the nation' and to reinforce the traditional notion that childcare and care of elderly people was a woman's responsibility. The policy also became a convenient justification for extensive government reductions in social security expenditure (Hayashi 1988: 23; Mioko and Jennison 1985: 122). As Yumiko Mikanagi explains, in the 1980s, the government 'initiated a curtailment of the social security system, calling for a *fortified* family function to offer private compensation for the reduced social security' (1998: 184). It argued that the Japanese family was a unique social institution imbued with cultural tradition and, as such, was an essential source of self-help in relation to the social security system (Takahashi 1997: 175). Discursively, the government adopted the catchphrase *welfare society with vitality* to describe the potential of the private sector – families and communities – for providing social services (ibid.: 173, 175). It also promoted the idea of a 'Japanese style social welfare model' based on the indigenous traditional principles of filial piety, and familial self-sufficiency and interdependence (see Goodman and Peng 1996). In order to achieve its objective of reducing social security expenditure, the government introduced a series of policies aimed at shifting the burden of care from the public to the private sector. Throughout the 1980s, the government reduced social security expenditure in a variety of areas, including medical services, child allowances, welfare for disabled people and services for the elderly. It also reduced the level of health insurance coverage and increased the entitlement age for national pensions. At the same time, the government adopted a range of policies to ensure that family members (namely women) would remain at home to bear the primary responsibility for childcare and care of the elderly (Mikanagi 1998: 184–5).

The series of changes in social security began with a revision in 1980 of the fee schedule for senior citizens' institutional care and accommodation. Prior to 1980, fees for using old-age welfare facilities were paid either by the user or by his or her legal guardian and were based on the individual's taxable income. After 1980, both the user and the guardian were obliged to pay the fees based on the total income of the household, including pension benefits. This legislative revision was followed by the enactment in 1982 of the Law for Health Care of the Aged, which eliminated subsidized medical care for the elderly, established in 1973. This law was further amended in 1986, with the introduction of special facilities for bedridden elderly people who were in need of care but did not require hospitalization. These facilities were designed purely for short-term respite rather than for long-term care. As Mikanagi explains, the purpose of the 1986 amendment was to shift long-term care for the elderly from public facilities and services to *zaitaku* (stay home) care, aided by complementary public assistance (1998: 184). In a bid to ensure that family members stayed at home to take care of the elderly, the government introduced a special tax credit in 1984 for a person living with and supporting aged parents (Osawa 1993: 176). In addition, the government introduced a series of tax measures that rewarded dependent wives of salaried workers at the expense of single workers and couples in full-time employment, thereby encouraging women to remain at home and provide care for their elderly relatives and children (Mikanagi 1998: 185). These gender-reinforcing social security reforms effectively neutralized any gender-rectifying gains made with the introduction of the EEOL.

Furthermore, despite Ministry of Labour claims to the contrary, the corporate sector either ignored the passage of the EEOL or simply developed strategies to circumvent the legislation. As Diana Helweg explains, following the introduction of the legislation, management 'studied methods to evade the law or pay it lip service without sacrificing any traditionally male prerogative of the workplace' (1991: 313). The most successful method devised by management to evade the legislation was the dual-track employment system, which divided employees into two groups – managerial and general clerical – at the time of recruitment. While management claimed that the dual-track employment system was designed to fulfil the equal treatment requirement of the EEOL by eliminating the past informal employer practice of discriminating against women at the point of entry to employment, in reality the system simply disguised the practice, thereby constituting an indirect form of sexual discrimination. As Lam explains, although management maintained that the selection for entry to the different career tracks was based solely on individual merit, in practice men were automatically assigned to the managerial track and women were rarely selected for it (1992: 130–1). Moreover, she argues,

> in the process of selection interviews with management, women were often challenged with tough questions about mobility and potential sacrifices of family life [while] men who intended to select the clerical (or non-mobile) career track were persuaded by [management] to change their mind.
>
> (ibid.: 131)

A common selection criterion for the managerial track was the *mobility requirement*, which involved the applicant being willing to accept company-wide transfers (Sugeno 1992: 132). Women often found it difficult to commit themselves to the mobility requirement at the beginning of their careers, and thus were excluded from the managerial track. More importantly, states Lam, the employment selection system automatically justified 'the differential wage systems, training and promotion opportunities accorded for the different *class* of employees in different career tracks' (1992: 131, 133).

Japanese feminists were vocal in their criticism of the dual-track employment system, arguing that the establishment of government guidelines concerning recruitment and hiring had failed to prevent discrimination in employment. The government rejected this criticism, maintaining that the dual-track employment system was not discriminatory and did not violate the EEOL, and refused to take further enforcement action. Moreover, in a bid to deflect further criticism, the Ministry of Labour rapidly conducted and published the results of a series of surveys indicating a positive shift in management attitudes and policy orientations following the enactment of the legislation. According to the surveys conducted or sponsored by the ministry, the EEOL had induced progressive changes in the areas of recruitment and conditions of employment, and job assignment and retirement.[5] However, according to Lam, these findings should be viewed with caution because of 'the inherent political incentives for the government to emphasise positive results' (1992: 119). Incensed by the government's apparent indifference to the discriminatory hiring practices of management and disillusioned by the government's gender-reinforcing changes to the social security system, feminists endeavoured to expose the contradictions in government regulatory measures and mediation. Furthermore, they demanded a role in the policy-making process.

Tensions between the Japanese government and feminists deepened in 1987, when the government decided to prepare and submit Japan's initial CEDAW report to the UN Committee on the Elimination of Discrimination Against Women without consulting NGOs or independent experts. In its consideration of Japan's initial report in New York in February 1988, the committee drew attention to this lack of consultation with domestic NGOs and expressed strong concern about the apparent disparity between the extraordinary industrial progress and the situation of women in a state that was one of the 'first economic powers in the world' (United Nations General Assembly 1988). It also maintained that such a 'prosperous [state] could afford an independent ministry for women's affairs' (ibid.: 1988). The committee criticized the government's lack of initiative regarding political representation and public childcare facilities, and disapproved of the fact that Japanese women were still discriminated against in employment in respect to recruitment, promotion and salaries (ibid.). The Japanese government responded by arguing that recommendations of international human rights treaty bodies such as the CEDAW committee were not legally binding and, therefore, it was under no obligation to obey the committee's recommendations. Despite pressure from Japanese feminists, who strongly criticized the government's initial CEDAW report, the government failed to initiate comprehensive legislative and public policy changes in accordance with the convention.

At the time, however, the LDP government was in a precarious political position. Acutely embarrassed by a bribery scandal involving high-ranking politicians and bureaucrats, and a sex scandal involving Prime Minister

Uno Sosuke, the government also faced a public backlash against a recently imposed consumption tax. All these were issues in which ordinary Japanese women had a stake, maintains Sally Ann Hastings (1996: 291), and on 3 March 1989 over 2,000 women rallied in Hibiya Park to call for the eradication of the consumption tax and for an investigation into the Recruit Scandal. When allegations of sexual misconduct against Sosuke surfaced a few weeks later, Japanese feminists backed calls for his resignation.[6] The Prime Minister initially refused to step down, and, already labouring under the weight of the Recruit Affair and the consumption tax, the government lost its majority for the first time since 1955 in the elections to half of the membership of the Upper House on 23 July 1989. The Japan Socialist Party (JSP), under the stewardship of Takako Doi (the first female chair of a Japanese political party), not only played an important role in the ruling party's defeat but also emerged as the 'big winner' in the elections (Herzog 1993: 192–3). The JSP put up a large number of female candidates in the elections, and Doi campaigned relentlessly on their behalf on a platform of the 'incorruptibility of women' (Hastings 1996: 291). A record twenty-one Upper House seats went to women in the elections, a phenomenon that was quickly dubbed the madonna boom by journalists (Tomoaki 1993: 105). Within a few months, however, the LDP government recovered its equilibrium and 'Japanese politics was back to business as usual' (Herzog 1993: 195).

The third period of state behavioural continuity: 1990–2004

On 6 June 1990, the Japanese government was forced to confront the subject of violence against women for the first time when Shoji Motooka, a Socialist member of the Upper House, raised the issue of and demanded a government investigation into Japanese military enforced prostitution during the Second World War. It was disclosed to Parliament that during the Second World War, the Japanese military had forcibly and deceptively conscripted approximately 200,000 women from Korea and other parts of Asia for use as military sexual slaves in so-called comfort stations. The LDP government promptly denied any involvement of the Japanese military in comfort-station operations and refused to conduct an investigation (Totsuka 1999: 49). The government's denial angered Korean NGOs that had been working on the issue of Japanese militarized prostitution and had persuaded the South Korean President, Roh Tae Woo, to raise the issue of Japanese government-run comfort stations during a state visit to Japan in May 1990. In July 1990, Korean feminists established the Korean Council for Women Drafted for Military Sex Slavery by Japan (KCWS) to put pressure on the Japanese government (Chung 1997: 234). In alliance with feminists in Japan, Taiwan, Burma, the Philippines and North Korea, the KCWS located and interviewed surviving comfort women (producing two volumes of testimony) and appealed to international bodies such as the UN, the ILO and the International Commission of Jurists (ICJ) for support in its campaign to ensure that the Japanese government admitted legal responsibility for the military enforced prostitution and paid compensation to the victims (Yang 1997: 54).

Encouraged by KCWS's success in piquing the interest of high-profile international bodies in the issue of Japanese military enforced prostitution, the first victims came forward in August 1991, and on 6 December 1991 three South Korean former comfort women filed a lawsuit against the Japanese government for violating their human rights (Watanabe 1994: 4). However, only one of the plaintiffs, Hak-sun Kim, was willing to reveal her name and speak out publicly against the Japanese government. Prior to then, former comfort women had remained silent, owing to the extreme social stigma and shame (see Kim 1997; O'Herne 1994). The case of Kim and her fellow plaintiffs was strengthened in January 1992, when the Japanese historian Professor Yoshimi Yoshikai unearthed official government documents in the archives of the Department of Defence revealing incontrovertible evidence of the Japanese government's direct involvement in the establishment and running of military brothels, or 'comfort stations', during the Second World War. The LDP government questioned the authenticity of the documents, and despite further disclosures by Japanese academics and former Japanese military personnel and despite the UN taking up the issue in February 1992 and again in May 1992, the Japanese government refused to issue a formal apology or admit legal responsibility.[7]

At the time, the Japanese government was desperately trying to deal with two new bribery scandals involving high-ranking politicians and government officials, and within a year, the LDP's thirty-eight years of uninterrupted conservative rule had come to an end.[8] In July 1993, the LDP government was replaced by a seven-party coalition government led by Hosokawa Morihiro, who, during his brief time as Prime Minister, reluctantly expressed regret for the Japanese government's past official involvement in militarized prostitution on an official visit to Seoul in November 1993 (Field 1997: 7). However, Hosokawa refused to admit legal responsibility and set the precedent, since maintained by the Japanese government, of ruling out compensation on the grounds that war compensation between Japan and Korea had already been settled in the 1965 Japan–Republic of Korea normalization agreement on war reparations and in subsequent bilateral treaties (see Hsu 1993: 101–5).

Less than a year, and two governments, later, Japan announced plans to establish a private charity fund – the Asian Women's Fund – to collect donations from the Japanese public as sympathy money for surviving comfort women. This gesture fell a long way short of the demands made by legal advocates representing the comfort women, who protested against the setting up of the fund because it failed to hold the Japanese government legally accountable and because it did not provide for direct compensation (Yoneda 1998: 238). Frustrated by the government's recalcitrance, Japanese human rights lawyers persuaded the ICJ to investigate the matter. The ICJ undertook a fact-finding mission to Japan, and in late November 1994 issued a 240-page report urging the Japanese government to provide full rehabilitation and financial restitution (Dolgopol and Parajape 1994). As an interim measure, the ICJ recommended that the government pay US$40,000 to each survivor. Within a week of the ICJ's report being issued, a group of 105 Japanese and Korean lawyers released a statement proclaiming the responsibility of the Japanese government to compensate former comfort women under international law (Soh 1996: 1237). In the meantime, the KCWS announced plans to file a complaint with the Permanent Court of Arbitration in The Hague in order to determine the extent of the Japanese government's international legal obligation to provide individual compensation. However, because the Japanese government repeatedly refused to agree to arbitration, the complaint could not be heard (International Labour Conference 1996b). Nevertheless, international pressure on the Japanese government to offer a formal apology and to pay restitution out of official funds continued to build.

At the fourth UN World Conference for Women, held in Beijing in 1995, a resolution was adopted supporting the comfort women, despite intense opposition from Japanese government representatives. In January 1996, the UN Special Rapporteur on Violence Against Women, Radhika Coomaraswamy, presented a detailed report on human rights abuses against comfort women to the UN Commission on Human Rights (Oh 2001: 18). In her report, Coomaraswamy described the comfort system as a practice of 'military sexual slavery' and held Japan legally responsible not only for providing compensation to the victims but also for punishing the perpetrators (United Nations Commission on Human Rights 1996). In February 1996, the UN Commission on Human Rights sent a statement to the Japanese government advising it to take legal responsibility for its predecessor's actions (Oh 2001: 18). The same year, the ILO Committee of Experts officially characterized the comfort system as 'sexual slavery' and maintained that it violated the ILO Forced Labour Convention, which, although no longer in force, was nevertheless in force at the time the comfort system was in operation (International Labour Conference 1996b). In 1998, UN Special Rapporteur Gay McDougall presented a report on sexual slavery in armed conflict to the UN Commission on Human Rights in which she described the comfort stations as 'rape centres'. Her report also recommended a series of measures to address the comfort-women issue, including the establishment of an international panel for the pursuit of criminal responsibility and realization of state compensation to individual survivors (United Nations Commission on Human Rights: Subcommission on Prevention of Discrimination and Protection of Minorities 1998).

These investigations and reports by international bodies were critical to the campaign for compensation because, according to Chunghee Sarah Soh,

[t]hey irrevocably transformed the nature of the comfort women debate from bilateral disputes over Japan's insufficiently acknowledged post-war responsibility toward Korean victims (as exemplified by the law-suit brought by Hak-sun Kim and her fellow plaintiffs) to an international indictment of Japan's violations of women's rights during the war.

(2000: 60)

In fact, she argues,

[t]he precedent-setting UN debate . . . resulted in a drastic shift in the paradigm for representing the comfort women. In contrast to the pre-UN debate view of the comfort women as prostitutes, the international community [came] to define them as victims of military sexual enslavement, a war crime perpetrated by the Japanese state.

(ibid.: 60)

However, despite the intense international scrutiny and pressure, the Japanese government continued to refuse to recognize any legal obligation to compensate the victims of the comfort system. Instead, Japanese government representatives contacted and met secretly with South Korean survivors to offer them money in exchange for their silence. A diplomatic crisis between Japan and its neighbour was averted only after the Japanese government agreed to refrain from further clandestine activities (Oh 2001: 19). Furthermore, any hopes the Japanese government may have had that the issue of compensation for the victims of military enforced prostitution would disappear were dashed on 27 April 1998, when a remote Japanese district court rendered a decision ordering the Japanese government to pay compensation to three Korean comfort women.[9]

In the case of *Ha* v. *Japan*, the Shimonoseki branch of the Yamaguchi Prefectural Court found the Japanese government liable to the three plaintiffs for the legislature's failure to enact compensation legislation. The plaintiffs argued that Japan had the 'duty of a moral state' to atone for its crimes, and invoked both international and Japanese law to establish a legal obligation on the part of the Japanese government to compensate victims of wartime aggression, including military sexual slaves (Meade 2002: 234–5). Although the court ultimately rejected these arguments, it nonetheless ruled in favour of the plaintiffs, calling the comfort system a form of sexual and racial discrimination, as well as a fundamental violation of human rights (Okada 1999: 99–100). According to Etsuro Totsuka, the plaintiffs and their legal representatives had chosen to file the lawsuit in the remote district court of Shimonoseki not only because it was the nearest Japanese court for the plaintiffs, who lived in the town of Pusan across the Korean Strait, but also because it 'represented a strategic choice of forum that might be more likely to serve justice instead of serving entrenched government interests' (Totsuka 1999: 54). He states:

> The plaintiffs, their lawyers, and their supporters assumed that conscientious judges willing to consider arguments contrary to governmental claims were not in top positions in large urban areas but, instead, were often transferred to remote districts like Shimonoseki. Thus, it was believed that the plaintiffs were more likely to receive an impartial hearing and a fair judgement in the Shimonoseki Court than in courts of larger cities.
>
> (1999: 54)

The plaintiffs and their supporters greeted the court's decision with jubilation, hailing it as a great victory for comfort women (Meade 2002: 236). However, their joy was short-lived. On 8 May 1998, the Japanese government appealed in the Hiroshima High Court against the Shimonoseki Court's decision and, as feared, the High Court overturned the landmark decision on 29 March 2001. The High Court's ruling affirmed the Japanese government's position that the Japan–Republic of Korea normalization agreement on war reparations settled all claims. The court also argued that 'compensation for former comfort women should be dealt with by the Diet, not by the courts' (ibid.: 237). The three Korean women subsequently filed an appeal with the Supreme Court of Japan but, as expected, the court dismissed their appeal on 25 March 2003 (Green 2003: 15).

Three days before the Hiroshima High Court handed down its decision, the Tokyo District Court dismissed the first-ever case filed by former comfort women in the Japanese courts – the case involving Hak-sun Kim. On 26 March 2001, almost ten years after the case was first filed, the Tokyo District Court ruled against the plaintiffs on the basis that the Japan–Republic of Korea normalization agreement on war reparations foreclosed any right to claim damages against the Japanese government (Meade 2002: 233). Moreover, the court ruled that, if it existed, the right to demand compensation had expired in 1985 – twenty years after the conclusion of the Japan–Republic of Korea agreement (ibid.: 233). Japanese courts have consistently used this argument to dismiss over forty cases brought against the Japanese state by former comfort women since 1991. Despite the lack of success that private group litigants had convincing Japanese courts that compensation and an official apology from the Japanese government were legally justified, former comfort women and their supporters continued their litigation campaign. However, they began to seek redress through the US legal system rather than the Japanese legal system (ibid.: 237). On 9 September 2000, a group of fifteen former comfort women filed a class-action lawsuit against the Japanese government with the District Court for the District of Columbia under the 1789

Alien Tort Claims Act (ATCA).[10] Providing US district courts with jurisdiction over certain violations of international law, ATCA had been successfully used in recent years to bring to justice individuals who had committed human rights atrocities in foreign states.[11] However, it had rarely been used against foreign states themselves because of jurisdictional restrictions under the Foreign Sovereign Immunities Act (FSIA). The plaintiffs in *Hwang* v. *Japan* argued, unsuccessfully, that Japan had explicitly waived immunity by signing the Potsdam Declaration at the end of the Second World War. The Japanese government promptly filed a motion to dismiss the case on 7 March 2001 on the grounds of sovereign immunity – a motion strongly supported by the US State Department. Taking its cue from the executive branch, the court granted Japan's motion to dismiss on 4 October 2001. The plaintiffs appealed against the decision, taking the case to the US Supreme Court, in vain. Their appeal was denied on 21 February 2006, much to the disappointment of survivors, two of whom had been touring US cities at the time in a series of speaking engagements (Gerona-Adkins 2001). The US State Department's open support of the Japanese government's move to dismiss the suit is unsurprising, given its long, covert financing of the Japanese LDP government and its direct influence in orchestrating Japanese historical amnesia in the immediate post-war period (Gluck 2003: 295, 293–4; Igarashi 2000; George Hicks 1997). Perhaps more significant is the indifference of Allied occupation forces to the plight of the comfort women, US military-controlled prostitution and the US government's failure to come to terms with the suffering it inflicted during its wars in Asia and elsewhere, or to provide restitution to its victims.[12]

Despite the failure of the litigation campaign in the United States, pressure continued to mount on the Japanese government in the form of the Tokyo Women's International War Crimes Tribunal, an international citizens' tribunal[13] convened by the Japan-based NGO Violence Against Women in War Network and with a Japanese and international audience of more than 1,300 in attendance. The tribunal was presided over by the former head of the Yugoslavia International War Crimes Tribunal, Gabrielle McDonald, and ran from 8 to 12 December 2000. During the controversial trial of the Japanese state, the tribunal heard testimonies from more than forty former comfort women, and in its final judgment found the State of Japan guilty of breaching international law by refusing to bring the perpetrators to justice or to acknowledge its own responsibility (Millet 2000). The tribunal also found the Japanese Emperor Hirohito guilty of war crimes. Despite the tribunal's lack of legal authority, this finding was significant because it highlighted the indelible link between the Emperor's impunity from prosecution and that of the Japanese government and high-ranking government officials (Hirofumi 2001: 579–80). The tribunal attracted enormous international media attention. Unfortunately, it also attracted a virulent backlash from conservative

Japanese political leaders and intellectuals, who attacked the legitimacy of the tribunal and the veracity of survivors' testimony and claims. This political backlash was, in fact, part of a wider campaign by Japanese neonationalists to expunge the past and reassert a 'healthy' sense of nationhood and national pride (see Igarashi 2000). These convictions are shared by many upper-echelon officials in the Japanese government, which refused to recognize the tribunal and disassociated itself from any legal responsibility to compensate victims of military enforced prostitution. The government is now looking for what it calls a biological solution to the comfort-women problem. For the Japanese administration, a sincere apology and compensation to survivors of the Japanese comfort system was not an issue of justice but rather a public relations problem that it hoped would fade away as the survivors died of old age or the lingering effects of war-inflicted injury or disease (Hahm 2001: 128).

In the early 1990s, the Japanese government was also forced to confront another issue concerning gender-based violence, namely sexual harassment in the workplace. Japanese feminists and lawyers were instrumental in bringing the issue of sexual harassment to the attention of both the general public and the political elite. Activists began to take advantage of sexual harassment lawsuits against American affiliates of Japanese corporations to raise the issue in Japan. Prior to 1990, the concept of sexual harassment simply did not exist in Japan because there was no term in the Japanese language for sexual harassment other than the vague and rarely used phrase *seiteki iyagarase* (sex-related unpleasantness). According to Rochelle Kopp (1998: 45, 49), Japanese feminists imported the term 'sexual harassment' directly from the United States and shortened it from *sekushuaru harasumento* to *sekuhara* in common language. In 1991, the Santama Association of Occupational Safety and Health surveyed 10,000 Japanese women concerning sexual harassment in the workplace, and by publicizing the results hoped to focus public and political attention on the problem (Hayashi 1994). The following year, on 16 April 1992, the Fukuoka District Civil Court ruled in favour of the complainant in the first sexual harassment case in Japan (Watanabe 1996: 33). With no existing national legislation explicitly prohibiting sexual harassment, the court was forced to invoke the Civil Code in its decision to hold Kyu Kikaku Publishing Company liable for failing to maintain a non-hostile working environment (Patterson 1993: 206).

The decision attracted even more media attention than when the case was originally filed in 1989. One newspaper editorialist proclaimed that the ruling marked Japan's alignment with the rest of the world, and another remarked that 'the decision reinforced the feeling that times were changing and that employers could no longer safely ignore workplace sexual harassment' (Patterson 1993: 206). Buoyed by the extraordinary media interest in the case, Japanese legal advocates began to examine the problem of sexual harassment and to analyse possible legal remedies. Soon, leading Japanese law journals and periodicals were publishing articles and even special editions dedicated to the issue of sexual harassment (Wolff 1996: 518–19). Advocates demanded that the government either make an amendment to the EEOL to include sexual harassment provisions or enact a separate piece of sexual harassment legislation (Patterson 1993: 221). Once again, the government adopted the tactic of trying to outlast domestic pressure by claiming that it needed time to study the issue. The Ministry of Labour announced that it would conduct an extensive survey to determine the extent of the problem and whether *formal* measures were necessary to combat sexual harassment in the workplace. After conducting the survey, the only action the government took was to distribute educational pamphlets to employers in 1994. However, the government came under renewed pressure to take legislative action on sexual harassment in early 1996, when the United States Equal Employment Opportunity Commission (EEOC) filed a large class action against the United States subsidiary of Mitsubishi Motors. As Kopp explains, 'the lawsuit against Mitsubishi Motors put a spotlight on the subject of sexual harassment in Japanese companies, both in their international operations and in Japan' (1998: 42). The EEOC lawsuit, which was filed in the Federal District Court in Peoria, Illinois, was filed on behalf of hundreds of women who had worked at the Mitsubishi Motors plant in Norma, Illinois, since 1990. According to Kopp, Japanese corporate management, both in the United States and Japan, paid close attention to the suit's potential damages of US$300,000 per employee, or US$150 million in total damages. Soon after the case was filed, the Japan Overseas Enterprises Association held an emergency seminar on sexual harassment, which attracted nearly 100 personnel managers from large Japanese corporations (ibid.: 42).

In mid-1996, at the request of Japanese feminists, the Vice President of the United States-based National Organization for Women (NOW), Rosemary Dempsey, travelled to Tokyo for a week-long series of events to raise awareness about sexual harassment, which culminated in international demonstrations against Mitsubishi Motors held simultaneously in the United States and Japan on 27 June. In Japan, the demonstration started with a press conference and a protest outside the annual shareholders' meeting of Mitsubishi Motors. During her trip to Tokyo, Dempsey met with government and union officials, business leaders, the Minister of Labour and representatives of Mitsubishi Motors (Corbin 1996). As a result, in August 1996, the Ministry of Labour pledged to provide employers with more specific guidelines and techniques for preventing sexual harassment (Kopp 1998: 49). The ministry also promised to consider including sexual harassment provisions in any amendments to the EEOL. However, as the EEOC class action floundered in the American courts, Japanese corporations lost interest in the issue of sexual harassment. According to Pauline Reich, corporations became complacent and believed that it was unnecessary to adopt preventive measures such as training Japanese managers before they were posted overseas (1988: 85). Eventually, Mitsubishi Motors Manufacturing of America agreed to pay a US$34 million out-of-court settlement to end the class-action sexual harassment lawsuit brought against it by the EEOC (Friedman 1999). The settlement, which was reached on 10 June 1998, was the largest ever such settlement in the United States, and both the Japanese government and the corporate sector took heed (BBC News 1999).

By this time, the Japanese government had reluctantly succumbed to intense international and domestic pressure to revise Japanese labour legislation and, in amending the EEOL in June 1997, had included a provision prohibiting sexual harassment. However, as Leon Wolff explains, the provision, Section 21, is far from bold and 'manages not to even use the term sexual harassment'. Even more disappointingly, he continues, it 'neither explicitly outlaws acts of sexual harassment nor provides penalties if corporations fail to provide a workplace free of sexual harassment' (2003: 158). For several years prior to these revisions, Japanese feminists had levelled criticisms at the original EEOL regarding a wide range of employment issues besides sexual harassment in the workplace. The Working Women's International Network (WWIN) had repeatedly brought complaints about the legislation before the ILO, CEDAW and the UN Human Rights Commission in an effort to draw public attention and embarrass the Japanese government. Other groups, such as the Working Women in the Shosha Trading Companies, had also submitted reports highly critical of the EEOL and the government's implementation of the law to the UN Commission on the Status of Women. In its 1992 report, the Shosha group argued that the EEOL had actually 'worsened the circumstances surrounding women's labour and even made their work more difficult' (Gelb 2003: 53).

The UN Committee on the Elimination of Discrimination Against Women had also criticized, among other practices, Japanese state employment policies. Furthermore, the mediation procedure attached to the EEOL had also been seriously challenged by private group litigation in the mid-1990s. In the early 1990s, the ILO Committee of Experts repeatedly criticized Japan's persistently high wage differential between men and women. The committee concluded that the seniority wage system, together with the concentration of women in lower-paid jobs and a lack of equal employment opportunities, appeared to be the primary cause of the wage gap and urged the Japanese government to introduce a wage system based on job content (UNCEDAW 1993). It also called on the government to execute 'additional measures to ensure that existing inequalities in recruitment and hiring, assignment, and promotion ... be remedied' (International Labour Conference 1992: 300). Furthermore, the committee demanded that the government implement the principle of equal pay for work of equal value in accordance with the ILO Equal Remuneration Convention (ibid.: 300).

However, the Japanese government failed to act on the ILO committee's recommendations. In a bid to deflect further international criticism, the Japanese government submitted a report to the ILO, in 1996, containing misleading information concerning the wage gap between men and women in Japan. According to the government report submitted to the ILO, the wage gap had narrowed to 20 per cent, whereas in fact it had widened to almost 40 per cent since the enactment of the EEOL in 1985. That the wage disparity was comparatively large and had been widening was apparent from a basic statistical survey on wage structure conducted by the Japanese Ministry of Labour in 1996, in which it was determined that the average wage of women under regular employment was only 60.4 per cent that of men (see JCLU 1998). Outraged by the government's distortion of the wage differential in Japan, the Japanese Workers' Committee for Human Rights, in partnership with the WWIN, sent a communiqué to the ILO disputing the government's statistic.[14] In October 1997, twelve members of the WWIN travelled to Geneva to brief the ILO and the UN Human Rights Committee on current discrimination in employment litigation in Japan and to present statistical data on existing employment conditions, including wages. According to a WWIN representative, the group went to Geneva in the hope that it would generate further international pressure on the Japanese government to revise national employment legislation and policies (Salem Hicks 1997).

The Japanese government was also under pressure from the UN CEDAW committee to modify its employment practices and to address the problems of women's political under-representation, discriminatory practices relating to civil rights (marriage and family relations), violence against women, and insufficient support for the reconciliation of work and family responsibilities. In late January 1994, the committee considered Japan's second and third periodic reports in New York. The committee criticized the state for submitting reports that were purely descriptive and lacked any 'critical analysis of the obstacles to full implementation of the convention in Japan' (United Nations General Assembly 1995). The committee also criticized the Japanese state for failing to recognize any specific problem areas or issues of sexual discrimination. With respect to employment, the committee criticized the state for failing to comply with the principle of equal pay for work of equal value, and for failing to implement adequate measures in the areas of employment opportunity and part-time employment. It argued that the dual-track employment system practised by the corporate sector indirectly discriminated against women in terms of promotion and wages, and that such practices 'needed to be prosecuted' (United Nations General Assembly 1994). Moreover, the committee demanded that the state take steps to ensure that the corporate sector eliminated such discrimination but questioned whether the Japanese government actually understood the concept of indirect discrimination. It urged the government to revise the EEOL to include the concept of indirect discrimination (ibid.).

When drafting Japan's second and third periodic CEDAW reports, the Japanese government, once again, failed to consult Japanese NGOs or independent experts.[15] Frustrated and disillusioned by this, a number of Japanese NGOs submitted shadow reports to the CEDAW committee, and twenty-four NGO representatives attended the committee meeting in New York to consider Japan's second and third periodic reports. Thirteen of the twenty-four NGO representatives were members of the Japanese Association of International Women's Rights (JAIWR), which had been established in 1987 and provided other Japanese NGOs with information and training on the CEDAW (Yoneda 2000: 68). The JAIWR also helped representatives of the Osaka Group Campaigning for the Abolishment of Discrimination Against Women set up an informal meeting with CEDAW committee members in New York to discuss employment issues confronting Japanese women. In a bid to reveal the real story of employment conditions in Japan, the Osaka Group had submitted a shadow report to the CEDAW committee, and group representatives were cheered by the moral support offered by committee members (see Osaka Group Campaigning for the Abolishment of Discrimination Against Women 1993). According to Masumi Yoneda, committee members encouraged the Osaka Group representatives to 'continue to fight the difficulties they faced in Japan' (Yoneda 2000: 69). On their return to Japan, the Osaka Group representatives decided to lend their support to private individual and group litigants filing lawsuits against the Sumitomo group of companies after government mediation under the EEOL had either failed or been refused.

The series of lawsuits filed against the Sumitomo group of companies in 1995 seriously challenged the Ministry of Labour's implicit policy of avoiding mediation in cases of employee complaints regarding promotion in employment. The litigation campaign against Sumitomo began when seven female employees from Sumitomo Metal Incorporated applied for mediation on 23 March 1994. However, mediation was deferred because the company reported to the Ministry of Labour that it would offer the complainants a settlement. In May, management met with the complainants to reach an agreement, but, in its settlement offer, Sumitomo Metal refused to acknowledge that its promotion practices discriminated against female employees. Insulted by the management's settlement offer, the complainants refused to negotiate with the company further and pressed for mediation. By mid-August, the Ministry of Labour became convinced that the dispute should go to mediation, and although Sumitomo Metal denied the allegation of sexual discrimination, it eventually agreed to mediation in order to clear its name. On 13 September, the ministry informed the seven complainants, through its Osaka Women and Minors Bureau, that mediation would take place. On 20 February 1995, the Osaka Equal Opportunity Mediation Commission delivered its recommendations (Kamiya 1995: 76–8). Being the first case of mediation conducted under the EEOL since the legislation was enacted in 1985, the Sumitomo Metal dispute attracted considerable media attention. However, neither Sumitomo Metal nor the complainants were willing to accept the Osaka commission's recommendations because, while Sumitomo Metal felt vindicated by the commission's recommendation that it merely *adjust* its dual-track employment system, the complainants 'felt that given the commission's refusal to match the complaints with individualized remedies and failure to state any findings concerning the alleged sexual discrimination, they had not been appropriately heard' (ibid.: 77).

At the same time that the Ministry of Labour was putting pressure on Sumitomo Metal to reach an in-house settlement with its complainants, it was also urging Sumitomo Chemicals Incorporated to do the same regarding a similar complaint made against the company. However, Sumitomo Chemicals refused to resolve the dispute in-house (Hayashi 2000). In other similar disputes involving Sumitomo Electric Incorporated and Sumitomo Life Insurance Incorporated, the Ministry of Labour decided against pressing the two companies to reach in-house settlements. In both cases, the ministry turned down the complainants' request for mediation on the basis that their allegations of discrimination were insupportable. With the support of the Osaka Group, the disgruntled employees in all four cases simultaneously filed lawsuits against the Sumitomo group of companies in August 1995. In the case of Sumitomo Electric, the complainants also sued the Japanese government for failing to implement Article 2 of CEDAW, claiming damages against the state and the company. The Japanese government responded by arguing that ratification of CEDAW did not demand the immediate elimination of discrimination against women in all fields, but rather the gradual elimination of discrimination over some time. However, as Yoneda points out, such an interpretation of the demands of ratification 'cannot be drawn from the wording of Article 2 of CEDAW or from its drafting history' (2000: 67).

Being the first case in which a Japanese court had had to interpret CEDAW, the *Sumitomo Electric* case attracted considerable media attention, which made the Japanese government very uneasy. As hearings in the case in the Osaka District Court dragged on, the government reluctantly yielded to mounting international and domestic pressure to revise the 1985 Equal Employment Opportunity Law. On 14 January 1997, the Ministry of Labour presented a draft bill amending the EEOL and other related provisions in the 1947 Labour Standards Law to the Diet. The bill was passed at the ordinary session of the Diet on 11 June 1997 and the revisions became effective on 1 April 1999. However, while the amended legislation extended the principle of sexual non-discrimination to the areas of recruitment, job assignment and promotion, prohibited sexual harassment and abolished the requirement of consent to begin mediation, it still lacked effective enforcement mechanisms to deter violations, and insisted on mediation to resolve disputes arising between employers and employees instead of legal redress. Moreover, under the amended legislation, the final settlement by mediation still depended on both parties' consent (Hanami 2000).

Only months after the revised EEOL became effective, the Japanese government came under renewed international pressure in the *Sumitomo Electric* case. On 15 October 1999, the director of the internationally accredited International Women's Rights Action Watch (IWRAW), Dr Marsha Freeman, submitted a statement to the Osaka District Court on behalf of the plaintiffs, outlining in detail CEDAW's requirements and the responsibility of the Japanese state and Sumitomo Electric to redress sexual discrimination in employment (Yoneda 2000: 72, n 14). IWRAW representatives also attended the occasional hearing in court (International Women's Rights Action Watch 1997). However, Dr Freeman's statement made no difference to the court's decision, with the presiding judge, Tetsuo Matsumoto, turning down the plaintiffs' claims for damages on 31 July 2000. In his judgment, Matsumoto argued that although Sumitomo Electric's policy of excluding high-school graduate female employees from managerial positions contravened Article 14 of the Japanese Constitution, at the time the plaintiffs were appointed in the 1960s such employment practices were the social norm and did not disturb the public order (Yoneda 2000: 72, n 14). He added that the EEOL did not oblige companies to redress discriminatory employment practices in place prior to the law's enactment in 1985 (Working Women's Network 2000). As for the responsibility of the state, the court ruled that the EEOL had no retroactive effect and, therefore, was inapplicable in the plaintiffs' case. Anticipating that the court would tolerate Sumitomo Electric's employment practices, lawyers representing the plaintiffs had made a preliminary requisition for such a case, arguing that the company had an obligation to redress its discriminatory management practices in due course (Miyachi 2000). The court turned down the plaintiffs' preliminary requisition, however, stating that the company was not obliged to redress its labour management practices, because they did not offend public standards of decency (ibid.).

Even small gains made with the 1997 amendments to the EEOL were offset by further changes to the social security system, when the Japanese government, confronted by a rapidly ageing society and falling birth rate, introduced measures that increased the burden of care on women. In 1998, a government white paper on welfare stated that, while the ageing population and diminishing birth rate will raise social security costs in the future, 'because the vitality of society and economy have to be maintained ... steps should be taken to make the social security benefits and premiums more efficient and rational' (Osawa 2000: 14). According to Mari Osawa, this meant that harsh fiscal restraints were, once again, imposed on the social security system and as much of the caring as possible was transferred from the public sector to the private sector (ibid.: 14–15). As both a counter-measure to the marked decline in the birth rate and an attempt to improve employee (female) availability to provide care-taking in the private, familial sector, the government introduced a revised Act on Childcare and Leave for Nursing in 1994, which provided up to twelve months' parental leave and leave for up to three months for the care of sick relatives – primarily care of frail elderly parents (Morozumi 1998: 60). The revised Act became effective on 1 April 1999. Ironically, the Japanese government based ratification of the ILO Workers with Family Responsibilities Convention on the original, unrevised legislation, the 1991 Childcare Leave Law. Ratification took place on 9 June 1995.

Finally, under domestic and international pressure following the UN World Conference for Women in Beijing in 1995, the Japanese government was forced to confront the issue of domestic violence. Japanese feminists returned from the Beijing conference determined to press the government to take action on the issue of domestic violence, which, because of the traditional notion of marital privacy, was considered a private matter protected from state intervention (Gaul 1998: 30). Predictably, the Japanese government responded by stating that it required time to study the issue of domestic violence. In 1999, the government conducted a nationwide survey to determine the extent of the problem, and, after further lobbying from Japanese feminists, it finally passed the Law for the Prevention of Spousal Violence and the Protection of Victims on 6 April 2001. However, while the domestic violence legislation, which became effective on 13 October 2001, gives victims some protection, it fails to make domestic violence a crime. The legislation permits district courts to issue six-month restraining orders against a perpetrator of domestic violence and to evict a perpetrator from the home for up to two weeks. If the restraining order is violated, the court can issue a jail term of up to a year and a fine of up to one million yen (approximately US$8,000). However, to obtain a restraining order under the legislation, the burden of proof is on the victim. Furthermore, the law does not include a provision for the courts to issue emergency injunctions against abusive partners without a hearing. There is also no recourse for women seeking legal protection from and redress for marital rape. Further, on numerous occasions, the courts have upheld the husband's right to coerce his wife into having sex (Rice 2001). In one such case, a Tokyo court actually blamed the plaintiff for having caused her husband to resort to sexual assault and found that, 'although it involved a certain degree of violent acts, it is within the range of the degree of force used in fights among ordinary married couples and, thus, does not warrant a special consideration [by the court]' (cited in Yoshihama 2000: 543).

Conclusion

Japan has been highly resistant to incorporating international norms of sexual non-discrimination and, despite considerable domestic and international criticism, has developed effective strategies and tactics to delay and avoid comprehensive legislative and public policy changes on the issues of women's civil, political and labour rights, and also on the issue of violence against women. With the exception of long-delayed revisions to citizenship and labour laws in 1985, and some modest legislative changes on the issues of employment and domestic violence in 1997 and 2001 respectively, there have been virtually no changes to state behaviour across the issue-areas studied since Allied occupation forces left Japan in 1952. The story of Japan's response to international norms of sexual non-discrimination since 1952 has been dominated, as we have seen, by three periods of state behavioural continuity in which the state created and consolidated a profoundly patrilineal corporate identity and resisted international and domestic pressure to ratify and comply with international conventions governing women's human rights. The last two periods of stasis were punctuated on occasion by changes to state practices compelled by a combination of external and internal pressure, but the changes were minimal and commonly neutralized by other, gender-reinforcing state policies. The pressure emanating from international criticism, domestic feminist activism and litigation, although sustained, has largely failed to generate substantial state behavioural change in accordance with international norms of sexual non-discrimination.

7 India

Since gaining independence from British rule on 14 August 1947, the Indian state has been extremely reluctant to incorporate international norms of sexual non-discrimination. In fact, in recent years, the state has been increasingly loath to do so. The most significant impediment to norm diffusion has been the gender-biased corporate identity of the state, which was politically and judicially reconstituted in the post-independence period as an implicitly communalist nation in which women are subordinate to various religious communities within the state. For although independent India was established as a secular state, successive Indian governments have given precedence to systems of personal law based on Hindu, Muslim, Christian or Parsi religious norms over other legal provisions that might have some bearing on the provisions of personal law. Also, in the post-independence period, government public policy-making was based on the notion of women as supplicants in need of the protection of the state. This imbued the corporate identity of the state with a paternalistic aspect. In recent years, the Indian government has tacitly sought to establish the supremacy of Hinduism and create a Hindu state predicated on asymmetric gender relations in both the familial and the social contexts. The deeply paternalistic and increasingly communalist corporate identity of the state has effectively prevented the diffusion of international norms of sexual non-discrimination.

This chapter examines why the Indian state has been antipathetic to incorporating international norms of sexual non-discrimination. It also examines why domestic feminist activism and international pressure have failed to induce substantive state legislative amendments and public policies that are extensive in their scope and implementation. It examines why the state resisted ratifying the primary international treaty on sexual non-discrimination, the United Nations (UN) Convention on the Elimination of Discrimination Against Women (CEDAW), and why it finally ratified the convention on 9 July 1993 with significant reservations. It also examines why the state has failed to comply with CEDAW and other ratified conventions. The chapter begins by tracing the political reconstitution of the paternalistic and implicitly communalist corporate identity of the state in the wake of independence, before examining how this identity construction has affected the diffusion of international norms of sexual non-discrimination. Applying the analytical argument elaborated in previous chapters, I investigate how and why the state has consistently resisted the incorporation of international norms of sexual non-discrimination. I argue that the state's response to these norms is one of behavioural continuity. We can identify four periods of state behavioural continuity between 1947 and 2004 in which social interaction tends to result in the reproduction of discriminatory state practices.

The first period of state behavioural continuity, from 1947 to 1974, saw the state ratify a number of key international conventions but fail to comply with any of these conventions. It saw Indian feminists of the pre-independence period form an alliance with the state that led to complacency among activists about their achievements and the state's commitment to gender equality. It also saw feminists and the state discursively share similar ideas concerning the role of women in society. Thus, there was no contentious discursive interaction between Indian feminists and the state. It was also a period in which state imperatives of national integration and political stability took precedence over eliminating highly discriminatory religious personal or civil laws. The second period of state behavioural continuity, from 1975 to 1984, saw the Indian government declare a state of emergency, from June 1975 to March 1977, and flirt openly with religious communal politics at the expense of secularism. It also saw domestic feminists become aware of the enormous disparities between urban-based middle- and upper-class Indian women like themselves and the vast majority of rural-based and lower-class women. Further, it saw Indian feminists exploit the government's recognition of the UN International Women's Year (IWY) to press for legislative and public policy changes on a range of issues, including violence against women. However, the government responded with empty promises and cosmetic changes.

The third period of state behavioural continuity, from 1985 to 1995, saw the state eventually ratify CEDAW but refuse to comply with the international convention. In fact, in this period, the state implemented civil legislation that directly contravened the convention. The period witnessed the state pandering to communal politics and resisting domestic feminist pressure to reverse its decision to implement regressive civil legislation. It also saw the state successfully resist feminist pressure to enact and implement substantive legislation on issues of gender-based violence. The fourth period of state behavioural continuity, from 1996 to 2004, saw the state attempt to silence its international and domestic critics and divert attention from its increasingly conservative agenda by appropriating and championing the domestic feminist political cause. It also saw the state attempt to stifle public debate and threaten to deregister feminist non-governmental organizations (NGOs) that criticized its policies.

Post-independence reconstruction of the gender-biased corporate identity of the state

In the post-independence period, the Indian government politically reconstituted a paternalistic and implicitly communalist corporate state identity based on a dualistic understanding of women as simultaneously supplicants in need of the protection of the state and subordinate to various religious communities within the state. Despite its much-vaunted commitment to gender equality, the Indian government implemented a range of public policies aimed at providing adequate social services to ensure that women were able to fulfil their 'legitimate role in the family' and protecting them from hazards in the labour force 'for which they were physically unfit' (Banerjee 1998: WS-4). Also, the Indian government, while professing secularism, refused to revise the highly discriminatory system of religious personal or family laws on the basis that the individual religious communities, rather than the state, should initiate legal change. In the aftermath of Partition, the Indian government argued that its primary responsibility was to reassure the religious communities, particularly the Muslim community, rather than exacerbate their anxieties about their status and future in independent India by imposing a common or uniform civil code (Hasan 1994: 61–2). Furthermore, in the immediate post-independence period, the government persuaded many pre-independence feminists involved with the nationalist movement to work in partnership with it to modernize India and, in the process, rid society of inequalities.

Often affiliated with major NGOs such as the Women's Indian Association, the National Council of Women in India, and the All India Women's Conference, some of these pro-independence feminists were elected or nominated to government legislative bodies, while others were appointed to public service positions in the expanding social welfare and educational sectors. For instance, when the government established the Central Social Welfare Board (CSWB) in 1953, a number of prominent pro-independence feminists were appointed to the board (Desai 1986: 287). The following year, Social Welfare Boards were set up in each state to assist and advise the CSWB, and were likewise largely staffed by pro-independence feminists (Caplan 1985: 24). Almost all these activists were from the urban middle and upper classes and had entered the pro-independence movement through voluntary social work, where they became conscious of social inequalities and privations suffered by women under colonial rule. For many, explains Geraldine Forbes, improving the status of Indian women seemed dependent on freedom from British imperialism (Forbes 1982: 533–4). The post-independence government exploited this and the belief of many activists in selfless, unpaid social work to provide an ad hoc social welfare system on the cheap. The government viewed social work as a natural extension of women's familial *service,* and both the CSWB and the State Social Welfare Advisory Boards were established on the basis of voluntary service.

The CSWB was established primarily to distribute a nationwide programme of government grants-in-aid to voluntary welfare organizations, which were encouraged by the government to view women as beneficiaries of, rather than active participants in, economic development. The government deliberately fostered this view of women by formulating economic policies based on a trickle-down theory of development and a belief in the welfare state as a means of alleviating poverty. The government drew up five-year economic development plans and asked prominent women's organizations to participate in the drafting process. These organizations agreed with the government that strong economic growth was a priority because they presumed that ordinary women would automatically gain from the expected prosperity (Forbes 1996: 225). Thus, while the five-year plans incorporated social objectives, these were subordinate to economic objectives. Moreover, in the First Five-Year Plan (1951–6), the government drew a clear distinction between social welfare and social services. Whereas the government reserved the scope of social welfare for the underprivileged and vulnerable in society – essentially women and children – it directed social services in health, housing and education to the 'betterment of human resources in general' (Government of India 1968: 403). This distinction meant that, while social services were administratively co-ordinated with an integrated national approach, social welfare issues were split between different ministerial departments with no clear objectives or priorities (Sharma 1988: xxiv). In fact, administering social welfare was left largely to the discretion of voluntary agencies and thus not included in the planned development process (ibid.: 82). With the activities of voluntary agencies determined by the programmes for which government grants were available, this meant that the social welfare administered by such agencies consisted of literacy programmes and courses in housewifery, nutritional programmes and the dispensing of medicines (Desai 1986: 292; Caplan 1985: 24). Furthermore, while successive post-independent governments allocated between 12 per cent and 20 per cent of the total budget of the various Plans to social services, they never allocated more than 0.3 per cent to social welfare (Caplan 1985: 23).

As they became increasingly allied with the government, feminist activists lost much of their pre-independence dynamism. The government's economic modernization programme best served urban middle- and upper-class women, who became beneficiaries of new educational and employment opportunities, and this strengthened the illusion of a marked improvement in the situation of Indian women in general. Since these classes dominated the leadership of the pre-independence women's movement, their advantaged position led them to believe they had achieved gender equality. According to Neera Desai, this inevitably had a detrimental effect on the post-independence women's movement as a whole. For although individual women and more radical feminists affiliated with the Communist Party voiced their dissatisfaction with government social policies and economic development plans, the drive and militancy of the movement rapidly faded as the core acquiesced and supported the status quo (1986: 293). Even the government's compromises with religious minority communities in the original constitutional debates failed to alter the perception among pre-independence feminists that they had achieved many of their objectives and that other beneficial changes would inevitably follow (Misra 1997: 29).

The original constitutional debates in the late 1940s were lengthy and intense, with the subjects of fundamental rights and directive principles of state policy attracting the most attention and criticism in the Constituent Assembly. In the course of Constituent Assembly deliberations, debate typically focused on the precise meaning of secularism and the attendant questions concerning the relationship between religion and the state, and the relationship between the right to equality and the right of religious denominations to organize their own affairs. The debate concerning the meaning of secularism and the state–religion relationship was further complicated by the question of a uniform civil code. Despite the central legislature's genuine commitment to creating a liberal democratic polity, the leading cabal or inner group of the Constituent Assembly successfully defended a constitutional definition of secularism that contrasted sharply with a liberal democratic conceptualization of secularism characterized by the complete separation between religion and the state. Influenced by the aftermath of Partition, the leading cabal of the Constituent Assembly favoured a definition of secularism based on the principle of equal respect for all religions – *saarva dharma samabhava*. Following from this dominant understanding of secularism, the question of a uniform civil code was relegated to the section on directive principles of state policy, despite the protest of progressive Constituent Assembly members.

In the Constituent Assembly, progressives disputed the claim by members belonging to the Muslim community that their personal law constituted part of their religion and should, therefore, remain outside the control or reach of the state (Parashar 1992: 212–13). Progressives argued in vain that

> [o]ne of the factors that have kept India back from advancing to nationhood has been the existence of the personal laws based on religion, which keep the nation divided into watertight compartments in many aspects of life. We are of the view that a uniform civil code should be guaranteed to the Indian people ... [and] therefore suggest that the Advisory Committee might transfer the clause regarding a uniform civil code from Part II to Part I.
>
> (Dhagamwar 1993: 218)

The uniform civil code remained consigned to the section on directive principles of state policy of the Constitution rather than being reassigned to the section on fundamental rights, which meant that the state could shelve the enactment of a common civil code indefinitely. This was because constitutional directive principles were not judicially enforceable and represented an indefinite agenda for social change. The question of a uniform civil code was also inextricably linked with wider political considerations of national integration and political stability. The government, confronted with the challenge of unifying a nation deeply divided along religious lines in the wake of Partition, was wary of taking any legislative steps that might be construed as prejudicial by the minority religious communities, especially the Muslim community. The government feared that any attempt to reform or replace religious personal laws with a uniform civil code would jeopardize integration because it would engender a sense of helplessness and alienation among the already apprehensive minority religious communities (Parashar 1992: 159).

The government's decision not to revise religious personal laws was also a reaction to the rising influence of the *ulema* (theologians) and other Muslim conservatives, who exploited heightened communal tensions after Partition to conflate Islamic personal law and community identity. Muslim conservatives argued that secularism would become meaningless if the central legislature amended Muslim personal law (which had been codified in 1937 within the framework of the *Shariat*) without their support. Furthermore, they argued that only the *ulema* were competent to approve legislative changes to the *Shariat* (Hasan 1993: 7). The government accepted the argument of Muslim leaders that the *Shariat* was immutable, and by doing so, states Archana Parashar, 'gave priority to its responsibility to integrate the minorities into the national mainstream over the need to ensure legal equality for women' (1992: 159). Progressives and feminists tried to convince the government that having different personal laws actually threatened the integrity of the nation and that, by endorsing such a system of civil law, the state risked impeding legislative changes in other areas. Moreover, they argued that the government's failure to secularize family law through the enactment of a uniform civil code was likely to fan the flames of communal strife rather than quell communal tensions (Tummala 1993: 60). The government reacted by reassuring progressives and feminists that its decision not to interfere with minority personal laws was only temporary and that once India was ready, it would replace religious personal laws with a uniform civil code.

Yet the government gave no indication as to when it would initiate proceedings to dissociate civil law from religion. However, shortly after the new Constitution came into effect in the summer of 1951, the government initiated proceedings to reform the religious personal law of the majority Hindu community. According to Parashar, the government's underlying motive for doing so was the same as its motive for not intervening and revising minority religious personal laws: national integration. However, whereas in the case of the latter, the government relied on non-intervention to pacify minority communities and achieve their national integration, in the case of the former, the government relied on intervention to increase its sphere of authority over the majority religious community and further national integration. Despite its claims to the contrary, argues Parashar, ensuring gender equality was never the government's intention in deciding whether or not to intervene and revise religious personal laws (1992: 268). Nevertheless, the government's decision to revise Hindu personal law met with vehement opposition from conservative quarters within the Congress government itself and from within the wider Hindu community. Even progressives within the ruling government resisted changes to Hindu personal law because they felt that revising the personal law of only one religious community amounted to a 'secular state encouraging communalism' (Kapur and Cossman 1996b: 57).

Despite the staunch opposition, the government pressed ahead with the revisions to Hindu personal law, not because it intended to ensure gender equality, as it claimed publicly, but because it was determined to integrate 85 per cent of the Indian population and establish state authority over the Hindu religious community. For it had become clear to the government that it could not rely on Hindu community leaders to support its plans to modernize and industrialize India. Therefore, the government decided that it had to try to replace individual allegiance to the Hindu religious community with an allegiance to the new state and the social values that it wanted to inculcate (Parashar 1992: 77–8, 140). The government believed that the most effective way of asserting its authority over the Hindu religious community was through the revision of Hindu personal law. The government's proposed revisions to Hindu personal law were finally debated in Parliament in one long and heated session in 1951. Conservatives opposed to the Hindu Code Bill argued that the legislative amendments violated the constitutional principle of religious freedom and discriminated against religious communities. Progressives opposed to the bill argued that the revisions violated the constitutional principles of secularism and equality. The government argued, to the contrary, that the Constitution gave the state the authority to reform or intervene in religious personal laws. The Law Minister, Dr B. R. Ambedkar, explained the position of the government by stating that 'the Constitution permitted it to treat different communities differently without attracting the charge of practising discrimination'. He argued that 'although the Constitution permitted people to profess and practise their religion and to have their personal law because personal law was embedded in religion, the state had always retained its right to interfere in the personal law of any community' (ibid.: 97). Ambedkar also refuted any suggestion that by codifying only Hindu personal law, the state was departing from its declared intention to secularize civil law. He maintained that 'the reason there was no reform of

Muslim law or that of other religious communities was that these communities had not been consulted and it would be unfair to impose reforms on them without consultation' (ibid.: 97–8).

However, despite the Law Minister's efforts to defend the Hindu Code Bill, the legislative amendments seemed destined for defeat, and when the Prime Minister, Jawaharlal Nehru, withdrew his support for the bill, Ambedkar resigned. In his resignation statement, Ambedkar criticized Nehru for capitulating to those who opposed the bill. He stated:

> I got the impression that the Prime Minister although sincere had not the earnestness and determination required to get the Hindu Code Bill through. The Bill was the greatest social reform measure ever undertaken by the legislature in the country. To leave untouched the inequality between class and class, between sex and sex, and to go passing legislation relating to economic problems is to make a farce of our Constitution and so build a palace on a dung heap.
>
> (quoted in Lateef 1994: 52)

Following the Law Minister's resignation, the bill lapsed when the provisional parliament was dissolved in late 1951. However, the Congress government renewed its push to revise Hindu personal laws when it was re-elected in 1952. However, it decided to reintroduce the Hindu Code Bill to Parliament as several separate bills rather than as a complete piece of legislation. Political opposition to the revisions remained formidable, however, with the same objections made against a unified Hindu code being raised to the separate bills. Eventually, the government agreed to dilute the revisions to reach a level of minimum parliamentary consensus in order for the individual bills to be passed.[1] This meant that the legislative changes were far from progressive and were indicative of the government's intention, not to ensure gender equality but, rather, to establish its authority over the Hindu religious community. With the exception of Hindu personal laws, successive post-independent governments made no effort to revise discriminatory religious personal laws. Gradually, the government's policy of non-intervention in minority religious personal laws became a permanent principle of government practice.

Furthermore, in the event of a conflict between a woman's claim to her fundamental constitutional rights and her status under religious personal law, the Indian judiciary in the post-independence period invariably upheld the primacy of the latter, thus reinforcing the politically constituted communalist corporate identity of the state. For instance, in 1952, the Bombay High Court held that religious personal laws were immune from judicial interpretation on the basis that personal law was not law within the meaning of Article 13 of the Constitution because it was religious textual law and, hence, could not be challenged (Jaising 1996: i). In *Narasu Appa Mali* v. *State of Bombay*, the court also held that if, by force of the Constitution itself, personal laws were rendered no longer in effect, the constitutional directive principle of a uniform civil code would become redundant (Mansfield 1993: 150). This meant that, as far as the Bombay High Court was concerned, women were not entitled to claim that they were being discriminated against in relation to any aspect of family law (Jaising 1996: i). Also in 1952, the Madras High Court, in *Srinivasa Aiyar* v. *Saraswati Ammal*, held that even if personal laws were subject to constitutional fundamental rights, they did not violate these rights (Agnes 1999a: 88). The courts also consistently upheld discriminatory personal laws relating to succession to property, as well as the right to polygamy among the Muslim community. The courts maintained that the institution of polygamy was not discriminatory because it was 'vital and compelling to those who believed in the sanctity of their personal laws' (Sorabjee 1990: 110). In a series of judgments upholding the remedy of restitution of conjugality under the 1955 Hindu Marriage and Divorce Bill, the judiciary consistently took the view that it was a woman's sacred duty to live with her husband in a matrimonial residence of his choosing. In all the cases, the women had left the family home to take up employment, and even though they were contributing to the family income, their husbands filed for restitution (Agnes 1999a: 84).

The remedy of restitution, which aimed to preserve the marital unit in the Hindu community, allowed for the forcible return of a spouse who was judged to have left the matrimonial home without cause. Originally only available to the husband, the Hindu Marriage and Divorce Bill made the remedy equally available to both men and women. However, it was invariably men who resorted to the remedy, and the courts consistently dismissed the respondent's arguments for leaving the marital home. As Ratna Kapur and Madhu Mehra explain, the judiciary constantly judged the reasonableness of a woman's conduct in leaving the matrimonial home against the standard of the ideal good and dutiful wife (1997: 3). For instance, in 1964, in *Tirath Kaur* v. *Kirpal Singh*, a lower court disallowed the wife's argument that she had taken up employment away from the matrimonial residence because of her husband's financial austerity. The respondent stated that she sent part of her salary to her husband, but when she could no longer meet his demands for more money, he commanded her to resign. She said that, while she wanted the marriage to continue, she was not prepared to resign her position. The trial court found that the wife's refusal to give up her job amounted to desertion and granted the husband a decree of restitution. The wife appealed against the decision but her appeal was dismissed by the High Court, which concluded that unless a wife could prove that she was compelled to leave the matrimonial home because of her husband's misconduct, she was duty bound to reside there and fulfil her marital obligations. Similar judicial decisions were made in a series of subsequent cases spanning from 1966 to 1978 (Kapur and Cossman 1996b: 114–16). Thus, in the post-independence period, the judiciary 'erected an insurmountable obstacle for gender equality within personal laws by providing a legal basis for the continuation of discriminatory personal laws' (Agnes 1999a: 89).

The first period of state behavioural continuity: 1947–74

The politically constituted and judicially reinforced communalist corporate state identity created in the post-independence period had an immediate and lasting inhibiting effect on the diffusion of international norms of sexual non-discrimination. Between 1957 and 1961, the Indian state ratified three major international conventions but failed to comply fully with any of these conventions. The Indian state ratified the ILO Equal Remuneration Convention and the Discrimination (Employment and Occupation) Convention in 1958 and 1960 respectively, and ratified the UN Convention on the Political Rights of Women in 1961. It also signed, but refused to ratify, the UN Convention on the Nationality of Married Women in 1957. It signed and ratified these various international conventions during a period of active involvement in the UN and its specialized agencies because it was eager for international recognition following independence. The Indian government was also confident that the new national Constitution met the requirements of the conventions. In addition, it believed that the 1948 Minimum Wages Act met the specific requirements of the ILO Equal Remuneration Convention. However, the Minimum Wages Act made no reference to the principle of equal pay for work of equal value. Moreover, it did not apply to the agricultural sector, where 80 per cent of women worked, or to contract labour, the category of workers most female employees fell under.

During the 1950s and 1960s, the level of political mobilization and activism in India in general was relatively low and, as we have seen, pre-independence feminists were, by and large, incorporated into the fold of successive Congress governments via legislative and bureaucratic administrative bodies. Furthermore, discursively, pre-independence feminists did not deviate substantially from the politically held view of women as supplicants in need of the protection of the state. For instance, Durgabai Deshmukh, one-time head of the CSWB and a member of the national Planning Commission, spoke of women primarily as supplementary earners and social welfare recipients (Banerjee 1998: WS-6). Congress's commitment to gender equality was not seriously questioned until 1974, when the national Committee on the Status of Women in India (CSWI) compiled a damning report on the situation of women in India (Forbes 1996: 226). The CSWI, which had been appointed by the Ministry of Education and Social Welfare on 22 September 1971, was due to submit its report, entitled *Towards Equality: The Report of the Committee on the Status of Women in India,* on the eve of the UN International Women's Year (IWY). The CSWI had been established in response to repeated requests by the

UN to member states to submit a report on the status of women following the General Assembly's adoption of the Declaration on the Elimination of Discrimination Against Women in 1967.

The UN's request had initially been directed to the Indian Ministry of External Affairs, which redirected it to the Ministry of Education and Social Welfare because it appeared to be the only government administrative body that had 'something to do with women' (Mazumdar 1985: 209–10). The Minister of Education and Social Welfare at the time, Dr Phulrena Guha, put up a note to Cabinet requesting that a commission on the status of women be set up to meet the UN's request. A pre-independence feminist, Dr Guha argued, in vain, that the UN's request provided the government with the opportunity to conduct the first review of a segment of the population to whom all kinds of promises were made at the time of independence, and that such a review warranted a commission. Dr Guha was eager for a commission to be established rather than a committee because once a commission was constituted under the Commission of Enquiries Act and a budget approved, it automatically became an autonomous body able to conduct a completely independent inquiry. A commission was able to order a range of investigations, call in academics to undertake studies, and hold public hearings. Furthermore, unlike the report of a committee, the government was unable to suppress the report of a commission (Mazumdar 2001).

Although disappointed that the government had decided to set up a committee instead of a commission, Dr Guha accepted the position of committee chair and, after making some changes in the composition of the committee, settled on eleven members, including a political scientist (Vina Mazumdar), a social anthropologist (Leela Dube) and a law professor (Lotika Sarkar). The new Minister of Education and Social Welfare, Nurul Hasan, supported Dr Guha's choice of committee members and commissioned the Indian Council of Social Science Research (ICSSR) to provide the committee with research support (Mazumdar 1985: 210). Between 1971 and 1973, the committee commissioned nearly eighty studies and surveys by top-ranking social and political scientists, established task forces and study groups, and informally interviewed approximately 10,000 women of different classes across India (Mazumdar 2001). The committee based its extensive research on a dual frame of reference supplied by the government. According to this dual frame of reference, the committee was to measure the existing situation of women in India against existing national legislative and public policy provisions and the objective of those provisions, which was 'to enable women to play their full and proper role in building up the nation' (Misra 1997: 30; Committee on the Status of Women in India 1975: 1).

Prior to its submission, the government had expected that the committee's report would provide it with its IWY *pièce de résistance*: demonstrating the achievements of a female Prime Minister of a state that was committed to gender equality. Indira Gandhi had been Prime Minister since 1966 and was keen to show the international community that Indian women were emancipated. However, the committee's lengthy and thoroughly researched report showed that the status of Indian women had declined significantly since independence, and documented patent inequalities between men and women. The report's condemnation of a socio-economic and political system that pervasively discriminated against women diverged sharply from the image of women's independence about to be presented at government-sponsored IWY events across India (Calman 1992: 51). Anticipating that the report would cause considerable discomfort within Congress, the Minister of Education and Social Welfare ordered that it be kept secret throughout January 1975. Hasan wanted to ensure that the report did not suffer the same fate as other committee reports submitted around this period, which were never publicly released because they did not find favour with the government ('Report: the making of a founding text' 1998: 110).

Two months before the submission of the report, says Mazumdar, Hasan

> put up a very bland note to Cabinet saying that, even though the Committee on the Status of Women in India had not been set up by a resolution of parliament, since it was the first review of such an important matter, the report should be tabled before parliament.
>
> ('Report: the making of a founding text' 1998: 110)

Unaware of its damaging content, Cabinet agreed to table the report, and by doing so ensured its public release. To further insure the report against government suppression, Hasan also took the risk of arranging a press conference on the report for 18 February 1975 without the Prime Minister's knowledge, to be addressed by the committee's chair, Dr Guha, and member-secretary Mazumdar (Mazumdar 2001). Members of every major international press agency attended, including journalists from the *International Herald Tribune*, the London *Times* and the *Manchester Guardian*, and gave the report wide international coverage. Angered and embarrassed by the committee's report, and distracted by a deepening domestic political crisis, Prime Minister Indira Gandhi decided against attending the UN IWY Conference in Mexico (19 June–2 July 1975).

The second period of state behavioural continuity: 1975–84

Despite her decision not to attend the UN IWY Conference in Mexico, Indira Gandhi selected a delegation to deliver a government-prepared statement at the conference that, on her instructions, made no reference to the CSWI report and painted a rosy picture of the status of women in India. However, the delegation, which included CSWI member Vina

Mazumdar, decided that it would be foolish, given the international press coverage of the *Towards Equality* report, to present anything but an accurate assessment of the situation of Indian women, and therefore rewrote the statement (Mazumdar 2001). The delegation also bravely decided to distribute approximately fifty copies of the *Towards Equality* report at the conference. While the delegation was attending the conference in Mexico, the domestic political crisis took a turn for the worse, with the Allahabad High Court, on 12 June 1975, finding Indira Gandhi technically guilty of corrupt election practices in the 1971 general election. The judicial decision prompted widespread calls for the Prime Minister's resignation, but instead of stepping down, Indira Gandhi declared a state of emergency on 25 June 1975, citing internal threats to national security. The Constitution was immediately suspended, all key opposition leaders and dissidents were arrested and held for months without being charged, and the press was subjected to strict censorship. Moreover, a number of ordinances were promulgated that, in the name of internal security, trampled on the democratic rights of citizens (Krishna 1995: 168). Among them, the Foreign Contribution (Regulation) Act was enacted in 1976 in a bid to restrain NGO activism through the regulatory control and monitoring of foreign financial backing.

During the twenty-one months of the Emergency, Indira Gandhi centralized authority within herself and a select circle of friends and relatives, especially her son Sanjay Gandhi, whom she promptly elevated to the position of de facto deputy Prime Minister (Krishna 1995: 166, 168). She also continued to undermine the Congress Party's organization and openly flouted the legislature (Kumar 1995b: 60). Further, Indira Gandhi's near-authoritarian Congress government subverted secular principles by making compromises with Hindu majoritarianism. Indira Gandhi was a devout Hindu and promoter of Hindu fundamentalism, despite political sloganeering to the contrary (Mazumdar 1992: 15), and in 1976 the government amended the 1954 Special Marriage Act to deprive Hindu women access to secular succession law and deter Hindu men from marrying non-Hindu women. If a Hindu man married a non-Hindu woman, under the new amendments he forfeited his right to ancestral property. Yet in the same year that it enacted these discriminatory legislative amendments, the government also adopted seemingly progressive employment legislation in the form of the Equal Remuneration Act. However, the Equal Remuneration Act was a purely cosmetic piece of legislation aimed at deflecting international criticism of the Emergency generated at the IWY Conference in Mexico and by the international distribution of the CSWI's report. Also, as part of its bid to deflect international criticism, the government established a Cell on Women's Employment within the Ministry of Labour and a National Committee on Women under the chairmanship of the Prime Minister. However, these administrative bodies served no concrete public policy purpose.

The 1976 Equal Remuneration Act was a superficial piece of legislation, because, apart from the fact that it made no reference to the internationally recognized principle of equal pay for work of equal value, it applied to less than 20 per cent of the labour force and was not implemented or enforced. The Act applied only to the industrial sector; it did not apply to the agricultural sector, where almost 80 per cent of all women workers were employed. In the agricultural sector, the government even legislated gender-based pay scales with lower wages for female workers (Left and Levine 1998: 300). The scope of the Act did not extend beyond hiring and pay, and only government-appointed inspectors were permitted to file a complaint against an employer for violating the Act. The penalty for violating the Act consisted of a token fine, which employers, on the rare occasions complaints were filed, usually found more economical to pay rather than comply with the law. Moreover, employers frequently segregated jobs or used a piece-rate system of payment to avoid being accused of discrimination. Finally, female employees in the industrial sector were often reluctant to come forward or make a complaint for fear of losing their jobs, and because the burden of proof for establishing that the law had been violated lay with the complainant.

For those women working in the unprotected agricultural sector, the only legal remedy available to them was the 1947 Industrial Disputes Act, which provided for arbitration by government agencies in the case of an industrial dispute. However, the Act made no reference to the principle of sexual non-discrimination, and its procedural requirement made it extremely difficult for individual complainants to make a claim. First, while the Act covered industrial disputes between employers and employees across the public and private sectors – including the agricultural sector – to qualify for arbitration, the dispute had to qualify as an *industrial dispute*. In order for an individual employee's grievance to qualify as an industrial dispute, it required the sponsorship of a trade union or, in the case where no trade union existed, the sponsorship of co-workers. The vast majority of female employees worked in the informal or unorganized sectors where there were no trade unions. Thus, female complainants were reliant on the support of co-workers, which was often difficult to rally. Even if a female employee were unionized, the probability of a union taking a grievance involving sexual discrimination to court was extremely low because the union would have to pay the costs of litigation (Andiappan 1979: 403, 408). Second, if a complaint were made, it was difficult to prove discrimination and secure the necessary legal redress unless the act of discrimination was flagrant (Menon 1966: 352).

Although the political conditions during the state of emergency were unconducive to feminist activism, the CSWI's report, *Towards Equality*, stimulated and inspired many activists. For instance, among the many thousands of citizens arbitrarily arrested and detained during the emergency, Pramila Dandavate recalls receiving a copy of the summary of

Towards Equality in prison and forming a small study group with inmates to discuss issues raised in the document ('Report: the making of a founding text' 1998: 109). Ordinarily, individuals would not see government reports such as *Towards Equality*, but the ICSSR had published a paperback summary of the 480-page report just prior to the emergency, making it more accessible to the general public (Calman 1992: 70, n 9). Members of the CSWI also became political activists after being shocked and dismayed by the committee's findings. While some committee members admit that they had been aware that Indian women were victims of discrimination before research for the report began, they maintain that they were unaware of the full complexity and extent of women's subordination and oppression. One such member, Sakina Hasan, says that although she was 'generally aware that, in spite of the constitutional safeguards, discrimination against women was there in most walks of life', she also felt the committee 'did not know enough about women's situation and it was necessary to identify specific problems' (Editor's Note (Discussion Forum) 1985: 81).

Other committee members confess that they were completely ignorant of the inequalities in Indian society and knew very little about the traditions and social attitudes that affected women's status prior to the preparation of the report. Mazumdar states:

> To tell you the truth, when I was first informed about the committee, I could not understand why the government wanted a committee to look at the status of women. It seemed to me that this was a settled question, and I had no clue that there were still problems about women's status.
>
> (Editor's Note (Discussion Forum) 1985: 82)

Female intellectuals and researchers in the wider academic community were also surprised and shaken by the committee's findings. Reflecting on the content of *Towards Equality*, Neera Desai and Maithreyi Krishnaraj write:

> Three decades after independence, and after three decades of planned development, the picture of women's position that emerged was startling in its grimness. . . . Women's position was worsening in practically every sphere, with the exception of some gains in education and employment for middle-class women.
>
> (1987: 5)

The realization that the vast majority of Indian women had not benefited, as they had done, from post-independence government economic policies mobilized these hitherto complacent urban-based middle- and upper-class women to protest against social injustice following the end of the emergency.

The state of emergency ended in March 1977, when elections brought the first post-independence non-Congress government to power. Sankaran Krishna argues that, while it is hard to fathom the precise reasons for Indira Gandhi's decision to relax the Emergency and call for elections on 24 January 1977, it is evident 'that she badly miscalculated the degree of alienation from her regime and to the *excesses* of the emergency' (Krishna 1995: 168). Sudipta Kaviraj adds that Indira Gandhi's intelligence system appears to have misled her into believing that she and her government would win the elections. Kaviraj speculates that this was because 'in times of authoritarianism it is not wise to carry anything but good news' (1986: 1705). Given that the centre was taking more and more decisions and that it had stifled the press, the government remained ignorant of the widespread disillusionment among the rural poor. The government also underestimated the strength of the coalition of opposition parties. Indira Gandhi and her government were comprehensively defeated in the March elections by a coalition of five opposition parties – the Janata Party – which promised to restore democracy to India. The end of the emergency also brought a wave of feminist activism against the growing powers of the central government and the subordination of women at almost every level of society (Forbes 1996: 244).

While Indian feminists initially focused on addressing the concerns raised in the *Towards Equality* report of the CSWI, they quickly moved beyond these concerns to fight against gender-based violence, especially dowry-related deaths, and rape (Misra 1997: 30). The catalyst for this broadening of the feminist political agenda was the dowry murder of a young Delhi woman called Tarvinder Kaur and the police custodial rape of a young tribal girl called Mathura (Katzenstein 1989: 62). It is worth noting that, at this time, the international legal framework did not deal with issues of gender-based violence, hence Indian feminist intervention on such issues pre-dates the development of international norms aimed at preventing and eliminating such practices. In May 1979, Kaur made a deathbed statement to the police, accusing her in-laws of dousing her with kerosene and setting her alight because her parents could not meet the in-laws' ever-increasing demands for more dowry. Despite her statement, the police recorded Kaur's death as a suicide. A loose coalition of feminists, the Delhi-based branch of Stree Sangharsh Sanghatan (Women's Struggle Organization), took up the case and drew widespread public attention to dowry-related crimes. On 1 June 1979, Stree Sangharsh Sanghatan organized a widely publicized anti-dowry demonstration in Delhi, which was followed in the next few weeks by further demonstrations against dowry deaths (Kumar 1995a: 67). However, demonstrators often faced considerable public hostility and on one occasion were driven out of an area by the neighbours of a victim's in-laws who had perpetrated the dowry-related crime (Palriwala and Agnihotri 1996: 508). The demonstrations attracted the attention of the press, and a heated public debate on dowry and dowry-related crimes erupted (Kumar 1995a: 67).

However, Congress, which had returned to power with Indira Gandhi at the helm in January 1980 following the collapse of the Janata government from internal factionalism and defections, was reluctant to interfere in what it regarded was a private, familial issue. Finally, in January 1981, as a result of persistent pressure from feminist activists and non-Congress parliamentarians, the government appointed a Joint Committee of Parliament to review the operation of the 1961 Dowry Prohibition Act (Mazumdar 1999: 354, n 41). However, the government established the joint committee in a bid to stall feminist political intervention on the issue, and after the committee delivered its report, over eighteen months later, on 11 August 1982, no legislative action was taken on the committee's recommendations for another two years. In the interim, the government embarked on a discursive campaign to convince the media and the general public that what it called the social evil of dowry and dowry-related crimes was solely attributable to the degeneration of moral, social and familial values. By doing so, say Rajni Patriwala and Indu Agnihotri, the government hoped to escape a wide-ranging examination and critique of its economic policies and civil laws that had contributed to women's subjugation in the family and Indian society (1996: 507). Feminists tried, unsuccessfully, to challenge the government's representation of the issue by discursively locating the root of the problem in gender inequalities in the family and in the polity (Bush 1992: 599).

The government finally enacted the Dowry Prohibition (Amendment) Act in 1984, but the amended legislation was neither substantial nor enforceable. Indian feminists described the dowry amendment bill as a piece of toothless legislation. They were angered by what they described as the mindless callousness shown in the government's legislative amendments and the 'lack of political will towards the problem of dowry' (Gandhi and Shah 1991: 220). As Nandita Gandhi and Nandita Shah explain,

> [o]n the one hand, [the amendments] enlarge the definition of dowry to make it easier to prove but, on the other, they leave several loopholes, which render the law ineffective. Firstly, the law holds both the giver and taker of dowry guilty. If the giver is guilty who will provide the evidence? The giver or the bride's family are in a particularly vulnerable position. Before marriage it becomes a matter of the family's honour and after marriage every demand is like a ransom note with the usual threats of cruelty and torture if its conditions are not met. Thus, to indict those who are forced to give is to take away their initiative to approach the law. Secondly, section 3 condones dowry by providing some safeguards: if presents are given to the bride or groom, the law stipulates that a list of such presents be maintained can quite easily be bypassed. This provision simply changes one form

of dowry to another: that of presents. Thirdly, there are no provisions for better implementation of the law.

(ibid.: 220)

By the time these amendments were passed, the feminist anti-dowry campaign had become a more or less spent force, with activists questioning their handling of the issue and the level of mobilization declining (Palriwala and Agnihotri 1996: 510). Nevertheless, argue Palriwala and Agnihotri, there was sufficient pressure generated by the campaign to ensure further amendments to the Dowry Prohibition Act in 1986 (ibid.: 510). Once again, however, these amendments were insubstantial. This is evident in the fact that, despite the legislative changes, the number of dowry deaths or bride burnings continued to rise, and few convictions were secured.

The obvious disparity between government legislation and its effective implementation left many feminists feeling embittered that the government had easily sidetracked their demands by enacting ineffective legislation. Activists were similarly disappointed by the perfunctory attention given by the Congress government to the issue of rape, particularly police custodial rape. Co-ordinated feminist activism on rape began in early 1980 and was prompted by an open letter by four university law professors against a judgment in a case of police custodial rape in Maharashtra. The Mathura rape case, already mentioned, had occurred several years earlier and involved a 16-year-old tribal girl, Mathura, who was raped by two local police officers while in custody (Kumar 1995a: 69–70, 72). Initially, the lower Sessions Court acquitted the police officers after finding that the complainant was of loose morals (Patel 1988: 254). This ruling was subsequently overturned by the Nagpur branch of the Bombay High Court, which decided that the complainant had been 'subjected to forcible sexual intercourse' and sentenced each of the police officers to seven and a half years in prison. However, on appeal, the Supreme Court reversed this decision and acquitted the police officers. The Supreme Court dismissed the complainant's testimony as a tissue of lies on the grounds that there was no evidence that she had resisted or shouted for help and because there was proof that she was not a virgin (Sharma 1991: 59). The court thus held that the complainant had consented to having sexual intercourse with the defendants (Baxi 1994: 254). The Supreme Court decision appalled Professor Upendra Baxi, who came across a reference to the case in a volume of *Supreme Court Cases* one September evening in 1979. The next morning Baxi discussed the case with his colleague Lotika Sarkar and, together with Raghunath Kelkar and Vasudha Dhagamwar, signed an open letter urging the Chief Justice to review the case.[2] The letter was also circulated to feminist political organizations, urging them to put pressure on the Supreme Court to reopen the case (Desai 1997: 113).

At first there was no reaction to the letter from either the Chief Justice, the media or feminist organizations. According to Baxi, feminists simply 'did not know how to cope with this *crie de coeur*' (1994: 71). Then, unfortunately, he continues, there was a backlash from colleagues reproaching us for 'sensationalizing' judicial discourse and acting unprofessionally. The national press refused to publish the open letter, on the basis that it did not constitute news and bordered on contempt of court. Eventually, a leading daily English-language newspaper of Pakistan, the *Dawn* in Karachi, published the open letter in its entirety, and feminists began to mobilize around the Mathura case and the issue of police custodial rape in general (ibid.: 71; Katzenstein 1989: 62). Four months after the open letter had been signed, a series of demonstrations and rallies were held in Ahmedabad, Napur, Bombay and, lastly, New Delhi (Mazumdar 1999: 351). Organizations such as Stree Sangharsh Sanghatan and the Bombay-based Forum Against Rape (established specifically to address the issue of custodial rape), political activists and civil rights lawyers lobbied the government and submitted a petition to the state legislator and the Prime Minister's office demanding a review of the Mathura case and changes in the rape law (Gothoskar and Patel 1982: 94–5). The Supreme Court dismissed the review petition on technical grounds and stopped lawyers from intervening on behalf of feminist organizations on the basis that

> [t]he privilege of intervention was wholly at the discretion of the court and in this case it was rightly to be declined, given the behaviour of women's groups in criticising the court and holding protest at the Supreme Court. Furthermore, if such tendencies were to be encouraged every group disgruntled at the court's decision could subvert the finality of the apex court's determination.
>
> (Baxi 1994: 74)

The Supreme Court's dismissal of the petition provoked further demonstrations in New Delhi and Bombay.

Meanwhile, according to Radhu Kumar, protests by feminists, local neighbourhood groups and trade union-based groups concerning other incidences of police custodial rape were being widely reported in the press. Unfortunately, this extensive press coverage 'encouraged national parties to use the issue of custodial rape as a political lever against their rivals' (1995a: 71). When yet another case of custodial rape, involving a young woman named Maya Tyagi, hit the headlines in June 1980, Congress's Home Minister, Zail Singh, travelled to Baghpat in Haryana State, where the rape had taken place, and promptly ordered a judicial inquiry into the incident. While Singh was in Baghpat, the opposition party Lok Dal publicly decried the incident as an example of Congress misrule (ibid.: 71, 74). At this time, another case of police rape took place in Dabwali, Haryana, and the Bharatiya Janata Party (BJP) demanded the resignation of the Haryana government for failing to protect the 'lives, property, and honour' of Dabwali residents. The Delhi unit of the BJP launched a one-week campaign against what it described as outrageous atrocities and attacks on women in the city (Akerkar 1995: WS-15). This was followed by the leader of the Janata (S) Party, Raj Narain, announcing his resignation as party leader and threatening to go on an indefinite hunger strike unless the Congress government took appropriate action 'to protect the dignity and honour of women' against custodial rape (Kumar 1995b: 64). Shortly afterwards, several parliamentary members used the issue to demand the resignation of the Home Minister during parliamentary debates regarding the dramatic increase in the incidents of rape. Unfortunately, says Kumar,

> the highly publicised nature of the campaign and the speed with which rape was used by mainstream political parties in a welter of accusation and counter-accusation placed feminists in the invidious position of having to rescue the issue from political opportunists.
>
> (1995a: 71)

The task of activists in rescuing the issue of custodial rape from becoming a political football for fractious politicians was complicated by the fact that the government promised that it would take decisive legislative steps to deal with the problems of custodial rape and rape in general.

In August 1980, the government proposed what appeared, at first glance, to be substantial changes to existing criminal law to deal with the problems of custodial rape, and rape in general. The draft legislation gave the impression of being radical because it defined the categories of custodial rape and specified a mandatory prison sentence of ten years, in-camera trials and a shift in the onus of proof on to the accused. However, as Flavia Agnes explains, the proposed amendments were far from progressive because they allowed the minimum sentence to be reduced for undefined 'adequate and social reasons' and the burden of proof clause did not extend beyond cases of custodial rape (1999b: 81116). The draft legislation also permitted the victim's past sexual history and general conduct to be used as evidence (ibid.: 81116). Furthermore, it was proposed that any publication relating to a rape trial be made a non-bailable offence with a prison sentence of up to three years. Acutely aware of the important role played by the press during the anti-rape campaign, feminists strongly opposed its virtual censorship during rape trials. Equally important, the proposed amendments did not address the issues of pre-trial procedures and police registering of complaints. The proposed legislative changes were referred to a Joint Committee of Parliament in December 1980 for discussion and, after soliciting public opinion, the committee finally submitted its report in November 1982.

Almost a year later, Parliament finally debated the Criminal (Amendment) Bill over a four-hour period, during which the fifteen parliamentarians present revealed their desire to deflect attention from the state's complicity in normalizing and sustaining gender-based violence. In the parliamentary debate, according to Pratiksha Baxi, the act of rape was treated as a criminal aberration and the role of the state was represented as that of protecting the honour of a chaste woman (2000: 1198–9). This is most evident in the discussion over whether or not to criminalize the publication of the name of the rape victim and any matter relating to the trial. This discussion, says Baxi, was discursively framed in terms of the loss of chastity and the subsequent social stigma and shame attributed to the rape victim. Those who supported the criminalization of publication argued that the law must not allow any publicity of the rape trial because the victim would inevitably suffer further stigmatization and ostracism by her community, and possibly be forced to live the life of a prostitute (ibid.: 1197). The legislator decided to make publication of rape trials into a bailable offence. In the parliamentary debate, the role of the state was also represented as that of protecting honourable men from false accusations of rape. This is evident in the discussion over whether or not to retain the legislative provision concerning character evidence. It was agreed that the provision be retained because it was important to know a woman's character, especially her sexual history, so that respectable men could be protected from being falsely accused by unscrupulous women (ibid.: 1198).

When it came to the question of criminalizing (adult) marital rape, the legislator decided against recognizing marital rape as a crime. However, on the recommendation of the Joint Committee, the legislator decided to criminalize as 'illicit sexual intercourse' the rape of a woman separated from her husband. The Joint Committee's recommendation read:

> In the case where the husband and wife are living separately under the decree of judicial separation, there is a possibility of reconciliation between them until a decree of divorce is granted. Hence, the intercourse by the husband with his wife without her consent during such period should not be treated as or equated with rape ... [it] should be treated as illicit sexual intercourse.
>
> (Baxi 2000: 1198)

Parliament enacted the Criminal (Amendment) Bill on 25 December 1983. Despite its obvious flaws and glaring weaknesses, feminists presumed that the legislation would have a positive judicial impact and make it easier for victims of rape to seek legal redress. However, following the enactment of the legislation, the incidence of rape steadily rose and of the cases registered and tried, there were very few convictions (Sarkar 1994: 81). In fact, judicial decisions in the post-amendment period convey a dismal picture of regressive interpretations of the legislation and acquittals on minimal grounds, with, claims Agnes, 'the same old notions of chastity, virginity, premium on marriage and fear of female sexuality reflected in the judgements' (Agnes 1999b: 81116).

The preoccupation of Indian feminists and the press with domestic issues of gender-based violence meant that the UN mid-decade Conference for Women in Copenhagen and India's signing of CEDAW on 30 July 1980 went virtually unnoticed except by those activists attending the conference and pressing the government to sign the convention before the conference's end. Finally, the government signed CEDAW on the last day of the Copenhagen conference to avoid international embarrassment, but refused to ratify the convention or comply with its provisions. By signing CEDAW, the Indian state was expected to ratify promptly and to refrain from acts that would defeat the object and purpose of the convention. It was also obligated to abide by the spirit of the convention. However, the Indian government openly flouted its obligations by refusing to amend or remove discriminatory religious personal laws and by failing to take substantive legislative and public policy initiatives in accordance with the convention. Within just over three years of signing CEDAW, Indira Gandhi's second term in office had ended with her assassination on 31 October 1984 by two of her Sikh bodyguards. Immediately following her death, her only surviving son, Rajiv Gandhi, was sworn in as Prime Minister, and in the December 1984 general election, Congress won by a landslide on the strength of a sympathy wave.

The third period of state behavioural continuity: 1985–95

Soon Rajiv Gandhi's government clashed with Indian feminists over its decision to enact the Muslim Women's (Protection of Rights on Divorce) Bill on 6 May 1986, which denied divorced Muslim women the right to maintenance under Indian constitutional law. This bill directly contravened CEDAW (Rahman 1990: 486). Before the passage of this bill, Muslim women could, like women from other religious communities, petition for maintenance under the secular Code of Criminal Procedure if their ex-husbands refused or failed to provide them with financial support. The bill was the legislative outcome of the government's decision to take steps to reverse an April 1985 ruling of the Supreme Court, commonly referred to as the *Shahbano* decision. In *Mohammad Ahmed Khan* v. *Shahbano Begum*, the Supreme Court dismissed Khan's appeal against the decision of the Madhya Pradesh High Court to award his ex-wife, Shahbano, maintenance under the Code of Criminal Procedure. Shahbano was an elderly Muslim woman who had been pursuing her ex-husband for maintenance through the court system for ten years, after he threw her out of the house in 1975. Khan, a prominent lawyer on a five-figure income, initially paid his wife a small amount of maintenance after ordering her to leave the marital home but soon stopped paying her maintenance altogether. In response, Shahbano filed a prevention of destitution provision of 500 rupees a month under the Code of Criminal Procedure (Coomaraswamy 1994: 53).

However, while the Judicial Magistrates' Court in Indore was considering Shahbano's claim, Khan divorced his wife of forty-three years using the triple *talaq*, the Islamic method of divorce that requires only that one party say 'I divorce you' three times. As required by Islamic personal law, Khan returned to Shahbano the *mehr* or marriage settlement that she had originally brought into the marriage, and paid her maintenance of 200 rupees a month during the period of *iddat* (three months from the date of divorce). Despite arguing that his payment of maintenance and settlement relieved him from any further obligations under Muslim personal law, the local magistrate directed Khan to pay maintenance of twenty-five rupees a month. In 1980, Shahbano filed a revised application for increased maintenance, and the Madhya Pradesh High Court raised the amount to 179 rupees a month. Khan then appealed, but the Supreme Court upheld the High Court's decision. The Supreme Court ruling provoked an intense public debate unwitnessed by previous judicial decisions granting Muslim women maintenance under the Code of Criminal Procedure.

In order to understand why the *Shahbano* decision was so controversial, we need to understand the nature of the judicial decision itself and the domestic political context in which it was made. As Zoya Hasan explains, whereas previous judicial decisions granting Muslim women maintenance under the Code of Criminal Procedure had been framed in terms of social justice, the *Shahbano* decision, by contrast, was framed in terms of the discriminatory aspects of the Islamic legal system (1989: 45, 46). The Chief Justice of the Supreme Court's provocative decision was also made at a time of heightened communal tension, which was the legacy of Indira Gandhi's last period in power, and at a time when Congress was facing crucial by-elections. In his lengthy opinion, the Chief Justice of the Supreme Court openly criticized the way in which the Islamic legal system degraded women and allowed Muslim men to discard their wives whenever they chose to, without any reason (Nussbaum 2000: 173). Although a Hindu, the Chief Justice also interpreted various Islamic sacred texts and argued that, in his opinion, there was no textual justification for providing inadequate maintenance for Muslim women. He also admonished the state for failing to enact and implement a uniform civil code as constitutionally directed. The Chief Justice maintained that a uniform civil code was essential for national integration and that the role of social reformer had to be assumed by the courts because of the state's vacillation on the code (Mody 1987: 939).

The *Shahbano* decision came on the heels of Indira Gandhi's assassination in October 1984 and accompanying communal riots. Following Indira Gandhi's death, a long-running dispute about the status of a

Muslim mosque, the Babri Masjid, in Ayodhya in the northern state of Uttar Pradesh, flared as Hindu fundamentalists agitated to have a shrine in the mosque's precinct declared the birthplace of the god Ram and a Hindu temple built on the site. The Islamic clergy and the Muslim Personal Board argued that the *Shahbano* decision and Hindu claims of ownership of the Babri Masjid site were part of a Hindu communal onslaught on Muslims. Muslim fundamentalists were outraged by the *Shahbano* decision because they saw it as an incursion into Muslim personal law and a violation of their constitutional right to exercise religion. The Muslim Personal Law Board threatened to set up Islamic courts in order to dispense justice according to *Shariat* law, and the *ulema* issued a warning that the Supreme Court ruling violated the teachings of Islam (Kumar 1995a: 78). Muslim fears were exacerbated by the entrance into the public debate surrounding the *Shahbano* decision of the Hindu nationalist BJP, which seized on the *Shahbano* decision to assert itself in national politics. The BJP used the decision to accuse the Congress government of favouritism towards religious minorities and to whip up anti-Muslim sentiment (Ram 2000: 72). Appropriating Congress's discourse of national integration, the BJP demanded that the government enact a uniform civil code for the sake of national unity. However, the BJP's demand was motivated not by a desire to ensure gender equality in civil law, but by the chance to standardize all personal law under a nominally civil but actually Hindu code of family law (Desai 1997: 118). The enthusiastic support extended by the BJP to the *Shahbano* decision and a uniform civil code convinced Islamic leaders that Muslim cultural identity was under serious threat and, with militant fervour, they mobilized a large segment of the community to agitate against any outside intervention in their religious personal law (Hasan 1989: 47).

Caught in the communal crossfire, feminists and Muslim moderates disputed the claim by Muslim fundamentalists that the community was unanimously opposed to the *Shahbano* decision and rejected their discursive position on cultural identity (Hasan 1989: 47; Ram 2000: 73). They mobilized against the conservative backlash by setting up committees, such as the Committee for the Protection of Muslim Women, in Calcutta, Trivandrum and Delhi, and organizing conventions and public meetings across India to draw attention to the issue. They also submitted memoranda to the Prime Minister's office exhorting the government to protect the rights of minority Muslim women. Legal experts on the *Shariat* joined the fray by endorsing the *Shahbano* decision and, together with feminist organized protests, demonstrated that the Muslim community did not unanimously hold fundamentalist views. The government itself initially welcomed the *Shahbano* decision, but the loss of a number of crucial seats in Muslim constituencies in December 1985 by-elections prompted Congress to execute a volte-face on the decision. With the traditional alliance between Congress and the Muslim orthodox Jamiyyat-ul-Ulama at risk following the by-elections, and Muslims holding nearly a third of parliamentary seats, Congress, fearing further electoral losses, took steps to assuage the feelings of the Muslim community as a whole (Hasan 1989: 47; Frykenberg 1993: 248). The government held discussions with members of the Muslim Personal Law Board regarding the contents of a bill that would reverse the Shahbano decision, and at the All-Momin conference Prime Minister Rajiv Gandhi assured delegates that Muslim personal law would not be altered as a result of the Supreme Court judgment (Hasan 1989: 47).

On 25 February 1986, the government introduced the Muslim Women's (Protection of Rights on Divorce) Bill into Parliament, which deprived Muslim women of their right to seek maintenance under the Code of Criminal Procedure. According to Hasan, the government's decision to introduce the bill when it did was based on a desire to prevent further electoral losses and to stem Muslim anger over the reopening of the disputed Babri Masjid shrine three weeks earlier (Hasan 1989: 48). Congress initially tried to defend the bill as a means of protecting minority women's rights, but a massive outcry against the proposed legislation by feminists and Muslim moderates forced the government to ditch this defence. Instead, the government claimed it had drafted the bill 'in deference to the wishes of the Muslim community' (ibid.: 49). The government went so far as to claim that, even though it was not totally in agreement with the legislative provisions, it had no choice but to draft the legislation because the Muslim community perceived the *Shahbano* decision to be a fundamental threat to its religious and cultural identity. In doing so, argues Hasan, the government was trying to transfer responsibility for the bill to the Muslim fundamentalists (Hasan 1989: 49). In parliamentary debates to consider the bill, the government defended the bill on the twin basis of maintaining national unity and non-interference in religious personal law. The government argued that it was obliged to introduce the bill primarily out of respect for a minority community's right to cultural autonomy (Hasan 1999: 75). The Law Minister, Asoke Sen, reminded Parliament that, since independence, the state had accepted that minority personal law would not be modified without a community's consent and that it was 'the consistent policy of the government that in matters pertaining to a community priority would be given to the leaders of the community' (Hasan 1989: 48). According to Hasan, this recognition of Muslim religio-political leaders meant that the government 'had no choice but to disregard the view of so many Muslim groups who had expressed their opposition to the bill' (ibid.: 48).

Furthermore, argues Hasan, the passage of the Muslim Women's (Protection of Rights on Divorce) Bill on 6 May 1986 conferred legitimacy on Muslim religio-political leaders as the sole spokesmen of the Muslim community. Despite the opposition of feminists and Muslim moderates to the bill, and despite dissent within Congress ranks, the government refused to withdraw the bill. Arif Mohammad Khan led internal party opposition to the bill. Angered by Congress's decision to rely solely on the opinion of Muslim conservatives and ignore progressive views within the Muslim community, Khan resigned. His resignation emboldened other party members to speak out against the bill, but the groundswell of internal opposition was stifled by the issuing of a government whip directing party members to vote in favour of the bill. However, a substantial number of Congress Party members refused to comply with the party whip, which was to have far-reaching political implications for the government in the near future (Mody 1987: 950). Feminists and Muslim moderates also refused to give up and challenged the validity of the bill in a joint petition to the Supreme Court. They contended that the bill violated women's constitutional rights. However, as of late 2004, the writ was still pending in the court. The Supreme Court's failure to hear the petition in a timely fashion, according to Ratna Kapur, served to 'encourage the fundamentalist voice and the state's search for legitimacy in religion'. It also demonstrated to Kapur that 'the judiciary, as an arm of the state, [had] become implicated in the relationship fostered between the state and religious fundamentalism' (1992: 37).

Meanwhile, Shahbano Begum found herself not only physically threatened but also made to feel responsible for the communal conflict following the Supreme Court decision in her case (Chhachi 1991: 168). Eventually succumbing to enormous Islamic community pressure, Shahbano surrendered the right she had long fought for and publicly renounced the maintenance awarded to her by the Supreme Court (Kumar 1995a: 79). Thus, according to Sudesh Vaid, 'she was made to accept her *mistake*' (1988: 23). The Hindu Right, which included the BJP political party and its allied quasi-political organizations – the Rashtriya Swayamsevak Sangh and the Vishwa Hindu Parishad, and the extremist Shiva Sena party – exploited the victimization of Shahbano and the government's staunch defence of the Muslim Women's (Protection of Rights on Divorce) Bill to establish itself as a self-proclaimed civilizing force in India and to build a critique of the Congress government. Commandeering the discourse of gender equality, the Hindu Right attacked the Muslim community for its discriminatory practices and promised to do what it charged the government with failing to do: that is, reform punitive and backward Islamic personal law. The Hindu Right also accused the government of putting Muslim community interests ahead of national unity and, in the process, sacrificing women's rights, which, it argued, could only be restored by the introduction of a uniform civil code. This argument contrasted sharply with Congress's long-held belief that national unity could only be achieved by accommodating Muslim community interests such as retaining their personal law (Hasan 1999: 72, 78). However, the Hindu Right's idea of national unity consisted of Hindu majoritarianism, and its notion of a uniform civil code consisted of a code modelled on Hindu law. Moreover, the Hindu Right considered a uniform civil code modelled on Hindu law as a necessary precondition for the promotion of Hindu nationalism (Bano 1995: 2981). The Hindu Right also exploited the government's enactment of the Muslim Women's (Protection of Rights on Divorce) Bill to accuse it of practising a form of pseudo-secularism by failing to treat religious communities equally. However, the Hindu Right's idea of equal treatment of religious communities was to establish 'majority (Hindu) norms as the ostensibly neutral norms against which all others are judged' (Cossman and Kapur 1996: 2622). By questioning the government's secular credentials, argues Hasan, the Hindu Right hoped to displace Congress from the centre of politics, and, even though its motives were quite transparent, the Hindu Right continued to present its objectives in terms of progressive legislative reform and achieving gender equality (Hasan 1999: 80).

The Hindu Right also accused feminists and Muslim moderates of promoting pseudo-secularism by making claims derived from Western values and without any understanding of *real* Hindu values (Desai 1997: 121, n 7). Confronted by the careless manner in which the Hindu Right appropriated and interpreted various concepts and issues such as secularism and a uniform civil code to suit its political agenda, Indian feminists were forced to rethink their position and demand for a uniform civil code. As Kumar explains, the experiences of activists during the Shahbano controversy consisted of a series of bitter lessons. She states:

> Discovering the ease with which a 'community in danger' resorts to fundamentalist assertions, among which control over women is one of the first, feminists also confronted the ease with which the Indian state chose to accommodate communalism (by taking no action against the Vishwa Hindu Parishad agitation) and balance this by a concession to fundamentalism (allowing personal law to cut into the application of uniform laws such as section 125 of the Code of Criminal Procedure).
>
> (1995a: 78)

During the *Shahbano* controversy, activists also confronted the ease with which Muslim religious leaders mobilized the Islamic community against them by raising the symbol of the Muslim woman as the real woman and portraying feminists as unnatural creatures trying to erase Muslim female identity (ibid.: 79). However, before feminists had a chance to rethink their strategies and tactics in dealing with politicized religion, a communal storm erupted over an act of sati (widow immolation) in Deorala, in the state of Rajasthan, in September 1987.

The Deorala sati incident ignited a furious public and legal debate that spanned questions of religious identity and communal autonomy, the identity and social position of Hindu women, and the role of the law and the state in society. Given that the practice of sati had long been illegal and that previous incidents, which were rare and highly localized in independent India, had attracted little attention, the reaction to the Deorala sati incident and the extraordinary debate it aroused was surprising (Kumar 1995a: 80–1). Sati had been banned by colonial legislation in 1829. Of the estimated forty instances of the practice since independence, twenty-eight had occurred in Rajasthan.[3] In a way, argues Kumar, the extraordinary debate surrounding the Deorala sati incident 'can be understood only as part of a process of political reorganization in which the death of Roop Kanwar, the girl who was immolated, became the symbol of Rajput identity politics' (1995a: 81). When Indian feminists denounced the incident and the glorification of sati that followed immediately after the immolation, the issue quickly became inextricably linked to Rajput community identity, and the Hindu Right intervened to defend Rajput chivalric tradition (Kapur and Cossman 1996b: 64). The Hindu Right argued that sati was a cultural tradition justified by religious texts and that a widow's unique sacrifice was incomprehensible to modern Indian women bent on imposing their Western-derived views of equality and liberty on a 'society that had once given noble, spiritual women the respect they deserved' (Oldenburg 1994: 105). In part, the debate also can only be understood in the context of the recent political erosion of democratic principles and secular law. Local authorities had prevented previous sati incidents without any pressure from feminists or the government, observes Lotika Sarkar, indicating that existing legislation was adequate (1995: 12). However, the government, by playing fast and loose with the secular Criminal Procedure Code in the wake of the *Shahbano* decision and flirting with communalism, was rendered incapable of acting on the Deorala incident. The combination of government inaction and the religious justification for the Deorala sati served as a warning to feminists that women's fundamental rights were under threat, making the issue of sati a matter of urgent attention.

The feminist political campaign against sati began with a small number of activists in Jaipur expressing their shock and anger at the girl's immolation and the failure of the Rajasthan administration to respond to the crime (Jain, Misra and Srivastava 1987: 1891).[4] Learning of the death of Kanwar from a brief report in the local daily newspaper, these local activists promptly called on the Chief Minister of Rajasthan to demand that the perpetrators of the crime be charged and that the planned celebration (the *chunari mahotsav*) be prevented.[5] Although both demands were ignored, a case for abetment of suicide was registered and Kanwar's fifteen-year-old brother, who lit the pyre, was arrested. Yet the excitement over the planned *chunari* ceremony grew unchecked as prominent members of the newly formed Sati Dharm Raksha Samiti (Organization for the Defence of the Religious-Ethical Ideal of Sati) promoted the glorification ceremony, and the local press ran daily reports on the build-up to the event. Thousands of pilgrims from across Rajasthan began arriving in Deorala, and Samiti decided to run the site as a commercial venture and form a trust to collect donations. Stalls were set up selling memorabilia and cassettes of devotional songs, and handbills informing visitors of the *chunari* ceremony were distributed (Oldenburg 1994: 107).

Frustrated by the Rajasthan administration's failure to act, local feminists met to co-ordinate a public demonstration on 14 September 1987 to demand that the Chief Minister enforce the law and stop the planned celebration for 16 September. They also sent telegrams to the Prime Minister, Rajiv Gandhi, and the Women's Welfare Minister, Margaret Alva, urging Congress to intervene. Over 300 anti-sati protestors, including scholars and academics, journalists, and professionals, marched in silence to the state legislator in Jaipur, only to find the Chief Minister unavailable to receive their memorandum. Finally, the Chief Minister's secretary accepted the memorandum. Activists decided to make a last-ditch appeal to the Jaipur High Court, before it closed that day, to direct the state government to prohibit the glorification ceremony on the grounds that it was illegal (Oldenburg 1994: 107). The next day, 15 September, the High Court issued an injunction against the glorification ceremony. However, despite announcing that it would comply with the court's directive, the Rajasthan administration proceeded to allow the ceremony to take place. In fact, many Rajasthan Legislative Assembly members visited the site in Deorala to pay their respects, including the President of the state Janata Party, the acting President of the Rajput Sabha, and prominent members of the BJP and the Congress Party. The President of the Janata Party, Kalyan Singh Kalvi, openly agreed with those who saw the Deorala incident as an opportunity to reinvigorate Rajput identity and reassert the community's political significance. Kalvi not only participated in the activities of Samiti but also attended a press conference held by the organization, where it affirmed its support of *voluntary* sati and warned that 'hurting Rajput sentiments could be dangerous' (Joseph 1991: 1025).

The central Congress government broke its long silence only after the glorification celebrations were safely over, when the Women's Welfare Minister expressed her anguish in a telegram to the Centre for Women's Studies at Jaipur University, and Rajiv Gandhi dispatched Home Minister Chidambaram to Rajasthan on 19 September to 'inquire into the matter' (Oldenburg 1994: 108). According to Veena Oldenburg, the Home Minister met with local feminists to

> deliver the government's assurances that the situation was now under control, since the main culprits – Roop Kanwar's father-in-law and his three sons – had been arrested, and that no temple would be permitted to be built on the site to glorify the alleged sati.
>
> (ibid.: 108)

Later, the Home Minister also met with several hundred young Rajput men who had driven through the main streets of Jaipur brandishing swords and demanding an audience with the minister unchecked by local police. Angered by the minister's firm stand against sati, the youths departed, vowing to protect *sati dharma* (ibid.: 108–9). The following day, feminist anti-sati activists began receiving death threats (Jain *et al.* 1987: 1893). Adding to the tension, the head priests of several major Hindu temples in centres such as Benares and Puri issued statements defending the practice of sati as a noble aspect not only of Rajput culture but also of Hinduism (Kumar 1995a: 82). The priests also maintained that 'issues such as sati should be placed under their purview as arbiters of Hindu personal law and not that of the state' (ibid.: 82). Further, they claimed that Hinduism was in danger of being eroded (ibid.: 82).

The head priests' cry of Hinduism in danger was echoed by the Hindu Right, which organized a series of pro-sati demonstrations and charged the Congress government with neglecting the rights of the majority community. Referring to the recent enactment of the Muslim Women's (Protection of Rights on Divorce) Bill, the Hindu Right accused the government of acceding to the demands of minority communities at the expense of the majority community. As the Hindu Right's pro-sati campaign gathered momentum, it attracted the support of many Hindu women. This allowed the Hindu Right to claim that it represented the *true* wishes of Hindu women and to accuse feminists of being out of touch with the *real* women of India (Kumar 1995a: 82). This argument found support among a number of academics and public intellectuals, including Ashis Nandy, who, in a series of articles, questioned whether middle-class feminists had any right to speak on behalf of rural women, especially those who believed in sati, when they showed little understanding of the complex relationship between the traditional custom of sati and religious community identity (see Nandy 1987, 1988a, b). Nandy maintained that the reaction of feminists to Kanwar's death was driven by a desire to gain political power by virtue of a presumed 'superior knowledge and morality' rather than by a deep understanding of the issues raised by Kanwar's death. He claimed that the 'feigned panic' and 'hyperbole' with which feminists greeted Kanwar's death obscured important questions concerning the 'psychological basis' of the events in Deorala. Nandy argued that the Deorala incident was rooted in the erosion of traditional lifestyles by new and modern social, economic and cultural forces (see Nandy 1989, 1995).

Indian feminists responded to these attacks by conducting their own fact-finding missions in Deorala and mobilizing support among rural and urban women in Rajasthan against sati. Moreover, by interviewing Hindu women who had taken part in pro-sati demonstrations, activists demonstrated that these women supported *satipuja* (the worship of sati) but not *sati* (the actual practice of widow sacrifice). The interviews also revealed that most of the women who had participated in the pro-sati marches were urban, middle-class women (Desai 1997: 119). Also, prominent scholars Imrana Qadeer and Zoya Hasan challenged the claims of Nandy by arguing that his explanation of sati and the Deorala episode was fundamentally flawed. In an article published in November 1987, Qadeer and Hasan stated:

> By blaming 'market morality' as the villain of the piece, [Nandy's] explanation exonerates the role of tradition – hindu or otherwise – in reviving and glorifying sati and looks at the protests as an expression of conflict between tradition and modernity. Both these propositions are deceptive. Much of the evidence either about Roop Kanwar's sati or the recorded evidence about satis in earlier periods point to coercion of the woman.
>
> (1987: 1948)

Feminists also argued that the Hindu Right was using sati to create a *tradition* for its own political purposes. They claimed that sati, like the Muslim personal law, had 'become a symbol of identity for certain powerful sections and a basis for quick mobilisation' (ibid.: 1948). In conjunction with Hindu moderates, they also pressed the Congress government to strengthen existing legislation against sati.

Despite government promises to the contrary, however, the 1988 Commission of Sati (Prevention) Bill replicated many of the caveats and ambiguities of the original legislation of the East India Company Regulation of 1829 and added a few of its own. As Oldenburg explains, 'instead of making a law that prohibits an incontestable crime against women, the framers of the new law succeeded in defining sati as a woman's crime' (1994: 126). The enactment of the bill in January 1988 prompted further protests by feminists, who argued that the legislation was ambiguous and negated the fundamental social reality that sati was not a voluntary act comparable to suicide but rather an act of coercion and murder (Palriwala and Agnihotri 1996: 521). They also accused the government of compromising with fundamentalist and communal politics. In response, the central government tried to appease feminists by promising to focus its attention on women's rights in the future (Upreti and Upreti 1991: 98). In 1988, the government released two major reports containing recommendations for government action, but, according to Agnihotri and Mazumdar, the only purpose these reports served was to show the widening divergence between the perspectives of the government and feminists on 'gender roles, issues and participation' (1995: 1875). Already wary of the government's motives and empty legislative promises, activists were angered but not surprised to find that they had not been consulted during the drafting phase of the first of the two reports, the *National Perspective Plan for Women, 1988–2000* (NPP) (ibid.: 1875).

The first that activists knew of the NPP's existence was when it was placed before a national committee headed by Prime Minister Rajiv Gandhi for policy endorsement. Activists promptly demanded that the government hold a national debate before the document was adopted as policy, but their demand fell on deaf ears. Faced with the government's refusal to discuss the contents of the NPP, seven national women's NGOs convened a meeting in Delhi to debate the plan, which was attended by activists representing thirty-nine NGOs from across India. This debate was then followed by several state-level discussions and the publication of a critique of the NPP, entitled *The National Perspective Plan for Women, 1988–2000: A Perspective from the Women's Movement* (Agnihotri and Mazumdar 1995: 1875). The main concern of feminists was that the NPP included a myriad of recommendations but made no mention of how these recommendations would be implemented or who in government would be accountable for their implementation (Kishwar and Vanita 1989: 147, 149). Yet according to Madhu Kishwar and Ruth Vanita,

> [i]n almost every section, the plan recommends setting up yet another government department. The numerous existing government bodies dealing with women's issues such as the Central Social Welfare Board, the Women's Welfare and Development Bureau, the Department of Women and Child Development, are barely distinguishable from one another and yet, the plan recommends setting up many more similar organisations on the national, state, and local levels, among them, a National Resource Centre for Women; Women's Development Corporations; Resource Centres on media at centre and state levels; a special division of law enforcement in the Department of Women and Child Development; and a number of advisory committees and cells.
>
> (ibid.: 149)

Activists argued that the government report failed to provide any evidence that such a radical expansion of administrative machinery was justified or necessary. Instead, they exhorted the government to establish statutory, autonomous commissions on women at the centre and state level as recommended by the Committee on the Status of Women in India in 1975 (Kasturi 1996: 136). They also demanded that the government focus on women's employment rights and establish appropriate childcare facilities to enable women to work (Agnihotri and Mazumdar 1995: 1875). Further, they demanded that the government ratify CEDAW and immediately incorporate Article 2 of the convention into the Indian Constitution.[6]

Although the second of the government's reports, *Shramshakti: Report of the National Commission on Self-Employed Women and Women in the Informal Sector*, was prepared by a commission headed by the prominent feminist Ela Bhatt, it also failed to outline how and by which government department(s) its many recommendations would be implemented (Agnihotri and Mazumdar 1995: 1875). The commission employed various task forces of activists and scholars to conduct extensive field studies and interview self-employed women and women working in the informal sector. This research revealed that government loans to women in these sectors often failed because of unrealistically high repayment and interest rates. It also revealed that government social welfare programmes failed to meet the needs of self-employed women and women working in the informal sector, and that these women faced a high degree of harassment and extortion from police and municipal authorities. The Shramshakti Report criticized the state for failing to protect self-employed women and women working in the informal sector. It also criticized the state's dismal record on delivering social welfare programmes that reached and benefited these women (Kasturi 1996: 130). However, the report made no mention of holding the state accountable for its failings. Furthermore, the release of the Shramshakti Report and the NPP were overshadowed by an economic and political crisis that threatened to destroy the Congress government. Congress's economic liberalization programme had stalled and Prime Minister Rajiv Gandhi was facing allegations that in 1987 he had been involved in pay-offs resulting from the state's purchase of artillery from the Swedish armaments manufacturer Bofors. The crisis deepened when Gandhi's Finance Minister, Vishwanath Pratap Singh, resigned over the Bofors controversy to help form the National Front opposition, which questioned the Prime Minister's public and political credibility and launched a scathing attack on Congress's economic policies (Denoon 1998: 52).

In a desperate bid to shore up its rural support, which was swinging away to the Left as lower-income groups struggled with accelerating inflation, Congress announced plans for a new, decentralized *panchayat raj*, or local self-government system, giving more powers to the *panchayats* (village councils) (Gala 1997: 33; Kumar 1995b: 65). The government's plan exploited the fact that the *panchayat* system had held popular political appeal since Mahatma Gandhi expounded his vision of a polity consisting of self-reliant villages with little dependence on higher levels of government (Sudarshan 1990: 60). The government's intention with the plan was to undermine the opposition's campaign leading into the December 1989 general election. In a bid to further undermine the opposition's election campaign and in the hope of appealing to rural female voters, the government promised to introduce a 30 per cent reservation of seats for women at both *panchayat* and *zilla* (district) levels (Kumar 1995b: 65). Campaigning on the slogan 'Power to the People', Rajiv Gandhi addressed the National Conference on Panchayat Raj and Women and announced that his government would not only introduce a 30 per cent reservation but extend this reservation to 50 per cent within another two years. On 15 May 1989, Gandhi introduced to Parliament a constitutional amendment increasing the powers of the *panchayat raj* and reserving 30 per cent of seats for women. During the parliamentary debates on the 64th Constitution (Amendment) Bill, Congress hailed the proposed changes to the *panchayat raj* as a revolutionary approach to governance and an opportunity to realize Mahatma Gandhi's dream. Congress also boasted that it had already prevented women from committing suicide and sati, and now the proposed changes to the *panchayat raj* would liberate women (Sharma 2000: 69). The opposition responded by accusing Congress of trying to undermine Indian federalism by bringing the *panchayats* under the direct control of the central government, and of risking needless disruption to the *panchayat* system just to find an election slogan (Sudarshan 1990: 59). The opposition also argued that a mandatory quota for women was nothing more than a cheap manoeuvre by Congress to build a vote bank (Sharma 2000: 70). The bill was passed by the Lok Sabha (Lower House) on 16 August 1989 but was narrowly defeated in the Rajya Sabha (Upper House), and thus not enacted.

The December 1989 general election resulted in a hung parliament, and although Congress won enough seats to return as the largest parliamentary group, the National Front, a coalition of seven parties led by the socialist Janata Dal, formed the government. However, Prime Minister Vishwanath Pratap Singh's minority coalition collapsed eleven months later when the BJP withdrew its support. Subsequently, Congress propped up a breakaway socialist government, headed by Chandra Shekhar, for five months before it collapsed in the midst of a major economic crisis. During the ensuing election campaign, Rajiv Gandhi was assassinated at an election rally in Tamil Nadu, but despite his death, Congress won the election and formed a government in July 1991 with P. V. Narashima Rao as Prime Minister. However, the BJP also emerged from the election stronger, having campaigned on a promise to build a Hindu temple at the disputed site of the Babri Masjid mosque in Ayodhya. These events and the subsequent threat to women's rights of new economic structural adjustment programmes and escalating communal tension led many Indian feminists to seek both greater political representation at all levels of government and ratification of CEDAW.[7]

Finally, the government ratified CEDAW on 9 July 1993. However, the impetus for ratification came less from domestic feminist pressure than from the government's desire to avoid international embarrassment following the UN Human Rights Conference in Vienna in June 1993. In what Kapur describes as a cynical public relations exercise, the Indian government ratified CEDAW with significant reservations, declaring that

[w]ith regard to Articles 5(a) and 16(1) ... the Government of India declares that it shall abide and ensure these provisions in conformity with its policy of non-interference in the personal affairs of any community without its initiative and support.

(Kapur 2001a; UNCEDAW 1996)

The government's rationale for this declaration was that it needed to safeguard the constitutionally enshrined rights of religious and ethnic minorities. However, by refusing to amend or remove discriminatory religious personal laws, the government not only denied equality to women but also flouted its legal obligation to abide by the spirit of the convention (Rahman 1990: 486). Following ratification, moreover, the government failed to amend other domestic legislation and public policies that conflicted with the convention, and to submit its initial periodic CEDAW report on time.

The fourth period of state behavioural continuity: 1996–2004

In the general election of May 1996, Congress suffered its worst defeat since independence, winning only 140 seats in an extremely fragmented parliament. The Hindu nationalist BJP emerged from the election stronger and formed a minority government under Prime Minister Atal Behari Vajpayee but lost power after only twelve days. For the next eighteen months, Congress served as a key supporter to two shaky governments of the centre-left United Front, headed first by H. D. Deve Gowda and then by Inder Kumar Gujral. In the lead-up to the election, feminists had lobbied intensely for one-third reservations in Parliament and state assemblies, and the major political parties had accepted their demand, incorporating it into their election manifestos (Mazumdar 1999: 368; Sharma 2000: 70). However, political support for reservations was short-lived and in the election, political parties gave less than 15 per cent of the total number of tickets to women. Following the election, all political parties, including those in the United Front coalition government, deliberately derailed legislation providing for a quota at the parliamentary level. This suggests that their initial support for reservations was based on political expediency. When the United Front coalition government led by Gowda introduced the 81st Constitution (Amendment) Bill to Parliament in September 1996, it was greeted with derision. Medha Nanivadekar speculates that this was because members perceived reservations in Parliament as a direct threat to their political survival (Nanivadekar 1998: 1815). Prime Minister Gowda was content not to push the legislation and referred the bill to a Joint Select Committee of Parliament for further consideration (Sharma 1998: 25).

Indian feminists continued to press for reservations but became concerned when the BJP appropriated for itself this and other gender equality issues, claiming a mission to reform discriminatory laws. Installed as the ruling party in the March 1998 mid-term election, the BJP also continued to champion a uniform civil code, creating a dilemma for feminists about whether and how to lobby for a uniform civil code and other gender equality reforms without being associated with the BJP on the issues. Equally problematic for feminists was the extent of support among Hindu women for the BJP and the level of their participation in the activities of BJP-affiliated organizations (see Sarkar 1993a, b; Mazumdar 1995). As they debated how to respond to these dilemmas, the BJP coalition government, under international pressure, prepared and submitted India's initial CEDAW report on 2 February 1999. According to Kapur, the report, which was five years overdue, failed to mention the fact 'that not a single law had been repealed or legal reforms enacted in compliance with the convention' (2001b). However, this did not pass unnoticed by the CEDAW committee, which, in its consideration of India's initial report in late January 2000, criticized the state for entering reservations to CEDAW and for failing to comply with the convention. The committee criticized the state for failing to intervene in religious personal laws, arguing that the state's policy of non-intervention served to perpetuate sexual stereotypes and was discriminatory. It also berated the state for failing to act to prevent and eliminate both state-based and societal-based violence against women. Further, it criticized the state for failing to protect NGOs, feminist activists and human rights defenders from acts of 'violence and harassment in the communities in which they work' (United Nations General Assembly 2000: 14). The committee exhorted the state to 'introduce comprehensive legislative reform to promote equality and the human rights of women', and to enact a uniform civil code (ibid.). It also pressed the state to strictly enforce existing legislation and to introduce affirmative action programmes in the areas of political and judicial representation, and employment. Further, it commanded the state to introduce gender sensitization and human rights training programmes for the police, security forces and medical professionals (ibid.: 12).

The BJP-led National Democratic Alliance government elected on 13 October 1999 refused to act on the CEDAW committee recommendations other than to make rhetorical statements of intent. The government declared 2001 to be Women's Empowerment Year and announced ambitious plans to mark the year, but, as feminists predicted, none of these plans was realized. The government also promised to address the issue of domestic violence and to increase both the number of women in the police force and the number of police units dealing with crimes against women. However, despite accepting as a model the Domestic Violence Against Women (Prevention) Bill drafted by the Lawyer's Collective Women's Rights Initiative, the government failed to table any such legislation in Parliament (Lawyer's Collective Women's Rights Initiative 2000).[8] The government also promised to address the issue of sexual harassment following two Supreme Court decisions in 1997 and 1999.[9] However, despite considerable domestic pressure from feminists and sustained international pressure, particularly from the ILO Committee of Experts, the government failed to enact legislation prohibiting sexual harassment in the workplace. Instead, it issued a circular to all government employees informing them of the Supreme Court guidelines of 1997, and distributed a copy of the guidelines to employers in the private sector.

The real agenda of the BJP-led coalition government was to strengthen the communalist corporate identity of the state by restoring women to the position they once enjoyed in the glorious and ancient past as *matrishakti* (the power and primordial energy of Mother) (Kapur and Cossman 1996a: 97). The BJP's ideal woman, according to Tanika Sarkar, was one who had a strong 'intellectual grasp of the values of Hindu culture and devotional attachment to the ideals of Hindu womanhood' (Sarkar 1991: 2061). Further, she continues, the government's intention was to introduce policies that reinforced women's role in the family as wives and mothers (ibid.: 2061). The government's policies became infused with the idea of women as *matrishakti* and the belief in the natural and essential differences between men and women (Kapur and Cossman 1996b: 245). The government used the language of gender equality and rights as a 'tool for dismantling the rights of religious minorities and masquerading the continued inequalities of gender and community' (Kapur and Cossman 1996a: 102). As feminists struggled to extricate the demand for gender equality from the government's Hindu nationalist discourse, the BJP coalition government became increasingly difficult to negotiate with as it narrowed avenues for public debate and undermined any notion of political accountability (Kapur 2001a). Symptomatic of the government's desire to stifle public debate was its use of an anachronistic, Emergency-era statute, the Foreign Contribution (Regulation) Act of 1976, to restrict the activities of NGOs, especially feminist NGOs. In late 1999, the Home Ministry threatened thirteen feminist NGOs with deregistration under the Act, after two BJP officials complained about the NGOs' sponsorship of a newspaper advertisement criticizing the government's position on women's rights (Voice of the Asia-Pacific Human Rights Network 1999).

The party officials accused the feminist NGOs of being anti-national and anti-Indian, and demanded an investigation into their activities. Another NGO, the Volunteer Action Network India, subsequently leapt to the defence of the feminist NGOs, only to find itself threatened with deregistration by the Home Ministry. The Home Ministry justified its actions on the basis that the NGOs were 'associated with the release of certain advertisements in the press and with certain documents of a political nature' (Voice of the Asia-Pacific Human Rights Network 1999). Combined with the government's imposition of an arbitrary clearance requirement for NGOs organizing international conferences, the Home Ministry's enforcement of the Foreign Contribution (Regulation) Act signalled an increasing unwillingness on the part of the government to tolerate criticism and dissent (ibid.). Furthermore, the government's determination to restrict access to information about government plans and activities indicated a retreat from democratic principles. In this climate of mutual distrust, the government became increasingly hostile towards international norms of sexual non-discrimination.

Conclusion

Since independence in 1947, India has ratified several international conventions of sexual non-discrimination, including CEDAW, but refused to comply with any of these conventions. Always resistant to incorporating international norms of sexual non-discrimination, the state became increasingly recalcitrant in the mid-1990s. Despite considerable internal and external pressure, the state developed effective strategies and tactics to delay and avoid comprehensive legislative and public policy change on the issues of women's civil, political and labour rights, and violence against women. In the mid-1990s, the state became ultra-conservative and progressively hostile towards international norms of sexual non-discrimination. The history of India's response to these norms since 1947 has been dominated, as we have seen, by four periods of state behavioural continuity in which the state created and consolidated a paternalistic and communalist corporate identity, and resisted international and domestic pressure to ratify and comply with international conventions. The state repeatedly evaded external and internal pressure to incorporate international norms of sexual non-discrimination, either by making empty promises to implement gender-rectifying policies or by enacting ineffective legislation. Recently, the state attempted to divert attention away from its increasingly conservative agenda by appropriating the language of gender equality and aligning itself with women's rights issues. It also tried to silence Indian feminists by legally restraining their activities and restricting their access to information about government plans and policies.

Conclusion

This book has examined the emergence, growth and efficacy of international norms of sexual non-discrimination. In particular, it has addressed several important questions regarding the diffusion of such norms into domestic state practices: to what extent have international norms of sexual non-discrimination diffused and impacted on state behaviour? Why, how and under what conditions have these norms influenced the actions of states? Why have particular norms diffused more readily than others and why have certain norms failed to diffuse into domestic state practices? Through what processes and promoted by which agents have states come under pressure to comply with these norms? What has motivated states to agree, or refuse, to incorporate these norms into domestic practices? And what, if anything, can those operating in the field learn from this comparative study on norm diffusion?

Despite the expansion of international and European norms of sexual non-discrimination since the end of the Second World War, the diffusion and efficacy of these norms have received little explicit attention. While feminist international legal scholars have critiqued the conceptual and procedural origins of international norms of sexual non-discrimination, they have not examined their diffusion. While international relations scholars have debated the role of numerous norms in international politics, they have paid scant attention to the diffusion and efficacy of international norms of sexual non-discrimination. The very existence of a comprehensive set of international and European norms of sexual non-discrimination makes examining the diffusion and efficacy of these norms worthwhile. The fact that *half the world's population* is potentially affected by these norms makes investigating their diffusion and influence imperative. As I argue in Chapter 2, the explanation for why states respond the way they do to international norms of sexual non-discrimination lies in the complex interaction between international and domestic socio-cultural structures and agents. Whether or not a state incorporates these norms into domestic practices also depends on the strength of the gender-biased corporate identity of the state, which is politically constituted and reconstituted within the state at various points in time.

Feminist international legalism is unequipped to explain the diffusion and efficacy of international norms of sexual non-discrimination, as it assumes these norms are inconsequential, based on inadequate international enforcement mechanisms and patriarchal states. Rationalist perspectives in international relations are also ill-equipped to explain the diffusion and efficacy of these norms, as they treat diffusion, or rather compliance, as a purely instrumental response by states to the efficacy of norms. Both neoliberalism and liberal intergovernmentalism invoke arguments about utility maximization, claiming that compliance is determined by the rational calculations of states or individuals respectively. Interpretive perspectives in international relations appear, at first glance, to be better equipped to explain the diffusion and efficacy of international norms of sexual non-discrimination. Sociological institutionalism predicts pervasive diffusion and isomorphic effects 'driven by the rationalised culture of the Western-derived world polity' (Schofer 1999: 265). Constructivism, in its various guises, views diffusion and the internalization of norms as the product of socialization, a process whereby states are inducted 'into the ways of behaviour preferred by [international] society' (Risse 1999: 529). However, while both sociological institutionalism and constructivism help explain the durability and constitutive influence of norms, they struggle to explain the variance in state responses to international norms of sexual non-discrimination or the limited overall impact these norms have had on state behaviour.

Recapping the argument

The central argument of this study is that, while the gender-biased corporate identity of many states is a serious impediment to the diffusion of international norms of sexual non-discrimination, certain conditions arise under which particular norms diffuse and influence state behaviour. These preconditions emerge as a result of historically and locationally specific structural–agential interaction. The notion of the gender-biased corporate identity of the state is primarily intended to surmount the problems that patriarchy, as conceived by feminist international legal scholars, has in dealing with the historical and cross-national variation in state systems of gender relations and the dynamics of change. It is also designed to overcome the problems that international relations theories have in explaining the relative intransigence of states towards complying with or incorporating international norms of sexual non-discrimination. As I argue in Chapter 2, the gender-biased corporate identity of the state presents a formidable but not insurmountable barrier to internationally derived change. Thus, it is crucial to understand how the gender-biased corporate identity of the state is created and maintained, and to explain the motivation of states to resist or accept the idea that they should incorporate international norms of sexual non-discrimination into domestic practices. This requires analysing the relationship between structure and agency, which are the defining components of international and domestic society and, accordingly, of the explanation of norm diffusion and efficacy. This also requires an examination of the contentious discursive relationship between various actors, as well as the operations of power in social interaction.

In Chapter 2, I argue that a theoretical approach drawing on insights from critical realism provides a useful way to conceptualize the relationship between structure and agency for the purpose of explaining not only the diffusion and efficacy of international norms of sexual non-discrimination but also the emergence and expansion of these norms. This approach traces the historical process by which structural–agential interaction and contentious discursive interaction between various agents enable or constrain norm formation and diffusion. Using this approach, Chapter 3 traces the origins and development of international and European norms of sexual non-discrimination. Also using this approach, Chapters 4–7 examine the extent to which various international norms of sexual non-discrimination have diffused into the domestic practices of Germany, Spain, Japan and India respectively. The four cases examined in this study highlighted how the gender-biased corporate identity of the state, in its various guises, acted as a significant barrier to the diffusion of international norms of sexual non-discrimination. These cases, with the exception of India also showed how, despite the inhibiting effect of the gender-biased corporate identity of the state, particular norms diffused at particular points in time as a consequence of external and/or internal pressure generated by certain actors.

In Chapter 3, I trace the emergence and development of salient international and European norms of sexual non-discrimination in the post-Second World War era. These included norms related to women's civil, political and labour rights, and the issue of violence against women. I identified three historical periods of norm elaboration in which social interaction generated change, and two interim periods of norm continuity in which social interaction restrained the development of new norms. In each of the three periods of norm elaboration, the main impetus behind the changes came from international feminists, who exploited favourable international political and legal conditions to press for the creation of certain norms. In their fight to create effective norms, activists seized on and refashioned the dominant international political discourse of the time to articulate their claims and assert their demands. However, securing revisions to the international and European legal systems was not easy, with state representatives time and again contesting and watering down proposed changes. In each of the two interim periods of norm continuity, the opportunities for international feminists to act effectively – that is, to exercise meaningful influence on international and European policy – narrowed considerably.

In Chapter 4, I examine the effects of international norms of sexual non-discrimination on the domestic practices of Germany. I argue that despite its long-standing reputation as an exemplary member of the international and European communities, Germany has, until recently, resisted incorporating such norms. I also argue that the Christian-occidental, paternalistic corporate state identity reconstructed in the wake of the Second World War proved highly resistant to internationally derived change. In the light of this, I identify three periods of state behavioural continuity, between 1945 and 1997, in which social interaction tended to result in the reproduction of discriminatory state practices. However, both the first and the last of these periods of stasis were punctuated by instances of either regionally or domestically derived state behavioural change. I also identify a single period of state behavioural change, from 1998 to 2004, in which social interaction mediated by contentious discursive interaction between a range of actors resulted in the adoption of certain non-discriminatory state practices.

In the German case, we saw how the state repeatedly resisted internal pressure from German feminists to alter its behaviour. We saw how domestic feminists seized political opportunities at certain historical junctures in the late 1960s and late 1980s and attempted, without success, to influence state practices. I suggested that one of the reasons for this was that activists failed to discursively challenge and cast doubt on the state's conservative conception of gender relations. However, while internal pressure failed to generate state behavioural change, the European Commission's threat to initiate infringement proceedings against Germany in May 1979 for failing to implement European directives by their designated deadlines induced a noticeable, albeit minimal, change to national labour practices. In 1994, the state made further minor adjustments to national employment practices as a result of domestic electoral pressure. Following a dramatic changing of the guard at the elite level in 1998, the state became more receptive to incorporating international norms of sexual non-discrimination, but state behavioural change was guaranteed only by a combination of internal and external pressure. The internal pressure emanated from feminists within the new political elite, who discursively challenged the traditional conception of gender relations and pursued a range of legislative and public policy changes designed to bring state practices into line with international and European norms. The external pressure was generated by international bodies, which pressed for state behavioural change through their reporting systems.

In Chapter 5, I investigate the effects of international norms of sexual non-discrimination on the domestic practices of Spain. I argue that Spain's receptiveness to such norms vacillated over time. I also argue that the neoconservative, paterfamilias corporate state identity created following the Spanish Civil War remained impervious to internationally derived change until 1976 and the democratic transition. Moreover, this

National-Catholic corporate state identity continued to have a residual inhibiting effect on diffusion following the democratic transition. In light of this, I identify a period of state behavioural continuity, from 1945 to 1975, in which social interaction resulted in the reproduction of discriminatory state practices. Following the re-establishment of democracy in 1976, Spain experienced two consecutive periods of state behavioural change in which social interaction resulted in the adoption of non-discriminatory state practices. In 1996, a second period of state behavioural continuity began that continued to 2004.

In the Spanish case, we saw how the authoritarian state established at the end of the Civil War in 1939 implemented a range of discriminatory measures that contravened international law. At the same time, the authoritarian state crushed any internal dissent or opposition to its policies. Following the death of General Francisco Franco and the democratic transition in 1976, the state became increasingly receptive to incorporating international norms of sexual non-discrimination, but state behavioural change was ensured only by a combination of internal and external pressure. The internal pressure emanated from feminists, who exploited the democratic state's desire for international and European recognition to press for legislative and public policy initiatives. Spanish feminists also seized on and used to great effect the discourse of European integration, which resonated with the political elite. The external pressure was generated by international bodies, which pressed for state behavioural change through their reporting systems, and by the European Union, which demanded that Spain meet certain conditions of membership. Following a conservative changeover at the elite level in 1996, the attitude of the state towards international norms of sexual non-discrimination hardened and it became far less receptive to incorporating such norms into domestic practices. The state ignored international and domestic criticism of its attempts to re-establish a more traditional corporate state identity and implement gender-reinforcing policies.

In Chapter 6, I examine the effects of international norms of sexual non-discrimination on the domestic practices of Japan. I argue that despite progressive constitutional and policy reforms implemented by Allied occupation forces between 1945 and 1952, Japan has been extremely reluctant to incorporate such norms. I also argue that the patrilineal corporate state identity reconstructed in the immediate post-occupation period proved highly resistant to internationally derived change. In the light of this, I identify three periods of state behavioural continuity between 1952 and 2004, in which social interaction tended to result in the reproduction of discriminatory state practices. The second and third of these periods of stasis were punctuated by instances of state behavioural change, but in each instance the change was minimal, and commonly offset by other, gender-reinforcing state policies.

In the Japanese case, we saw how the state repeatedly resisted internal and external pressure to modify its behaviour. We saw how Japanese feminists and private individual litigants grasped political opportunities at certain points in time and attempted, with little success, to influence state behaviour. I suggest that the primary reason for this is that the state developed effective strategies to deflect internal criticism, including the practice of *paralysis by analysis*, which involved the state taking an inordinate amount of time to study the compatibility between Japanese and international law, and concession-making. For instance, when activists and litigants campaigned for changes to national labour laws in the early 1980s, the state responded by making modest legislative concessions. However, these changes to Japanese labour laws were promptly undermined by gender-reinforcing social security measures introduced by the state. Moreover, these social security measures acted to reinforce the patrilineal corporate identity of the state. From 1990 onwards, the state resisted intense international and domestic pressure to admit legal responsibility for and pay compensation to victims of state-sponsored military prostitution during the Second World War. The state also resisted pressure to meet its international legal obligations under a number of conventions regarding sexual non-discrimination. When international bodies and Japanese feminists and litigants criticized the state and applied pressure on it to change, the state responded by making legislative concessions in certain areas. However, these legislative changes were minimal and they were often offset by other, gender-reinforcing policies.

In Chapter 7, I investigate the effects of international norms of sexual non-discrimination on the domestic practices of India. I argue that despite its self-proclaimed commitment to gender equality, India has steadfastly refused to incorporate such norms. In fact, recently, India became increasingly loath to incorporate and internalize such norms. I also argue that the paternalistic, communalist corporate state identity constructed initially in the post-independence period, and reinforced in recent years, has proved virtually impervious to internationally derived change. In the light of this, I identify four periods of state behavioural continuity, between 1947 and 2004, in which social interaction tended to result in the reproduction of discriminatory state practices.

In the Indian case, we saw how the state repeatedly resisted internal and external pressure to alter its behaviour. We saw how Indian feminists grasped political opportunities at certain points in time and attempted, with little success, to influence state behaviour. I suggest that the principal reason for this is that the state developed several effective delaying strategies to avoid modifying its behaviour, including making empty promises and adopting ineffective legislation. For instance, when Indian feminists campaigned for changes to the Dowry Prohibition Act in the early 1980s, the state responded by enacting amendments that were insubstantial and unenforceable. From 1996 onwards, the state became increasingly averse to incorporating international norms of sexual non-discrimination. The state not only resisted intense international pressure to meet its legal obligations under a number of conventions regarding sexual non-discrimination but also attempted to silence domestic feminist political critics by appropriating their oppositional discursive repertoire for itself and legally restraining their activities.

Theoretical and practical implications

The argument developed in this study has several implications for the examination of the diffusion and efficacy of international norms in international relations. It also has important implications for the *structure–agency problematique* in international relations, in terms both of ontological assumptions and of empirical analysis. In addition, the argument developed in this study has implications for the blind spots of feminist international legalism regarding the consequences of international norms of sexual non-discrimination. Furthermore, the cross-national analysis of state responses to these norms has practical implications for those operating in the field.

Implications for studying the diffusion and efficacy of international norms in international relations

In 1993, Peter Katzenstein argued that

> our analysis of international and domestic politics will remain incomplete if it neglects the normative context that helps define the interests of actors. Incompleteness is of course essential to the enterprise of developing compelling explanations in the social sciences. But the assumption that actors know their interests, though convenient for analytical purposes, sidesteps some of the most important political and intriguing analytical questions in contemporary politics.
>
> (1993a: 294)

Since then, constructivists in international relations have shown why and how the international normative context shapes the identity and interests of states. Recent constructivist scholarship has emphasized the socialization process by which international norms diffuse into states. Socialization is defined as the process by which new members are inducted into the ways of behaviour that are preferred in international society (see Finnemore 1996b; Finnemore and Sikkink 1998; Cortell and Davis 2000). In this process, states' identities and preferences are defined and redefined by international norms. In turn, the practices of states define and redefine international normative structures. The identity referred to here is the social identity of the state. This argument renders the corporate aspect of state identities insignificant in explaining the diffusion and efficacy of international norms. However, as I have explained, in this study the corporate aspect of state identities is understood to play a crucial role in determining the behavioural responses of states to international norms of sexual non-discrimination. As we have seen in the cases of Germany and Japan, the social or external identity of the state has little bearing on its behavioural response to these norms in comparison with the corporate or internal identity of the state. Despite its highly 'internationalized' and 'Europeanized' social identities, Germany has been almost as reluctant to incorporate international norms of sexual non-discrimination as Japan, which is commonly understood to identify 'relatively weakly with international society' (Gurowitz 1999: 422). It is important, therefore, not to ignore or underestimate the importance of the corporate aspect of state identities in analysing and explaining international norm diffusion and efficacy. So, while constructivism has addressed the shortcomings of rationalism and broadened our understanding of the durability and constitutive influence of international norms, it has failed to explain adequately why certain norms affect certain states and not others at certain times and in certain ways. It has also failed to explain adequately why well-established international regimes as a whole sometimes fail to have a significant effect on the behaviour of states.

As I demonstrate in this study, explaining why norms fail to diffuse and affect state behaviour is as important as explaining why norms diffuse and influence domestic state practices. In Chapter 2, I argue that the major impediment to the diffusion of international norms of sexual non-discrimination is the gender-biased corporate identity of the state, which is politically constituted and reconstituted within the state. Thus, it is important to understand how the gender-biased corporate identity of the state is created and maintained. This requires tracing the process by which political elites and other dominant actors within the state, such as the Church, construct and consolidate a corporate identity based on certain ideas and beliefs about gender relations in the public and private spheres. Yet as we have seen in Chapters 4–7, despite the formidable barrier to diffusion presented by the gender-biased corporate identity of the state, international organizational pressure and/or domestic pressure emanating from feminist political activism and/or private individual litigation facilitate diffusion on occasion and induce state behavioural change. Therefore, this study suggests that the inclusion of an analysis of the construction of the corporate aspect of state identities, and of the relationship between this aspect of state identities and various international and domestic agents pressing for changes to the behaviour of states, may take us a step closer to developing a general theory of international norm diffusion.

Implications for the structure–agency problematique in international relations

The *structure–agency problematique* has recently been the subject of keen debate in the study of international relations but it has yet to be resolved. As Walter Carlsnaes explains,

> [a]t the heart of this problem lies the increasingly widespread recognition that, instead of being antagonistic partners in a zero-sum relationship, human agents and social structures are in a fundamental sense dynamically interrelated entities, and hence that we cannot account fully for the one without invoking the other. The 'problem' is that although such views of reciprocal implication suggest that the properties of both agents and social structures are relevant to a proper understanding of social behaviour (including the study of change), we nevertheless ... '*lack a self-evident way to conceptualize these entities and their relationship*'.
>
> Carlsnaes (2001: 344; emphasis added to indicate where Carlsnaes
> quotes Alexander Wendt)

While I do not pretend to have solved the structure–agency problematique in international relations, I suggest that the argument developed in this study regarding social interaction between structures and agents offers a new and meaningful way to analyse and explain variation in the extent to which international norms diffuse and are internalized by states. In Chapter 2, I propose that a useful way to explain the significant variation in the extent to which international norms of sexual non-discrimination are incorporated into domestic practices is to trace the historical sequences of social interaction which lead to state behavioural change or continuity. This requires a conceptualization of structure and agency that treats the two elements of social interaction as autonomous, irreducible entities and explicitly includes time as a variable linking structures and agents. For although social interaction is continuous, it is necessary to accept the temporal separation of structure and agency if we are to obtain analytical purchase on those processes that are accountable for determinate state behavioural change or continuity (Archer 1998: 376). It is also necessary to acknowledge that socio-cultural structures and agents are separate entities possessing distinct emergent properties in order to examine their interplay over time. By using an ontology of emergent properties, we can trace how, over time, international and domestic social contexts and agents interact, with agency resulting in state behavioural change or continuity. If we are to explain state responses to international norms of sexual non-discrimination adequately, it is also necessary to acknowledge the role that contentious discursive interaction plays in motivating states to act in certain ways at certain points in time. Contentious discursive interaction involves a relational struggle between various agents over the meaning of social situations or issues such as the gendered social order, family–state relations and domestic violence. It also involves a relational struggle between domination and resistance, or power.

Implications for feminist international legalism

Feminist international legal scholars, as I explain in Chapter 1, presume that international norms of sexual non-discrimination have virtually no effect on the behaviour of states, because the regime in which these norms are embodied lacks enforcement mechanisms, and because state patriarchal interests are profoundly inhibiting. However, this comparative study of the diffusion of international norms of sexual non-discrimination has highlighted the importance of examining the effects of such norms before trivializing their relevance or dismissing them as inconsequential. As we have seen in each of the four cases examined in this study, the problem of norm ineffectiveness lies not in the international regime itself but in the lack of political will on behalf of state elites to incorporate norms of sexual non-discrimination that conflict with domestically embedded ideas and values of gender differentiation – in other words, the gender-biased corporate identity of the state.

In each of the four cases, we saw how political elites produced and reproduced a corporate identity based upon certain predominant ideas about gender roles and relations. The gender system within each state differed both in nature and in degree of strength, thus producing a distinct corporate identity. By examining the political constitution and reconstitution of the gender-biased corporate identity within each state, this study revealed cross-national variation and historical differences in gender systems, which, in turn, affected the diffusion of norms in different ways. I suggest, therefore, that the notion of the gender-biased corporate identity of the state provides an explanatory power that is lacking in the concept of patriarchy as it is employed in feminist international legalism. Contrary to the assumption by feminist international legal scholars that international norms of sexual non-discrimination are inconsequential, this study has also demonstrated that these norms are consequential for state behaviour. However, their influence has not been as extensive as it should be, and this is a matter of great concern.

Practical implications for those operating in the field

There are several lessons that can be drawn from this study for those operating in the field. First, international and domestic agents trying to promote state behavioural change need to pay close attention to how state elites create and maintain the gender-biased corporate aspect of state identities. Second, international and regional bodies need to find ways to generate positive attitudinal change among state elites and among other dominant actors within states, such as the Church, religious communities and the judiciary. Third, international and regional bodies need to create positive incentives to encourage state compliance. These might take the form of financial and technical assistance, clear and precise reporting guidelines, educational training programmes for policy-makers, and judicial educational programmes (Alston 2000: 524–5; United Nations 2000). Fourth, international and regional bodies need to strengthen and, more importantly, develop the political will to apply such mechanisms and hold states accountable to their agreements. However, international and regional bodies must remain aware that even if they apply enforcement procedures, there is no guarantee that states will fully respect their international legal obligations. As we saw in the German case, despite being held accountable to its European legal obligations by the European Court of Justice in the mid-1980s, the state resisted making the appropriate changes to national employment law. Fifth, it is important for international bodies to support those fighting for progressive change from within states, including private individual and group litigants. International support for domestic feminist activists fighting for change might take the form of outreach training programmes and advisory services, legal literacy programmes, translating international legal provisions into national languages, and facilitating information exchange between activists in various states. Finally, advocates struggling for change at the domestic level need to be aware that discursively challenging political elites' ideas of proper and appropriate gender roles and relations in society contributes to generating state behavioural change. If political elites within states make empty promises or misappropriate gender equality issues, domestic feminist activists need to find ways to shift the terms of the political debate surrounding such issues. And, in my view, academics and feminists working together and making greater use of international law can expose and critique the discursive tactics of political elites and create new ways of thinking and talking about gender equality issues, as well as open avenues for action.

Notes

Introduction

1 The infringement procedure allows the European Commission to bring a state in front of the European Court of Justice on charges of non-compliance. The term 'Germany' is used throughout the study to refer to the Federal Republic of Germany, and the term 'European Union' is generally used throughout the study to refer also to the European Economic Community and the European Community.

2 The terms 'gender-rectifying' and 'gender-reinforcing' are taken from Mikanagi (1998).

3 All four states examined in this study ratified various existing international conventions of sexual non-discrimination during this period but no appropriate changes to national legislation or public policy were made.

4 Japan ratified these conventions in 1967 and 1955 respectively but failed to comply with either convention.

1 Existing explanations of international norm diffusion

1 Inconvenient commitments being defined by Keohane (1992: 178–9) as 'those commitments that oblige governments (1) to take actions that they would, apart from their commitment, not undertake; or (2) not to take actions in which they would, apart from their commitment, engage.'

2 Sidney Jones (1996: 271) speculates that the diversity of the Asian region, the lack of any existing institutional framework, and the lack of disinterest, or hostility, on the part of many states in the region towards concern shown by the international community about their human rights records make the establishment of a regional human rights system highly unlikely.

3 For work on epistemic communities in international relations, see Haas (1990); for work on transnational advocacy networks, see Keck and Sikkink (1998).

2 International norms of sexual non-discrimination and changing state practices

1 In the case of the United Nations, these action plans emanated from four world conferences held between 1975 and 1995.

2 The modern sovereign state, to use Stephen Krasner's definition (1984: 224), is a form of political organization consisting of government 'personnel who occupy positions of decisional authority' and a 'normative order' constructed in large part by political elites.

3 These questions were first raised by Allen (1999: 54).

3 Origins and development of international norms of sexual non-discrimination

1 Individualization refers to treating couples as individuals as opposed to breadwinner and dependant or a member of a family group (Hoskyns 1996: 110).
2 The European Council has since adopted such measures: Council Directive of 3 June 1996 on the Framework Agreement on Parental Leave, Council Directive of 15 December 1997 on the Burden of Proof in Cases of Discrimination Based on Sex, Council Directive of 15 December 1997 on the Framework Agreement on Part-time Work, and Council Resolution of 6 June 2000 on the Balanced Participation of Women and Men in Family and Working Life.
3 The European Commission's Women's Bureau was established in 1976 and later renamed the Equal Opportunities Unit.
4 The missions include field trips to Korea and Japan in 1995 on the issue of military sexual slavery; to South Africa on the issue of rape, Brazil on the issue of domestic violence, and Poland on the issue of trafficking and forced prostitution in 1996; to Rwanda in 1997 on the issue of gender-based violence during armed conflict; and to the United States in 1998 on the issue of gender-based violence in detention or prison.
5 For a discussion of CEDAW's enforcement mechanisms and significance of the optional protocol, see Hoq (2001).
6 The European Parliament passed a resolution on violence against women on 14 July 1984, which was drafted by the Committee on Women's Rights and called on the European Community to take action on issues of gender-based violence, including sexual harassment.
7 Directive 2002/73/EC amending Council Directive 76/207/EEC on the Implementation of the Principle of Equal Treatment for Men and Women as Regards to Employment, Vocational Training and Promotion, and Working Conditions.

4 Germany

1 Allied occupation forces oversaw the drafting and passage of the new post-war Constitution, and the inclusion of the principle of equality was ensured primarily by the courageous and tenacious intervention of a feminist within the SDP, Elisabeth Selbert.
2 The CDU–CSU coalition government revived the 1938 Act on Working Time and other Legal Provisions Concerning Special Protective Measures for Women Workers, and introduced the 1952 Law for the Protection of Mothers.
3 Germany finally ratified the 1957 UN Convention on the Nationality of Married Women in 1974, and the 1962 UN Convention on Consent to Marriage in 1969.
4 The Decree against Radicals was enacted in direct response to the violent terrorism of the Red Army Faction and other extremists, but according to many critics was used by the state to suppress any criticism of its own behaviour.
5 Direct effect establishes that EU law can be used directly by individual litigants to challenge national policies.
6 Articles 611a (equal treatment in employment, promotion, and dismissal), 611b (advertisement of vacancies) and article 612 paragraph 3 (pay) were inserted into the Civil Code.
7 Progressive state and local governments included those of Hessen, Hamburg, North Rhine-Westphalia, Bremen and Berlin.
8 The UFV was founded in East Berlin on 3 December 1989 as a national umbrella organization for a diverse range of feminist political groups and initiatives. In 1998, the UFV was disbanded as a national organization.

9 East and West German feminist political advocates were drawn together on one issue – abortion – and the issue was discussed in parliamentary discussions on unification.

10 According to an EU study published in October 2002, *The Life of Women and Men of Europe*, Germany had the largest gender wage gap in both the public and the private sectors in the EU; the average gross hourly earnings of women were 77 per cent of men's earnings in the public sector and 73 per cent in the private sector, compared with average EU figures of 87 per cent in the public sector and 82 per cent in the private sector (Eurostat 2002).

11 Prior to the September 2002 election, there were only enough childcare providers to cover 7 per cent of children under three years of age, and most primary schools sent pupils home by 1 p.m. at the latest.

5 Spain

1 Falangist doctrine was the official doctrine of the Falange Española Tradicional-ista y de las Juntas Ofensivas Sindicalistas, the fascist state party formed by Franco in 1937.

2 The fundamental laws of the authoritarian regime were said to serve the same purpose as that of a liberal democratic constitution and pledged loyalty to 'the doctrine of the Holy, Apostolic, Roman Catholic Church, the only true faith, inseparable from the nation's conscience, inspiration of its legislation' (Boetsch 1985: 144).

3 The Spanish Communist Party (PCE) was eventually legalized on 9 April 1977.

4 The Spanish state eventually adopted Act 11/1994 of 19 May, Article 28 of which substituted the term 'work of equal value' for the term 'equal work' but failed to implement or enforce the legislation.

5 The Law 11/1981 of 13 May was entitled Promotion of the Financial and Civil Equality of Marriage Partners and Protection of the Rights of the Children.

6 In 1989, the Spanish government introduced legal provisions for unpaid parental leave to be taken by either parent, and in 1990 the government incorporated an article reversing the burden of proof in the Spanish Labour Court Proceedings Law (Threlfall 1997: 20–1).

6 Japan

1 In the end, the Supreme Court's ruling made no difference in the outcome for the accused in the Fukuoka Patricide Case, because the Fukuoka District Court sentenced him again to three years' imprisonment, suspending the penalty for a period of three years, basing its conviction this time on Article 205(2), the constitutionality of which had now been confirmed.

2 Article 200 of the Criminal Code punishes murderers of lineal ascendants with death, or life imprisonment.

3 On both occasions, Japanese feminists pressured the government into reversing its decision to abolish the Women and Minors Bureau in the Ministry of Labour. See Jones (1976: 217).

4 The UN Human Rights Committee, in its consideration of Japan's initial report under the International Covenant on Civil and Political Rights, condemned the Japanese Nationality Law as discriminatory.

5 The Ministry of Labour sponsored surveys conducted by the Japan Economic Research Centre and the National Institute of Employment and Vocational Research.

6 For details of the Recruit Scandal and the sex scandal involving Sosuke, see Herzog (1993).

7 The issue of Japanese military enforced prostitution during the Second World War was first raised by the UN Commission on Human Rights in February 1992 and again in May 1992 for the UN Working Group on Contemporary Forms of Slavery.

8 For details of the two bribery scandals, see Herzog (1993: 188–9).

9 The three Korean comfort women were Ha Sun-nyo, Park Tu-ri and Lee Sun-dok.

10 The Alien Tort Act allows US district courts to hear suits by aliens alleging torts committed anywhere in violation of international law.

11 Recent successful cases using ATCA include *Kadic* v. *Karadzic*, 74 F.3d 232 (2d Cir. 1995) (using the statute to exercise jurisdiction and find liability in a case involving war crimes and crimes against humanity in Bosnia); and *Trajano* v. *Marcos*, 978 F.2d 493 (9th Cir. 1992) (asserting a wrongful death claim by a Philippine citizen for the torture death of her son).

12 Allied occupation forces knew about the Japanese comfort women but chose to ignore the issue. It is clear that the Allied forces had ample evidence of Japanese military enforced prostitution in the form of reports such as the *Amenities in the Japanese Armed Forces* report prepared in 1945 by the Allied Translator Interpreter Service and the *Japanese Prisoner of War Interrogation Report, No. 49* prepared by the Psychological Warfare Team attached to the US Army forces in the India–Burma theatre. The prisoners of war interrogated for this latter report were twenty Korean women forced to act as prostitutes for the 114th Infantry Regiment of the Japanese Imperial forces stationed in Burma. Moreover, the Allied authorities not only tolerated Japanese organized prostitution for US occupying troops but also regulated the practice. Upon landing in Japan, US Army officers promptly inspected red-light districts and set up prophylactic stations. The Japanese, in the meantime, established comfort stations for the occupation troops in numerous prefectures, the largest being set up in Tokyo by the Special Comfort Facilities Association, which was soon renamed the Recreation and Amusement Association. See Tanaka (2003) and Lie (1997).

13 International citizens' tribunals, although not formal bodies, stress adherence to legal procedures in order to enhance their legitimacy (Klonghoffer and Apter Klinghoffer 2002: 8).

14 The Working Women's Network was established by the Osaka Group Campaigning for the Abolition of Discrimination Against Women in October 1995, and was supported by female lawyers.

15 The CEDAW committee, however, was under the mistaken impression that the Japanese government had consulted Japanese NGOs. See United Nations General Assembly (1994).

7 India

1 Accordingly, the Special Marriage Act was passed in 1954, the Hindu Marriage and Divorce Bill in 1955, the Hindu Minority and Guardianship Bill in 1956, the Hindu Succession Bill in 1956 and the Hindu Adoptions and Maintenance Bill in 1956.

2 Upendra Baxi, Raghunath Kelkar and Lotika Sarkar had all been members of the CSWI legal task force.

3 For a historical account of sati, see Thapur (1988).

4 Jaipur is sixty-five kilometres from Deorala and was the home town of Kanwar's parents.

5 The *chunari mahostav* is a ritual held thirteen days after the immolation, when a red veil is placed on a trident at the site of the burning.

6 Article 2 of CEDAW expects state parties to condemn discrimination against women in all its forms, agree to pursue by all appropriate means and without delay a policy of eliminating discrimination against women and, to this end, undertake: a) to embody the principle of the equality of men and women in their national constitutions or other appropriate legislation if not yet incorporated therein and to ensure, through law and other appropriate means, the practical realization of this principle; b) to adopt appropriate legislative and other measures, including sanctions where appropriate, prohibiting all discrimination against women; c) to establish legal protection of the rights of women on an equal basis with men and to ensure through competent national tribunals and other public institutions the effective protection of women against any act of discrimination; d) to refrain from engaging in any act or practice of discrimination against women and to ensure that public authorities and institutions shall act in conformity with this obligation; e) to take all appropriate measures to eliminate discrimination against women by any person, organization or enterprise; f) to take all appropriate measures, including legislation, to modify or abolish existing laws, regulations, customs and practices which constitute discrimination against women; g) to repeal all national penal provisions which constitute discrimination against women.

7 For details about India's economic structural adjustment policies and their impact on women, see Ranadive (1994), Dewan (1999), Ghosh (1994) and Shah *et al.* (1994).

8 The Lawyer's Collective Women's Rights Initiative is an NGO of lawyers and law students established in New Delhi in 1980 to provide community legal services and campaign for legal reform.

9 In August 1997, the Supreme Court had invoked CEDAW in support of its decision to issue a set of guidelines for the prevention of sexual harassment and abuse in the workplace. In *Vishaka* v. *the State of Rajasthan,* the court stated that it felt compelled to issue the guidelines in the absence of domestic legislation to deal with what it described as the 'evil of sexual harassment', and directed that the guidelines be strictly observed in all workplaces until such time as the government enacted suitable legislation in this area. In 1999, the Supreme Court reconfirmed its position on sexual harassment in the subsequent case *Apparel Export Promotion Council* v. *Chopra.* The court held that the message of international instruments such as CEDAW and the Beijing Declaration unmistakably 'cast an obligation on the Indian state to gender sensitize its laws' and on the courts to ensure that this message was not lost on the state. Moreover, it maintained that courts and counsel must never forget the core principles embodied in international conventions and instruments, and as far as possible to give effect to them.

References

Adler, Marina A. (1996) 'Impact of German unification on the status of women in rural east and west', *Sociological Focus*, 29(4): 291–310.

Aeberhard-Hodges, Jane (1996) 'Sexual harassment in employment: recent judicial and arbitral trends', *International Labour Review*, 135(5): 499–533.

Agnes, Flavia (1999a) *Law and Gender Equality: the politics of women's rights in India*, New Delhi: Oxford University Press.

—— (1999b) 'Violence against women: review of recent enactments', in Swapna Mukhopadhyay (ed.), *In the Name of Justice: women and law in society*, New Delhi: Manohar Publications, p. 81116.

Agnihotri, Indu and Mazumdar, Vina (1995) 'Changing terms of political discourse: women's movement in India, 1970s-1990s', *Economic and Political Weekly*, 22 July: 1869–78.

Akerkar, Suriya (1995) 'Theory and practice of women's movement in India: a discourse analysis', *Economic and Political Weekly*, 29 April: WS-2–WS-23.

Allen, Amy (1999) *The Power of Feminist Theory: domination, resistance, solidarity*, Boulder, CO: Westview Press.

Almeda, Elisabet and Sarasa, Sebastia (1996) 'Spain: growth to diversity', in Vic George and Peter Taylor-Gooby (eds), *European Welfare Policy: squaring the welfare circle*, New York: St Martin's Press, pp. 155–76.

Alston, Philip (2000) 'Beyond them and us: putting treaty body reform into perspective', in Philip Alston and James Crawford (eds), *The Future of UN Human Rights Treaty Monitoring*, Cambridge: Cambridge University Press, pp. 501–25.

Alter, Karen J. (2001) *Establishing the Supremacy of European Law: the making of an international rule of law in Europe*, Oxford: Oxford University Press.

Andiappan, P. (1979) 'Public policy and sex discrimination in employment in India', *Indian Journal of Industrial Relations*, 14(3): 395–415.

Archer, Margaret S. (1982) 'Morphogenesis versus structuration: on combining structure and agency', *British Journal of Sociology*, 33(4): 455–83.

—— (1995) *Realist Social Theory: the morphogenetic approach*, Cambridge: Cambridge University Press.

—— (1998) 'Realism and morphogenesis', in Margaret Archer, Roy Bhaskar, Andrew Collier, Tony Lawson and Alan Norrie (eds), *Critical Realism: essential readings*, London: Routledge, pp. 356–81.

—— (2000) *Being Human: the problem of agency*, Cambridge: Cambridge University Press.

—— (2003) *Structure, Agency and the Internal Conversation*, Cambridge: Cambridge University Press.

Arranz, Fatima, Quintanilla, Beatriz and Velázquez, Cristina (2000) 'Making women count in Spain', in Fiona Beveridge, Sue Nott and Kylie Stephen (eds), *Making Women Count: integrating gender into law and policy-making*, Aldershot, UK: Ashgate, pp. 107–29.

Ashworth, Georgina (1999) 'The silencing of women', in Tim Dunne and Nicholas J. Wheeler (eds), *Human Rights in Global Politics*, Cambridge: Cambridge University Press, pp. 259–76.

Astelarra, Judith (1992) 'Women, political culture, and empowerment in Spain', in Jill M. Bystydzienski (ed.), *Women Transforming Politics: worldwide strategies for empowerment*, Indianapolis, IN: Indiana University Press, pp. 41–50.

—— (1995) 'Policy measures on the division of paid and unpaid work: Spain', in Tineke Willemsen, Gerard Frinking and Ria Vogels (eds), *Work and Family in Europe: the role of policies*, Tilburg, The Netherlands: Tilburg University Press, pp. 167–79.

Bakirci, Kadriye (1998) 'Sexual harassment in the workplace in relation to EC legislation', *International Journal of Discrimination and the Law*, 3: 3–28.

Banaszak, Lee Ann (1996) *Why Movements Succeed or Fail: opportunity, culture, and the struggle for woman suffrage*, Princeton, NJ: Princeton University Press.

Banerjee, Nirmala (1998) 'Whatever happened to the dreams of modernity: the Nehruvian era and women's position', *Economic and Political Weekly*, 25 April: WS-2–WS-7.

Bano, Sabeeha (1995) 'Muslim women's voices: expanding gender justice under Muslim law', *Economic and Political Weekly*, 25 November: 2981–2.

Barker, Colin and Lavalette, Michael (2002) 'Strategizing and the sense of context: reflections on the first two weeks of the Liverpool docks lockout, September–October 1995', in David S. Meyer, Nancy Whittier and Belinda Robnett (eds), *Social Movements: identity, culture, and the state*, Oxford: Oxford University Press, pp. 140–56.

Baxi, Pratiksha (2000) 'Rape, retribution, state: on whose bodies?', *Economic and Political Weekly*, 1 April: 1196–200.

Baxi, Upendra (1994) *Inhuman Wrongs and Human Rights: unconventional essays*, New Delhi: Har-Anand Publications.

BBC News (1999), 'World: America's record payment in US sex harassment case', www.bbc.co.uk/1/hi/world/americas/11113.htm (accessed 12 April 1999).

Bercusson, Brian and Dickens, Linda (1997) *Equal Opportunities and Collective Bargaining in Europe: defining the issues*, Luxembourg: Office for the Official Publications of the European Communities.

Berghahn, Sabine (1995) 'Gender in the legal discourse in post-unification Germany: old and new lines of conflict', *Social Politics: International Studies in Gender, State, and Society*, 2(1): 37–50.

Bericht der Bundesregierung über die Situation der Frauen in Beruf, Familie und Gesellschaft (1966) Bundestag Drucksache V/909, Bonn.

Berkovitch, Nitza (1999a) 'The emergence and transformation of the international women's movement', in John Boli and George M. Thomas (eds), *Constructing World Culture: international non-governmental organizations since 1875*, Stanford, CA: Stanford University Press, pp. 100–26.

—— (1999b) *From Motherhood to Citizenship: women's rights and international organizations*, Baltimore, MD: Johns Hopkins University Press.

Berman, Sheri (2001) 'Ideas, norms, and culture in political analysis', *Comparative Politics*, 33(2): 231–50.

Bertelsmann, Klaus and Rust, Ursula (1995) *Equality in Law between Men and Women in the European Community: Germany*, London: Martinus Nijhoff.

Beveridge, Fiona and Mullally, Siobhan (1995) 'International human rights and body politics', in Jo Bridgeman and Susan Millns (eds), *Law and Body Politics: regulating the female body*, Aldershot, UK: Dartmouth, pp. 240–72.

Beveridge, Fiona and Nott, Sue (1998) 'A hard look at soft law', in Paul Craig and Carol Harlow (eds), *Lawmaking in the European Union*, London: Kluwer Law International, pp. 285–309.

Bijnsdorp, Mireille G. E. (2000) 'The strength of the optional protocol to the United Nations Women's Convention', *Netherlands Quarterly of Human Rights*, 18(3): 329–55.

Boetsch, Laurent (1985) 'The church in Spanish politics', in Thomas D. Lancaster and Gary Prevost (eds), *Politics and Change in Spain*, New York: Praeger, pp. 144–67.

Boli, John (1987) 'Human rights or state expansion? Cross-national definitions of constitutional rights, 1870–1970', in George M. Thomas, John W. Meyer, Francisco O. Ramirez and John Boli (eds), *Institutional Structure: constituting the state, society, and the individual*, London: Sage, pp. 133–49.

Boli, John and Thomas, George M. (1997) 'World culture in the world polity: a century of international non-governmental organization', *American Sociological Review*, 62(2): 171–90.

—— (1999a) 'Introduction', in John Boli and George M. Thomas (eds), *Constructing World Culture: international non-governmental organizations since 1875*, Stanford, CA: Stanford University Press, pp. 1–10.

—— (1999b) 'INGOs and the organizations of world culture', in John Boli and George M. Thomas (eds), *Constructing World Culture: international non-governmental organizations since 1875*, Stanford, CA: Stanford University Press, pp. 13–49.

Boling, Patricia (1998) 'Family policy in Japan', *Journal of Social Policy*, 27(2): 173–90.

Boyd, Susan B. (1997) 'Challenging the public/private divide: an overview', in Susan B. Boyd (ed.), *Challenging the Public/Private Divide: feminism, law, and public policy*, Toronto: University of Toronto Press, pp. 3–24.

Braddick, Michael J. (2000) *State Formation: early modern England c.1550–1700*, Cambridge: Cambridge University Press.

Brown, Catherine W. (1988) 'Japanese approaches to equal rights for women: the legal framework', in John O'Haley (ed.), *Law and Society in Contemporary Japan: American perspectives*, Dubuque, IA: Kendall/Hunt, pp. 197–220.

Bryant, Taimie L. (1991) 'For the sake of the country, for the sake of the family: the oppressive impact of family registration on women and minorities in Japan', *University of California Law Review*, 39(1): 109–68.

Buckley, Sandra (1993) 'Altered states: the body politics of being-woman', in Andrew Gordon (ed.), *Postwar Japan as History*, Berkeley, CA: University of California Press, pp. 347–72.

—— (1994) 'A short history of the feminist movement in Japan', in Joyce Gelb and Marian Lief Palley (eds), *Women of Japan and Korea: continuity and change*, Philadelphia, PA: Temple University Press, pp. 150–86.

Buergenthal, Thomas (1997) 'Modern constitutions and human rights treaties', *Columbia Journal of Transnational Law*, 36: 211–23.

Bunch, Charlotte (1993a) 'Feminist visions of human rights in the twenty-first century', in Kathleen E. Mahoney and Paul Mahoney (eds), *Human Rights in the Twenty-first Century*, Dordrecht: Martinus Nijhoff, pp. 967–77.

—— (1993b) 'Organizing for women's human rights globally', in Joanna Kerr (ed.), *Ours by Right: women's rights as human rights*, London: Zed Books, pp. 141–9.

Bunch, Charlotte and Reilly, Niamh (1994) *Demanding Accountability: the global campaign and the Vienna Tribunal for Women's Human Rights*, New Brunswick, NJ: Center for Women's Global Leadership Program, Rutgers University.

Burrows, Noreen (1984) 'Monitoring compliance of international standards relating to human rights: the experience of the United Nations Commission on the Status of Women', *Netherlands International Law Review*, 31(3): 332–54.

—— (1985) 'The 1979 Convention on the Elimination of All Forms of Discrimination Against Women', *Netherlands International Law Review*, 32(3): 419–60.

Bush, Diane Mitsch (1992) 'Women's movements and state policy reform aimed at domestic violence against women: a comparison of the consequences of movement mobilization in the US and India', *Gender and Society*, 6(4): 587–608.

Bustelo, Mara R. (2000) 'The Committee on the Elimination of Discrimination Against Women at the crossroads', in Philip Alston and James Crawford (eds), *The Future of UN Human Rights Treaty Monitoring*, Cambridge: Cambridge University Press, pp. 79–111.

Butragueno, Maria de los Angeles Jimenez (1982) 'Protective legislation and equal opportunity and treatment for women in Spain', *International Labour Review*, 121(2): 185–98.

Byrnes, Andrew (1988–9) 'Women, feminism, and international human rights law – methodological myopia, fundamental flaws or meaningful marginalisation? Some current issues', *Australian Year Book of International Law*, 12: 205–40.

—— (1997) 'Slow and steady wins the race? The development of an optional protocol to the women's convention', Paper presented at American Society of International Law, Ninety-first Annual Meeting, Washington, DC, 12 April.

Calman, Leslie J. (1992) *Toward Empowerment: women and movement politics in India*, Boulder, CO: Westview Press.

Caplan, Pat (1985) 'Women's voluntary social welfare work in India: the cultural construction of gender and class', *Bulletin of Concerned Asian Scholars*, 17(1): 20–31.

Carbayo-Abengozar, Mercedes (2000) 'Feminism in Spain: a history of love and hate', in Lesley Twomey (ed.), *Women in Contemporary Culture: roles and identities in France and Spain*, Bristol: Intellect Books, pp. 111–25.

Carlsnaes, Walter (2001) 'Foreign policy', in Walter Carlsnaes, Thomas Risse and Beth A. Simmons (eds), *Handbook of International Relations*, London: Sage, pp. 331–49.

Carney, Larry S. and O'Kelly, Charlotte G. (1990) 'Women's work and women's place in the Japanese economic miracle', in Kathryn Ward (ed.), *Women Workers and Global Restructuring*, Ithaca, NY: Cornell University Press, pp. 113–45.

Carr, Raymond and Aizpurua, Juan Pablo Fusi (1979) *Spain: dictatorship to democracy*, London: Allen & Unwin.

Chamberlayne, Prue (1991) 'The mothers' manifesto and the concept of mutterlichkeit', in Eva Kolinsky (ed.), *The Federal Republic of Germany: the end of an era*, Oxford: Berg, pp. 199–216.

—— (1993) 'Women and the state: changes in roles and rights in France, West Germany, Italy, and Britain, 1970–1990', in Jane Lewis (ed.), *Women and Social Policies in Europe: work, family, and the state*, Aldershot, UK: Edward Elgar, pp. 170–93.

—— (1994) 'Women and social policy', in Jochen Clasen and Richard Freeman (eds), *Social Policy in Germany*, London: Harvester Wheatsheaf, pp. 173–90.

Charlesworth, Hilary (1995) 'Worlds apart: public/private distinctions in international law', in Margaret Thornton (ed.), *Public and Private: feminist legal debates*, Oxford: Oxford University Press, pp. 243–60.

Charlesworth, Hilary and Chinkin, Christine (1994) 'Violence against women: a global issue', in Julie Stubbs (ed.), *Women, Male Violence, and the Law*, Sydney: Institute of Criminology, pp. 13–33.

—— (2000) *The Boundaries of International Law: a feminist analysis*, Manchester: Manchester University Press.

Charlesworth, Hilary, Chinkin, Christine and Wright, Shelley (1991) 'Feminist approaches to international law', *American Journal of International Law*, 85(4): 613–45.

Chayes, Abram and Chayes, Antonia Handler (1993) 'On compliance', *International Organization*, 47(2): 175–205.

Checkel, Jeffrey T. (1997) 'International norms and domestic politics: bridging the rationalist-constructivist divide', *European Journal of International Relations*, 3(4): 473–95.

—— (1998) 'The constructivist turn in international relations theory', *World Politics*, 50(2): 324–48.

—— (1999) 'Norms, institutions, and national identity in contemporary Europe', *International Studies Quarterly*, 43(1): 83–114.

—— (2000) 'Bridging the rational/constructivist gap? Theorizing social interaction in European institutions', Arena Working Paper Series WP00/11 (Oslo: University of Oslo Centre for European Studies).

—— (2001a) 'The Europeanization of citizenship?', in Maria Green Cowles, James Caporaso and Thomas Risse (eds), *Transforming Europe: Europeanization and domestic change*, Ithaca, NY: Cornell University Press, pp. 180–97.

—— (2001b) 'Why comply? Social learning and European identity change', *International Organization*, 55(3): 553–88.

Chen, Martha Alter (1995) 'Engendering world conferences: the international women's movement and the United Nations', *Third World Quarterly*, 16(3): 477–93.

Cherry, Kittredge (1987) 'Part-time jobs', *Womansword*, New York: Kodansha International.

Chhachhi, Amrita (1991) 'Forced identities: the state, communalism, fundamentalism, and women in India', in Deniz Kandiyoti (ed.), *Women, Islam, and the State*, London: Macmillan, pp. 144–75.

Chinkin, Christine (1999) 'A critique of the public/private dimension', *European Journal of International Law*, 10(2): 387–95.

Choi, Young Jong and Caporaso, James (2002) 'Comparative regional integration', in Walter Carlsnaes, Thomas Risse and Beth A. Simmons (eds), *Handbook of International Relations*, London: Sage, pp. 480–99.

Chung, Chin Sung (1997) 'The origin and development of the military sexual slavery problem in imperial Japan', *Positions East Asia Cultures Critique*, 5(1): 219–53.

Clark, Steve (2001) 'Earnings of men and women in the EU: the gap narrowing but slowly', *Statistics in Focus: Theme 3, Population and Social Conditions*, Luxembourg: Eurostat, 29 May.

Collins, Chik (1996) 'To concede or contest? Language and class struggle', in Colin Barker and Paul Kennedy (eds), *To Make Another World: studies in protest and collective action*, Aldershot, UK: Avebury, pp. 69–91.

Collins, Evelyn (1996) 'European Union sexual harassment policy', in R. Amy Elman (ed.), *Sexual Politics and the European Union: the new feminist challenge*, Oxford: Berghahn Books, pp. 23–33.

Comas, Cristina Garcia (2001) 'Law on reconciliation of work and family life examined', Working Paper, Barcelona: Centre for European Initiatives and Research in the Mediterranean, 28 July.

Committee on the Status of Women in India (1975) *Status of Women in India: a synopsis of the report of the National Committee on the Status of Women (1971–1974)*, New Delhi: Indian Council of Social Science Research.

Connors, Jane (1996) 'NGOs and the human rights of women at the United Nations', in Peter Willetts (ed.), *The Conscience of the World: the influence of nongovernmental organizations in the UN system*, Washington, DC: Brookings Institution, pp. 147–80.

Cook, Alice H. (1980) 'Legislation and collective bargaining: strategies for change', in Ronnie Steinberg Ratner (ed.), *Equal Employment Policy for Women: strategies for implementation in the United States, Canada, and Western Europe*, Philadelphia, PA: Temple University Press, pp. 53–78.

—— (1984) 'Federal Republic of Germany', in Alice H. Cook, Val R. Lorwin and Arlene Kaplan Daniels (eds), *Women and Trade Unions in Eleven Industrialised Countries*, Philadelphia, PA: Temple University Press, pp. 63–94.

Cook, Alice H. and Hayashi, Hiroko (1980) *Working Women in Japan: discrimination, resistance, and reform*, Ithaca, NY: Cornell University Press.

Cook, Rebecca (1989–90) 'Reservations to the Convention on the Elimination of All Forms of Discrimination Against Women', *Virginia Journal of International Law*, 30: 643–716.

Coomaraswamy, Radhika (1994) 'To bellow like a cow: women, ethnicity, and the discourse of rights', in Rebecca J. Cook (ed.), *Human Rights of Women: national and international perspectives*, Philadelphia, PA: University of Pennsylvania Press, pp. 39–57.

—— (1999) 'Reinventing international law: women's rights as human rights in the international community', in Peter Van Ness (ed.), *Debating Human Rights: critical essays from the United States and Asia*, London: Routledge, pp. 167–83.

Cooper, Norman (1976) 'The Church: from crusade to Christianity', in Paul Preston (ed.), *Spanish Crisis: the evolution and decline of the Franco regime*, New York: Harper & Row, pp. 48–81.

Corbin, Beth (1996) 'Global campaign aims to end "Seku Hara": protests by US and Japanese feminists', www.now.org/nnt/11-96/mitsu.html (accessed 14 June 2006).

Cortell, Andrew P. and Davis, James W., Jr (2000) 'Understanding the domestic impact of international norms: a research agenda', *International Studies Review*, 2(1): 65–87.

Cossman, Brenda and Kapur, Ratna (1996) 'Secularism: bench-marked by the Hindu right', *Economic and Political Weekly*, 21 September: 2613–30.

Council of Europe Press (1995) *Human rights: a continuing challenge for the Council of Europe*, Strasbourg: Council of Europe Publishing and Documentation.

Cousins, Christine (1995) 'Women and social policy in Spain: the development of a gendered welfare regime', *Journal of European Social Policy*, 5(3): 175–97.

Dauenhauer, Bernard P. (1998) *Paul Ricoeur: the promise and risk of politics*, Oxford: Rowman & Littlefield.

Denoon, David B. H. (1998) 'Cycles in Indian economic liberalization, 1966–1996', *Comparative Politics*, 13(10): 43–60.

Desai, Manisha (1997) 'Reflections from contemporary women's movements in India', in Jodi Dean (ed.), *Feminism and the New Democracy: re-siting the political*, London: Sage, pp. 110–23.

Desai, Neera (1986) 'From articulation to accommodation: women's movement in India', in Leela Dube, Eleanor Leacock and Shirley Ardeneur (eds), *Visibility and Power: essays on women in society and development*, New Delhi: Oxford University Press, pp. 287–99.

Desai, Neera and Krishnaraj, Maithreyi (1987) *Women and Society in India*, Bombay: Ajanta Publications.

Dewan, Ritu (1999) 'Gender implications of the new economic policy: a conceptual overview', *Women's Studies International Forum*, 24(4): 425–9.

Dhagamwar, Vasudha (1993) 'Women, children, and the constitution: hostages to religion, outcaste by the law', in Robert D. Baird (ed.), *Religion and Law in Independent India*, New Delhi: Manohar Publications, pp. 215–56.

Diaz-Ambrona, Juan Antonio Ortega (1984) 'The transition to democracy in Spain', in Christopher Abel and Nissa Torrents (eds), *Spain: conditional democracy*, London: Croom Helm, pp. 21–39.

Dolgopol, Ustinia and Parajape, Snehal (1994) *An Unfinished Ordeal: special report of the International Commission of Jurists on Comfort Women*, Geneva: International Commission of Jurists.

Donnelly, Jack (1999) 'The social construction of international human rights', in Tim Dunne and Nicholas J. Wheeler (eds), *Human Rights in Global Politics*, Cambridge: Cambridge University Press, pp. 71–102.

Donner, Laura A. (1993–4) 'Gender bias in drafting international discrimination conventions: the 1979 Women's Convention compared with the 1965 Racial Convention', *California Western International Law Journal*, 24(2): 241–54.

Duran, Maria Angeles and Gallego, Maria Teresa (1986) 'The women's movement in Spain and the new Spanish democracy', in Drude Dahlerup (ed.), *The New Women's Movement: feminism and political power in Europe and the USA*, London: Sage, pp. 200–16.

Eccleston, Bernard (1989) *State and Society in Post-War Japan*, Cambridge: Polity Press.

ECR (European Court Reports) (1971) Case 80/70, *Defrenne* v. *Belgium State* (*Defrenne I*).

—— (1976) Case 43/75, *Defrenne* v. *Societe Anonyme Belge de Navigation Aerienne Sabena* (*Defrenne II*).

—— (1990) Case 322/88, *Grimaldi (Salvatore)* v. *Ford des Maladies Professionelles*.

Editor's Note (Discussion Forum) (1985) 'From the Committee on the Status of Women in India to the end of the women's decade: some personal reflections', *Samya Shakti: A Journal of Women's Studies*, 2(1): 80–91.

Elder-Vass, Dave (2005) 'Emergence and the realist account of cause', *Journal of Critical Realism*, 4(2): 315–38.

Ellina, Chrystalla (1999) 'The role of international institutions in promoting women's rights: a multilevel analysis of the politics of gender in the European Union', PhD dissertation, Department of Political Science, University of Missouri-St. Louis.

Ellis, Evelyn (1988) *Sex Discrimination Law*, Aldershot, UK: Gower.

Enders, Victoria Loree (1992) 'Nationalism and feminism: the Sección Femenina of the Falange', *History of European Ideas*, 15(4–6): 673–80.

Enders, Victoria Loree and Radcliff, Pamela Beth (1999) 'Work identities: introduction to Part II', in Victoria Loree Enders and Pamela Beth Radcliff (eds), *Constructing Spanish Womanhood: female identity in modern Spain*, New York: State University of New York, pp. 125–30.

Escobedo, Anna (1999) 'New law promotes reconciliation of work and family life', Working Paper, Barcelona: Centre for European Initiatives and Research in the Mediterranean, 28 November.

European Commission's Expert Group on Gender and Employment (2001) *Gender Equality and the European Employment Strategy: an evaluation of the national action plans for employment 2001*, Manchester: University of Manchester Institute of Science and Technology EGGE Publications.

European Parliament (1989) *Report Drawn Up on Behalf of the Committee on Women's Rights on the Position of Women in Spain and Portugal as Regards Their Conditions of Work and Employment*, Document A2-0067/88, 10 May.

Eurostat (2002) *The Life of Women and Men of Europe: a statistical portrait*, Luxembourg: Eurostat.

Fellmeth, Aaron Xavier (2000) 'Feminism and international law: theory, methodology, and substantive reform', *Human Rights Quarterly*, 22: 658–733.

Ferree, Myra Marx (1987) 'Equality and autonomy: feminist politics in the United States and West Germany', in Mary Fainsod Katzenstein and Carol McClurg Mueller (eds), *The Women's Movements of the United States and Western Europe: consciousness, political opportunity, and public policy*, Philadelphia: Temple University Press, pp. 172–95.

—— (1993) 'The rise and fall of mummy politics: feminism and unification in (East) Germany', *Feminist Studies*, 19(1): 89–115.

—— (1995) 'Making equality: the women's affairs office in the Federal Republic of Germany', in Dorothy McBride Stetson and Amy G. Mazur (eds), *Comparative State Feminism*, London: Sage, pp. 95–113.

Ferree, Myra Marx and Gamson, William A. (1999) 'The gendering of the abortion debate: assessing global feminist influence in the United States and Germany in a globalizing world', in Donatella della Porta and Hanspeter Kriesi (eds), *Social Movements in a Globalizing World*, London: Macmillan, pp. 40–56.

Field, Norma (1997) 'War and apology: Japan, Asia, the fiftieth, and after', *Positions East Asia Cultures Critique*, 5(1): 1–49.

Finnemore, Martha (1996a) *National Interests in International Society*, Ithaca, NY: Cornell University Press.

—— (1996b) 'Norms, culture, and world politics: insights from sociology's institutionalism', *International Organization*, 50(2): 325–47.

Finnemore, Martha and Sikkink, Kathryn (1998) 'International norm dynamics and political change', *International Organization*, 52(4): 887–917.

Forbes, Geraldine (1982) 'Caged tigers: the first wave feminists in India', *Women's Studies International Forum*, 5(6): 525–36.

—— (1996) *Women in Modern India*, Cambridge: Cambridge University Press.

Forman, John (1982) 'The equal pay principle under Community law: a commentary on article 119 EEC', in Law Review of the Europa Instituut: University of Amsterdam, *Legal Issues of European Integration*, Deventer: Kluwer Law and Taxation Publishers, pp. 17–36.

Fraser, Arvonne S. (1995) 'The Convention on the Elimination of All Forms of Discrimination Against Women (The Women's Convention)', in Anne Winslow (ed.), *Women, Politics, and the United Nations*, Westport, CT: Greenwood Press, pp. 77–94.

—— (2001) 'Becoming human: the origins and development of women's human rights', in Marjorie Agosin (ed.), *Women, Gender, and Human Rights: a global perspective*, Piscataway, NJ: Rutgers University Press, pp. 15–64.

Frevert, Ute (1989) *Women in German History: from bourgeois emancipation to sexual liberation*, Oxford: Berg.

Friedman, Sherman M. (1999) 'Avoid sexual harassment suits', www.office.com/syb_sexualharass.html (accessed 12 January 2000).

Frykenberg, Robert Eric (1993) 'Hindu fundamentalism and the structural stability of India', in Martin E. Marty and R. Scott Appleby (eds), *Fundamentalism and the State: remaking polities, economies, and militance*, Chicago, IL: University of Chicago Press, pp. 233–55.

Fujimura-Fanselow, Kumiko (1995) 'Introduction', in Kumiko Fujimura-Fanselow and Atsuko Kameda (eds), *Japanese Women: new feminist perspectives on the past, present, and future*, New York: City University of New York Feminist Press, pp. xvii–xxxviii.

Gala, Chetna (1997) 'Empowering women in villages: all-women village councils in Maharashtra, India', *Bulletin of Concerned Asian Scholars*, 29(2): 31–45.

Gandhi, Nandita and Shah, Nandita (1991) *The Issues at Stake: theory and practice in the contemporary women's movement*, New Delhi: Kali for Women.

Gaul, Elise (1998) *Legislative Guide: domestic violence against women*, Philadelphia, PA: Soroptimist International of the Americas.

Gelb, Joyce (2003) *Gender Policies in Japan and the United States: comparing women's movements, rights, and politics*, Basingstoke, UK: Palgrave Macmillan.

Gerona-Adkins, Rita M. (2001) 'Demonstrators bash Bush support for Japan in "comfort women" suit: US DC court hold hearing; judge's ruling expected this month', *Asian Fortune*, www.asianfortune.com/Sept01/Comfort%20women.htm (accessed 1 August 2006).

Ghosh, Jayati (1994) 'Gender concerns in macro-economic policy', *Economic and Political Weekly*, 30 April: WS-2–WS-11.

Gluck, Carol (2003) 'The end of the postwar: Japan at the turn of the millennium', in Jeffrey K. Olick (ed.), *States of Memory: continuities, conflicts, and transformations in national retrospection*, Durham, NC: Duke University Press, pp. 289–314.

Gomez, Aurora Morcillo (1999) 'Shaping true Catholic womanhood: Francoist educational discourse on women', in Victoria Loree Enders and Pamela Beth Radcliff (eds), *Constructing Spanish Womanhood: female identity in modern Spain*, New York: State University of New York, pp. 51–69.

Goodman, Roger and Peng, Ito (1996) 'The east Asian welfare states: peripatetic learning, adaptive change, and nation-building', in Gosta Esping-Andersen (ed.), *Welfare States in Transition: national adaptation in global economies*, London: Sage, pp. 192–224.

Gothoskar, Sujata and Patel, Vithubai (1982) 'Documents from the Indian women's movement', *Feminist Review*, 12 (October): 92–103.

Government of India (1968) *Fourth Five Year Plan*, New Delhi: Planning Commission.

Graham, Helen (1995) 'Gender and the state: women in the 1940s', in Helen Graham and Jo Labanyi (eds), *Spanish Cultural Studies: an introduction: the struggle for modernity*, Oxford: Oxford University Press, pp. 182–95.

Graham, Robert (1984) *Spain: change of a nation*, London: Michael Joseph.

Green, Shane (2003) 'Sex slaves fail in compensation bid', *Age*, 27 March, p. 15.

Grugel, Jean and Rees, Tim (1997) *Franco's Spain*, London: Arnold.

Guerra, Luis Lopez (1998) 'The application of the Spanish model in constitutional transitions in Central and Eastern Europe', *Cardozo Law Review*, 19(6): 1937–51.

Guillen, Ana and Matsaganis, Manos (2000) 'Testing the social dumping hypothesis in southern Europe: welfare policies in Greece and Spain during the last 20 years', *Journal of European Social Policy*, 10(2): 120–45.

Gurowitz, Amy (1999) 'Mobilizing international norms: domestic actors, immigrants, and the Japanese state', *World Politics*, 51(3): 413–45.

Haas, Peter M. (1990) *Saving the Mediterranean*, New York: Columbia University Press.

Hageman-White, Carol (2003) Email correspondence with author, 7 January.

Hahm, Dongwoo Lee (2001) 'Urgent matters: redress for surviving comfort women', in Margaret Stetz and Bonnie B. C. Oh (eds), *Legacies of the Comfort Women of World War II*, New York: M. E. Sharpe, pp. 128–41.

Hanami, Tadashi (1981) 'The influence of ILO standards on law and practice in Japan', *International Labour Review*, 120(6): 765–79.

—— (1984) 'Japan', in Alice H. Cook, Val R. Lorwin and Arlene Kaplan Daniels (eds), *Women and Trade Unions in Eleven Industrialised Countries*, Philadelphia, PA: Temple University Press, pp. 215–38.

—— (2000) 'Equal employment revisited', *Japan Labor Bulletin*, 39(1): 5.

Hantrais, Linda (1994) 'Comparing family policy in Britain, France, and Germany', *Journal of Social Policy*, 23(2): 135–60.

Harrington, Mona (1992) 'What exactly is wrong with the liberal state as an agent of change?', in V. Spike Peterson (ed.), *Gendered States: (re)visions of international relations theory*, Boulder: Lynne Rienner, pp. 65–82.

Harvey, Ruth A. (1990) 'Equal treatment of men and women in the work place: the implementation of the European Community's equal treatment legislation in the Federal Republic of Germany', *American Journal of Comparative Law*, 38: 31–71.

Hasan, Zoya (1989) 'Minority identity, Muslim women's bill campaign, and the political process', *Economic and Political Weekly*, 7 January: 44–50.

—— (1993) 'Communalism, state policy, and the question of women's rights in contemporary India', *Bulletin of Concerned Asian Scholars*, 25(4): 5–15.

—— (1994) 'Minority identity, state policy, and the political process', in Zoya Hasan (ed.), *Forging Identities: gender, communities, and the state*, New Delhi: Kali for Women, pp. 59–73.

—— (1999) 'Gender politics, legal reform, and the Muslim community in India', in Patricia Jeffery and Amrita Basu (eds), *Resisting the Sacred and the Secular: women's activism and politicized religion in South Asia*, New Delhi: Kali for Women, pp. 71–87.

Hastings, Sally Ann (1996) 'Women legislators in the postwar diet', in Anne E. Inamura (ed.), *Re-imaging Japanese Women*, Berkeley, CA: University of California Press, pp. 271–99.

Hayashi, Hiroko (2000) 'The Japanese equal employment opportunity law and its limitations', Paper presented at the Workshop on Sex Discrimination in Japan: Sumitomo Litigation, New York University, 5 June.

Hayashi, Yoko (1988) 'Myth and reality: institutional reform for women', *AMPO: Japan–Asia Quarterly Review*, 18(2–3): 18–23.

—— (1994) 'Violence against women: endeavours made by women in Japan', *International Forum on Intercultural Exchange: 1993*, Japan: National Women's Education Centre.

—— (1995) 'Legal issues in employment', *AMPO: Japan-Asia Quarterly Review*, 25(4)-26(1): 42–8.

Heineman, Elizabeth (1996) 'Complete families, half families, no families at all: female-headed households and the reconstruction of the family in the early federal republic', *Central European History*, 29(1): 19–60.

Heinrich Boll Foundation (1999) *On the National Implementation of the Platform for Action of the 4th World Conference on Women in Beijing: Comment on the Response of the Federal Government by German Non-Governmental Organizations*, December, www.iiav.nl/european-womenaction-2001/countries/reports/germany1.html (accessed 21 November 2001).

Helweg, M. Diana (1991) 'Japan's equal employment opportunity act: a five-year look at its effectiveness', *Boston University International Law Journal*, 9: 293–320.

Hervey, Tamara (1993) *Justifications for Sex Discrimination in Employment*, London: Butterworths.

Herzog, Peter (1993) *Japan's Pseudo-democracy*, Folkestone, UK: Japan Library.

Hevener, Natalie Kaufman (1986) 'An analysis of gender based treaty law: contemporary developments in historical perspective', *Human Rights Quarterly*, 8(1): 70–88.

Heywood, Paul (1995) *The Government and Politics of Spain*, London: Macmillan.

Hicks, George (1997) *The Comfort Women: Japan's brutal regime of enforced prostitution in the Second World War*, New York: W. W. Norton.

Hicks, Salem (1997) 'Women take job bias fight abroad: group tells ILO, UN of Japan's misleading statistics, inequities', *Japan Times*, 12 October, p. 3.

Hirofumi, Hayashi (2001) 'The Japanese movement to protest wartime sexual violence: a survey of Japanese and international literature', *Critical Asian Studies*, 33(4): 572–602.

Hoq, Laboni Amena (2001) 'The women's convention and its optional protocol: empowering women to claim their internationally protected rights', *Columbia Human Rights Law Review*, 32(3): 677–725.

Hoskyns, Catherine (1985) 'Women's equality and the European Community', *Feminist Review*, 20 (June): 71–88.

—— (1986) 'Women, European law, and transnational politics', *International Journal of the Sociology of Law*, 14: 299–315.

—— (1988) 'Give us equal pay and we'll open our own doors: a study of the impact in the Federal Republic of Germany and the Republic of Ireland of the European Community's policy on women's rights', in Mary Buckley and Malcolm Anderson (eds), *Women, Equality, and Europe*, London: Macmillan, pp. 33–55.

—— (1996) *Integrating Gender: women, law, and politics in the European Union*, London: Verso.

Hoskyns, Catherine and Luckhaus, Linda (1989) 'The European Community directive on equal treatment in social security', *Policy and Politics*, 17(4): 321–35.

Hsu, Yvonne Park (1993) 'Comfort women from Korea: Japan's World War II sex slaves and the legitimacy of their claims for reparations', *Pacific Rim Law and Policy*, 2(1): 97–129.

Igarashi, Yoshikuni (2000) *Bodies of Memory: narratives of war in postwar Japanese culture, 1945–1970*, Princeton, NJ: Princeton University Press.

ILO (International Labour Organization) Committee of Experts on the Application of Conventions and Recommendations (1999) *Individual Observation Concerning Convention no. 100, Equal Remuneration 1951: Germany*, Geneva: International Labour Office.

—— (2000) *Individual Observation Concerning Convention no. 100, Equal Remuneration 1951: Germany*, Geneva: International Labour Office.

—— (2001) *Individual Observation Concerning Convention no. 100, Equal Remuneration 1951: Germany*, Geneva: International Labour Office.

International Labour Conference (1986) *Equal Remuneration: general survey by the committee of experts on the application of conventions and recommendations*, Seventy-second Session, Geneva: International Labour Office.

—— (1988) *Equality in Employment and Occupation: general survey by the committee of experts on the application of conventions and recommendations*, Seventy-fifth Session, Geneva: International Labour Office.

—— (1992) *Report of the Committee of Experts on the Application of Conventions and Recommendations*, Seventy-ninth Session, Geneva: International Labour Office.

—— (1995) *Summary of Reports*, Report III (Parts 1, 2 and 3), Eighty-second Session, Geneva: International Labour Office.

—— (1996a) *Equality in Employment and Occupation: special survey on equality in employment and occupation in respect to convention no. 111*, Eighty-third Session, Geneva: International Labour Office.

—— (1996b) *Report of the Committee of Experts on the Application of Conventions and Recommendations*, Eighty-third Session, Geneva: International Labour Office.

—— (1997) *Report of the Committee of Experts on the Application of Conventions and Recommendations*, Eighty-fifth Session, Geneva: International Labour Office.

International Women's Rights Action Watch (1997) 'When we make it work for us', *The Women's Watch*, 11(1), June.

Iwasawa, Yuji (1998) *International Law, Human Rights, and Japanese Law: the impact of international law on Japanese law*, Oxford: Clarendon Press.

Jacobs, Monica (1978) 'Civil rights and women's rights in the Federal Republic of Germany today', *New German Critique*, 13 (Winter): 165–74.

Jacobson, Roberta (1995) 'The Committee on the Elimination of Discrimination Against Women', in Philip Alston (ed.), *The United Nations and Human Rights: a critical appraisal*, Oxford: Clarendon Press, pp. 444–72.

Jain, Sharada, Misra, Nirja and Srivastava, Kavita (1987) 'Deorala episode: women's protest in Rajasthan', *Economic and Political Weekly*, 7 November: 1891–4.

Jaising, Indira (1996) 'Introduction', in Indira Jaising (ed.), *Justice for Women: personal laws, women's rights, and law reform*, Mapusa: The Other Indian Press, pp. i–v.

JCLU (Japan Civil Liberties Union) (1998) *Counter Report: Gender Equality (Article 3) 1998*, www.villagec.infoweb.nc.jp/katsudou/counter_report_1998/article_03. html (accessed 13 June 1999).

Jelin, Elizabeth (1996) 'Women, gender, and human rights', in Elizabeth Jelin and Eric Hershberg (eds), *Constructing Democracy: human rights, citizenship, and society in Latin America*, Boulder, CO: Westview Press, pp. 177–96.

Jenson, Jane and Valiente, Celia (2003) 'Comparing two movements for gender parity: France and Spain', in Lee Ann Banaszak, Karen Beckwith and Dieter Rucht (eds), *Women's Movements Facing a Reconfigured State*, Cambridge: Cambridge University Press, pp. 69–93.

Joachim, Jutta (1999) 'Shaping the human rights agenda: the case of violence against women', in Mary K. Meyer and Elisabeth Prugl (eds), *Gender Politics in Global Governance*, Lanham, MD: Rowman & Littlefield, pp. 142–59.

Jones, Anny Brooksbank (1995) 'Work, women, and the family: a critical perspective', in Helen Graham and Jo Labanyi (eds), *Spanish Cultural Studies: an introduction: the struggle for modernity*, Oxford: Oxford University Press, pp. 386–93.

—— (1997) *Women in Contemporary Spain*, Manchester: Manchester University Press.

Jones, H. J. (1976) 'Japanese women and party politics', *Pacific Affairs*, 49(2): 213–34.

—— (1976–7) 'Japanese women and the dual-track employment system', *Pacific Affairs*, 49(4): 589–606.

Jones, Sidney (1996) 'Regional institutions for protecting human rights in Asia', *Australian Journal of International Affairs*, 50(3): 269–78.

Joseph, Ammu (1991) 'Political parties and sati', *Economic and Political Weekly*, 20 April: 1025–6.

Kaji, Chizuko (1984) 'The postwar wife – no longer competent: civil code revisions and equality for women', *Japan Quarterly*, 31(1): 11–18.

Kamiya, Masako (1986) 'Women in Japan', *University of British Columbia Law Review*, 20(1): 447–69.

—— (1995) 'A decade of the Equal Employment Opportunity Act in Japan: has it changed society?', *Law in Japan*, 25: 40–83.

Kaplan, Gisela (1992) *Contemporary Western European Feminism*, London: Allen & Unwin.

Kapur, Ratna (1992) 'Feminism, fundamentalism, and rights discourse', *Indian Journal of Social Science*, 5(1): 33–40.

—— (2001a) Interview with author, New Delhi, 9 January.

—— (2001b) Interview with author, New Delhi, 11 January.

—— (2001c) Interview with author, New Delhi, 18 January.

Kapur, Ratna and Cossman, Brenda (1996a) 'Communalising gender engendering community: women, legal discourse and the saffron agenda', in Tanika Sarkar and Urvashi Butalia (eds), *Women and the Hindu Right: a collection of essays*, New Delhi: Kali for Women, pp. 82–119.

—— (1996b) *Subversive Sites: feminist engagements with law in India*, New Delhi: Sage.

Kapur, Ratna and Mehra, Madhu (1997) *Submissions Pertaining to Discrimination Against Women in Response to the Government's Third Periodic Report under the International Covenant on Civil and Political Rights*, New Delhi: Centre for Feminist Legal Research.

Kasturi, Leela (1996) 'Development, patriarchy, and politics: Indian women in the political process, 1947–1992', in Valentine M. Moghadam (ed.), *Patriarchy and Economic Development: women's positions at the end of the twentieth century*, Oxford: Oxford University Press, pp. 99–144.

Katzenstein, Mary Fainsod (1989) 'Organizing against violence: strategies of the Indian women's movement', *Pacific Affairs*, 62(1): 53–71.

Katzenstein, Peter J. (1990) 'Comparative political economy: nationalization in France and Italy thirty years later', in Peter J. Katzenstein, Theodore Lowi and Sidney Tarrow (eds), *Comparative Theory and Political Experience*, Ithaca, NY: Cornell University Press, pp. 167–87.

—— (1993a) 'Coping with terrorism: norms and internal security in Germany and Japan', in Judith Goldstein and Robert O. Keohane (eds), *Ideas and Foreign Policy: beliefs, institutions, and political change*, Ithaca, NY: Cornell University Press, pp. 265–95.

—— (1993b) 'Taming of power: German unification, 1989–1990', in Meredith Woo-Cumings and Michael Loriaux (eds), *Past as Prelude: history in the making of a new world order*, Boulder, CO: Westview Press, pp. 59–81.

—— (1995) 'The role of theory in comparative politics: a symposium', *World Politics*, 48(1): 1–49.

—— (1996a) *Cultural Norms and National Security: police and military in postwar Japan*, Ithaca, NY: Cornell University Press.

—— (1996b) 'Introduction: alternative perspectives on national security', in Peter J. Katzenstein (ed.), *The Culture of National Security: norms and identity in world politics*, New York: Columbia University Press, pp. 1–32.

—— (1997a) 'Introduction: Asian regionalism in comparative perspective', in Peter J. Katzenstein and Takashi Shiraishi (eds), *Network Power: Japan and Asia*, Ithaca, NY: Cornell University Press, pp. 1–44.

—— (ed.) (1997b) *Tamed Power: Germany in Europe*, Ithaca, NY: Cornell University Press.

—— (1997c) 'The smaller European states, Germany, and Europe', in Peter J. Katzenstein (ed.), *Tamed Power: Germany in Europe*, Ithaca, NY: Cornell University Press, pp. 251–304.

—— (1997d) 'United Germany in an integrating Europe', in Peter J. Katzenstein (ed.), *Tamed Power: Germany in Europe*, Ithaca, NY: Cornell University Press, pp. 1–48.

Katzenstein, Peter J. and Shiraishi, Takashi (1997a) 'Conclusion: regions in world politics: Japan and Asia – Germany in Europe', in Peter J. Katzenstein and Takashi Shiraishi (eds), *Network Power: Japan and Asia*, Ithaca, NY: Cornell University Press, pp. 341–81.

—— (eds) (1997b) *Network Power: Japan and Asia*, Ithaca, NY: Cornell University Press.

Kaviraj, Sudipta (1986) 'Indira Gandhi and Indian politics', *Economic and Political Weekly*, 20–27 September: 1697–708.

Kawashima, Yasuhide (1983) 'Americanization of Japanese family law', *Law in Japan*, 16: 54–68.

Kawashima, Yoko (1995) 'Female workers: an overview of past and current trends', in Kumiko Fujimara-Fanselow and Atsuko Kameda (eds), *Japanese Women: new feminist perspectives on the past, present, and future*, New York: City University of New York Feminist Press, pp. 271–93.

Keck, Margaret and Sikkink, Kathryn (1998) *Activists beyond Borders: advocacy networks in international politics*, Ithaca, NY: Cornell University Press.

Kenyon, Olga (1995) 'Women under Franco and PSOE: the discrepancy between discourse and reality', in Bernard McGuirk and Mark I. Millington (eds), *Inequality and Difference in Hispanic and Latin American Cultures*, New York: Edwin Mellen Press, pp. 51–61.

Keohane, Robert O. (1982) 'The demand for international regimes', *International Organization*, 36(2): 325–55.

—— (1984) *After Hegemony: cooperation and discord in the world political economy*, Princeton, NJ: Princeton University Press.

—— (1992) 'Compliance with international commitments: politics within a framework', *American Society of International Law Proceedings*, 176–80.

Kim, Hyun Sook (1997) 'History and memory: the comfort women controversy', *Positions East Asia Cultures Critique*, 5(1): 73–106.

Kishwar, Madhu and Vanita, Ruth (1989) 'Indian women: a decade of new ferment', in Marshall M. Bouton and Philip Oldenburg (eds), *India Briefing, 1989*, Boulder, CO: Westview Press, pp. 131–51.

Klonghoffer, Arthur Jay and Apter Klinghoffer, Judith (2002) International Citizens' Tribunals: mobilizing public opinion to advance human rights, New York: Palgrave Macmillan.

Klotz, Audie (1995) *Norms in International Relations: the struggle against apartheid*, Ithaca, NY: Cornell University Press.

—— (2000) 'Transnational activism and global transformations: the anti-apartheid and abolitionist experiences', *European Journal of International Relations*, 8(1): 49–76.

—— (2001) 'Can we *speak* a common constructivist language?', in Karin M. Fierke and Knud Erik Jorgensen (eds), *Constructing International Relations: the next generation*, New York: M. E. Sharpe, pp. 223–35.

Knapp, Kiyoko Kamio (1995) 'Still office flowers: Japanese women betrayed by the equal employment opportunity law', *Harvard Women's Law Journal*, 18: 83–137.

Koch, Angelika (2003) 'Equal employment policy in Germany: limited results and prospects for reform', *Review of Policy Research*, 20(3): 443–57.

Kolinsky, Eva (1988) 'The West German Greens: a women's party?', *Parliamentary Affairs: A Journal of Comparative Politics*, 41(1): 129–48.

—— (1989) 'Women in the Green Party', in Eva Kolinsky (ed.), *The Greens in West Germany: organization and policy making*, Oxford: Berg, pp. 189–221.

—— (1996a) 'Women in the new Germany', in Gordon Smith, William E. Paterson and Stephen Padgett (eds), *Developments in German Politics 2*, Durham, NC: Duke University Press, pp. 267–85.

—— (1996b) 'Women in the 1994 federal election', in Russell J. Dalton (ed.), *Germans Divided: the 1994 Bundestag elections and the evolution of the German party system*, Oxford: Berg, pp. 265–89.

Kopp, Rochelle (1998) 'Ricochet effect of US sexual harassment suit', *Japan Quarterly*, 43(4): 42–50.

Krasner, Stephen D. (1984) 'Approaches to the state: alternative conceptions and historical dynamics', *Comparative Politics*, 16(2): 223–46.

Kratochwil, Friedrich (2000a) 'Constructing a new orthodoxy? Wendt's social theory of international politics and the constructivist challenge', *Millennium: Journal of International Studies*, 29(10): 73–101.

—— (2000b) 'How do norms matter?', in Michael Byers (ed.), *The Role of Law in International Politics: essays in international relations and international law*, Oxford: Oxford University Press, pp. 35–67.

Krauss, Ellis S. (2000) 'Local politics in Japan: welcoming the third wave', in Sheila A. Smith (ed.), *Local Voices, National Issues: the impact of local initiative in Japanese policy-making*, Ann Arbor, MI: Center for Japanese Studies, University of Michigan, pp. 1–8.

Krishna, Sankaran (1995) 'Constitutionalism, democracy, and political culture in India', in Daniel P. Franklin and Michael J. Baun (eds), *Political Culture and Constitutionalism: a comparative approach*, New York: M. E. Sharpe, pp. 161–83.

Kumar, Radhu (1995a) 'From Chipko to sati: the contemporary Indian women's movement', in Amrita Basu (ed.), *The Challenge of Local Feminism: women's movements in global perspective*, Boulder, CO: Westview Press, pp. 58–86.

—— (1995b) 'Political women and women's politics in India', in Alida Brill (ed.), *A Rising Public Voice in Politics Worldwide*, New York: The Feminist Press, pp. 59–72.

Lam, Alice C. L. (1992) *Women and Japanese Management: discrimination and reform*, London: Routledge.

Landau, Eve C. (1985) *The Rights of Working Women in the European Community*, Luxembourg: Office for Official Publications of the European Communities.

Lateef, Shahida (1994) 'Defining women through legislation', in Zoya Hasan (ed.), *Forging Identities: gender, communities, and the state*, New Delhi: Kali for Women, pp. 38–58.

Laurent, Andre (1986) 'The elimination of sex discrimination in occupational social security schemes in the EEC', *International Labour Review*, 125(6): 675–83.

Lawyer's Collective Women's Rights Initiative (2000) *Domestic Violence Against Women (Prevention) Bill 2000: a lawyer's collective proposal*, New Delhi: Gondals Press.

Leary, Virginia A. (1997) 'Labour', in Christopher C. Joyner (ed.), *The United Nations and International Law*, New York: American Society of International Law and Cambridge University Press, pp. 208–31.

Left, Naomi and Levine, Ann D. (1998) *Where Women Stand: an international report on the status of women in 140 countries: 1997–1998*, New York: Random House.

Lemke, Christiane (1993) 'Old troubles and new uncertainties: women and politics in united Germany', in Michael G. Huelshoff, Andrei S. Markovits and Simon Reich (eds), *From Bundesrepublik to Deutschland*, Ann Arbor, MI: University of Michigan Press, pp. 147–65.

Lie, John (1997) 'The state as pimp: prostitution and the patriarchal state in Japan in the 1940s', *Sociological Quarterly*, 38(2): 251–63.

Liedtke, Boris N. (1999a) 'Compromising with the dictatorship: US–Spanish relations in the late 1940s and early 1950s', in Christian Leitz and David J. Dunthorn (eds), *Spain in an International Context, 1936–1959*, New York: Berghahn Books, pp. 265–75.

—— (1999b) 'Spain and the United States, 1945–1975', in Sebastian Balfour and Paul Preston (eds), *Spain and the Great Powers in the Twentieth Century*, London: Routledge, pp. 229–44.

Linz, Juan L. (1993) 'Innovative leadership in the transition to democracy and a new democracy: the case of Spain', in Gabriel Sheffer (ed.), *Innovative Leaders in International Politics*, New York: State University of New York, pp. 141–85.

Loenen, Titia (1993) 'Remarks', *Contemporary International Law Issues: opportunities at a time of momentous change*, Proceedings of the Second Joint Conference held in The Hague, the Netherlands, 22–24 July 1993, Dordrecht: Martinus Nijhoff.

Lubin, Carol Riegelman and Winslow, Anne (1990) *Social Justice for Women: the International Labour Organization and women*, Durham, NC: Duke University Press.

Lukes, Stephen (1986) 'Introduction', in Stephen Lukes (ed.), *Power*, New York: New York University Press, pp. 1–18.

Lutz, Ellen L. and Sikkink, Kathryn (2000) 'International human rights law and practices in Latin America', *International Organization*, 54(3): 633–59.

Lycklama a Nijeholt, Geertje, Swiebel, Joke and Vargas, Virginia (1998) 'The global institutional framework: the long march to Beijing', in Geertje Lycklama a Nijeholt, Virginia Vargas and Saskia Wieringa (eds), *Women's Movements and Public Policy in Europe, Latin America, and the Caribbean*, New York: Garland, pp. 25–48.

McAdam, Doug and Rucht, Dieter (1993) 'The cross-national diffusion of movement ideas', *Annals of the American Academy of Political and Social Science*, 528(1): 56–74.

McKean, Warwick (1983) *Equality and Discrimination under International Law*, Oxford: Clarendon Press.

Mackie, Vera (2003) *Feminism in Modern Japan*, Cambridge: Cambridge University Press.

MacLennan, Julio Crespo (2000) *Spain and the Process of European Integration, 1975–85*, Basingstoke, UK: Palgrave Macmillan.

McNeely, Connie L. (1998) 'Constituting citizens: rights and rules', in Connie L. McNeely (ed.), *Public Rights, Public Rules: constituting citizens in the world polity and national policy*, New York: Garland, pp. 3–37.

Maier, Friederike (2001) *Evaluation of the 2001 German National Action Plan for Employment*, Manchester: University of Manchester Institute of Science and Technology EGGE Publications.

Maki, John M. (1964) *Court and the Constitution of Japan: selected supreme court decisions: 1948–60*, Seattle, WA: University of Washington Press.

Mansfield, John H. (1993) 'The personal laws or a uniform civil code?', in Robert C. Baird (ed.), *Religion and Law in Independent India*, New Delhi: Oxford University Press, pp. 139–77.

Marfording, Annette (1997) 'Cultural relativism and the construction of culture: an examination of Japan', *Human Rights Quarterly*, 19: 431–48.

Markovits, Andrei S. and Gorski, Philip S. (1996) 'The new women's movement', in Michael G. Huelshoff, Andrei S. Markovits and Simon Reich (eds), *From Bundesrepublik to Deutschland*, Ann Arbor, MI: University of Michigan Press, pp. 137–45.

Marks, Michael (1997) *The Formation of European Policy in Post-Franco Spain*, Aldershot, UK: Ashgate.

Martin, Lisa L. (1995) 'Heterogeneity, linkage and common problems', in Robert O. Keohane and Elinor Ostrom (eds), *Local Commons and Global Interdependence*, London: Sage, pp. 71–91.

Martin, Lisa L. and Simmons, Beth A. (1998) 'Theories and empirical studies in international institutions', *International Organization*, 52(4): 729–57.

Mattli, Walter and Slaughter, Anne-Marie (1998) 'Revisiting the European Court of Justice', *International Organization*, 52(10): 177–209.

Mazey, Sonia (1998) 'The European Union and women's rights: from the Europeanization of national agendas to the nationalization of a European agenda', *Journal of European Public Policy*, 5(1): 131–52.

Mazumdar, Sucheta (1992) 'Women, culture, and politics: engendering the Hindu nation', *South Asia Bulletin*, 12(2): 1–24.

—— (1995) 'Women on the march: right-wing mobilization in contemporary India', *Feminist Review*, 49 (Spring): 1–28.

Mazumdar, Vina (1985) 'Role of research in women's development: a case study of the ICSSR programme of women's studies', in R. S. Ganapathy, S. R. Ganesh, Rushikesh M. Maru, Samuel Paul and Ram Mohan Rao (eds), *Public Policy Analysis in India*, New Delhi: Sage, pp. 208–51.

—— (1999) 'Political ideology of the women's movement's engagement with law', in Amita Dhanda and Archana Parashar (eds), *Engendering Law: essays in honour of Lotika Sarkar*, Lucknow: Eastern Book Company, pp. 339–74.

—— (2001) Interview with author, New Delhi, 15 January.

Meade, Christopher P. (2002) 'From Shanghai to globocourt: an analysis of the comfort women's defeat in *Hwang v. Japan*', *Vanderbilt Journal of Transnational Law*, 35(1): 211–89.

Mendez, Maria Teresa Gallego (1994) 'Women's political engagement in Spain', in Barbara J. Nelson and Najma Chowdhury (eds), *Women and Politics Worldwide*, New Haven, CT: Yale University Press, pp. 661–89.

Menon, P. M. (1966) 'Towards equality of opportunity in India', *International Labour Review*, 94(4): 350–74.

Mertus, Julie and Goldberg, Pamela (1994) 'A perspective on women and international human rights after the Vienna declaration: the inside/outside construct', *Journal of International Law and Politics*, 26(2): 201–34.

Meyer, John W., Boli, John and Thomas, George M. (1987) 'Ontology and rationalization in the Western cultural account', in George M. Thomas, John W. Meyer, Francisco O. Ramirez and John Boli (eds), *Institutional Structure: constituting state, society, and the individual*, London: Sage, pp. 12–37.

Meyer, John W. and Jepperson, Ronald L. (2000) 'The actors of modern society: the cultural construction of social agency', *Sociological Theory*, 18(1): 100–20.

Mikanagi, Yumiko (1998) 'Japan's gender-biased social security policy', *Japan Forum*, 10(2): 181–96.

Millet, Michael (2000) 'Hirohito named a war criminal', *Age*, 13 December, p. 10.

Mills, Sarah (2004) *Discourse*, London: Routledge.

Ministry for Family, Senior Citizens, Women and Youth (1999) (Bundesministerium für Familie, Senioren, Frauen und Jugend), 'Action plan of the federal government to combat violence against women', www.bmfsfj.de/anlage5407/Aktionsplan.pdf (accessed 14 June 2006).

Ministry of Social Affairs: Women's Institute (1988) *Equal Opportunities for Women Plan of Action 1988–1990*, Madrid: Women's Institute.

—— (1995) *Spanish Women on the Threshold of the 21st Century: report submitted by Spain to the Fourth World Conference on Women*, Madrid: Women's Institute.

Mioko, Fujieda and Jennison, Rebecca (1985) 'The UN decade for women and Japan: tools for change', *Women's Studies International Forum*, 8(2): 121–3.

Misra, Kalpana (1997) 'Indian feminism and the post-colonial state', *Women and Politics*, 17(4): 25–43.

Miyachi, Mitsuko (2000) 'On the unjust court ruling over the Sumitomo Electric gender-based wage discrimination case', wimmin.hp.infoseek.co.jp/MIYAJI.htm (accessed 1 August 2006).

Mody, Nawaz B. (1987) 'The press in India: the Shahbano judgement and its aftermath', *Asian Survey*, 27(8): 935–53.

Moeller, Robert G. (1993) *Protecting Motherhood: women and the family in the politics of postwar West Germany*, Berkeley, CA: University of California Press.

—— (1997) 'Reconstructing the family in reconstruction Germany: women and social policy in the Federal Republic, 1949–1955', in Robert G. Moeller (ed.), *West Germany under Construction: politics, society, and culture in the Adenauer era*, Ann Arbor, MI: University of Michigan Press, pp. 109–34.

Molto, Maria Luisa and Valiente, Celia (2000) *Gender Mainstreaming in the Spanish National Action Plan 2000*, Report for the European Commission's Group of Experts, Gender and Employment, Luxembourg: European Union.

—— (2001) *Evaluation of the Spanish National Action Plan 2001 from a Gender Perspective*, Report for the European Commission's Group of Experts, Gender and Employment, Luxembourg: European Union.

Moravcsik, Andrew (1997) 'Taking preferences seriously: a liberal theory of international politics', *International Organization*, 51(4): 513–53.

—— (1999) 'Is something rotten in the state of Denmark? Constructivism and European integration', *Journal of European Public Policy*, 6(4): 669–81.

—— (2000) 'The origins of human rights regimes: democratic delegation in postwar Europe', *International Organization*, 54(2): 217–52.

Morgan, Kimberly (2001) 'Gender and the welfare state: research on the origins and consequences of social policy regimes', *Comparative Politics*, 34(1): 105–24.

Morozumi, Michiyo (1998) 'Protection of the established position in Japanese labour law: basic normative patterns under the long-term employment system', *International Journal of Comparative Labour Law and Industrial Relations*, 14(1): 41–63.

Moxon-Browne, Edward (1989) *Political Change in Spain*, London: Routledge.

Muramatsu, Michio and Krauss, Ellis S. (1990) 'The dominant party and social coalitions in Japan', in T. J. Pempel (ed.), *Uncommon Democracies: the one-party dominant regime*, Ithaca, NY: Cornell University Press, pp. 282–305.

Naftulin, Lois J. (1980) 'Women's status under Japanese laws', *Feminist International*, 2: 13–16.

Nakanishi, Tamako (1983) 'Equality or protection? Protective legislation for women in Japan', *International Labour Review*, 122(5): 609–21.

Nandy, Ashis (1987) 'The sociology of sati', *Indian Express*, 5 October.

—— (1988a) 'Sati in Kaliyuga', *Economic and Political Weekly*, 17 September.

—— (1988b) 'The human factor', *Illustrated Weekly of India*, 17 January.

—— (1989) *At the Edge of Psychology: essays in politics and culture*, New Delhi: Oxford University Press.

—— (1995) *The savage Freud and other essays on possible and retrievable selves*, Princeton, NJ: Princeton University Press.

Nanivadekar, Medha (1998) 'Reservations for women: challenge of tackling counterproductive trends', *Economic and Political Weekly*, 11–18 July: 1815–19.

Nash, Mary (1991) 'Pronatalism and motherhood in Franco's Spain', in Gisela Bock and Pat Thane (eds), *Maternity and Gender Policies: women and the rise of the European welfare state, 1880s–1950s*, London: Routledge, pp. 160–77.

Neilson, June (1998) 'Equal opportunities for women in the European Union: success or failure?', *Journal of European Social Policy*, 8(1): 64–79.

Nielsen, Ruth (1983) *Equality Legislation in a Comparative Perspective: towards state feminism?*, Copenhagen: Women's Research Centre in Social Science.

Nielsen, Ruth and Szyszczak, Erika (1991) *The Social Dimension of the European Community*, Copenhagen: Handelshøjskolens Forlag.

Nussbaum, Martha C. (2000) *Women and Human Development: the capabilities approach*, Cambridge: Cambridge University Press.

Oh, Bonnie B. C. (2001) 'The Japanese imperial system and the Korean comfort women of World War II', in Margaret Stetz and Bonnie B. C. Oh (eds), *Legacies of the Comfort Women of World War II*, New York: M. E. Sharpe, pp. 3–25.

O'Herne, Jan Ruff (1994) *Fifty Years of Silence*, Sydney: Editions Tom Thompson.

Okada, Taihei (1999) 'The comfort women case: judgement of April 27, 1998, Shimonoseki Branch, Yamaguchi Prefectural Court, Japan', *Pacific Rim Law and Policy Journal*, 8(1): 63–108.

Oldenburg, Veena Talwar (1994) 'The Roop Kanwar case: feminist responses', in John Hawley Stratton (ed.), *Sati, the Blessing, and the Curse: the burning of wives in India*, Oxford: Oxford University Press, pp. 101–29.

Olson, Frances E. (1993) 'International law: feminist critiques of the public/private distinction', in Dorinda Dallmeyer (ed.), *Reconceiving Reality: women and international law*, Washington, DC: American Society of International Law, pp. 157–69.

Osaka Group Campaigning for the Abolishment of Discrimination Against Women (1993) *A Perspective on Equality: a nongovernmental evaluation of the efficacy of Japan's 2986 law of equal opportunity*, Osaka: Law Office of Noriko Ishida.

Osawa, Mari (1993) 'Bye-bye corporate warriors: the formation of a corporate-centred society and gender-biased social policies in Japan', *Annals of the Institute of Social Science*, 35: 157–94.

—— (2000) 'Government approaches to gender equality in the mid-1990s', *Social Science Japan Journal*, 3(1): 3–19.

Ostner, Ilona (1993) 'Slow motion: women, work, and the family in Germany', in Jane Lewis (ed.), *Women and Social Policies in Europe: work, family, and the state*, Aldershot, UK: Edward Elgar, pp. 92–115.

Ostner, Ilona and Lewis, Jane (1995) 'Gender and the evolution of European social policies', in Stephan Leibfried and Paul Pierson (eds), *European Social Policy: between fragmentation and integration*, Washington, DC: Brookings Institution, pp. 159–93.

Palan, Ronen (2000) 'A world of their making: an evaluation of the constructivist critique in international relations', *Review of International Studies*, 26(4): 575–98.

Pallmert, Ulrike (1984) 'Aid for battered women: the second women's house', in Edith Hoshino Altback, Jeanette Clausen, Dagmar Schultz and Naomi Stephan (eds), *German Feminism: readings in politics and literature*, Albany: State University of New York Press, pp. 178–80.

Palriwala, Rajni and Agnihotri, Indu (1996) 'Tradition, the family, and the state: politics of the contemporary women's movement', in T. V. Sathyamurthy (ed.), *Region, Religion, Caste, Gender, and Culture in Contemporary India*, New Delhi: Oxford University Press, pp. 503–32.

Parashar, Archana (1992) *Women and Family Law Reform in India: uniform civil code and gender equality*, New Delhi: Sage.

Parkinson, Loraine (1989) 'Japan's equal employment opportunity law: an alternative approach to social change', *Columbia Law Review*, 89: 604–61.

Patel, Vibhuti (1988) 'Emergence and proliferation of autonomous women's groups in India: 1974–1984', in Rehana Ghadrally (ed.), *Women in Indian Society*, New Delhi: Sage, pp. 249–55.

Paterson, William E. (1989) 'The Greens: from yesterday to tomorrow', in Peter H. Merkl (ed.), *The Federal Republic of Germany at Forty*, New York: New York University Press, pp. 340–63.

Patterson, Nancy (1993) 'No more *naki-neiri?* The state of Japanese sexual harassment law: judgment of April 16, 1992, Fukuoka Chiho Saibansho, Heisei Gannen (1989) (wa) no. 1872, Songai Baisho Jiken (Japan)', *Harvard International Law Journal*, 34(1): 206–23.

Payne, Stanley G. (1987) *The Franco Regime: 1936–1975*, Madison, WI: University of Wisconsin Press.

Peek, John M. (1992) 'Japan, the United Nations, and human rights', *Asian Survey*, 32(3): 217–29.

Peters, Anne (1999) *Women, Quotas, and Constitutions: a comparative study of affirmative action for women under American, German, and European Community and international law*, London: Kluwer Law International.

Pietila, Hilkka and Vickers, Jeanne (1996) *Making Women Matter: the role of the United Nations*, London: Zed Books.

Pollack, Benny (1987) *The Paradox of Spanish Foreign Policy: Spain's international relations from Franco to democracy*, London: Pinter.

Portero, Florentino (1999) 'Spain, Britain and the Cold War', in Sebastian Balfour and Paul Preston (eds), *Spain and the Great Powers in the Twentieth Century*, London: Routledge, pp. 210–28.

Preston, Paul (1986) *The Triumph of Democracy in Spain*, London: Methuen.

—— (1999) 'Franco's foreign policy: 1939–1953', in Christian Leitz and David J. Dunthorn (eds), *Spain in an International Context: 1936–1959*, New York: Berghahn Books, pp. 1–17.

Pridham, Geoffrey (1991) 'The politics of the European Community, transnational networks and democratic transition in southern Europe', in Geoffrey Pridham (ed.), *Encouraging Democracy: the international context of regime transition in southern Europe*, Leicester: Leicester University Press, pp. 212–45.

Prugl, Elisabeth and Meyer, Mary K. (1999) 'Gender politics in global governance', in Mary K. Meyer and Elisabeth Prugl (eds), *Gender Politics in Global Governance*, Lanham, MD: Rowman & Littlefield, pp. 3–16.

Qadeer, Imrana and Hasan, Zoya (1987) 'Deadly politics of the state and its apologist', *Economic and Political Weekly*, 14 November: 1946–9.

Rae, Heather (2002) *State Identities and the Homogenisation of Peoples*, Cambridge: Cambridge University Press.

Rahman, Anika (1990) 'Religious rights versus women's rights in India: a test case for international human rights law', *Columbia Journal of Transnational Law*, 28(2): 473–98.

Ram, Kalpana (2000) 'The state and the women's movement: instabilities in the discourse of rights in India', in Anne-Marie Hilsdon, Martha Macintyre, Vera Mackie and Maila Stivens (eds), *Human Rights and Gender Politics*, London: Routledge, pp. 60–82.

Ramirez, Francisco O. and McEneaney, Elizabeth H. (1997) 'From women's suffrage to reproduction rights? Cross-national considerations', *International Journal of Comparative Sociology*, 38(1–2): 6–24.

Ramirez, Francisco O., Shanahan, Suzanne and Soysal, Yasemin (1997) 'The changing logic of political citizenship: cross-national acquisition of women's suffrage rights, 1890–1990', *American Sociological Review*, 62(5): 735–45.

Ranadive, Joy R. (1994) 'Gender implications of adjustment policy programme in India', *Economic and Political Weekly*, 30 April: WS-12–WS-18.

Real, Carlota Bustelo Garcia del (1996) 'Progresos y obstáculos en la aplicación de la convención para la eliminación de todas las formas de discriminación contra la mujer', in Fernando M. Marino Menendez (ed.), *La Protección Internacional de los Derechos de la Mujer tras la Conferencia de Pekin de 1995*, Madrid: Universidad Carlos III de Madrid, pp. 31–55.

Reanda, Laura (1995) 'The Commission on the Status of Women', in Philip Alston (ed.), *The United Nations and Human Rights: a critical appraisal*, Oxford: Clarendon Press, pp. 265–303.

—— (1999) 'Engendering the United Nations: the changing international agenda', *European Journal of Women's Studies*, 6(1): 49–68.

Reich, Pauline C. (1998) 'The Mitsubishi motors cases: hindsight and analysis', *US–Japan Women's Journal: English Supplement*, 14: 84–120.

Reiko, Inoue (1986) 'Strengthening the web: 15 years of Japanese women's activism', *AMPO: Japan-Asia Quarterly Review*, 18(2–3): 12–17.

'Report: the making of a founding text' (1998) *Indian Journal of Gender Studies*, January–June: 87–113.

Rhodes, Martin (1997) 'Southern European welfare states: identity, problems, and prospects for reform', in Martin Rhodes (ed.), *Southern European Welfare States: between crisis and reform*, London: Frank Cass, pp. 1–22.

Rhoodie, Eschel M. (1989) *Discrimination against Women: a global survey of the economic, educational, social, and political status of women*, Jefferson, NC: McFarland.

Rice, Melinda (2001) 'Japan adopts tough domestic violence law', *Women's e News*, 2 December.

Richards, Michael (1998) *A Time of Silence: civil war and the culture of repression in Franco's Spain, 1936–1945*, Cambridge: Cambridge University Press.

Ricoeur, Paul (1991) 'Narrative identity', *Philosophy Today*, 35(1): 73–81.

—— (1995) 'Reflections on a new ethos for Europe', *Philosophy and Social Criticism*, 21(5/6): 3–13.

—— (1996) 'Entre mémoire et histoire', *Projet*, 248.

Ringmar, Erik (1997) 'Alexander Wendt: a social scientist struggling with history', in Iver B. Neumman and Ole Waever (eds), *The Future of International Relations: masters in the making?*, New York: Routledge, pp. 269–89.

Risse, Thomas (1999) 'International norms and domestic change: arguing and communicative behaviour in the human rights area', *Politics and Society*, 27(4): 529–59.

—— (2000) '"Let's argue!": communicative action in world politics', *International Organization*, 54(1): 1–39.

Risse, Thomas and Sikkink, Kathryn (1999) 'The socialization of international human rights norms into domestic practices: introduction', in Thomas Risse, Stephen C. Ropp and Kathryn Sikkink (eds), *The Power of Human Rights: international norms and domestic change*, Cambridge: Cambridge University Press, pp. 1–38.

Risse, Thomas, Cowles, Maria Green and Caporaso, James (2001) 'Europeanization and domestic change: introduction', in Maria Green Cowles, James

Caporaso and Thomas Risse (eds), *Europeanization and Domestic Change: transforming Europe*, Ithaca, NY: Cornell University Press, pp. 1–20.

Robins-Mowry, Dorothy (1983) *The Hidden Sun: women of modern Japan*, Boulder, CO: Westview Press.

Roggeband, Conny (1999) Email correspondence with author, 6 January.

Rollin, Hillary (1995) 'Women, employment, and society in Spain: an equal opportunity?', *Association for Contemporary Iberian Studies*, 18(2): 45–60.

Rossilli, Mariagrazia (1999) 'The European Union's policy on the equality of women', *Feminist Studies*, 25(10): 171–81.

Rubenstein, Michael (1992) 'Sexual harassment: European recommendation and code of practice', *Industrial Law Journal*, 21(1): 70–4.

Rudolph, Hedwig, Appelbaum, Eileen and Maier, Friederike (1994) 'Beyond socialism: the uncertain prospects for East German women in a unified Germany', in Nahid Aslanbeigui, Steven Pressman and Gale Summerfield (eds), *Women in the Age of Economic Transformation: gender impact of reforms in post-socialist and developing countries*, London: Routledge, pp. 11–26.

Ruttley, Philip (2002) 'The long road to unity: the contribution of law to the process of European integration since 1945', in Anthony Pagden (ed.), *The Idea of Europe: from antiquity to the European Union*, Cambridge: Cambridge University Press, pp. 228–59.

Sarkar, Lotika (1994) 'Rape: a human rights versus a patriarchal interpretation', *Indian Journal of Gender Studies*, 1(1): 69–92.

—— (1995) 'Women's movement and the legal process', Occasional Paper no. 24, New Delhi: Centre for Women's Development Studies.

Sarkar, Tanika (1991) 'The woman as communal subject: Rashtrasevika Samiti and Ramjanmabhoomi', *Economic and Political Weekly*, 31 August: 2057–65.

—— (1993a) 'The women of the Hindutva brigade', *Bulletin of Concerned Asian Scholars*, 25(4): 16–24.

—— (1993b) 'Women's agency within authoritarian communalism: the Rashtrasevika Samiti and Ramjanmabhoomi', in Gyanendra Pandey (ed.), *Hindus and Others: the question of identity in India today*, New Delhi: Viking Press, pp. 24–45.

Sawer, Marian (1993) 'Reclaiming social liberalism: the women's movement and the state', *Journal of Australian Studies*, special edition on Women and the State: Australian Perspectives, 37: 1–21.

Sawyer, R. Keith (2005) *Social Emergence: societies as complex systems*, Cambridge, Cambridge University Press.

Scheele, Alexandra (2001) *Government–Employer Agreement Prevents Equal Opportunities Law*, Düsseldorf: WSI in der Institut in der Hans-Bockler-Stiftung, 28 July.

Schiek, Dagmar (2000) 'Germany', *Bulletin Legal Issues on Equality*, no. 2/2000, Luxembourg: European Commission Directorate-General for Employment and Social Affairs.

—— (2001) 'Germany', *Bulletin Legal Issues on Equality*, no. 2/2001, Luxembourg: European Commission Directorate-General for Employment and Social Affairs.

Schissler, Hanna (2001) 'Normalization as a project: some thoughts on gender relations in West Germany during the 1950s', in Hanna Schissler (ed.), *The Miracle Years: a cultural history of West Germany, 1949–1968*, Princeton, NJ: Princeton University Press, pp. 359–75.

Schmid, Carol (1990) 'Women in the West German Green Party: the uneasy alliance of ecology and feminism', in Guida West and Rhoda Lois Blumberg (eds), *Women and Social Protest*, Oxford: Oxford University Press, pp. 225–42.

Schoepp-Schilling, Hanna Beate (1995) 'The impact of German unification on women: losses and gains', in Alida Brill (ed.), *A Rising Public Voice: women in politics worldwide*, New York: City University of New York, pp. 27–40.

—— (2000) 'Germany', in Marilou McPhedran, Susan Bazilli, Moana Erickson and Andrew Byrnes (eds), *The First CEDAW Impact Study*, Toronto: Centre for Feminist Research, York University and the International Women's Rights Project, pp. 55–62.

Schofer, Evan (1999) 'Science associations in the international sphere, 1875–1990: the rationalization of science and the scientization of society', in John Boli and George M. Thomas (eds), *International Nongovernmental Organizations since 1875*, Stanford, CA: Stanford University Press, pp. 249–66.

Schulten, Thorsten (1997) *EIRO Comparative Study on Gender Pay Equity: the case of Germany*, Düsseldorf: Institute for Economic and Social Research (WSI).

Seigel, Jerrold (2005) *The Idea of the Self: thought and experience in Western Europe since the seventeenth century*, Cambridge: Cambridge University Press.

Shaeffer-Hegel, Barbara (1992) 'Makers and victims of unification: German women and the two Germanies', *Women's Studies International Forum*, 15(1): 101–9.

Shah, Nandita, Gothoskar, Sujata, Gandhi, Nandita and Chhachhi, Amrita (1994) 'Structural adjustment, feminization of the labour force, and organizational strategies', *Economic and Political Weekly*, 30 April: WS-39–WS-48.

Share, Donald (1986) *The Making of Spanish Democracy*, New York: Praeger.

Sharma, Kalpana (1991) 'Cosmetic changes in rape law', in Subhadra Patwa (ed.), *The Law and Gender Justice*, Bombay: Research Centre for Women's Studies, p. 59.

Sharma, Kumud (1988) *National Specialised Agencies and Women's Equality*, New Delhi: Centre for Women's Development Studies.

—— (1998) 'Transformative politics: dimensions of women's participation in panchayati raj', *Indian Journal of Gender Studies*, 5(1): 23–47.

—— (2000) 'Power and representation: reservation for women in India', *Asian Journal of Women's Studies*, 6(1): 47–87.

Sharp, Ingrid and Flinspach, Dagmar (1995) 'Women in Germany from division to unification', in Derek Lewis and John R. P. McKenzie (eds), *The New Germany: social, political, and cultural challenges of unification*, Exeter: Exeter University Press, pp. 173–95.

Shaw, Jo and More, Gillian (1995) *New Legal Dynamics of the European Union*, Oxford: Clarendon Press.

Shaw, Josephine (1991) 'Recent developments in the field of labour market equality: sex discrimination law in the Federal Republic of Germany', *Comparative Labor Law Journal*, 12(1): 18–44.

Shubert, Adrian (1990) *A Social History of Modern Spain*, London: Unwin Hyman.

Sibeon, Roger (2004) *Rethinking Social Theory*, London: Sage.

Sikkink, Kathryn (1991) *Ideas and Institutions: developmentalism in Brazil and Argentina*, Ithaca, NY: Cornell University Press.

—— (1993) 'The power of principled ideas: human rights policies in the United States and Western Europe', in Judith Goldstein and Robert O. Keohane (eds), *Ideas and Foreign Policy: beliefs, institutions, and political change*, Ithaca, NY: Cornell University Press, pp. 139–70.

Singh, Aruna (1998) 'No light at the end of the tunnel', *The Tribune*, 7 November.

Singh, Rina (1998) *Gender Autonomy in Western Europe: an imprecise revolution*, London: Macmillan.

Soh, Chunghee Sarah (1996) 'The Korean comfort women', *Asian Survey*, 36(12): 1226–40.

—— (2000) 'From imperial gifts to sex slaves: theorizing symbolic representations of the comfort women', *Social Science Japan Journal*, 3(1): 59–76.

Sorabjee, Soli J. (1990) 'Equality in the United States and India', in Louis Henkin and Albert J. Rosenthal (eds), *Influence of the United States Constitution Abroad*, New York: Columbia University Press, pp. 94–124.

Stein, Eric (1981) 'Lawyers, judges, and the making of a transnational constitution', *American Journal of International Law*, 75(1): 1–27.

Steinberg, Marc W. (2002) 'Toward a more dialogic analysis of social movement culture', in David S. Meyer, Nancy Whittier and Belinda Robnett (eds), *Social Movements: identity, culture, and the state*, Oxford: Oxford University Press, pp. 208–25.

Steiner, Kurt (1956) 'A Japanese *cause célèbre*: the Fukuoka patricide case', *American Journal of Comparative Law*, 5(1): 106–11.

Strang, David and Chang, Patricia Mei Yin (1993) 'The International Labour Organization and the welfare state: institutional effects on national spending, 1960–80', *International Organization*, 47(2): 253–62.

Strang, David and Meyer, John W. (1993) 'Institutional conditions for diffusion', *Theory and Society*, 22(4): 487–511.

Sudarshan, R. (1990) 'The quest of the state: politics and judiciary in India', *Journal of Commonwealth and Comparative Politics*, 28(1): 44–69.

Sugeno, Kazuo (1992) *Japanese Labour Law*, Seattle, WA: University of Washington Press.

Sugimoto, Yoshio (1997) *An Introduction to Japanese Society*, Cambridge: Cambridge University Press.

Sullivan, Donna (1994) 'Women's human rights and the 1993 world conference on human rights', *American Journal of International Law*, 88(1): 152–67.

—— (1995) 'The public/private distinction in international human rights law', in Julie Peters and Andrea Wolper (eds), *Women's Rights Human Rights: international feminist perspectives*, New York: Routledge, pp. 126–34.

Takahashi, Mutsuko (1997) *The Emergence of Welfare Society in Japan*, Aldershot, UK: Ashgate.

Tanaka, Yuki (2003) *Japan's Comfort Women: sexual slavery and prostitution during World War II and the US occupation*, London: Routledge.

Thapur, Romila (1988) 'In history', *Seminar*, 342 (February): 14–19.

Thomas, Nick (2003) *Protest Movements in 1960s West Germany: a social history of dissent and democracy*, Oxford: Berg.

Thompson, Karen Brown (2002) 'Women's rights as human rights', in Sanjeev Khagram, James V. Riker and Kathryn Sikkink (eds), *Restructuring World Politics: transnational social movements, networks, and norms*, Minneapolis, MN: University of Minnesota, pp. 96–122.

Threlfall, Monica (1985) 'The women's movement in Spain', *New Left Review*, 151 (May–June): 44–73.

—— (1986) 'The role of women in the opposition to Francoism and the transition to democracy: questions for feminist research', paper presented at the European Consortium for Political Research Joint Sessions, Gothenburg, 1–6 April.

—— (1996) 'Feminist politics and social change in Spain', in Monica Threlfall and Sheila Rowbotham (eds), *Mapping the Women's Movement: feminist politics and social transformation in the north*, London: Verso, pp. 115–51.

—— (1997) 'Spain in social Europe: a laggard or compliant member state?', *South European Society and Politics*, 2(2): 1–33.

—— (1998) 'State feminism or party feminism? Feminist politics and the Spanish institute for women', *European Journal of Women's Studies*, 5: 69–93.

—— (1999) Email correspondence with author, 8 May.

Tinker, Irene and Jaquette, Jane (1987) 'UN decade for women: its impact and legacy', *World Development*, 15(3): 419–27.

Tomoaki, Iwai (1993) 'The madonna boom: women in the Japanese Diet', *Journal of Japanese Studies*, 19(1): 103–20.

Tons, Katrin and Young, Brigitte (2001) 'The case of Germany', in Ute Behning and Amparo Serrano Pascual (eds), *Gender and Mainstreaming in the European Employment Strategy*, Brussels: European Trade Union Institute, pp. 129–56.

Toshitani, Nobuyoshi (1980) 'Family policy and family law in modern Japan: II', *Annals of the Institute of Social Science*, 21: 130–76.

Totsuka, Etsuro (1999) 'Commentary on a victory for comfort women: Japan's judicial recognition of military sexual slavery', *Pacific Rim Law and Policy Journal*, 8(1): 47–61.

Tummala, Krishna K. (1993) 'Religion and politics in India', *Asian Journal of Political Science*, 1(2): 57–76.

United Nations (1998) *The United Nations and the Advancement of Women 1945–1996*, Blue Book Series, Volume VI, New York: United Nations Department of Public Information.

—— (2000) *Bringing International Human Rights Law Home: judicial colloquium on domestic application of the Convention on the Elimination of All Forms of Discrimination Against Women and the Convention on the Rights of the Child*, New York: United Nations.

United Nations Commission on Human Rights (1996) *Report of the Special Rapporteur on Violence Against Women, its Causes and Consequences: report on the mission to the Democratic People's Republic of Korea, the Republic of Korea, and Japan on the issue of military sexual slavery*, Fifty-second Session, Provisional Agenda Item 9(a), UN Doc.E/CN.4/1996, 53/Add.1.

United Nations Commission on Human Rights: Subcommission on Prevention of Discrimination and Protection of Minorities (1998) *Contemporary Forms of Slavery, Systematic Rape, Sexual Slavery, and Slavery-like Practices During Armed Conflict*, 50th Session, Provisional Agenda Item 6, UN Doc.E/CN.4/Sub.2/1998/13.

UNCEDAW (United Nations Committee on the Elimination of Discrimination Against Women) (1990) *Consideration of Reports Submitted by States Parties Under Article 18 of the Convention*, CEDAW/C/SR.152, 5 February.

—— (1993) *Reports Provided by Specialized Agencies of the United Nations on the Implementation of the Convention in Areas Falling within the Scope of their Activities: International Labour Organization*, CEDAW/C/1994/Add.2, 18 October.

—— (1996) *Meetings of States Parties to the Convention on the Elimination of Discrimination Against Women*, CEDAW/SP/1996/2, 29 February.

—— (1999) *Concluding Observations of the Committee on the Elimination of Discrimination Against Women: Spain*, CEDAW/C/1999/L.2/Add.6, 1 July.

UNDAW (United Nations Division for the Advancement of Women) (2000) *The*

Convention on the Elimination of All Forms of Discrimination Against Women, the Optional Protocol: Text and Materials, New York: United Nations Publications.

United Nations General Assembly (1987) *Report of the Committee on the Elimination of Discrimination Against Women*, Official Records, Forty-second Session, Supplement no. 38 (A/42/38).

—— (1988) *Report of the Committee on the Elimination of Discrimination Against Women*, Official Records, Forty-third Session, Supplement no. 38 (A/43/38).

—— (1990) *Report of the Committee on the Elimination of Discrimination Against Women*, Ninth session, Official Records, Forty-fifth Session, Supplement no. 38 (A/45/38).

—— (1993) *Report of the Committee on the Elimination of Discrimination Against Women*, Official Records, Forty-seventh Session, Supplement no. 38 (A/47/38).

—— (1994) *Report of the Committee on the Elimination of Discrimination Against Women*, Official Records, Forty-ninth Session, Supplement no. 38 (A/49/38).

—— (1995) *Report of the Committee on the Elimination of Discrimination Against Women*, Official Records, Fiftieth Session, Supplement no. 38 (A/50/38).

—— (2000) *Report of the Committee on the Elimination of Discrimination Against Women*, Twenty-second session and Twenty-third session, Official Records, Fifty-fifth Session, Supplement no. 38 (A/55/38).

United Nations Secretary General (1994) *Report of the Secretary General to the General Assembly on the Improvement of the Status of Women in the Secretariat*, November, A/49/587.

United States Department of Justice (1993) *Spain: human rights practices*, 31 January, Washington, DC: US Department of Justice.

Uno, Kathleen S. (1993) 'The death of good wife, wise mother?', in Andrew Gordon (ed.), *Postwar Japan as History*, Berkeley: University of California Press, pp. 293–322.

Upham, Frank K. (1987) *Law and Social Change in Postwar Japan*, Cambridge, MA: Harvard University Press.

—— (1993) 'Unplaced persons and movements for place', in Andrew Gordon (ed.), *Postwar Japan as History*, Berkeley, CA: University of California Press, pp. 325–46.

Upreti, H. C. and Upreti, Nandini (1991) *The Myth of Sati: some dimensions of widow burning*, Bombay: Himalaya Publishing House.

Ussel, Julio Iglesias de (1991) 'Family ideology and political transition in Spain', *International Journal of Law and the Family*, 5(3): 277–95.

Vaid, Sudesh (1988) 'Politics of widow immolation', *Seminar*, 342 (February): 20–3.

Valiente, Celia (1995) 'The power of persuasion: the Instituto de la Mujer in Spain', in Dorothy McBride Stetson and Amy G. Mazur (eds), *Comparative State Feminism*, London: Sage, pp. 221–36.

—— (1996a) 'El feminismo institucional en España: el Instituto de la Mujer, 1983–1994', *Revista Internacional de Sociología*, 13: 163–204.

—— (1996b) 'Partial achievements of central-state public policies against violence against women in post-authoritarian Spain', in Chris Corrin (ed.), *Women in a Violent World: feminist analyses and resistance across Europe*, Edinburgh: Edinburgh University Press, pp. 166–85.

—— (1996c) 'The rejection of authoritarian policy legacies: family policy in Spain (1975–1995)', *South European Society and Politics*, 1(1): 95–114.

—— (1997a) 'Gender, segmented labour markets, continental welfare states, and equal employment policies: the case of Spain', in Jan Holmer and Jan C. H. Karlsson (eds), *Work – Quo Vadis? rethinking the question of work*, Aldershot, UK: Ashgate, pp. 195–218.

—— (1997b) 'State feminism and gender equality policies: the case of Spain (1983–95)', in Frances Gardiner (ed.), *Sex Equality Policy in Western Europe*, London: Routledge, pp. 127–41.

—— (1997c) 'The regulation of sexual harassment in the workplace in Spain', in Barbara Hobson and Anne Marie Berggren (eds), *Crossing Borders: gender and citizenship in transition*, Stockholm: Swedish Council for Planning and Co-ordination of Research, pp. 179–200.

—— (1998) 'Sexual harassment in the workplace: equality policies in post-authoritarian Spain', in Terrell Carver and Veronique Mottier (eds), *Politics of Sexuality: identity, gender, citizenship*, London: Routledge, pp. 169–79.

—— (2001) 'Implementing women's rights in Spain', in Jane H. Bayes and Nayereh Tohidi (eds), *Globalization, Gender, and Religion: the politics of women's rights in Catholic and Muslim contexts*, New York: Palgrave Macmillan, pp. 107–25.

Vallance, Elizabeth and Davies, Elizabeth (1986) *Women of Europe: women MEPs and equality policy*, Cambridge: Cambridge University Press.

Vinas, Angel (1999) 'Franco's dream of autarky shattered: foreign policy aspects in the run-up to the 1959 change in Spanish economic strategy', in Christian Leitz and David J. Bunthorn (eds), *Spain in an International Context, 1936–1959*, New York: Berghahn Books, pp. 299–318.

Vincent, Mary (1996) 'Spain', in Tom Buchanan and Martin Conway (eds), *Political Catholicism in Europe: 1918–1965*, Oxford: Clarendon Press, pp. 97–128.

Vogelheim, Elisabeth (1988) 'Women in a changing workplace: the case of the Federal Republic of Germany', in Jane Jenson, Elisabeth Hagen and Ceallaigh Reddy (eds), *Feminization of the Labour Force: paradoxes and promises*, Oxford: Oxford University Press, pp. 106–19.

Vogel-Polsky, Elaine (1985) 'New social needs: the problems of women', in Jacques Vandamme (ed.), *New Dimensions in European Social Policy*, London: Croom Helm, pp. 95–114.

—— (1991) *Social Policy in a United Europe*, Research and Documentation Papers Social Policy Series 9, EN-9-91, Luxembourg: European Parliament Directorate-General for Research.

Vogt, Andrea and Zwingel, Susanne (2003) 'Asking fathers and employers to volunteer: a (de)tour of reconciliation policy in Germany?', *Review of Policy Research*, 20(3): 459–77.

Voice of the Asia-Pacific Human Rights Network (1999) *The Purse Strings as the Noose: Indian NGOs face new challenges*, New Delhi: South Asia Human Rights Documentation Centre.

Warner, Harriet (1984) 'EC social policy in practice: community action on behalf of women and its impact in the member states', *Journal of Common Market Studies*, 23(2): 141–67.

Watanabe, Kazuko (1994) 'Militarism, colonialism, and trafficking of women: comfort women forced into sexual labor for Japanese soldiers', *Bulletin of Concerned Asian Scholars*, 26(4): 3–16.

—— (1996) 'Fighting against sexual harassment on campus in Japan: a court case and statistical survey', *Australian Feminist Studies*, 11(23): 33–7.

Weitz, Eric D. (2001) 'The ever-present other: communism in the making of West Germany', in Hanna Schissler (ed.), *The Miracle Years: a cultural history of West Germany, 1949–1968*, Princeton, NJ: Princeton University Press, pp. 219–32.

Wendt, Alexander (1994) 'Collective identity formation and the international state', *American Political Science Review*, 88(2): 384–96.

—— (1997) 'Identity and structural change in international politics', in Yosef Lapid and Friedrich Kratochwil (eds), *The Return of Culture and Identity in IR Theory*, Boulder, CO: Lynne Rienner, pp. 47–64.

—— (1999) *Social Theory of International Politics*, Cambridge: Cambridge University Press.

—— (2000) 'On the via media: a response to the critics', *Review of International Studies*, 26(1): 165–80.

—— (2006) '*Social Theory* as Cartesian science: an auto-critique from a quantum perspective', in Stefano Guzzini and Anna Leander (eds), *Constructivism and International Relations: Alexander Wendt and his critics*, London: Routledge.

Whitworth, Sandra (1994) 'Gender, international relations and the case of the ILO', *Review of International Studies*, 20(4): 389–405.

Wolff, Leon (1996) 'Eastern twists on western concepts: equality jurisprudence and sexual harassment in Japan', *Pacific Rim Law and Policy Journal*, 5(3): 509–35.

—— (2003) 'Japanese women and the *new* administrative state', in Jennifer Amyx and Peter Drysdale (eds), *Japanese Governance: Beyond Japan Inc.*, London: Routledge, pp. 156–69.

Working Women's Network (2000) 'The Sumitomo trial', wimmin.hp.infoseek.co.jp/Sumitomo.htm (accessed 14 June 2006).

Wright, Shelley (1993) 'Human rights and women's rights: an analysis of the United Nations Convention on the Elimination of All Forms of Discrimination Against Women', in Kathleen E. Mahoney and Paul Mahoney (eds), *Human Rights in the Twenty-first Century*, Dordrecht: Martinus Nijhoff, pp. 75–88.

Yang, Hyunah (1997) 'Revisiting the issue of Korean military comfort women: the question of truth and positionality', *Positions East Asia Cultures Critique*, 5(1): 51–71.

Yoko, Nuita, Mitsuko, Yamaguchi and Kimoko, Kubo (1994) 'The UN Convention on Eliminating Discrimination Against Women and the status of women in Japan', in Barbara J. Nelson and Najma Chowdhury (eds), *Women and Politics worldwide*, New Haven, CT: Yale University Press, pp. 398–414.

Yoneda, Masumi (2000) 'Japan', in Marilou McPhedran, Susan Bazilli, Moana Erickson and Andrew Byrne (eds), *The First CEDAW Impact Study: final report*, York: York University for Feminist Research and the International Women's Rights Project, pp. 63–76.

Yoneda, Sayoko (1998) 'Sexual and racial discrimination: a historical inquiry into the Japanese military's comfort women system of enforced prostitution', in Ruth Roach Pierson and Nupur Chaudhuri (eds), *Nation, Empire, Colony: historicizing gender and race*, Indianapolis, IN: Indiana University Press, pp. 237–50.

Yoshihama, Mieko (2000) 'Policies and services addressing domestic violence in Japan: from non-interference to incremental changes', *Women's Studies International Forum*, 25(5): 541–53.

Young, Brigitte (1999) *Triumph of the Fatherland: German unification and the marginalization of women*, Ann Arbor, MI: University of Michigan Press.

Zippel, Kathrina (2002) *Sexual Harassment and Transnational Relations: why those concerned with German–American relations should care*, Washington, DC: American Institute for Contemporary German Studies, Johns Hopkins University.

Zoelle, Diana G. (2000) *Globalizing Concern for Women's Human Rights: the failure of the American model*, London: Macmillan.

Index